FORTRAN
for Humans

*

FORTRAN
for Humans
SECOND EDITION

Rich Didday

Rex Page

WEST PUBLISHING CO.
St. Paul • New York • Boston
Los Angeles • San Francisco

This book is dedicated
to all Rana pipiens, *everywhere*

Library of Congress Cataloging in Publication Data

Didday, Richard L
    Fortran for humans.

    Includes index.
        1. FORTRAN (Computer program language) I. Page,
Rex L., joint author. II. Title.
QA76.73.F25.D52 1977   001.6′424   76-54331

ISBN 0-8299-0125-6

PREFACE

"Just what the world needs—another book on Fortran!"

—ANONYMOUS

We have written this book because we feel that most books specifically about Fortran teach programming as an application of Fortran rather than the reverse. There are, of course, many books designed for use in an introductory computer science course that dwell primarily on programming and skip the details of a particular language. These books are appropriate in a course for computer science majors, but they are not particularly appropriate for a general studies course on Fortran programming.

Because most students learn to program in general studies Fortran courses, we feel that there is a need for a book that provides coordinated introduction to both the rules of Fortran and the creative process of designing algorithms.

We do not present Fortran as if it were the ultimate programming language. There are many languages that would probably be both easier for a student to learn and provide a wider variety of data structures. But Fortran is widely available. That alone is a good reason for teaching it. Not only is Fortran widely available, it is found in the same form everywhere. ANSI Standard Fortran is provided, at least as a subset, in virtually every Fortran system. This means that programs written in Fortran can be adapted for use at almost any computer installation, a feature of tremendous practical value. We attempt to present Fortran in the light of recent trends in programming languages. We emphasize aspects of Fortran that were precursors to newer languages, and de-emphasize aspects that are holdovers from assembly languages. We attempt to give the student a logical framework for thinking about programming.

We believe that a first course in programming should teach more than how to tack together some sequence of legal statements that produce the desired numbers. We believe that the most effective programmers write programs that make their meaning obvious to other humans as well as to computers. Effective programmers spend far more time in the analysis and design phases of problem solving than they spend in writing down Fortran statements. These notions are often referred to by the phrase **structured programming**. Accordingly, this book concerns itself both with program organization and documentation and with the specifics of Fortran.

In order to avoid the problem of confusing footnotes explaining the details of different systems, we have adhered closely to the standards established by the

American National Standards Institute, Inc. ANSI Fortran is described in "FOR-TRAN vs. Basic FORTRAN—a programming language for information processing on automatic data processing systems," *Comm ACM*, vol. 7, no. 10, 1964, pp. 591–625 and following reports in 1969 and 1971. The report is also available in the publication ANSI X3.9–1966. However, we have made two exceptions where we feel the improvement in clarity and ease of learning is overwhelming. The most ubiquitous of these is the use of quoted character strings in FORMAT statements. Our only other departure from the standards is our use of arbitrary INTEGER-valued expressions as array subscripts. To bring our programs into strict accordance with the standards would be a trivial matter, but we feel the revised versions would be more difficult for students to understand.

We have found that we can cover Chapters 1 through 9 in a ten-week, three-hour, beginning course in programming. If students are having trouble understanding arrays, the first sections of Chapter 11 may be helpful. Chapters 1 through 13 provide enough material for a serious sixteen-week programming course. The first seven chapters present a good basic introduction to programming and provide enough material for an elementary course. Since each of these chapters depends strongly on previous material, there is little choice in the order of presentation. Chapters 8 through 13 are almost independent of one another and can be rearranged to suit student interest or the goals of the course.

DO-loops are introduced in Chapter 8. We feel it is best to delay their introduction until the student is well versed in the construction of all kinds of loops; otherwise, there is a tendency to terminate loops with counters when other termination conditions would be more appropriate. However, Chapter 8 doesn't depend on any material beyond assignments, expressions, and arrays, and can therefore be covered quite early in the course. In fact, the first section of the chapter introduces the notion of a DO-loop without mentioning arrays, so that DO-loops could be introduced in the course simultaneously with Chapter 3 without having to deviate from the text in any important way.

> *Boxes throughout the text summarize important points and provide additional information.*

In this, the second edition, we have made three types of changes. First, we have revised, edited, and polished the examples in the text and the problems at the ends of the chapters to make them more relevant to the topics under consideration. We have expanded the exercises at the ends of the sections and the appendix of answers to help students evaluate their understanding of the material. New terms in the text are emphasized with **boldface type**.

Second, we have markedly increased the ease with which the book can be used as a reference. As in the first edition, we have arranged the material in the order that we feel is the most pedagogically sound. In many cases this means introducing restricted versions of certain statements first and covering the more general versions later. This is a valuable teaching technique, but it causes some problems when the text is used as a reference book. We have included four features which will alleviate these problems. (1) We have written an ANSI Fortran MiniManual summarizing the language definitions in one place for easy reference. (2) Non-ANSI features covered in the MiniManual are marked in gray. (3) We have prepared a quick reference index that lists examples of each type of statement keyed to relevant pages in the text. (4) We have included optional sections on advanced topics in relevant chapters, thus keeping similar material together for easy reference without creating artificial dependencies among the chapters.

Third, we have included a great deal of material on program design in the text. In the first edition, these ideas were expressed mainly by example.

The response to the first edition was very encouraging. Comments from users of the original text have convinced us to retain the overall organization, approach, and style in this revision. We owe much to Douglas Haden, Robert Percherer, Lansing Hatfield, and others for their suggestions which have helped us improve the examples and the format of the text.

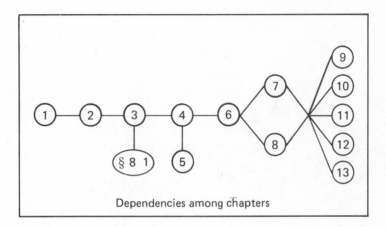

Dependencies among chapters

Acknowledgments

We would like to thank our students, who taught us how to teach Fortran, Ed Noyce for giving us the idea and getting us started, Walter Orvedahl for his encouragement and philosophical influence, and Jennifer Scrivner, Beverly Page, and Carolee Drotos for not giving up.

We would also like to thank Pat Mohilner, Jim George, Gary Sager, Janice Kurasz, Jerome A. Smith, Adolpho Guzman, John Backus, R. J. Beeber, S. Best, R. Goldberg, H. L. Herrick, R. A. Hughes, L. B. Mitchell, R. A. Nelson, R. Nutt, D. Sayre, P. B. Sheridan, H. Stern, I. Ziller, Merl Miller, Walt Kelley, Halliday and Resnick, Mort Drucker, Rector Page, Maj. C. S. Brown, Ryo Arai, E. K. "Mo" Moyer, Nora Huff, Harwood Kolsky, R. A. Didday, Mamie K. Moyer, Warren Page, Mildred Hill, Althea G. Hoerner, Bertrand Russell, William Hill, Herman C. Didday, Ruby G. Latham, Adolph Coors, E. W. Dijkstra, David Ossman, Philip Proctor, Philip Austin, and Peter Bergman for the parts they played.

Larimer County, Colorado   R. L. Didday
                                                                  R. L. Page

CONTENTS

*Starred sections may be skipped without loss of continuity.

*Starred sections may be skipped without loss of continuity.

†

1 BASIC IDEAS

Section 1 1

Advice to You Who Are about to Learn Fortran

You will probably find learning to program a new kind of experience. Insofar as programming is like planning a task, it is a familiar process. What makes it difficult is that the planning must be much more complete than most people are used to.

For example, suppose a carpenter decides to write a set of directions for hanging a door. The difficulty of his task would depend to a large extent on his audience. It would be much easier for him to write a set of directions addressed to another carpenter than it would be to write directions addressed to the general public. For the public the directions would have to be much more complete because most people know little about carpentry. In fact, a layman who happened to know how to hang a door would probably write better instructions for the general public than would the expert carpenter. While the carpenter might be tempted to say "rout strike box in jamb," the layman would realize that he would have to explain what a door jamb is, what the strike of a lock is, and what routing is before he could make any such statement.

It is usually the case that the programmer, like the carpenter, knows much more than his audience, the computer, about the process he is trying to describe. The computer does know some things in the sense that it can perform certain operations, but it is up to the programmer to describe the process in terms the computer understands. If a computer system accepts Fortran, then it already can perform all the operations specified in Fortran. It is up to the programmer to describe the process in terms of those operations.

To learn to do this is not easy for most people. However, it seems easier once you get the hang of it. It is also fun. Since it is easy and fun for those who know, you will no doubt have lots of friends who want to help you learn to program. Most of them will help you by writing a program which solves the problem you are working on. It should be fairly obvious that this does *not* help you learn to program. You can't learn to swim by having your friend do it for you. But it may not be so obvious that this form of help is often detrimental rather than merely unhelpful. It is detrimental primarily because your helper is likely to use statements you have never seen before. (It might be interesting for you to keep track of the number of times someone says to you: "Oh, that's no good. Why don't you do it this way?'') These things you've never seen before will fall into one of four categories:

1 (OK) They are described in the text and you will learn them soon.
2 (POOR) They are advanced constructions and shouldn't be used until you know more about the basics.
3 (BAD) They are outmoded ways of doing things which are holdovers from more primitive languages.
4 (FREQUENT) They don't exist at all.

We offer this advice: Listen politely to friends who want to help, but always try to write the program yourself using techniques you know about from the part of the text you have read.

The exercises at the end of each section should help you confirm that you understand the material in the section. Answers for virtually all the exercises appear at the end of the book.

Although the first few chapters contain many new concepts, you will probably be able to grasp them quickly. Later chapters contain more and more complex combinations of these basic concepts and will probably require more thought. You can't learn to program in a day. It will take lots of thought and practice, but we think you will find it an enjoyable experience.

---

blanks: Although people rarely draw attention to them, blank characters are very important in written communications. A blank serves as an unobtrusive separator.

////Imagine/reading/a/sentence/like/this.////
Oronewithnoseparatorsatalllikethis.

You may not be used to thinking of a blank character as the same sort of thing as an a or b or a ! But on a line printer (as on a typewriter) it takes a definite action to produce a blank just as it requires a definite action to produce an a.

One of the reasons we have numbered sections the way we have in this book is to draw attention to the blank as a legitimate character.

A typical usage is "Figure 13 4 1," read "figure thirteen four one," identifying the first figure in the fourth section of Chapter 13.

Section 1 2

Background

This book is intended to help you learn to program computers using the programming language Fortran. In practice, the only way to learn to program is to do it, so this book is really only an aid to reduce the number of errors in your trial-and-error learning process.

Fortran is a **computer language**, a language with which to communicate commands to a computer. **A computer** is a machine that manipulates symbols by following the instructions in a computer program (written in a computer language, of course). Humans may interpret these symbols as they please. For example, a person might want to interpret a certain set of

> *computer: a machine which can perform arithmetic operations, make logical decisions, and perform many other symbol manipulation tasks automatically by following the instructions in a computer program*

symbols as the results of a number of questionnaires, and he might write a program (a sequence of commands) in Fortran which would cause some of the symbols to be matched up in pairs. He might then call this process "computer dating" and make a lot of money.

Motivation for development of computers comes from efforts to mechanize symbol manipulation tasks. An adding machine is a familiar

> *program: a sequence of instructions*

device which manipulates symbols and, in so doing, winds up with symbols that we call the sum of the symbols we put in. Early computers were little more than assemblages of devices which added, multiplied, divided, and so on, and could do these operations in sequence. Thus, a person who wanted to add a large list of numbers, then divide the sum by another number, then subtract this from yet another number, could write down a series of commands which would be *stored in the machine* and carried out in order automatically. The key word here is *stored*. The instructions which the computer is to follow are stored in the machine, and they can be changed by the user of the computer, the programmer.

> *machine language: a set of commands which a computer is built to perform. Different computers have different machine languages. A machine language program runs with no need for translation. Most machine languages bear little similarity to human languages.*

In the early days, one of the programmer's biggest problems was keeping up with changes in computers. There was, and still is, a continuing introduction of newer, faster, different computers. In the early fifties a group of programmers began an attempt to get around this problem. It had become apparent that if something weren't done, programmers would be spending large portions of their lives just learning the language for one new computer after another. Since the process of learning new languages was both gruesome and time-consuming, they designed a computer language closer to English than typical machine languages. They called their new language **Fortran**. It was a higher-level language. Since there had never been any widely used higher-level languages before that time, and since the problems involved in translating complex higher-level statements into efficient machine language programs had only begun to be studied, their first successful effort didn't look very much like English. They wanted Fortran to provide a way of giving commands to computers that was easy for programmers to learn, general enough to handle a great variety of problems, and designed so that the commands would be meaningful in terms of any computer's internal workings. Hopefully, manufacturers of new computers would provide machine language programs for translating Fortran programs into commands for their new machines. Programmers, then, wouldn't have to learn too much about the new machine to be able to program it and could continue to write their programs in Fortran, relying on the company's translation program to convert Fortran statements to machine commands.

> *higher-level language: a computer language which appears more like a human language than a machine language and is designed to be used on many different brands of computers*

Even though the new language wasn't really much like English, it was a big improvement over machine languages. It was concerned largely with arithmetic computing, and it promised to bring the use of the computer within reach of a large number of technically oriented people who would not have been willing to write programs before. Although the first version of Fortran was never widely available, Fortran II (introduced in 1958) became the first popular, commercially available higher-level language.

Through the years, as people have become more and more familiar with what is involved in programming, they have found certain types of statements more useful than others. *Higher-level languages have evolved.* Fortran IV, the language you will be learning, was introduced in 1962. It is available at virtually all computing installations and is defined by a set of standards maintained by the American National Standards Institute. (See *Fortran*, ANSI X3.9–1966, American National Standards Institute, Inc., 1430 Broadway, New York, New York 10018.)

Many higher-level languages in addition to Fortran have been designed and used, and it is probable that sooner or later Fortran will no longer be so popular— a more modern language will take its place. At this time, however, Fortran is very widely used, and computer companies have spent a lot of time and effort making programs which translate Fortran into their machine languages. These programs are called **compilers**, perhaps because they work by compiling a long list of machine commands which will do just what your Fortran statements ask. Of all the compilers available at your computer center, it is likely that the 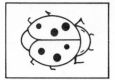Fortran compiler is the most reliable and the most convenient to use. As you learn more about computer programming, you will see why there are likely to be mistakes (or **bugs** as they are called) in any large computer program including a compiler. It is hard enough to write programs without having to worry about bugs in the compiler, so it is important to use a language whose compiler is as accurate as possible. Since this language will, on most computer systems, be Fortran, it is a valuable language to know.

> *compiler: a program which translates a higher-level language into machine language*

It is important to understand what it is that you are to learn about programming. We are not going to try to teach you to "think in Fortran"—in fact, this is undesirable. What you are encouraged to learn is first, how to analyze a problem from the real world and divide it into subproblems each of which you know how to solve, and second, how to communicate the results of your analysis to a computer in terms of a Fortran program. Figure 1 2 1 illustrates the process.

Phases 2 and 3 of Figure 1 2 1 are the most important to learn—and if you do learn them, you will be in a much better position to understand what can be done with computers. Unfortunately, they are virtually impossible to learn out of context. You will have to learn about reasonable analogies between real world processes and computer processes by learning about computers through programming.

Let's apply the scheme shown in Figure 1 2 1 to a specific problem. Figure 1 2 2 suggests a concrete example of a case in which it is very easy to make appropriate analogies. We don't expect you to understand all the details of the program, just the general idea.

Phase 1　You decide you want to know the average price per pound of laundry detergent.

Phase 2　The process you wish to carry out is to sum the individual brand prices and divide by the total number of brands.

$$\text{Average price} = \frac{\text{sum of prices}}{\text{total number of brands}}$$

Phase 3　You decide to let data locations in the computer represent the price per pound for each brand and the number of brands, and to use the addition and division operations to carry out your process.

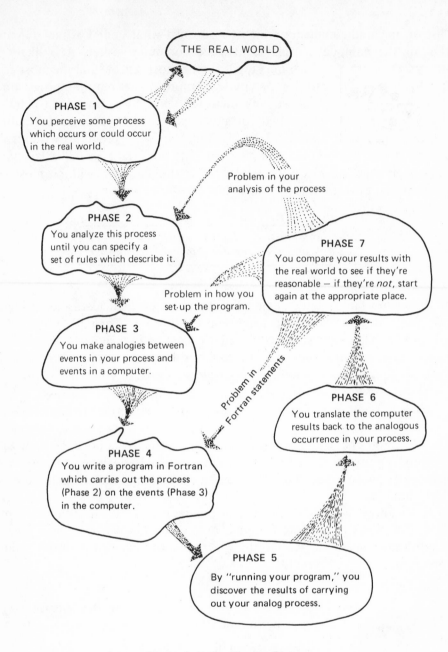

THE REAL WORLD

PHASE 1
You perceive some process which occurs or could occur in the real world.

Problem in your analysis of the process

PHASE 2
You analyze this process until you can specify a set of rules which describe it.

PHASE 7
You compare your results with the real world to see if they're reasonable — if they're *not*, start again at the appropriate place.

Problem in how you set up the program.

PHASE 3
You make analogies between events in your process and events in a computer.

Problem in Fortran statements

PHASE 6
You translate the computer results back to the analogous occurrence in your process.

PHASE 4
You write a program in Fortran which carries out the process (Phase 2) on the events (Phase 3) in the computer.

PHASE 5
By "running your program," you discover the results of carrying out your analog process.

Figure 1 2 1   The Big Picture

Phase 4

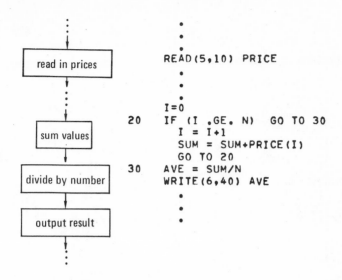

```
                        READ(5,10) PRICE
read in prices          •
                        •
                        •
                        I=0
sum values      20      IF (I .GE. N)   GO TO 30
                        I = I+1
                        SUM = SUM+PRICE(I)
                        GO TO 20
divide by number 30     AVE = SUM/N
                        WRITE(6,40) AVE
                        •
output result           •
                        •
```

Of course the statements shown in Phase 4 are unfamiliar to you. Perhaps, however, you can detect some of their meaning by just glancing at them. They include such actions as reading data (the detergent prices must be entered into the computation), computing the average price by first counting up the total and then dividing by N (the number of different brands), and finally, sending the result to be printed so we can see the answer.

Phase 5 You run your program and get the computed value.

Phase 6 That value should be the average price per pound.

Phase 7 If that number seems reasonable, accept it. If it doesn't, try to see where the problem lies, and start in again at the appropriate place.

Figure 1 2 2   Selecting a Laundry Detergent

Writing programs and using the results of computations is (or should be) a very logical process. The stories about credit card foul-ups, statements like "we have student numbers because that's easier for the computer," and the assumptions that computers are like people, only dumber and faster, show that unfortunately, many people don't understand the BIG PICTURE. As you go through this book, recalling the ideas in Figure 1 2 1 may help you to keep your perspective.

While the process of using the computer is basically logical, Phase 4, in which your ideas are translated into Fortran commands, may not seem to be. Don't worry if certain requirements in Fortran don't seem rational to you—they're probably not. Don't forget that Fortran was designed before anyone had used higher-level languages. Since then, committees and special-interest groups have added parts, usually trying to keep the new version enough like the old so that old programs will run on new compilers. Such an evolution is bound to produce some clumsy appendages. In this book we are trying to protect you from as many idiosyncrasies as possible; in fact, we will occasionally lie to you. That is, initially we will leave certain details out of the language we describe. But these will be only little white lies, and we think that they're for your own good (the details often add little but confusion at first). We fill in details when it becomes necessary so that by the end of Chapter 10 you have the whole picture.

By the way, you might consider that English, which was developed by a *huge* committee, isn't exactly logical either.

EXERCISES 1 2

1 Write down some of your current opinions about computers and how they work, what they do, what they will be able to do, how they affect the life of the average person, etc. Attach what you've written to the last page of this book so that when you've finished the book you can see in what ways your ideas about computers have changed.

2 Read more about the history of Fortran in the chapter on Fortran in *Programming Languages: History and Fundamentals* by Jean E. Sammet, New York, Prentice-Hall, 1969, pp. 143–172.

Section 1 3

Algorithms

Algorithm is a word used by the computing community to mean a rule, procedure, or sequence of instructions. An algorithm is a description of how to do some task, and each step of the description, while incompletely specified, is understood by the person or machine which is to perform the task. Each step will always be incompletely specified simply because it's impossible to describe anything *completely*. You just hope to be understood most of the time. Our first example of an algorithm is so incompletely specified that one important instruction is totally left out. Look at Figure 1 3 1 and see if you can discover what is missing.

Figure 1 3 1   The ZAPPO Algorithm

Since the ZAPPO instructions fail to tell you when to stop, you would wash your hair forever if you followed them unswervingly. There is little doubt that sometime, someone you know, maybe even (perish the thought) *you,* will write a program for the computer which acts like the ZAPPO directions in Figure 1 3 1. Saying "but that isn't what I *meant*" will get you sympathy but not results. Fear not, however; your program will not run forever. The infinite loop is a universal problem, and for that reason all programs are given some time limit. They run just so long, then they are thrown out whether they seem to be finished or not.

> *infinite loop: a list of instructions which cannot be performed in a finite amount of time*

The most important things to notice in the ZAPPO algorithm are:

1 When performed in order, the instructions lead you through the process of "washing your hair with ZAPPO"—presumably this is a difficult task which must be explained.

2 Each instruction is incompletely specified—if you don't know how to "lather," this algorithm is of no use to you.

3 Each step within the algorithm seems reasonable, but the overall effect is not reasonable (namely, it never stops).

A popular and useful way of depicting algorithms is **flowcharting**. Writing a flowchart helps people visualize how the individual parts of an algorithm fit together.

> *flowchart: a pictorial presentation of an algorithm*

Figure 1 3 2 shows a flowchart of the ZAPPO algorithm.

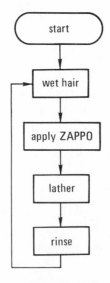

Figure 1 3 2

You will note that instruction 5 ("repeat") is not written out in the flowchart, and if you think about it a bit, you will realize that it is a different kind of instruction from the other four. Instructions 1 through 4 tell you to perform a specific act, whereas number 5 tells you where to get your next instruction. In a flowchart, arrows are used to indicate where to go next. We also added a box with *start* in it. If we read directions on a bottle, we assume we start at the top. In flowcharts this isn't always true.

So that you will be more comfortable thinking in terms of algorithms, we'll show you a few more examples. In each case we'll present a verbal description and a flowchart of the algorithm involved. Try to see how one relates to the other and see which is easier for you to use. Probably you'll want to use a combination of the two techniques.

The verbal description in the knitting algorithm may look strange to you, especially if you don't know that *sts.* means "stitches" and that *K2, P2* means "knit 2, purl 2," but this is a characteristic of programming languages—they contain symbols which mean precise things to the person or computer being instructed.

Knitting a Scarf

VERBAL DESCRIPTION
Starting at lower edge, cast on 116 sts. 1st row: *K2, P2. Repeat from * across. Repeat 1st row until total length is 60 inches.

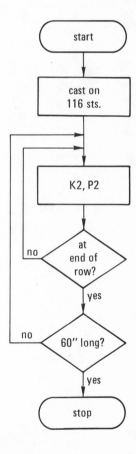

Figure 1 3 3   Knitting a Scarf

You will notice that a symbol (*) is used to identify a place to repeat from and that the "repeat from * across" instruction has become an arrow in the flowchart. Also, you will notice that, unlike the ZAPPO algorithm, the commands to "repeat" are conditional. You don't repeat forever; you repeat to the end of the row ("across"), or until the total length is 60 inches.

The flowchart for the knitting algorithm is relatively complicated, yet it is easy to understand. You probably won't write a program as complicated as this flowchart until you have read Chapter 3.

Get a Job (sha nana na sha nanananana)

Suppose you were out of work and wanted to get a job. One scheme would be:

VERBAL DESCRIPTION

START: Get the help wanted section of the newspaper and look at the first listing.

DECIDE: If you couldn't stand the job, proceed from the instruction called LOOP. If you could stand the job, call the people who placed the ad. If they seem reluctant to talk to you, try to convince them how great you would be at that job and check their response again. If they agree to talk to you, set up an appointment. If they turn you down, proceed to the next step.

LOOP: See if there are any more listings. If there are, look at the next one and repeat instruction DECIDE. If there aren't, be bitter, complain about the economy, and file for unemployment.

It may seem silly to you to write down an elaborate set of instructions for getting a job—after all, "everybody knows how to do that." That may be, but the point is most computer languages have been designed to do one fairly simple thing at a time, based on very little information, so when you are writing a computer

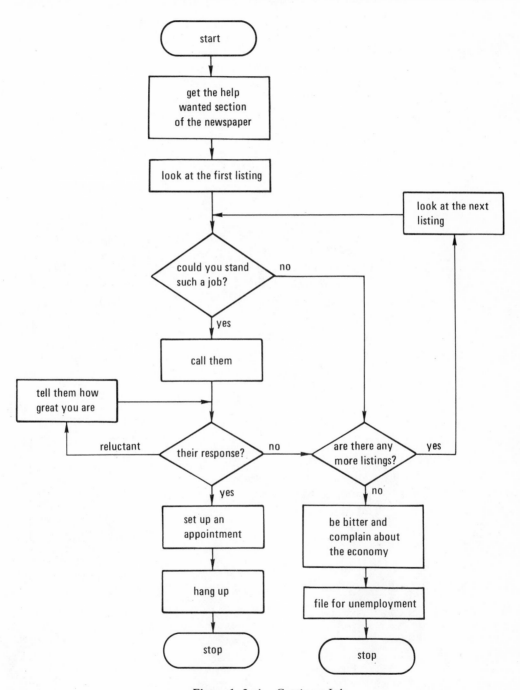

Figure 1 3 4   Getting a Job

program it is *you* who must figure out how to fit a number of basic instructions together to do a useful overall task. You will have to learn to describe the things you want done in simple terms. If you start thinking about all the little things you have to know to accomplish everyday tasks, it will give you some idea of the level of detail needed in computer programs.

Computing Compound Interest

Suppose you want to put some money in a savings account, and you want to decide whether it would be better to get 5 percent interest compounded quarterly or 4.85 percent interest compounded weekly. One way to find out which is better is to compute your interest for one year at each rate and then compare the results.

VERBAL DESCRIPTION

SETUP: Compute how many times a year you will receive interest (4 times with quarterly interest, 52 for weekly compounding). Call the number of times N.

UPDATE: Update the current principal by multiplying it by

$$1 + \frac{\text{interest rate}}{100 \times N}$$

Repeat this updating step until you have done it N times.

PROFIT: Subtract the initial deposit from the final principal to get the interest received.

Figure 1 3 5 Computing Compound Interest

This algorithm has a characteristic which is common to many algorithms—it repeats one of its statements several times. Computers are often used to perform difficult tasks by repeating many simple tasks, as in this example. Possibly this is where the characterization of computers as "high-speed idiots" comes from. This seems a little unfair since the computer *is* able to perform its program, and this is all we expect of it. Perhaps the *program* could be characterized as intelligent or idiotic, but the terms don't apply to the computer itself.

EXERCISES 1 3

1 Write a verbal description of and a flowchart for one or two of the following:

　　making a dessert (following a recipe)
　　making a desert (altering an ecosystem)
　　fixing a flat rear tire on a bicycle
　　computing your income tax
　　writing a haiku verse
　　buying a pair of shoes
　　figuring your grade-point average
　　getting a driver's license

Section 1 4

Machine Ideas

You will recall from Section 2 that Fortran was designed for use on many different computers. Fortran assumes that every computer has certain characteristics. These assumed characteristics can be described in simple terms and are helpful to know. The Fortran statements you will soon be learning will make sense if you visualize them as affecting the various parts of the **conceptual computer** shown in Figure 1 4 1.

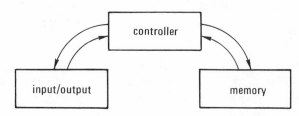

Figure 1 4 1　The Conceptual Computer

The conceptual computer has three parts, a **controller** which carries out the commands which make up your program, a **memory** which stores your program and any values it may use or produce, and **input and output devices** through which values are fed in and printed out. We'll describe each part in concrete terms.

The **memory** consists of some number of words or **cells**. A **memory cell** is a collection of two-state elements. At any point in time each element is in one or the other state. These two states are commonly named "1" and "0" by machine designers, and although we'll rarely think of memory cells in these terms,

> *memory: the part of a computer which stores programs and data*

the size of a memory cell is invariably given in **bits** (**binary digits**), the number of two-state elements making up the cell.

Each cell in memory has an **address** (denoting where it is) and a **value** (the particular pattern of 1's and 0's that it contains). In Fortran programs we give a **name** to each memory cell we wish to store a value in; the name can be thought of as the address of the memory cell. We can issue commands which will copy the value from a particular memory cell into another part of the machine by using

> *We use the terms* word, cell, memory word, memory location, *and* memory cell *interchangeably.*

the name of that memory cell. As the term *copy* implies, doing this does not disturb the value in the memory cell. We will also be able to store values in memory cells, and since there is only a fixed storage capacity (a fixed number of bits) in a cell, the value that used to be there is destroyed when a new value is stored.

The **controller** is the central coordinator of the conceptual computer. Your program, when stored in the memory, is really just a bunch of values (patterns of 1's and 0's) in a bunch of memory cells. The values that make up your program are examined by the controller, and the 1's and 0's work like electrical switches turning on the various subunits required to carry out the command. We're not trying to say that a computer is just a lot of 1's and 0's. That would be a vast oversimplification. But we want to emphasize that

> *controller: the part of a computer which carries out commands from a program*

the controller simply carries out the instructions or commands specified by bit patterns in memory cells. The controller can get values from memory cells, can manipulate them, can put new values back in memory, and can supervise the input and output devices.

Input and output devices (**I/O devices**) are the means of communication between human users and the machine. You will probably punch commands to the computer on cards, and these cards will be "read" by a **card reader,** an input device. The other I/O device you will use frequently is the **printer**, which will print your program and its results. TV and movie scenes involving computers always seem to focus on card readers, line printers, magnetic tape devices, or card sorters. The

> *input/output: the parts of a computer which allow communication between users and the computer*

first three are I/O devices often used to help communicate with a computer. A card sorter, on the other hand, stands alone, not connected to a computer. It can do several information processing tasks, but it cannot be considered a general-purpose computer. Probably these devices are shown because they move at a spectacular rate of speed. In the controller and the memory, on the other hand, nothing moves at all except electrons, and they're hard to see.

There are other types of I/O devices, but until you know more about computers, you'll be able to get by with just a card reader and a line printer. If you think we're being elusive, look at the manual describing the computer you will be using. Then you'll think we're as clear as Frank Zappa is weird.

Anyway, lest you think a card reader can actually *read*, let us emphasize that a card reader converts the holes in the card into electrical signals. These signals are put into the memory by the controller. Hence they become values stored in specific memory cells.

The card reader is commanded to "read" a card by the controller (when the controller has been instructed by your program). Similarly, the controller can send values to the printer and direct the printer to print them.

EXERCISES 1 4

1   Tour the computer you will be using and look at the various I/O devices, the controller (or **processor**), the various types of memory, etc.
2   Find out something about the machine you will be using—the number of bits per word, the number of words in the memory, the brand and model number, the price, what it smells like, etc.
3   List the parts of the "conceptual computer" and their functions.
4   What is the difference between the name of a memory cell and its value?

Section 1 5
A Program for the Conceptual Computer

To get an idea of how computers operate, it will be helpful for you to simulate a computer running a program. The idea is to play the roles of the various parts of the conceptual computer as it goes through the steps of a program. This is a realistic simulation. Every command is directly analogous to a Fortran statement, and all of the parts of the conceptual computer are used. The program you'll be simulating takes in two values and raises the first to the power designated by the second, using repeated multiplication. If the two values are 2 and 4, for example, the program will eventually arrive at the result 16 (2 times 2 times 2 times 2).

Begin as follows:

1 Get a stack of cards and label nine of them with the names STATEMENT 1, STATEMENT 2,..., STATEMENT 9. Label three more with the names A, B, and EXP. These twelve cards represent the memory. Spread them out so you can see them all at once, or at least so you can get to them easily.

2 Get a piece of paper and a pencil to use to write the output sent to the "printer."

3 Take three more cards and write

     2   3   on the first

     5   0   on the second

and 2 −1 on the third.

Place these cards face up in a stack with the first card on top for use by the "card reader."

4 Write the instructions (program statements) below on the cards labeled STATEMENT 1 through STATEMENT 9.

COMMENT: this program computes one number raised to the power of a second number.

STATEMENT 1   Remove the top card on the card reader stack, copy the first number on it into memory cell A, copy the second number into memory cell B, and then throw the card away.

STATEMENT 2   Look at the value in memory cell A and send it to the printer followed by the phrase TO THE POWER, then send the value of B to the printer, and finally send the word IS.

STATEMENT 3   Store the value 1 in memory cell EXP.

STATEMENT 4   Look at the value in memory cell B. If it is 0, take your next instruction from STATEMENT 8, otherwise go on to STATEMENT 5.

STATEMENT 5   Look at the values in memory cells EXP and A, multiply them together, and store the result in EXP.

STATEMENT 6   Take the value from memory cell B, subtract 1 from it, and place the new value back in B, erasing the old value.

STATEMENT 7   Get your next instruction from STATEMENT 4.

STATEMENT 8   Look at the value in memory cell EXP and send it to the printer.

STATEMENT 9   Get your next instruction from STATEMENT 1.

The program you will carry out does a fairly simple task; it reads in two numbers, *a* and *b*, and then multiplies *a* by itself *b* times. Figure 1 5 1 is a flowchart for the process.

In order to carry out the program, simply start with the instruction in memory cell STATEMENT 1, do exactly what it says, and then proceed to the next memory cell in sequence (i.e., to STATEMENT 2, and so on). Some of the instructions say to break the sequence. In this case, you again proceed sequentially after starting from the new STATEMENT. Go!

> *exponentiation: to compute a^b, just take*
> $$\underbrace{a \times a \times \ldots \times a}_{b \ factors}$$

There are a great many things to be learned from what you just did (assuming that you did the above simulation). The STATEMENTs that you (simulating the controller) carried out are very similar to the commands which can be written as statements in Fortran, so you now have a feeling for the degree of explicitness required to write programs. In addition, the algorithm we used has an unfortunate but altogether too common property—it works fine for some input values, and lousy for others. Hope you didn't go on too long with the last pair of input values

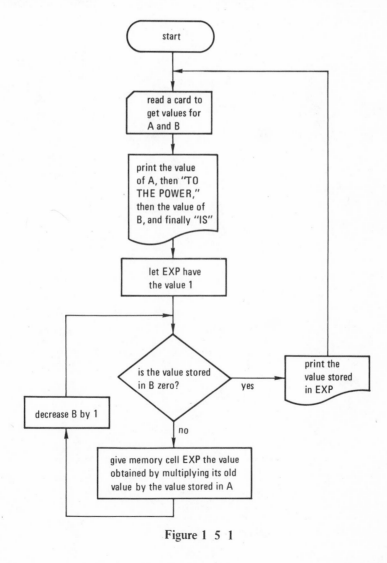

Figure 1 5 1

before you realized that something was desperately wrong. To be realistic, we should have given you a time limit, after which you (the controller) would stop executing the program whether you were finished or not.

The exercises below will give you a little more practice in choosing and expressing commands.

EXERCISES 1 5

1 Add another command into the exponentiation program so that it will just stop if the value in memory cell B is negative.

2 Write a program for the conceptual computer which computes the average of a bunch of numbers.

3 Write a program which finds the longest name in a list of names. Write a bunch of your friends' names on cards, and simulate a computer executing the program to find the longest name.

2 SIMPLE PROGRAMS

Section 2 1

Memory Cells

Of the three parts of the conceptual computer, the memory is probably the most confusing. The I/O apparatus's purpose is straightforward; the controller carries out commands, some of which you can imagine from your class simulation; and the memory is used to store values. This seems simple enough, but confusion seems to arise from the fact that each memory cell has a name. Because of the way computer programs are written, many people tend to confuse the name of a memory cell with the value stored in it, a mistake similar to confusing a box with its contents. Try to keep in mind that a memory cell is a container for a value.

We've said a number of things about memory already (that it's made up of cells, each of which has an address or name and a value, and that both your program and data are stored there). In this chapter we'll make these ideas more concrete and begin to get some ideas of how we use the computer's memory.

In order to use the memory in the Fortran language, you need a name for each memory cell you intend to use. The language is very considerate in that it allows you to name the memory cells in any way you like, as long as you follow a few rules.

> *rules for naming memory cells*
> - *start with a letter*
> - *use* only *letters and numerals*
> - *use no more than six characters*

As long as you follow these rules you have *complete freedom*! For example, you may name a memory cell DRAT, if you like, or any other four-letter word, or POT or CELL12 or COFFEE. But you may not name a memory cell MARI-JUANA or ASPIRINS because these names have too many characters, nor can you name one D--N because two of the characters in that name are neither letters nor numerals.

Once you have named a memory cell, the natural question arises: "What can you do with it?" The answer is that you can store any kind of information you want in it, as long as you can devise a way to represent the information.

By the time you get through this book, you will be able to create representations for whatever types of information you want to deal with. However, certain features of Fortran make it easier to deal with a few specific types of information. So, for a while we'll use only those types. In fact, in this chapter you'll see only two of those **data types**, as they are called.

> *data type: a collection of items of information organized in a standardized manner. A computer system or the programmer associates a special representation with each data type. Since a particular item of information, when stored in the computer's memory, is actually a string of 1's and 0's, this associated representation is essential for correct interpretation of the information item. Two different items of information may be stored in the computer's memory as the same string of 1's and 0's when the items have different data types. In this case the difference between them is determined solely by the difference in their associated representations.*

When you want to use a memory cell in a Fortran program, you must decide what kind of information it will contain; that is, you must choose its **type**. Within a program you may use many memory cells containing many different types of information, but any *one* memory cell is allowed to contain only *one* kind of information. That is, you will associate *one* name and *one* data type with each memory cell you use.

> FORTRAN *is not a legal memory cell name.*

There are several data types available in Fortran, but in this chapter we'll deal with only two of them: INTEGERs and REALs.

INTEGERs are whole numbers, like 1, 2, 3, 7, 11, –4, –1, and 0; numbers with no fractional parts. REALs are numbers with fractional parts and are always written with a decimal point, as in 137.9, 4932.1, 32.00, and –17.472. You might think it very picky to distinguish between whole numbers and numbers containing decimal fractions, especially if the two numbers happen to be 32, an INTEGER, and 32.00, a REAL. It *is* picky. But Fortran deals with the two numbers in vastly different ways, and the type you choose will seriously affect the result of a computation, so you may as well get used to the distinction. Numbers containing decimal points are REALs even if there is no fraction after the decimal point. Numbers without decimal points are INTEGERs.

> *In Fortran programs, numbers containing decimal points are known as* **REAL** *numbers. Thus, a REAL number is a sequence of digits with a decimal point located somewhere in the sequence. In addition, the sequence may be preceded by a plus or a minus sign.*
>
> | REALs | unREALs |
> |---|---|
> | *1497.3* | *1,497.3* |
> | *+83.0* | *+83* |
> | *–983.25* | *–983¼* |
> | *1.0* | *1* |
> | *0.5* | *½* |

> In Fortran programs, each INTEGER constant must be written
> as a series of digits which may be preceded by a plus or a minus
> sign:
>   1492
>   +83
>   −194
>   +0047
> A Fortran INTEGER may not contain any other kinds of
> symbols.
>   1,492 won't work.
>   +83.0 won't work either.

At the beginning of each Fortran program we use declaration statements to name the memory cells we intend to use and we say what type of information we intend to store in them. For example, the declaration statement

```
INTEGER TWO, M1, COUNT, A
```

gives names to four memory cells whose contents will be INTEGERs. On the other hand, the declaration statement

```
REAL X, Y, Z
```

gives names to three memory cells, X, Y, and Z, and decrees that each will be used to store REAL numbers. A memory cell must always contain the same kind of information. It can't contain an INTEGER value at one point and a REAL value at another point.

---

declaration statement

form
> type list
>
> *type* is the name of a Fortran data type (INTEGER or REAL, for example)
> *list* is a list of memory cell names, separated by commas

meaning
> instructs the compiler to attach the names in *list* to memory cells which will be used to store information of the *type* declared at the beginning of the statement

examples

```
INTEGER A, B, C, TWO, THREE, Q1
REAL W, ALPHA, Z27, STUDNT
REAL R, SP, TRACK
INTEGER M
```

---

1 Which of the following are legal names for memory locations? If not, why not?

```
23SKIDOO
SKIDOO23
SALE3
TORQUE
FLIMFLAM
JUICE
TONY THE TIGER
FORTRAN
```

2 Which of the following are legal declaration statements?

```
INTEGER A
INTEGER A, B
INTEGER VERYLONG
INTERGER Q
REAL J, Z, BETA
REAL HIGH,LOW
REAL A, 149.2
```

3 Write a Fortran statement which declares that we want to use two memory cells, AJAX and FOAM, to store INTEGERs.

4 Circle the INTEGERs and place a check mark by the REALs.

41.7

349

692.0

81

−49

−896.721

0

Section 2 2

The Assignment Statement

The question of how to get information into the memory cells you have named still remains. There are two ways. One is to assign values to the cells directly in the program; the other is to get their values from some source of data such as punched cards. Each method has its advantages in different contexts, but the former is the more important in learning to program.

An **assignment statement** gives values to memory cells directly in the program. The general form of the assignment statement is a memory cell name followed by the assignment operator (the equal sign, =), followed by the value which you wish to place into the memory cell. The assignment operator transfers the value on its right into the memory cell named on its left.

The assignment statement confuses many people, perhaps because the assignment operator (=) is a familiar sign, but the operation it designates is *not* familiar. The action in an assignment statement proceeds from *right to left:* the value on the right is placed into the memory cell named on the left. This is an important thing to remember, so important that you should probably read this paragraph again.

> =   *Remember! In Fortran the equal sign does not mean equals in the mathematical sense. A statement like* A = B *places the value in the memory cell* B *into the memory cell* A. *It is true that immediately after the statement is executed the values in* A *and* B *are the same, but at some later time the values in the two memory cells may be different. For example, the next statement in the program may assign a different value to* B. *This won't affect the value of* A, *so at that point* A's *value will be different from* B's.

Examples

```
TWO = 2
```
The value 2 is placed into the memory cell named TWO.
```
M1 = -1
```
The value −1 is placed into the memory cell named M1.
```
STUDNT = 3.982
```
The number 3.982 is placed into the memory cell named STUDNT.
```
TRACK = -1.95
```
The number −1.95 is placed into the memory cell named TRACK.
```
FOUR = 2
```
The value 2 is placed into the memory cell named FOUR. FOUR is a lousy name for a memory cell containing the value 2. The reason it's lousy has nothing to do with the rules of Fortran. The compiler doesn't care what names you associate with which values. But there are enough complications in writing programs without increasing the problems by choosing misleading names. Choose names which at least hint at the ways in which the values stored will be used.

Of course, in order for the above assignment statements to work properly, the declaration statements
```
INTEGER TWO, M1, FOUR
REAL STUDNT, TRACK
```
must appear at the beginning of the program.

It would soon get boring just writing programs that assigned values to a bunch of memory locations. Fortunately, the right-hand side of an assignment statement can be more complex than just a single number. It may be an **expression** involving some arithmetic computations. In Fortran, the familiar operations of addition, subtraction, multiplication, division, and exponentiation may be used in the usual ways (see Table).

operation	standard symbols	example	Fortran symbol	examples
addition	+	$a + b$	+	A+B 1+1
subtraction	−	$a - b$	−	A−B 3−2
multiplication	$\times$	$a \times b$	*	A*B 4*4
division	$\div$ — /	$a \div b \quad \dfrac{a}{b}$ a/b	/	A/B 10/2
exponentiation	superscript	a^b	**	A**B 2**10

The reason the multiplication and exponentiation symbols aren't the same as usual will become apparent if you look at a punched card. There would be no way of telling the multiplication sign $\times$ from the letter X, so an asterisk (*) is used instead. In addition, there's no way of punching superscript symbols, so we use ** instead.

Example

```
REAL TOTAL
TOTAL = 12.00*(1.0+0.05)
```

The value of the arithmetic expression above (namely 12.60) is placed into the memory cell named TOTAL.

Expressions can be considerably more general than the ones you have seen so far, which have involved only constants. It is also permissible to use memory cell names in an expression. Thus, names of memory cells may appear on both sides of an assignment statement, but the names are used in very different ways. As you already know, the name on the *left* side tells where to *store* the value which results from the computation on the right side. Memory cell names on the *right* side mean "go to this place in memory, and use whatever value is stored there in the computation." It is important to realize that the values of memory cells on the right remain unchanged by the process of evaluating the expression.

Example

```
INTEGER COUNT
COUNT = -M1*TWO
```

The value of the arithmetic expression on the right is placed into the memory cell named COUNT. To compute the value of the expression, the controller must first determine the contents of the memory cells M1 and TWO, then execute the indicated arithmetic operations. If we assume the values of the memory cells M1 and TWO haven't changed since the last time we used them in this chapter, then TWO has the value 2 and M1 has the value −1, so COUNT will be assigned the value −(−1)*2, that is, 2.

Example

```
COUNT = COUNT+1
```

The value of the expression on the right is placed into the memory cell named COUNT. This example may appear odd at first because the memory cell to be given a value is involved in the expression on the right. This is one time when it is especially important to remember that the action goes from right to left. First the computer looks up the current value of COUNT; our last assignment made that value 2. Adding 1 to 2, the value of the expression is 3, and this value is put into the memory cell COUNT. This assignment destroys the old value of COUNT.

In most cases, writing arithmetic expressions to make computations is quite natural and the results fit in pretty well with your past experience. However, there is one big difference to keep in mind. Remember that each memory cell is made up of a fixed number of elements or symbols, 1's and 0's. That means that some numbers will be too long to fit. For example, INTEGER memory cells in

IBM 360 and 370 computers cannot handle INTEGERs outside the range –2149531648 to +2149531647. This may not seem particularly restrictive, and usually it isn't, but it is important to realize that this doesn't include *all* integers. There are an infinite number of (mathematical) integers. If you are not careful, this restricted INTEGER range may cause you to get results you don't expect. If you multiply two big numbers together, the result may be too big to fit in one memory cell, and this will no doubt cause problems in your computation. (This type of error is known as an **overflow**.)

Another problem arises in evaluating expressions like 29/7. The result certainly cannot be computed to infinite precision, but what value should be computed? Fortran settles this question by convention: the value of an arithmetic operation involving only INTEGERs must be an INTEGER. Therefore, if the number 4 1/7 comes up as the quotient of two INTEGERs, the fractional part is dropped. Hence 29/7 equals 4 (in Fortran).

Arithmetic expressions will be dealt with in more detail later. For now, rely on your past experience with mathematics to guide you in using parentheses to denote groups of operations which are to be done before others. For example, $1 + (7 * 3)$ is 22, but $(1 + 7) * 3$ is 24. You may also rely on the usual algebraic rules of precedence: exponentiations are performed first, then multiplications and divisions, then additions and subtractions. For example, $10 + 7**2/12$ equals $10 + (7**2)/12$, which is 14. When you are uncertain about how an expression will be evaluated, use parentheses to make it perfectly clear.

EXERCISES 2 2

1 At the end of the following program fragment, what are the values of A and B?

```
INTEGER A, B
B = 10
A = B
B = 2
```

2 What values would be stored in INTEGER memory cell B by these assignment statements?

```
B = 2*3*4
B = (2/1) + 1
B = -19*2
```

3 Which of these are legal assignment statements? If not, why not? (Assume all variable names have been declared to be INTEGERs.

```
A = A*A + A
BO = 2
-AT = 2
CAT + DOG = FIGHT
CAT + DOG-3
FIGHT = CAT + DOG
```

4 What value will be stored in INTEGER memory cell SOUP by these assignment statements?

```
SOUP = 1 + (7*4)/2
SOUP = 123/2
SOUP = (19/20) + 1
SOUP = (21/20) + 1
SOUP = (8/16)*1024
```

5 Write statements which will

　　a declare an INTEGER memory cell named FIRST and assign FIRST the value 2,

　　b assign FIRST its old value times 4, and

　　c assign FIRST its old value plus 1.

Section 2 3

The WRITE Statement

So far you have learned how to attach names to memory cells and to place values into them. You can also make the computer perform computations involving INTEGER numbers. Unfortunately, however, you have no way at this point of finding out the results of the computations. The WRITE statement will solve this problem, as the following example demonstrates.

Suppose you are buying a car, and you want to compute the total price, including an optional FM radio and supersport airfoil spoiler. The computation might proceed like this:

　1　note the base price

　2　note the price of the FM radio option

　3　note the price of the airfoil spoiler option

　4　add the above three figures to get a subtotal

　5　compute 7 percent sales tax

　6　add tax to subtotal to get total cost

The program below makes these computations. You should be able to understand everything in the program except, possibly, the WRITE, FORMAT, STOP, and END statements. We'll explain those after you've looked the program over carefully.

```
        REAL    BASEPR, RADIO, SPOILR
        REAL    SUBTOT, TAX, TOTAL
        BASEPR = 4127.00
        RADIO = 232.00
        SPOILR = 248.00
        SUBTOT = BASEPR + RADIO + SPOILR
        TAX = SUBTOT*0.07
        TOTAL = SUBTOT+TAX
        WRITE(6,1000) BASEPR
 1000   FORMAT('1BASE PRICE     $',F7.2)
        WRITE(6,2000) RADIO
 2000   FORMAT('      RADIO     $',F7.2)
        WRITE(6,3000) SPOILR
 3000   FORMAT('    SPOILER     $',F7.2)
        WRITE(6,4000) SUBTOT
 4000   FORMAT('0TOTAL PRICE    $',F7.2)
        WRITE(6,5000) TAX
 5000   FORMAT('          TAX   $',F7.2)
        WRITE(6,6000) TOTAL
 6000   FORMAT('0PLEASE PAY CASHIER    $',F7.2)
        STOP
        END
```

output
```
        BASE PRICE    $4127.00
             RADIO    $ 232.00
           SPOILER    $ 248.00

        TOTAL PRICE   $4607.00
               TAX    $ 322.49

     PLEASE PAY CASHIER    $4929.49
```

Each of the WRITE statements in the program instructs the controller to send one line to the printer. To understand how this works, you need to understand the various parts of a WRITE statement. First of all, most computers have several output devices attached to them, including line printers, magnetic tapes, disks, and so forth. To send output to the printer, the WRITE statement must select that particular device out of the whole collection of devices attached to the computer. That is the purpose of the "6" in the WRITE statements of the above program. On the computer system we were using, as on many others, I/O unit 6 is the line printer. (Your system may denote the printer with a different number, perhaps 3 or 2. Check with a local expert.)

In addition, the WRITE statement must refer to a FORMAT which describes the basic layout of the line, what kinds of values go where, where the line goes on the page, and so forth (more on this later). This is the purpose of the "1000" in the first WRITE statement; it tells the controller to use FORMAT number 1000 to determine the layout of the line. The FORMAT, however, doesn't specify all the information which goes on the line. Some of it

Local Expert

comes from values stored in memory cells, and this is the purpose of BASEPR in the first WRITE statement. Thus, the first WRITE statement says to put the value of BASEPR on a line whose layout is described in FORMAT 1000 and send the line to unit 6, the printer.

WRITE statement

form

WRITE (*u, f*) *list*

u is an INTEGER constant or INTEGER memory cell name

f is an INTEGER corresponding to the label on a FORMAT statement

list is a list of memory cell names, separated by commas (*list* may be omitted if the FORMAT completely specifies the line so that no values from memory are needed)

meaning

sends the line described in FORMAT *f*, filled in with values from the memory cells in *list*, to the designated I/O unit *u*

examples

```
WRITE(6,1030) A, B, C
WRITE(6,2019) Q
WRITE(3,3000)
WRITE(N,2042) A,C,T
```

The FORMAT statement must describe the layout of the line in several ways. First, it must say where to put the line on the page. There are several possible choices, but the most important are (1) on the next available line, (2) on the second line down from the current line, leaving a blank line in between, and (3) at the top of the next page, leaving the rest of the current page blank. The particular choice is indicated by a **carriage control character** in the FORMAT. Character strings in FORMATs including the carriage control character are distinguished from other types of information by enclosing them in **quote marks** (actually, they look more like apostrophes, but we call them quote marks because of the way they're used). Any character string in a FORMAT is copied (without the quote marks) onto the line being written. The carriage control character is simply the first character on the line.

In other words, the printer refuses to print the first character on any line sent to it by the controller. Instead, the printer uses the first character to select one of the three choices for line positioning. The character "blank" (' ') selects the next available line, the character zero ('0') selects the second line down from the current line, and the character ('1') selects the top of the next page.

These character strings in FORMATs that are transmitted as is (less quote marks) to the output line are known as **literal descriptors** because they describe a part of a line literally, as it will stand. In order to leave a place in a line to insert values from memory, we use **data descriptors** in FORMATs. These data descriptors specify the type of information stored in memory which will be inserted at

literal descriptors

forms

    'string'   non-ANSI

    *n*H*string*   ANSI standard

    string is a sequence of one or more characters (letters, digits, and/or special characters like periods, slashes, etc.)

    n is an INTEGER indicating the number of characters in *string*

meaning

    denotes the sequence of characters *string* to be copied literally onto an output line from a FORMAT

examples

```
'ARCHETYPAL SYSTEMS INC.'
23HARCHETYPAL SYSTEMS INC.
','
1H,
```

note

    We will use the nonstandard form in our programs because we feel it is easier to read. If your system will accept only the ANSI standard form, known as the **Hollerith notation**, or if you want to conform strictly to the standards, you should have no trouble converting our literal descriptors to yours. In fact, it won't be long before you'll be able to write a program to make the conversion for you.

The Hollerith notation gets its name from Herman Hollerith, who invented some punch card processing equipment in the last decade of the nineteenth century. In large measure, it was because of Hollerith's equipment that the U.S. census of 1890 was finished before the start of the census of 1900.

---

carriage control characters

`' '` *or* `1H`	*(blank)*	*move down the page one line before printing*	*single space*
`'0'` *or* `1H0`	*(zero)*	*move down the page two lines before printing*	*double space*
`'1'` *or* `1H1`	*(one)*	*move to the top of the next page before printing*	*eject page*

this point in the line (INTEGER or REAL), the number of character positions to use to print the value, and in the case of REALs, the number of digits beyond the decimal point to print. Each data descriptor in a FORMAT will correspond to a memory cell in the WRITE *list*. The value from the first memory cell in the WRITE *list* goes into the spot on the line indicated by the first data descriptor in the FORMAT. The second memory cell in the WRITE *list* matches with the second data descriptor in the FORMAT, and so on.

For each type of value, there is a different kind of data descriptor. The I*w* data descriptor is used for INTEGER values; I6, for example, leaves six spaces in the line for an INTEGER from memory to be inserted. The F*w.d* data descriptor is used for REAL values; F7.2 leaves seven spaces in the line for a REAL value, rounded to two decimal places, to be inserted. It is essential in matching memory cells in the WRITE *list* with data descriptors in the FORMAT that the types of values in the memory cells be identical to the types of the data descriptors. If an INTEGER valued memory cell matches with an F*w.d* data descriptor, or if a REAL valued memory cell matches in sequence with an I*w* data descriptor, the

---

data descriptors

forms

F*w.d*

I*w*

w and *d* are unsigned INTEGER constants (*d* must be smaller than *w*)

meaning

describes a field of width *w* (i.e., *w* character positions) to be filled with a REAL value expressed to *d* decimal places in the case of F*w.d*, or an INTEGER value in the case of I*w*. The values are always **right justified** in the field (i.e., the last digit goes into the last position of the *w*-character field). If the value is negative, the number is preceded by a minus sign (−) which takes up one of the *w* character positions. In REAL values, the decimal point occupies one of the *w* character positions and the decimal fraction takes up *d* positions, leaving *w* − *d* − 1 character positions for the rest of the number (and minus sign if needed).

examples

```
      A = 479.12
      B = -7.86
      M = 12
      WRITE(6,1000) A,B,M
 1000 FORMAT(' ', F10.2, F7.1, I4)
      WRITE(6,1001) M,B,A
 1001 FORMAT(' SALES', I3, F7.2, '    RATE', F7.3)
```

printed lines

bbbb479.12bbb−7.9bb12   *b* means *blank*

SALESb12b479.12bbRATEb−7.860

results printed will be erroneous. If you are lucky, your computing system will detect the error. More likely, a mysterious, erroneous result will be printed with no explanation given.

Since WRITE statements must reference FORMAT statements, FORMATs must have labels. As you can see in the box on Fortran statement layout, labels on statements must be placed in columns 1 through 5. A **label** is simply an unsigned INTEGER of one to five digits, but not all zeros. Thus a FORMAT is a labeled statement consisting of the key word FORMAT followed by a parenthesized list of FORMAT descriptors (literal descriptors, data descriptors, and others we haven't covered yet).

Conventions concerning the physical appearance of Fortran statements are based on the assumption that the statements are punched on 80-column cards. Certain columns are used for certain purposes. There are four fields on a Fortran statement card:

1   the label field (columns 1–5)
2   the continuation field (column 6)
3   the statement field (columns 7–72)
4   the identification field (columns 73–80)

The identification field is completely ignored by the compiler but it is printed on your program listing and is often used for card numbering. In all fields, blanks are ignored; you should use blanks freely to make your program readable.

You write one statement on each card. However, if your statement is too long to fit in the statement field of one card, you may continue it into the statement field of the next card by placing any mark (other than zero) in the continuation field (column 6) of the second card. (This doesn't work for comment statements.)

There is one additional convention: a C in column 1 will cause the compiler to ignore the entire card. Since the card will be printed on the program listing, you may use this convention to intersperse your program with comments.

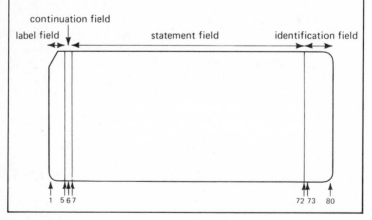

continuation field
label field   statement field   identification field

1   5 6 7   72 73   80

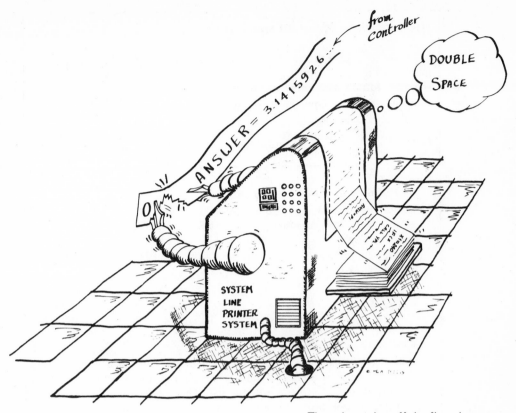

The printer rips off the first character on each line sent by the controller and uses it to decide how far to move the paper before printing.

The whole notion of FORMATs, data descriptors, literal descriptors, and the like probably seems unduly complicated to you. We sympathize. It *is* unduly complicated. In fact, FORMATs are a major hurdle for novice Fortran programmers. They're a real pain in the old wazoo. When you write FORMATs, try to visualize the line to be printed. It often helps to write out a prototype line, then write the FORMAT to match the prototype, inserting literal descriptors where you know exactly what the line will look like and data descriptors where computed results will be inserted.

If you look back at the program now, you should be able to understand how the WRITE statements work, using the FORMATs, to print results. However, you're still in the dark about the last two lines, the STOP and END statements. The STOP statement instructs the *controller* to stop executing your program and proceed to someone else's. The END statement instructs the *compiler* that there are no more statements in your program. The END statement must be, physically,

alternate forms of output statements

Most versions of Fortran provide other (non-ANSI) forms of input/outout statements. It is easy to convert the forms we use to the other forms (many of which are easier to use).

Probably the most common alternate form is one in which the unit number is not needed.

form

    PRINT *f*, *list*

conversion

    WRITE(6,*f*) *list* → PRINT *f*, *list*

    Notice the comma after the FORMAT number. There is no comma after the parenthesis in the ANSI standard form. No change is needed in the FORMAT itself or in the I/O list.

    An even more convenient form is the format-free I/O popularized by the WATFOR/WATFIV compilers:

form

    PRINT, *list*

conversion

    WRITE(6,*f*) *list* → PRINT, *list*

    Here there is a major change in the FORMAT. Most of it is (hooray!) thrown away. Literal descriptors are moved from the abandoned FORMAT into the *list*. The system chooses data descriptors itself. Carriage control characters cannot be used.

example conversions

```
      WRITE(6,1000) BASEPR
 1000 FORMAT(' BASE PRICE     $', F7.2)

      PRINT, 'BASE PRICE     $', BASEPR


      WRITE(6,2000) N, SUM, AVE
 2000 FORMAT(' N=', I3, ' SUM=', F8.3, ' AVE=', F10.5)

      PRINT, 'N=', N, 'SUM=', SUM, 'AVE=', AVE
```

the last card in your program, but the STOP statement may appear anywhere. Of course, after the STOP statement is executed, no other statement in your program will be executed, so it's difficult to see why you would want to put it anywhere except immediately preceding the END statement. In Chapter 3 we'll see examples where the difference between STOP and END statements is clearer. For now, just remember that the compiler, in translating your program to machine language, translates STOP into a command for the controller, but END is an instruction for the compiler itself and is not translated into a machine language command.

```
STOP statement

form
    STOP

meaning
    instructs controller to stop executing your program and to
    begin executing the next program
```

```
END statement

form
    END

meaning
    informs compiler that there are no more statements in your
    program
```

At this point you should be able to prepare a program and run it. Look around the computer center and find a sign describing the correct deck setup. It will include some statements (known as job control statements) other than the Fortran statements in order to direct your program to the correct subsystems built into your computer system (one of these subsystems is the Fortran compiler). You might try the first problem at the end of this chapter for starters.

EXERCISES 2 3

1 Which of the following statements are legal?

```
WRITE(6,1000) X
WRITE(6,2000) X+Y, 21,72, 3*2
WRITE, A, B, C
WRITE(6,3000)
WRITE(6,3000),A
```

2 What would the following program fragment print?

```
      INTEGER M
      REAL A
      A = 2.0*35.2
      M = 3+9
      WRITE(6,1000) A,M
 1000 FORMAT(' ', F5.2, I4)
```

Section 2 4

The READ Statement

In most cases the most convenient and efficient way to place values into memory cells is to use the assignment statement which we have just discussed. There is, however, a second way to give values to memory cells which, in certain cases, makes a program easier to use. We are speaking of the READ statement. Its main advantage is that it allows you to change the data that the program uses in its computations without changing the program itself. The following example illustrates the point.

Suppose you are tired of balancing your checkbook each month, especially since your balance often disagrees with the bank's. You know the bank uses a computer to figure your balance, so maybe if you use a computer too, you will have a better chance of agreeing with the bank. Let's try to think of a way to write a program to compute your bank balance.

Basically, the program must assign the old balance and amounts of the month's transactions to memory cells, compute the new balance, and print the result. One approach to writing such a program is described below:

1. declare one memory cell to store the amount for each check you wrote
2. declare one memory cell to store the amount for each deposit you made
3. declare a memory cell to store the old balance and one to store the new balance
4. assign values for the old balance and all the checks and deposits, using assignment statements
5. write an expression which computes the new balance and assign its value to the memory cell to be used for that purpose
6. print the new balance

The big disadvantage to a program like this one is that it must be changed every month. Each month you will write a different number of checks for different amounts, make a different number of deposits, and have a different old balance. Therefore, you will have to declare a different number of memory cells in each month's program and assign them different values.

A second approach would be to keep a running balance rather than to do all the totaling at the end. Then, instead of needing a memory cell for each check and deposit, you need only one cell for the current transaction (check or deposit) and one cell for the current balance. This approach is shown in Figure 2 4 1.

Although this approach is closer to what we want, there is still a problem: there is no way to stop and print out the final balance. The program just keeps going. You will learn a way to exit the loop to print results in Chapter 3, but for now we'll try another approach.

We are trying to avoid changing the program each month. Of course it is clear that something must be changed, since the amounts of the transactions will be

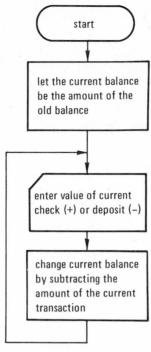

Figure 2 4 1

different each month, but it would be nice to have some way to give the program this information without having to change the program itself. To give data to the program from an outside source, in other words. This can be accomplished by using the READ statement.

The READ statement directs the controller to get values from the card reader and place them into memory cells. The card reader gets these values from **data cards**, which are not part of the program itself. A READ statement consists of the word READ followed by a unit number and FORMAT label in parentheses, followed by a list of memory cell names known as the **input list**. The memory cell names in the list must be separated by commas, just as they were in the WRITE statements you saw in Section 2 3. For many systems, the unit number associated with the card reader is 5, but as with the printer's unit number, you'll have to check with local experts to determine the correct number for your system.

The READ statement places a value into each memory cell in the input list, getting these values from a data card following your program. Just as output lines must be described by FORMATs, so must data cards be described by FORMATs. The READ statement refers to a FORMAT and matches each memory cell in the input list sequentially with the data descriptors in the FORMAT. The data descriptors specify the type of value which will be on the card and where the values will be. To look at it another way, the FORMAT divides the data card into fields, one for each data descriptor, and the READ statement takes values for the memory cells in its input list from these fields. The value from the first field goes into the first memory cell in the input list, and so on down to the last memory cell in the input list.

```
┌─────────────────────────────────────────────────────────────────┐
│ FORMAT statement (restricted form)                              │
│                                                                  │
│ form                                                             │
│    FORMAT (spec)                                                 │
│    spec is a list of FORMAT descriptors separated by commas      │
│                                                                  │
│ meaning                                                          │
│    describes an output line or data card                         │
│                                                                  │
│ note                                                             │
│    Every FORMAT must be labeled.                                 │
│                                                                  │
│ examples                                                         │
│    1001 FORMAT('0BALANCE=',F10.2)                                │
│    2000 FORMAT(I7, F10.0)                                        │
│    2001 FORMAT(2I0, I10, F8.0, I3)                               │
└─────────────────────────────────────────────────────────────────┘
```

As with WRITE statements, it is extremely important that the field types (REAL or INTEGER) match the types of the corresponding memory cells in the input list. If an F$w.d$ (REAL) data descriptor gets paired with an INTEGER type memory cell, the results can be a disaster, often without warning. Of course, pairing an Iw descriptor with a REAL type memory cell causes similar problems. Unlike FORMATs associated with WRITE statements, input FORMATs don't need carriage control characters; each time a READ statement is performed, a new data card is used (you can't back up). In fact, literal descriptors won't be of any use to us in FORMATs associated with READ statements, but the F$w.d$ and Iw descriptors are used to describe REAL and INTEGER fields of w characters on the data card. If a FORMAT contains several data descriptors, the corresponding fields on the data card lie one after the other, left to right across the card.

```
┌─────────────────────────────────────────────────────────────────┐
│ READ statement                                                   │
│                                                                  │
│ form                                                             │
│    READ(u,f) list                                                │
│    u is an unsigned INTEGER constant or an INTEGER memory        │
│    cell name                                                     │
│    f is a FORMAT statement label                                 │
│    list, an input list, is a list of memory cell names separated │
│    by commas                                                     │
│                                                                  │
│ meaning                                                          │
│    places values into the memory cells in list, taking the values│
│    from fields on a data card. The fields on the data card are de-│
│    scribed in FORMAT f and the data cards lie on unit u.         │
│                                                                  │
│ examples                                                         │
│    READ(5,1000)A, B, C                                           │
│    READ(5,2000)X                                                 │
└─────────────────────────────────────────────────────────────────┘
```

You may recall that in Chapter 1, when you were simulating a computer, the controller executed some statements similar to READ. It was a two-step process: first the controller told the card reader to read a card, and then it told certain memory cells to remember the values on that card. The Fortran READ statement is executed in the same way.

No data card can be read twice. Each time a READ statement is performed, it starts at the beginning of a new card.

data cards: cards with values punched on them which follow your program. They are not statements in your program, but they contain values to be stored in memory cells used by your program.

Data cards are placed after a special card put after the end of your program. This card varies from one computer system to the next, and again, you'll have to look around the computer center for a poster describing deck setup or consult a local expert on how to make up the card which separates your program from the data cards.

Now let's see how we can use the READ statement to solve the bank balance problem. Recall that we wanted to write the program in such a way that we could use it every month without change. Thus, the program itself can depend neither on the actual amounts of the checks and deposits nor on the number of transactions. This calls for careful planning, and we will take several stabs at the problem before coming up with a complete solution.

> *Since data cards come after your program and are not part of it, their use is not bound by the rules for punching Fortran statements. You may use any or all of the 80 columns available.*

Our first approach is to READ the amounts of the transactions one by one and keep a running total representing the current balance. Our program will assume that there are no more than 5 transactions in any one month. If you are a heavy check writer, you can easily change the program so that it will handle 25 or 50 transactions, but this dependence on a maximum number of checks is an objectionable feature which we will remove later in an improved version of the program. Read the program carefully, and try to understand what it does. We'll describe it in detail after you've read through it.

```
COMMENT:  THIS PROGRAM CALCULATES A NEW BANK BALANCE GIVEN
C         THE OLD BALANCE AND TRANSACTIONS.
C         TO USE THE PROGRAM, PUNCH SIX DATA CARDS.
C           CARD  1 :  OLD BALANCE
C           CARDS 2-6:  TRANSACTIONS (POSITIVE FOR CHECKS AND
C                                     NEGATIVE FOR DEPOSITS)
      REAL BALNCE, TRANS
      READ(5,1000) BALNCE
 1000 FORMAT(F5.0)
      READ(5,1000) TRANS
      BALNCE = BALNCE - TRANS
      READ(5,1000) TRANS
      BALNCE = BALNCE - TRANS
      READ(5,1000) TRANS
      BALNCE = BALNCE - TRANS
      READ(5,1000) TRANS
      BALNCE = BALNCE - TRANS
      READ(5,1000) TRANS
      BALNCE = BALNCE - TRANS
      WRITE(6,2000) BALNCE
 2000 FORMAT(' NEW BALANCE IS $', F7.2)
      STOP
      END
```

data
```
   456.03
    78.36
   -25.39
    45.25
    45.22
   -75.42
```

output
NEW BALANCE IS $ 388.00

There are several important things to notice about the above program. For one thing, the data descriptor F5.0 in FORMAT 1000 describes a data card with a REAL number in columns 1 through 5. The d part of an F$w.d$ data descriptor is ignored by the READ statement as long as there is a decimal point in the REAL number on the data card. For this reason, we normally let d be zero and always include the decimal point in a REAL number on a data card. If the decimal point is omitted, then the controller inserts one d places from the right-hand side of an F$w.d$ field.

> *numeric fields and blanks: On a data card, fields covered by an* F$w.d.$ *or* Iw *data descriptor are known as numeric fields. Numeric fields may contain blanks, but the blanks are interpreted as zeros. This will cause problems if a number with no decimal point does not extend all the way to the rightmost field position. Effectively, enough zeros are tagged onto the end of the number to fill out the field. Unless the programmer does this intentionally, aware of the results, he ends up with a much larger number than he intended.*

The second important thing to notice about the program is the high degree of redundancy. The statements READ(5,1000) TRANS and BALNCE = BALNCE – TRANS are repeated over and over again. There are always ways to avoid repeating the same statements over and over again, and you will learn one in the next chapter, but for now this will have to suffice.

The third important feature is the technique of computing the sum of the transactions using a single memory cell in which the running sum builds up. In this case, that memory cell is called BALNCE. First we put the amount of the old balance into BALNCE. This step is called **initialization**. Each time the computer gets the amount of a new transaction from a data card, it changes BALNCE by that amount. This technique, called **accumulating a sum**, is very common in computer programming. You will see it again and again. In this case the sum accumulates one term at a time in the memory cell BALNCE.

EXERCISES 2 4

1 Prepare some data cards for the above program, assuming that you wrote four checks in the amounts $4.27, $27.92, $132.00, and $9.42, made one deposit in the amount of $237.26, and had an old balance of $1.25. What results would be printed if the program were executed with these data cards?

2 Which of the following are legal Fortran I/O statements? If a statement is not legal, explain why.

```
READ(5,1000) A, B, D
WRITE(6,2000) A, B, D
READ(5,3000) A, A+B, 2
WRITE(6,4000),A
WRITE(6,5000)
READ(5,7000)X
```

3 Write a program which READs four INTEGERs from a card and WRITEs their sum.

PROBLEMS 2

1 Construct a program which prints your name and address (as they would appear on a mailing label), using one WRITE statement for each printed line. Sample output:

```
CHESTER P. FARNSWORTHY
1704 MONDO VERDE LN.
FERNLY, NEVADA 89408
```

2 Write a program to (a) print your name, (b) assign the result of a computation to an INTEGER memory cell, e.g., $N = 1 + 2 - (3*4)/5$, and (c) print the value of this integer variable below your name.

3 Write a program which computes and prints the sum of the squares of the first ten integers, $1^2 + 2^2 + 3^2 + \ldots + 10^2$.

4 Design a program which computes your car's gasoline mileage. Devise a FORMAT statement which causes three REAL values to be READ from one card. The three values are previous mileage reading, current mileage reading, and gallons of gas used. Be sure to print out the three input values as well as the computed mileage.

5 Write a program which READs the lengths of the sides of a rectangle (expressed as INTEGERs), and prints out those lengths followed by the area of the rectangle.

6 Design a program which helps you visualize the effects of inflation. READ in the inflation rate (say, 0.06 if the rate is 6 percent per year), and print out

a the amount of money you will need in four years to buy what $1.00 will buy today (if the rate is 6 percent, then this is given by $1.00 * 1.06 * 1.06 * 1.06 * 1.06)

b the amount of money you would have needed four years ago to buy what $1.00 will buy today ($1.00/(1.06 * 1.06 * 1.06 * 1.06))

7 Do problem 6 again, but change the program so that it accepts not only the rate of inflation, but also the number of years the comparison is to be made for. (Hint: use exponentiation.)

8 Write a program which figures out how long it will take to mow a rectangular lawn with a rectangular house on it. READ in the dimensions of the lawn and house. Assume you can mow at a rate of a hundred square feet per minute.

9 Do problem 8 again, but include more accurate information about your personal mowing habits. In addition to the input data which allows you to compute the area to be mown, use these three input values:

a the width of your mower's cut (e.g., 18 inches)

b your walking speed (e.g., 1.5 miles per hour)

c the fraction of the time you spend resting or drinking lemonade (e.g., 0.25 if you rest a quarter of the time)

3 LOOPS

Section 3 1

Introduction

By now you know enough to write programs which perform numerical computations and print out the results. You also know that the numbers used in the computations can either be written within the program itself or obtained from data cards outside the program. Thus you are able to use a computer to do computations similar to those you can do on a desk calculator. In some cases it might actually be more convenient to use a computer to do these calculations, but most of the time it would be easier to use the desk calculator. In one case, the numbers and arithmetic operation symbols are punched on cards; in the other case, they are entered directly into the machine through its keyboard—about the same amount of work. The computer might have a slight advantage if the expression is written with lots of parentheses which make it hard to untangle, and the calculator might have a slight advantage in simply totaling up a list of numbers (as in our checking account problem) since the procedure is simple enough to be remembered without being written down in the form of a program. Thus, the computer may not seem particularly useful to you right now, but by the end of this chapter you will begin to see how useful it can be.

Totaling a list of numbers on a calculator is a very repetitious task: enter a number, punch the add key, enter a number, punch the add key, and so forth. The program we wrote in Section 2 4 to total a list of numbers was also very repetitious:

```
        .
        .
        .
   READ(5,1000) TRANS
   BALNCE = BALNCE - TRANS
        .
        .
        .
```

It turns out that a repetitious program can always be written in a much more compact way using a program structure known as a **loop**. Instead of writing the same statements over and over, we tell the computer to repeat the statements. In order to tell the computer to repeat, we need to know a new kind of statement.

loop:

46

Section 3 2

Transfer of Control

If we come to a point in a program where we want to repeat a previous statement instead of proceeding in the usual sequence to the next statement, we must have some way of telling the controller where to begin that repetition. In Fortran this is done by placing a **label** on the statement to be repeated and referring to that label to initiate the repeat. To tell the controller to repeat from the statement whose label is *s*, we write

$$\text{GO TO } s$$

The label *s* is an unsigned INTEGER between 1 and 99999. The statement to be repeated will have the number *s* in its label field, columns 1 through 5 (see the box on page 34 describing the statement card format). Almost any statement may be labeled, but it is wise to put a label on a statement only if it is necessary to refer to the statement from some other point in the program.

> The only statements we've seen so far which may not be labeled are the declaration statements
>
>   INTEGER *list*
>   REAL *list*
>
> and the END statement.
> These are commands to the compiler, *not to the controller*.

Examine the following rewritten version of Section 2 4's bank balancing program.

```
column 7
    |
    ↓
      INTEGER BALNCE, TRANS
      READ(5,1000) BALNCE
1000  FORMAT(F5.0)
20    READ(5,1000) TRANS
         BALNCE = BALNCE - TRANS
      GO TO 20
      END
```

This version avoids having to rewrite statements in the program. Instead, the GO TO statement causes them to be repeated. Unfortunately, the program suffers from the same malady as the flowchart in Figure 2 4 1: it never stops to print the final balance.

We need some way to avoid repeating the important steps in the program indefinitely. We want to add a new transaction to the balance only if we haven't already finished adding all of this month's transactions. In other words, instead of always returning to statement 20, we want to return only under certain *conditions*. A conditional GO TO would solve the problem. You may recall that in

Section 1 3 we had a similar problem with the ZAPPO algorithm, but there was no problem with the knitting algorithm because it had a conditional repeat.

Fortunately, Fortran provides a way to construct a **conditional statement**: the IF statement. For our current purposes, the **IF statement** has the form

$$\text{If } (e_1 \text{ } rel \text{ } e_2) \text{ GO TO } s$$

where s is a statement label, e_1 and e_2 are arithmetic expressions like the right-hand side of an assignment statement, and rel expresses a relation between e_1 and e_2. The six possibilities for rel are shown below.

relation	usual symbol	Fortran symbol
less than	<	.LT.
less than or equal to	⩽	.LE.
equal to	=	.EQ.
not equal to	≠	.NE.
greater than or equal to	⩾	.GE.
greater than	>	.GT.

(Actually the IF statement can be more general than this, but we'll get to that later.) If $e_2 \text{ } rel \text{ } e_2$ is true, then the controller proceeds to statement s; otherwise, the controller continues from the statement following the IF statement in the usual sequence. For instance, the IF statement below

```
IF (TRANS .NE. 0.0)  GO TO 20
```

means "IF the value of memory cell TRANS is not equal to 0, then GO TO statement 20; otherwise, just go on to the next statement."

IF statement (restricted version)

form
IF $(e_1 \text{ } rel \text{ } e_2)$ GO TO s
e_1 and e_2 are arithmetic expressions
rel is a relational operator
s is a statement label

meaning
instructs the controller to decide whether or not the expressed relationship between the arithmetic expressions is true; if so, the controller proceeds from statement s; otherwise it continues from the next statement as usual

examples
```
IF (A+B .GT. 0)  GO TO 130
IF (3*(A/B) .GT. C*B)  GO TO 500
```

Now let's see how we can use the IF statement to fix our program. We want to say:

> "If the last transaction has not yet been added
> to the balance, repeat from statement 20."

There is no way to say this directly using the IF statement, so we will have to find a way to say it in the language we have available. To do this we need some way to tell when we have reached the last transaction. Of course, we have no way of knowing in advance exactly what the amount of the last transaction will be, but with a little thought we realize that we know something the last transaction won't be: it will *not* be zero. How can we use this fact?

Suppose that, after punching all of the month's transactions on cards, we punch one more card containing the transaction *zero*. When we come to a card containing zero, we will know that it must be the last transaction. Our program can use that fact to determine whether or not to continue the loop.

```
       REAL BALNCE, TRANS
       READ(5,1000) BALNCE
1000 FORMAT(F5.0)
20     READ(5,1000) TRANS
         BALNCE = BALNCE - TRANS
         IF (TRANS .NE. 0.0)  GO TO 20
       WRITE(6,2000) BALNCE
2000 FORMAT(' NEW BALANCE IS $', F7.2)
       STOP
       END
```

> Note that we've indented the statements that make up the loop.

data
```
  456.03
   78.36
  -25.39
   45.25
   45.22
  -75.42
    0.0
```

output
```
NEW BALANCE IS $ 388.00
```

The program places the beginning balance in memory cell BALNCE, then adds each transaction into the balance until it reaches the last transaction (zero). At that point, instead of returning to statement 20 to add in another transaction, it prints the final balance and stops.

Perhaps we should note that the program actually adds the phony zero transaction into the balance. Since zero doesn't change a sum, it doesn't affect the result, but that is really a fortunate coincidence. It would be better not to add the phony transaction into the balance at all. Can you think of a way to change the program so that it doesn't add the phony transaction (see Exercise 3 2 3)?

Simple as it may seem, the IF statement you have just learned about adds a great deal of power to the language. In fact, there is a mathematical theorem which says that any computation which can be done at all, no matter how complicated, can be programmed using statements you already know: the assignment statement, the WRITE statement, the GO TO statement, and the IF statement. The rest of the Fortran statements you will learn won't make the language any more powerful, but they will help you write programs in a more concise, efficient, and readable way than you could using only what you know now. Nevertheless, using only the statements you know now, you can program the computer to do a large variety of useful tasks, and these programs can be both efficient and clearly expressed. We hope this will give you some confidence when you attack the problems at the end of this chapter.

EXERCISES 3 2

1 What is the Fortran equivalent of the * which appears in the knitting algorithm of Section 1 3?

2 Which of the following IF statements are illegal?

```
IF (X .GT. Y)   GO TO 35
IF (X*2 +17 .LE. Y**2)   GO TO 100
IF (14 .EG. 2)   GO TO 10
IF (X .SGT. A)   GO TO 15
IF Y .EQ. 0, GO TO 20
```

3 Rewrite the bank balancing program so that it doesn't add in the phony transaction. (Hint: You will need to move the IF statement, change its GO TO statement, add another GO TO statement in the place where the IF now stands, and put a label on the WRITE statement.)

Section 3 3

Loops

To become more familiar with the IF statement, let's try to write a program to do the computations of the laundry detergent problem of Figure 1 2 2. In that problem we wanted to average the price per pound of a number of laundry detergents. Imagine that you have a bunch of cards and each card contains the price and weight of a different brand of detergent. The flowchart in Figure 3 3 1 shows what we want to do. Briefly, we want to accumulate a sum of prices, counting the number of terms in the sum as we go along, and divide the total by the number of terms to get the average price. You are already aware of a technique for accumulating a sum, so the part of the program which computes the sum of the prices should be easy to follow.

> *Counting the number of times some event happens (the number of cards read, for instance) is just a special case of accumulating a sum, namely the case in which each term in the sum is 1.*

Follow the flowchart in Figure 3 3 1 and try to see what it does. If you don't quite get it, make up some data cards and follow the instructions, performing the computations as you go. Once you understand the flowchart, try to see how you can convert each part of it to Fortran statements. Hopefully the only place you'll have any trouble at all is in translating the statement "does the card contain a price and weight?"

VERBAL
DESCRIPTION

Count number of detergents surveyed while accumulating sum of unit prices.

Divide sum of unit prices by number of detergents surveyed to get the average price.

Print results.

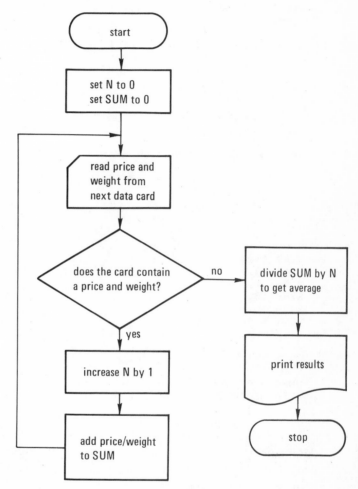

Figure 3 3 1   Computing the Average Price of a Laundry Detergent

How can the program know what is a price and weight and what isn't? The method we used in the check balancing program was to put a data card containing a phony value after the data cards containing legitimate values and testing for the phony value in the program. We can do the same thing here. We know that no company is going to pay you to take their detergent, so no brand will have a negative price. Thus, we can put a data card indicating a negative price at the end of the cards with legitimate prices. Then, to see if the card we just READ is the last card, we simply test to see if the value we READ is less than zero.

Follow through this program and convince yourself that it does what we want.

```
COMMENT:  FIND THE AVERAGE COST OF LAUNDRY DETERGENT
          REAL PRICE, WGT,  SUM, N,  AVG
C
C         GET PRICES AND WEIGHTS, KEEPING TRACK OF TOTAL UNIT
C         COSTS AND NUMBER OF BRANDS SAMPLED.
          N = 0.0
          SUM = 0.00
   10     READ(5,1000) PRICE,WGT
 1000     FORMAT(F5.0,F5.0)
C            HERE'S WHERE WE TEST FOR THE TERMINATION CARD
             IF (PRICE .LT. 0.00)  GO TO 20
C            AVERAGE IN THIS BRAND
             SUM = SUM + (PRICE/WGT)
             N = N+1.0
             GO TO 10
C
C         WE'VE GOT THE TOTAL UNIT COST.  NOW COMPUTE AVERAGE.
   20     AVG = SUM/N
          WRITE(6,2000) N
 2000     FORMAT(' NUMBER OF BRANDS SURVEYED:',F6.0)
          WRITE(6,2001) AVG
 2001     FORMAT(' AVERAGE PRICE PER POUND:    $',F6.2)
          STOP
          END
```

data

```
    4.49 15.0
    1.47  3.1
    2.96  4.7
    6.95 18.3
    5.36 15.8
   -1.1  0.00
```

output

```
NUMBER OF BRANDS SURVEYED:     5.
AVERAGE PRICE PER POUND    $    .42
```

Loops like the ones you have seen in the check balancing program and the detergent price program are an extremely important part of most computer programs. In fact, many programs would simply be impossible to write in Fortran without using loops. The loops you have seen so far have been quite simple, and you have probably had little difficulty in understanding what they do. but loops can get complicated quickly. (We'll show you a more complicated loop in the next section.) For this reason, it is advisable to construct loops carefully in an attempt to keep the program as well organized and straightforward as possible. Some rules to follow in writing loops are outlined in the accompanying box. We think that if you will keep these rules in mind when you write programs, you will be able to avoid many errors.

loop writing

one entry, one exit

In general, a loop should be entered only at the top. That is, there should not be any jump (GO TO) from outside the loop to a statement in the middle of a loop. One reason for this is that, when writing a loop, you will tend to make many assumptions about the values of the memory cells involved in the loop. A jump into the middle of the loop often makes these assumptions unjustified. Similarly, exits from the loop should be jumps to the first statement following the loop. Following this rule tends to keep the program more straightforward.

pre-test, post-test

In general, there should be only one statement in a loop which can terminate the loop, and this statement should be either at the very beginning of the loop (**pre-test**) or at the very end (**post-test**). Jumps out of the middle of a loop, especially if there are more than one of them, can lead to erroneous assumptions about the memory cells involved in the loop. Although the test in our detergent program is not the first statement of the loop, it is an inherent part of the first operation in the loop, namely the operation of obtaining a new piece of legitimate data. In a sense, it is reasonable to think of the test for legitimate input as a part of the READ statement itself, the first statement in the loop.

In fact, many versions of Fortran make this idea explicit by allowing the following (nonstandard) form of READ statement.

END condition READ (non-ANSI)

form

READ(u, f, END = s) *list*

u is a unit number (usually 5)

f is the label of a FORMAT statement

s is the label of an executable statement

list is a list of memory cell names

meaning

stores values from unit u in the memory cells in *list*, according to FORMAT f. If an end of file is reached (i.e., if there are no more data cards to be read), transfer control to statement s.

examples

```
READ(5,5000,END=20) TAXRT
READ(5,1000,END=100) PRICE,WGT
```

Even without this specialized READ statement it is always possible to convert a loop into a version which satisfies a strict interpretation of the *pre-test* (or *post-test*) concept. But the idea is to produce clear, simple constructs. Bending over backwards to suit some supposed ideal can cause clutter itself.

A loop is, conceptually, a single unit in a program and should be made to appear that way by formatting the program listing in some appropriate way. We do this by indenting each statement of the loop after the first. This simple practice makes a surprising difference in the readability of the programs.

EXERCISES 3 3

1 Any value that could not possibly be a price for a detergent can be used to signal the end of the data cards. Rewrite the IF statement in the detergent price program so that the value 999.9 is the last card signal.

2 Write a program that counts by fives, printing the successive counts as it goes. Terminate the count when it reaches 100.

3 (optional) Rewrite the detergent price program so that its loop is in post-test form.

Section 3 4

Nested Loops

We have decided to provide a bank balance computing service for our friends. At the end of each month our friends will bring us a record of their checking account transactions in the form of a deck of punched cards. We could simply take the first deck, use the program in Section 3 2 to compute the new balance, then take the next deck, run it, and so on. We would have to repeat this process until we had completed each of our friends' new balances; that is, until we had no decks left to run. We might be at the computer center all day.

Alternatively, we could let the computer do more of the work by adding a few statements to the bank balance program so that it automatically starts the process over for each friend's account.

Let's consider what sorts of things we would need to do to convert our old program to this new, more useful form. First we would need some way of making the correspondence between the new account balances and the person who gave us those cards. One way to do that would be to ask our friends to place a card punched with their social security number on it at the front of their deck. Other than that, they need make no changes—just as before, they put the old account

Our *friends would be somewhat offended by not being able to use their names instead of their social security number. We'll see how to do that in Chapter 4.*

balance on a card, follow it by their transactions for the month, and indicate the end of their deck by putting a card with a 0.0 on it at the end.

All we have to do now is add some statements to our program so that it repeats its computations once for each of our friends' accounts. It can tell when it is through with one deck by testing (just as before) for a 0.0 transaction card. But wait ... how can it tell when it has processed the last deck? After it completes the last deck, how is it to know that no deck follows?

So far we've imagined the program to have the form of Figure 3 4 1. After it has finished the last deck, it would just go back, expecting another name card. A

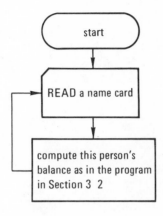

Figure 3 4 1

reasonable solution is for us to slap a special card at the very end—a card with a negative (hence impossible) social security number will do.

Our program will now have the form of Figure 3 4 2. It contains what is known as a **nested loop**, that is, a loop inside another loop. This structure is like that of the knitting algorithm in Section 1 3.

Our new program appears below. Although the general form of the program is familiar, some of the details are new. For example, it contains a new kind of IF statement. The statement to the right of the first IF statement is not

IF statement (restricted form)

form
    IF *(rel) s*
    rel is a relational expression
    s is an executable statement other than an IF (*s* is the **object** of
       the IF)

meaning
    performs *s* if *rel* is true

examples
```
IF (A .LT. B)   STOP
IF (G*Q .EQ. H)   A = 47*G + Q
IF (3*Z .GT. 96+H)  WRITE(6,1000)Z
```

a GO TO statement as it has always been before. It is a STOP statement instead. In general, any executable statement (READ, PRINT, assignment, or STOP) can be placed to the right of an IF. An exception is that an IF statement cannot be on the right of another IF. Of course, nonexecutable statements (e.g., compiler instructions like INTEGER A, REAL B, or END) cannot be objects of IF statements because that wouldn't make sense. In order to make sense of them, the compiler would have to check the value of the relational expression, but that can be done only when the controller executes the program.

VERBAL
DESCRIPTION

Get social security number of account holder.

Get old balance for this account.

Process transaction cards for this account.

Repeat.

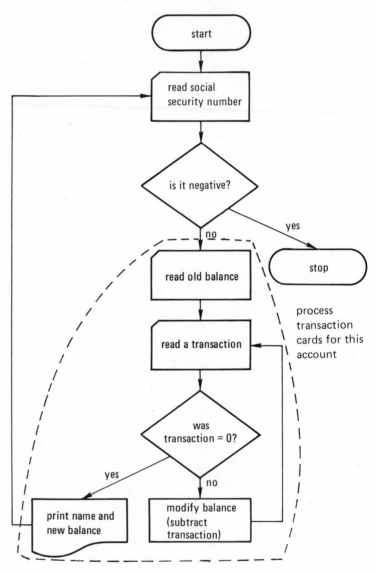

Figure 3 4 2

```
COMMENT:   THIS PROGRAM COMPUTES BANK BALANCES FOR A NUMBER
C          OF PEOPLE.  THE DATA CARDS MUST BE ORGANIZED IN
C          GROUPS, EACH GROUP STARTING WITH A SOCIAL SECURITY
C          NUMBER WHICH IDENTIFIES THE PERSON WHOSE BALANCE
C          IS TO BE COMPUTED.  THE SECOND CARD IN EACH GROUP
C          MUST CONTAIN THE PERSON'S OLD BALANCE.  EACH
C          ADDITIONAL CARD MUST CONTAIN A TRANSACTION ON THE
C          ACCOUNT, POSITIVE VALUES FOR WITHDRAWALS AND
C          NEGATIVE ONES FOR DEPOSITS.  EACH GROUP TERMINATES
C          WITH A CARD CONTAINING 0.0, AND THE FINAL CARD
C          (FOLLOWING THE LAST GROUP) MUST CONTAIN A NEGATIVE
C          VALUE (AN ILLEGITIMATE SOCIAL SECURITY NUMBER).
          INTEGER SOCSEC
          REAL BALNCE, TRANS
  100     READ(5,1000) SOCSEC
 1000 FORMAT(I9)
          IF (SOCSEC .LT. 0)   STOP
          READ(5,2000) BALNCE
 2000     FORMAT(F5.0)
  200     READ(5,2000)TRANS
          IF (TRANS .EQ. 0.00)   GO TO 300
          BALNCE = BALNCE - TRANS
          GO TO 200
  300     WRITE(6,3000) SOCSEC
 3000     FORMAT('0SOCIAL SECURITY NUMBER:', I10)
          WRITE(6,4000) BALNCE
 4000     FORMAT(' NEW BALANCE: $', F7.2)
          GO TO 100
          END
```

data

column 1

```
276407566
456.32
 22.98
 33.54
-291.55
 54.39
 0.0
175504244
332.53
 22.03
-329.41
 22.11
 0.0
        -1
```

output

```
SOCIAL SECURITY NUMBER: 276407566
NEW BALANCE: $ 636.60

SOCIAL SECURITY NUMBER: 175504244
NEW BALANCE: $ 617.40
```

EXERCISES 3 4

1 What parts of the knitting algorithm of Section 1 3 correspond to what parts of the program in this section?

2 Modify the program in Section 3 4 so that it prints a record of transactions as well as a balance for each person. If you can, have the program print each transaction as a positive number (even though deposits are negative on data cards) with the word DEPOSIT beside each deposit.

PROBLEMS 3

1 Write a program to READ two numbers per card and print these two numbers and their difference on one line; the last card will contain zeros.

2 Alter the bank account program of Section 3 2 so that it deducts a service charge of ten cents for each check (but makes no charge for deposits).

3 Alter the bank balancing program of Section 3 4 so that it prints the following pieces of information for each account it processes:
   a social security number
   b old balance
   c number of checks
   d total value of check written against the account
   e number of deposits
   f total amount deposited
   g new balance
   h a "THANK YOU" message

4 Write a program which READs in cards containing EPA mileage information. Each data card should have an INTEGER (car identification number) and two REALs (EPA highway gas mileage and EPA city driving gas mileage). Use a negative car identification number to signal the end of data. Print out the data on each car, plus the average of the two mileage figures. If a car's average is less than 16.0 miles per gallon, print THIS CAR IS A GUZZLER. If its average is greater than 30.0 miles per gallon, print out a complimentary message.

5 Write a program which will calculate the area of a right triangle given the lengths of the two legs. Each data card will contain two INTEGERs representing the length of the legs. Assume that the last data card will contain two zeros.

6 Write a program which computes the sum of the first n odd integers where the value of n comes from a data card.

7 Write a program which computes the first perfect square larger than 84,123. A perfect square is an integer which is the square of another integer (perfect square = $n*n$). Use a loop in your program. (An easy technique is to square each integer, starting at 1 and going up until you find a square larger than 84,123.)

8 One Denver Mint Tea tea bag makes one cup of strong, aromatic tea in eight minutes. Leaving the bag in longer than ten minutes has no further effect on the strength of the tea. If we say that strong (eight minutes) tea has relative strength 1.0, then the relative strength of tea steeped in a teapot for other lengths of time is

$$\text{number of bags} * \frac{\text{number of minutes}}{\text{number of cups}} * \frac{1 \text{ cup}}{8 \text{ minutes}}$$

if the steeping time is under ten minutes. For steeping times over ten minutes the relative strength is

$$\text{number of bags} * \frac{10 \text{ minutes}}{\text{number of cups}} * \frac{1 \text{ cup}}{8 \text{ minutes}}$$

Write a program which READs several data cards, each containing three values: (1) the number of bags used, (2) the number of cups of water used, and (3) the steeping time in minutes. Have your program compute and print out the relative strength of the tea for each data card. If the relative strength is less than 0.5, print HOPE YOU LIKE WEAK TEA, and if it's greater than 1.25, print HOPE YOU LIKE YOUR TEA STRONG. Continue processing cards until you come to one with a stopping value on it (e.g., a negative number of tea bags).

9 Bobby's mom gave him a new bike for his birthday. The gear ratios on his bike are

gear	ratio
1	3.3:1
2	2.02:1
3	1.52:1
4	1:1

and the speed of his bike is given by the formula

speed (miles per hour) = .02 * rpm/gear ratio

For example, his speed at 3300 rpm in low gear would be

.02 * 3300 * 1 / 3.3 = 20 mph

Write a program which READs data cards giving the rpm's where he shifts. For each shift point, have your program print out his top speed in each gear. If an rpm value over 6500 rpm comes in, print the message

BOBBY'S BIKE EXPLODED

and then STOP.

Bobby's New Bike

10 In making fudge candy, a thermometer is handy. Unfortunately, accurate candy thermometers are difficult to find. The ones we've used have been off by several degrees. To test thermometers for accuracy, we use them to measure the temperature of boiling water, and compare their readings to the (known) temperature of boiling water.

At sea level water boils at 212°F. At higher altitudes it boils at lower temperatures. Use the computer to print out a table of boiling points at various altitudes: sea level, 500 feet, 1000 feet, 1500 feet, and so on in steps of 500 feet up to 15,000 feet above sea level. The boiling point changes by about 1°F for each 550-foot change in altitude. You can use the formula below to compute the boiling point in Fahrenheit degrees when the altitude is measured in feet above sea level.

$$\text{boiling point} = 212 - \frac{\text{altitude}}{550}$$

11 If your thermometer reads in Celsius (centigrade) degrees and you know your altitude in meters, the formula is

$$\text{boiling point} = 100 - \frac{\text{altitude}}{170}$$

Use the computer to print a table of boiling points as in problem 10, but in steps of 100 meters up to 5000 meters above sea level.

4 EXPRESSIONS IN DETAIL

Section 4 1
Introduction

Recall that the computer's memory is made up of a number of **cells** and that we can place values into these cells as well as retrieve values placed there previously. We also mentioned that the interpretation of these values is pretty much up to us. In Fortran we can denote values of several different data types, and the system will automatically represent them as a pattern of 1's and 0's in memory cells. You're already familiar with the INTEGER and REAL data types. In this chapter we'll discuss the other available data types and explain the rules for the evaluation of expressions. Also, we'll fill in the details about FORMATs so you will have more control over input and output operations.

Section 4 2
INTEGERs and REALs

Before jumping directly into the details of arithmetic expressions, we'd like to review the characteristics of their basic elements, numbers—REALs and INTEGERs. An **INTEGER constant** is a signed or unsigned string of digits. Since

---

INTEGER constant

form
   string of decimal digits which may be preceded by a plus or
   a minus sign

(LEGAL)
   +1497
   −392
   −01124
   33421

(ILLEGAL)
   +1,497   *no commas allowed*
   −392.0   *no decimal point allowed*
   33,492.1

The Number of '54 Chevy's You've Seen
in Your Lifetime Is an INTEGER

each memory cell has a finite capacity, some numbers may be too large (+ or –) to fit. The exact values INTEGERs may take depends on which computer system you are using.

For the same reason, REALs have a finite range. In practice, the limitations imposed by the finite range of REALs seldom come into play, but their finite accuracy does. We didn't have the accuracy problem with INTEGERs because they are represented exactly. REAL numbers, on the other hand, are represented to some number of digits of accuracy (again, the exact number depends on which computer system you are using).

REAL constants are written as signed or unsigned strings of decimal digits containing a decimal point. There is an additional possibility. For writing super-big numbers like the national debt or super-small numbers like the diameter of a chlorine atom, Fortran provides a version of the widely used "scientific notation." This consists of writing a REAL constant in the usual form followed by a decimal point shift factor (which is an E followed by an INTEGER constant). The decimal point shift factor in a REAL constant indicates how far to move the decimal point in the number that precedes the E. Positive shifts indicate shifts to the right, negative shifts to the left.

This E-notation for REALs is something like the way the numbers are represented in the computer. The 1's and 0's in a REAL valued memory cell are divided into two parts, the fraction, or "mantissa," and the point shift, or "exponent." If a computation results in a number with an exponent which is too large, an **over-flow** occurs. On the other hand, computations may result in numbers whose exponent parts are too large in the negative direction to fit in the reserved space. Such a condition is called an **underflow** since the number is too small to be represented.

REAL constants

form

    x

    *x*E*s*

    x is a signed or unsigned string of decimal digits containing a
    decimal point
    s is an INTEGER constant

meaning

    specifies a number indicated by *x* with its decimal point shifted
    s places (positive *s* indicates right shift; negative *s*, left shift)

If You Measure a Pizza, You Get a REAL Number

examples of REAL constants

form		*meaning*
1.00		
−7.7254		
+.000137		
.472E5	LEGAL	47200.
+7.21E−2		.0721
−1.22E−12		−.00000000000122
+6.023E+23		Avogadro's Number
.002E3		Avis's Number
1,482.5	ILLEGAL	invalid, no comma allowed
723		invalid, needs decimal point
−4.18732E−.5		invalid, shift factor must be INTEGER

Overflows and underflows occasionally occur, but they don't cause nearly as many problems as the restricted accuracy in the mantissa. Limited accuracy makes it impossible to represent a number like

$$1./3. = .33333333333 \ldots$$

Any digits beyond those that fit into the memory word simply get lost. This can occasionally cause some embarrassing situations, because in Fortran

$$1./3. + 1./3. + 1./3.$$

doesn't quite equal 1.0! The errors due to this effect are called **roundoff errors**. In certain applications, roundoff errors, each one seemingly insignificant, can add up to make a final answer completely wrong. This is a serious problem, and numerical analysts have spent enormous effort trying to understand how to avoid getting such erroneous results.

EXERCISES 4 2

1   Which are legal INTEGER constants; which are not? If not, why not?

1	4*2
1.0	12.75
−12	−127.5
−134794	1275
12 + 2	−0

2   Which are legal REAL constants? If not, why not?

2	5.67
+2	5.67E0
+2.00	300E30.0
−2.01E3.2	−22.E+30
−2.1E3	−.0000021
−2.22E−22	

Section 4 3

Arithmetic Expressions

You have already seen many examples of arithmetic expressions. They were used as the right-hand side of assignment statements and in relational expressions in IF statements. We purposely kept those expressions quite simple in order to defer a detailed explanation of the rules of evaluation until now.

Arithmetic expressions are formed of memory cell names and arithmetic constants separated by arithmetic operators (+, −, *, /, **). In addition, parentheses may be used to force the controller to perform the operations in the desired order.

Consider the following examples of arithmetic expressions:

```
COUNT+1
```

Find value of COUNT and add 1 to it.

```
(1+BRATE-DRATE)*POPUL
```

Find value of BRATE, add it to 1, subtract the value of DRATE, and multiply the result by the value of POPUL.

```
PI*(R**2)
```

Raise the value of R to the power 2 (i.e., square R) and multiply the result by the value of PI.

In each of these examples the meaning of the expression is not hard to see, but consider a more complicated expression like

```
SUMXSQ/(N-1.0)  -  SUMX**2/(N*(N-1.0))
```

In this case the expression appears ambiguous because it is not clear which operations should be performed first. Should we proceed from left to right, from right to left, or by some other set of rules? Surely we should perform the operations grouped by the parentheses first, but after that there is still ambiguity. Are we to raise SUMX to the power 2 or to the power $2/(N*(N − 1.0))$? Do we divide SUMXSQ by $(N − 1.0)$ or by $(N − 1.0) − SUMX$? The expression would be easier to interpret if we didn't have to write it all on one line, but Fortran requires us to do so.

> *in normal algebraic notation the expression is*
>
> $$\frac{sumxsq}{n-1} - \frac{sumx^2}{n(n-1)}$$

In Fortran the order of operations proceeds according to the following rules of precedence, which are the same as those used in ordinary algebra.

( )   First   compute the expressions within parentheses

**   Second   perform exponentiations

*, / Third   perform multiplications and divisions

+, – Fourth   perform additions and subtractions

→   Tiebreaker   perform adjacent additive operations
      (non-ANSI)   (+, –) from left to right
                        perform adjacent multiplicative operations
                        (*, /) from left to right
                        perform adjacent exponentiations
                        (**) from right to left

Now no ambiguity remains. The expression is equivalent to

`(SUMXSQ/(N-1.0)) - ((SUMX**2)/(N*(N-1.0)))`

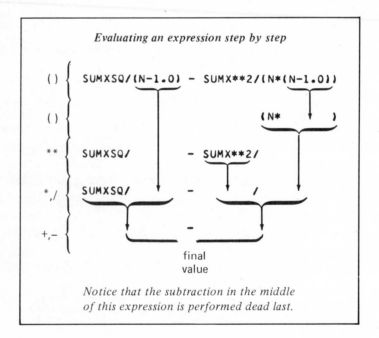

Evaluating an expression step by step

final
value

*Notice that the subtraction in the middle
of this expression is performed dead last.*

Consider this expression:

$$A/B*C - D + E$$

The rules of precedence tell us to perform multiplications and divisions before additions and subtractions. Therefore A/B*C must be evaluated first. But does that mean (A/B)*C or A/(B*C)? Using the tiebreaker rule, (A/B)*C would be the interpretation.

Arithmetic operators may be used with either REALs or INTEGERs, so that both 2/4 and 2.0/4.0 are legal expressions, which yield the values 0 and 0.5 respectively. But how should something like 2/4.0 be interpreted? The first value is an INTEGER constant, the second a REAL. The ANSI standards solve this problem by forbidding it. Such an expression, which combines values (or memory cells) of differing types, is said to be **mixed mode**. Versions of Fortran which adhere strongly to the standards will issue an error message and refuse to run the program. Most versions of Fortran are more lenient, however. Unfortunately, since such situations are not covered in the standards, different versions of Fortran make different assumptions about what the programmer means by the expression. This makes it advantageous to avoid mixed mode expressions altogether.

One exception is in the case of exponentiation. Here is one place where it is desirable to mix REAL and INTEGER in the same expression, and so this *is* permitted by the standards. For example, the expression 4.73**8 means to form a product containing eight factors, 4.73 times itself eight times. The result of this computation is quite naturally a REAL.

It is also possible to raise a REAL to a REAL power, but the computation which is performed is very different. For example, 4.73**1.79256 clearly cannot mean to multiply 4.73 times itself 1.79256 times. In order to make this computation, the controller first computes the logarithm of the base in the exponentiation, multiplies that by the exponent, getting a product p, and finally raises $e = 2.7182818 \ldots$ to the power p. Since logarithms of negative numbers do not generally result in REAL values, *it is illegal to raise a negative number to a REAL power.* No logarithms are involved in raising a number to an INTEGER power, however, so there is nothing wrong with an expression like $$x^y = e^{y \, \log(x)}$$ (−4.73)**8 even though the expression (−4.73)**8.0 would be illegal. Use INTEGERs for exponents whenever you can. There is one other thing that can cause trouble. We said that INTEGER constants could be numbers like −2 or 3 and that you could use an arithmetic operator between two constants; however, 3*−2 is illegal in Fortran. In addition to the rules for forming arithmetic expres-

A**3	A**3.0
↑	↑
use this	*not this*

sions that you've seen so far, there is the rule that *no two operator symbols (*, /, +, −, **) may come in a row*, no matter what they're used for. The expression 3 * −2 can be written legally as 3 * (−2).

---

arithmetic expressions

form
　　　basic arithmetic elements (numeric memory cells, unsigned numeric constants, or parenthesized subexpressions) separated by arithmetic operators (+, −, *, /, or **) with an optional sign (+ or −) at the beginning of the expression

meaning
　　　specifies a numeric value, namely the value obtained by following the rules of precedence and carrying out the operations denoted by the arithmetic operators

examples

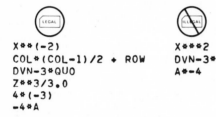

```
X**(-2)              X***2
COL*(COL-1)/2 + ROW  DVN-3*
DVN-3*QUO            A*-4
Z**3/3.0
4*(-3)
-4*A
```

Now that we know how to create and interpret arithmetic expressions, let's return to the assignment statement. Recall that an assignment statement is a memory cell name followed by the assignment operator (=) followed by an expression. The assignment statement tells the controller to evaluate the expression and store the result in the memory cell named to the left of the assignment operator. In this way the controller gives the cell a new value. For example, if we had made the declarations

```
INTEGER PURCH1, PURCH2, TOTAL, CENTS
REAL DOLARS
```

then these assignment statements

```
PURCH1 = 75
PURCH2 = 50
TOTAL = PURCH1 + PURCH2
CENTS = 125
DOLARS = 125.0/100.0
```

would leave the memory cells with these values:

PURCH1	75
PURCH2	50
TOTAL	125
CENTS	125
DOLARS	1.25

Everything was nice and easy—each expression on the right was of the same type as the memory cell named on the left, so it was obvious what to store. But what if a statement like

```
CENTS = DOLARS*100.00
```

has appeared? The memory cell named on the left is an INTEGER: the expression on the right is REAL. A very important rule about assignment statements takes care of this situation. (Notice that this is *not* an example of a mixed mode expression. The expression on the right involves the multiplication of two REAL values.)

The rule is that *the expression to the right* of the replacement operator *is evaluated first* without any concern being given to the memory location named on the left. After the expression has been evaluated, a check is made to see if the type of the result agrees with the type of the memory cell where the result is to be stored. If it does not agree, then *the value stored in the memory cell is the value of the expression after being converted to the data type required by the memory cell.*

So, in the example above, first DOLARS * 100.0 is evaluated to get the REAL value 125.0, and then, since CENTS is declared to be an INTEGER, the corresponding INTEGER value 125 is stored in CENTS.

This is a very important rule to understand. Let's see it in action again.

Suppose at some point in a program we need to compute a term N/M. Since we've been counting with M and N, they are declared INTEGERs, but the use we make of the term requires it to be REAL. Since we're not certain how our compiler treats mixed mode operations, we will use assignment statements to control the conversions ourselves. Can you see why these two program fragments produce different results?

```
INTEGER M,N                INTEGER M,N
REAL TERM,FRAC,NUM         REAL TERM,NUM,DENOM
N=2                        N=2
M=3                        M=3
NUM=N                      NUM=N
FRAC=1/M                   DENOM=M
TERM=NUM*FRAC              TERM=NUM/DENOM
```

M	3
N	2
NUM	2.0
FRAC	0.0
TERM	0.0

M	3
N	2
NUM	2.0
FRAC	3.0
TERM	0.666666

The key difference is caused by the statement

```
FRAC = 1/M
```

The INTEGER expression 1/M is evaluated first (giving the INTEGER value 0). Then (and only then) the computed value is converted to REAL (0.0), and stored in FRAC.

EXERCISES 4 3

1 Using the precedence rules, compute the value of the expression (−1**4).

2 Use parentheses to make the meaning of the following arithmetic expressions perfectly clear. When the expression is ambiguous, use the non-ANSI tiebreaker rule we gave.

```
MOUSE + CAT*DOG**2
SEX + DRUGS - SKIN*FLICK + BUSTER**BROWN**SHOES
ROCK/ER/FELLOW
```

3 Suppose A has the value −3.7. Then A**2 is legal, but A**2.0 isn't. Why?

4 In the following program, SNAFO takes on several different values at different times. What values are they?

```
INTEGER A,B,C
REAL SNAFO, R1, R2
R1=1
R2=2
A=1
B=4
C=16
SNAFO=R1*R2
SNAFO=A*R2
SNAFO=B/(A+B)
SNAFO=B
SNAFO=C/B
STOP
END
```

5 In algebraic notation we write the product of two terms like a and b as ab. Why isn't this allowed in Fortran?

Section 4 4

Other Operators

Many people write programs which involve finding the logarithm of some value. Although not as many people use the logarithm operation as, say, addition, it still would be a terrible waste for each person to have to rediscover his own algorithm for computing logarithms. Fortran provides a number of additional commonly used operators which may be used in expressions. The following program uses two of these operators: ALOG for logarithms and SQRT for square root.

```
      REAL X, T, SQRX, SQRT, ALOG
      X = 144.0
      SQRX = SQRT(X)
      WRITE(6,1000) SQRX
1000 FORMAT(' SQUARE ROOT OF 144=',F5.2)
      T = ALOG(X/12.0)
      WRITE(6,2000) T
2000 FORMAT(' LOGARITHM OF 144/12=',F5.2)
      STOP
      END
```

output
```
SQUARE ROOT OF 144=12.00
LOGARITHM OF 144/12= 2.48
```

Notice that the operators appear just before the expression we wish them to operate on, and that that expression is enclosed in parentheses. Also notice that we have declared that the operators will yield REAL values by listing their names in a type statement.

The quantity in parentheses after an operator is called its **argument**. Probably this term is familiar to you from mathematics. Some operators have more than one argument, and in that case the arguments are separated by commas. In fact, some built-in operators may be given a different number of arguments at different times (MIN0, for example, which yields the minimum value of all its arguments, no matter how many there may be).

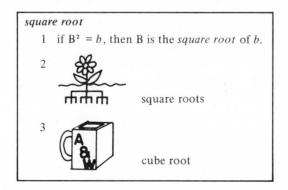

A number of commonly used operators (or built-in FUNCTIONs, as they are often called) are shown in Figure 4 4 1. The rest of the built-in FUNCTIONs are described in the ANSI Fortran MiniManual at the end of this book.

Some useful built-in FUNCTIONs

The argument should be REAL valued if shown as r and INTEGER if shown as i.

FUNCTION	value computed	type of result
SQRT(r)	$\sqrt{r}$	REAL
ALOG10(r)	log to the base 10 of r	REAL
ALOG(r)	natural logarithm of r	REAL
EXP(r)	e^r, where e is the base of natural logarithms	REAL
SIN(r)	trigonometric sine of r radians	REAL
COS(r)	cosine of r radians	REAL
ATAN(r)	the angle $\left(-\dfrac{\pi}{2} \text{ to } \dfrac{\pi}{2} \right)$ whose tangent is r	REAL
ABS(r)	the absolute value of r $\lvert r \rvert$	REAL
IABS(i)	$\lvert i \rvert$	INTEGER
FLOAT(i)	REAL version of i FLOAT(2) is 2.0	REAL
INT(r)	INTEGER version of r INT(−3.7) is −3	INTEGER
MAX0($i_1, i_2, \ldots, i_n$)	largest value of $i_1, i_2, \ldots, i_n; n \geqslant 2$	INTEGER
MIN0($i_1, i_2, \ldots, i_n$)	smallest value of $i_1, i_2, \ldots, i_n, n \geqslant 2$	INTEGER
AMAX1($r_1, r_2, \ldots, r_n$)	largest value of $r_1, r_2, \ldots, r_n; n \geqslant 2$	REAL
AMIN1($r_1, r_2, \ldots, r_n$)	smallest value of $r_1, r_2, \ldots, r_n; n \geqslant 2$	REAL

Figure 4 4 1   Built-in FUNCTIONs

You will probably find most of the functions familiar even if their names seem a little strange. The reason some of the names have extra letters stuck in front of them (ALOG, AMIN1, IABS. . .) is because of the Fortran implicit typing convention, which is covered in Section 4 6. The reason the minimum and maximum functions have numbers tacked on the end (AMIN1, MAX0) is to identify the type of arguments each takes (0 for INTEGER, 1 for REAL). We've listed the most commonly used functions here. More are listed in the MiniManual.

EXERCISES 4 4

1 What values do these expressions have?

```
SQRT(4.0)
MIN0(-1,-2,-2,4,7)
INT(3.1415926)
ABS(AMAX1(-1.0,-3.0,-2.5))
ABS(AMIN1(-1.0,-3.0,-2.5))
ALOG(EXP(1.0001))
```

2 There is no operator for the trigonometric tangent function in ANSI Fortran. Is this a gross oversight?

Section 4 5 *

Using Truncation

> This section may be skipped without loss of continuity.

You are probably wondering why Fortran chooses to deal with two different kinds of numbers instead of sticking with one kind as we normally do in our hand computations. The answer probably lies in the fact that experience has shown that integers and numbers with fractional parts are used in basically different ways in most computations. It is also true that the difference allows for greater flexibility in our programs. For example, INTEGER division, with its truncation property, can often be used to advantage. The following question can be dealt with easily in Fortran because INTEGER division drops the remainder.

Question: Is the INTEGER value stored in N evenly divisible by 2?

Answer: If (N/2)*2 is equal to N, then yes, otherwise no.

Explanation: If N is evenly divisible by 2, then N/2 will not have any fractional part to lose, so (N/2)*2 will equal N. If, however, N is not even, then the division will lose a fractional part and (N/2)*2 will be different from N.

Examples: If N = 6, then
(N/2) = 3 and 3*2 is equal to 6.
If N = 7, then
(N/2) = 3 and 3*2 is not equal to 7.

There are many other ways in which the differences between INTEGERs and REALs are useful. Our next example uses the fact that if an assignment statement has a REAL on the right-hand side and an INTEGER memory cell on the left, an INTEGER version of the right-hand side is stored in the cell. Another way of saying this is that the fractional part is truncated or **chopped** so that the value can be expressed as an INTEGER.

A bar graph is a popular way to summarize data. Figure 4 5 2 is a bar graph summarizing the data pictured in Figure 4 5 1.

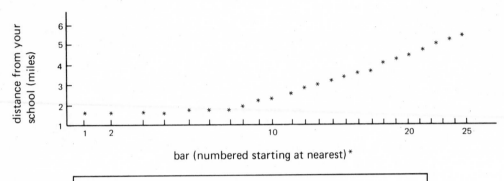

bar (numbered starting at nearest)*

*Bars are numbered rather than named to avoid giving free publicity to the Dutch Goose, Menlo Park.

Figure 4 5 1

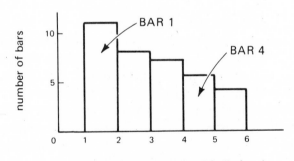

distance from your school (miles)

Figure 4 5 2

How might we convert our data from the first form to the second? Basically what our program will do is to read information about one bar at a time and decide which data summary, BAR0, BAR1, BAR2, BAR3, BAR4, or BAR5, the information should be added to. For example, if we find an establishment 3.27 miles from school, we would count it in BAR3, since the height of BAR3 indicates the number of establishments between 3.00 and 4.00 miles away. A flowchart for the program which organizes the data in this way is shown in Figure 4 5 3.

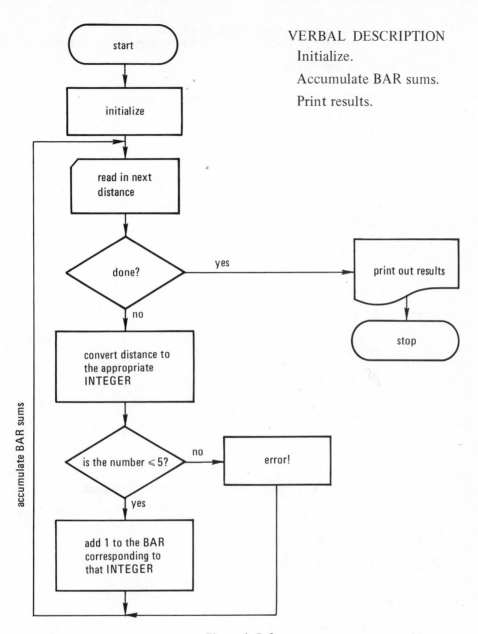

VERBAL DESCRIPTION
Initialize.
Accumulate BAR sums.
Print results.

Figure 4 5 3

```
COMMENT:  MAKE A BAR GRAPH FROM DISTANCE DATA.
       INTEGER BAR0, BAR1, BAR2, BAR3, BAR4, BAR5, NUMB
       REAL DIST
C      INITIALIZE BAR HEIGHTHS
       BAR0=0
       BAR1=0
       BAR2=0
       BAR3=0
       BAR4=0
       BAR5=0
C      READ DISTANCES AND ACCUMULATE BAR SUMS
 10    READ(5,1000) DIST
 1000  FORMAT(F10.0)
       IF (DIST .LT. 0.0)  GO TO 200
C      DROP FRACTIONAL PART TO DETERMINE BAR SUM AFFECTED
 18    NUMB = DIST
C      FIGURE OUT WHICH BAR IT FITS IN
       IF (NUMB .NE. 0)  GO TO 20
          BAR0 = BAR0+1
          GO TO 10
 20    IF (NUMB .NE. 1)  GO TO 30
          BAR1 = BAR1+1
          GO TO 10
 30    IF (NUMB .NE. 2)  GO TO 40
          BAR2 = BAR2+1
          GO TO 10
 40    IF (NUMB .NE. 3)  GO TO 50
          BAR3 = BAR3+1
          GO TO 10
 50    IF (NUMB .NE. 4)  GO TO 60
          BAR4 = BAR4+1
          GO TO 10
 60    IF (NUMB .NE. 5)  GO TO 100
          BAR5 = BAR5+1
          GO TO 10
C      ERROR ...
 100   WRITE(6,1001) DIST
 1001  FORMAT(' DISTANCE',F12.2,' IS OUT OF RANGE')
       GO TO 10
C      PRINT RESULTS
 200   WRITE(6,2000)
 2000  FORMAT('1BAR    HEIGHT')
       WRITE(6,4000) BAR0
 4000  FORMAT('  0',I7)
       WRITE(6,4001) BAR1
 4001  FORMAT('  1',I7)
       WRITE(6,4002) BAR2
 4002  FORMAT('  2',I7)
       WRITE(6,4003) BAR3
 4003  FORMAT('  3',I7)
       WRITE(6,4004) BAR4
 4004  FORMAT('  4',I7)
       WRITE(6,4005) BAR5
 4005  FORMAT('  5',I7)
       STOP
       END
```

Statement number 18 is the heart of the program. Let's see how it works. Suppose READ statement number 10 gives DIST the value 1.275. Then, since NUMB is an INTEGER,

```
18      NUMB = DIST
```

will *convert* the value 1.275 to an INTEGER before storing it in NUMB. So in this case, NUMB would be given the INTEGER value 1.

Given data corresponding to Figure 4 5 1

```
1.9
0.4
0.9
3.9
17.5
2.8
4.5
4.1
3.2
5.8
6.9
4.5
3.7
2.9
5.2
-1.0
```

our program would finally print out

```
DISTANCE        17.50 IS OUT OF RANGE
DISTANCE         6.90 IS OUT OF RANGE


BAR    HEIGHT
 0       2
 1       1
 2       2
 3       3
 4       3
 5       2
```

Using this information, we drew Figure 4 5 2.

EXERCISES 4 5

1 Write an assignment statement which computes the number of nickels in CENTS pennies.

2 What BARs do these values go in?

4.715	−2.98
3.2	496.1
0.96	

Section 4 6*

Implicit Typing

Fortran does not require memory cell names to be listed in type statements. If a memory cell name is not explicitly given a type, Fortran makes an assumption. The convention is, if the memory cell name starts with I, J, K, L, M, or N, it is assigned the type INTEGER; otherwise, the type assigned is REAL.

This has one side effect which may have already brought you grief. If you make a keypunching mistake and misspell a memory cell name, the compiler won't print an error message. Instead, it assumes you want to have a memory cell of that name and assigns it a type according to the convention. The result is a program which may look like it works, but produces incorrect results.

The question of whether or not to explicitly type INTEGER and REAL variables can lead to heated debate (believe it or not). Here are some arguments.

pro: It's crucial for the programmer to be aware of the use he or she intends to make of each memory cell. Explicitly naming the type ensures that the programmer is conscious of each memory cell, its name, and its type.

con: If you don't follow the naming rules, you have to look all the way up to the top of the program to see what type a given memory cell is. That takes your mind off what you're doing.

pro: It's important to choose memory cell names which are strongly suggestive of the use made of the cell. Often six letters are inadequate to the task, and further restricting the choice of the first letter to fit the implicit typing convention becomes unbearable.

con: There's too big a deal made of using fancy memory cell names. People see a memory cell named IDEAS and think that the program does something significant. It's better to use names like A, B, and C—they don't mislead anyone about what the computer is actually doing.

pro: You have to use type statements for all the Fortran data types besides INTEGERs and REALs—why not be consistent and do it for all of them?

con: Consistency is the hemoglobin of small minds. Besides, it's just a waste of time to punch the type statements. Let the compiler figure out what types the memory cells have.

.
.
.

Section 4 7*

Other Numeric Data Types

REALs and INTEGERs are the most commonly used types of Fortran numbers, but there are two other types. One of them, DOUBLE PRECISION, makes it easy to deal with numbers which have more digits than are allowed in REALs. Typically, DOUBLE PRECISION constants have more than twice the accuracy of REALs.

> **DOUBLE PRECISION** *constants*
>
> *examples*
>   129.748239
>   −49734004.88
>   1.00000000
>   −4.72D−8
>   .31415926535898D+01
>   2.7182818204590D0
>   5.77215664901D−01

DOUBLE PRECISION variables are declared using the usual form of a declaration statement with the *type* position occupied by the phrase DOUBLE PRECISION, as below.

`DOUBLE PRECISION A, D, Z`

DOUBLE PRECISION constants and variables may be mixed with REAL values in arithmetic expressions, and the result is a DOUBLE PRECISION value. As with REALs, and for the same reason, negative DOUBLE PRECISION values cannot be raised to non-INTEGER powers. Thus (−4.7D00)**0.5 is not a legal expression.

COMPLEX is the other type of Fortran number. COMPLEX numbers have two parts, a real part and an imaginary part, and are written in the form (*r part, i part*) where *r part* (the real part) and *i part* (the imaginary part) are REAL constants.

> **COMPLEX** *constants*
>
> *examples*
> (1.0, 0.0)
> (0.0, 1.0)
> (1.0, −1.0)
> (4.93, 7.948)
> (−5.221, 6.14)

COMPLEX variables are declared in exactly the way you would expect.

`COMPLEX ZETA, MU, A`

As with the other types of Fortran numbers, COMPLEX values can be used in arithmetic expressions, and they can be mixed with REAL values to produce a COMPLEX result, using +, −, /, or *. There are two restrictions to be aware of: (1) the exponent in a ** operation can never be COMPLEX, and (2) if the base in a ** operation is COMPLEX, the exponent must be of type INTEGER.

> *number* **COMPLEX *is illegal*
> COMPLEX**INTEGER *is legal*
> COMPLEX**non-INTEGER *is illegal*

EXERCISES 4 7

1 What are the values of the following expressions?
    a 2.0*(1.4, 3.7)
    b (0.0, 1.0)**2
    c A*(1.0, 0.0) + B*(0.0, 1.0), where A and B are REALs
    d ZETA*(1.0, −1.0), where ZETA is COMPLEX

2 Does the following statement make sense?
    `IF (ZETA .GE. (1.4,3.72)) STOP`

3 Which of these statements are true? (The ANSI Fortran MiniManual gives details of the FUNCTIONs used here.)
    `DOUBLE PRECISION X,Y,Z`
    a `IDINT(DBLE(3.14159))` equals 3
    b `SNGL(DBLE(3.14159))` equals 3.0
    c `INT(SNGL(DABS(X)))` always equals IDINT (X)
    d `SNGL(X+Y+Z)` always equals `SNGL(X)+SNGL(Y)+SNGL(Z)`

4 Which are true?

`COMPLEX Z, CLLOWY`

a (1.0, −1.0) equals CONJG(CMPLX(1.0, 1.0))

b CONJG(Z) always equals CMPLX(CABS(Z), 0.)

c CABS(CONJG(Z)) always equals CABS(Z)

d CABS(CLLOWY) always equals ABS(REAL(CLLOWY)) + ABS(AIMAG(CLLOWY))

Section 4 8

LOGICALs

Numbers aren't the only sorts of information that can be conveniently manipulated in Fortran. There is also a LOGICAL data type.

In Chapter 3 we used tests like

IF (X. GT. 2.0) STOP

The expression within parentheses is an example of a LOGICAL expression. Its value is either .TRUE. or .FALSE. depending, of course, on whether or not the value of memory cell X is greater than 2.0. The statement to the right (STOP in this case) is carried out only if the LOGICAL expression has the value .TRUE. The expressions in IF statements can be more elaborate than those we've seen so far, and they can be used in places other than IF statements.

> **LOGICAL**: *a data type with only two possible values—.TRUE. and .FALSE.—corresponding to Boolean (two-valued) logic*

A **LOGICAL expression** is formed of basic LOGICAL elements separated by LOGICAL operators (.AND., .OR., and .NOT.) and grouped by parentheses. A basic **LOGICAL element** can be one of three things:

1 a LOGICAL constant (.TRUE. or .FALSE.)

2 the name of a memory cell which has been declared to have type LOGICAL

3 a relational expression (like those we've seen in IF statements)

The simplest basic LOGICAL element is a LOGICAL constant (either .TRUE. or .FALSE.). The second kind of basic LOGICAL element is a memory cell name which has been declared to be of type LOGICAL. For example, the statement

`LOGICAL X, Y, Z`

declares X, Y, and Z to be memory cells containing LOGICAL values. Any of them could then be basic LOGICAL elements in a LOGICAL expression.

If you aren't familiar with formal logic or Boolean algebra, you may become confused by trying to see too deep an analogy between the symbols .TRUE. and .FALSE. and the familiar philosophical, ethical, moral concepts "true" and "false." Try to keep firmly in your mind that a LOGICAL memory cell always has exactly one value at a given point in time (just as an INTEGER variable may have only one value at a time). That value is either .TRUE. or .FALSE.. There are no in-betweens. No LOGICAL value is partly true and partly false. This isn't much like real life, and perhaps that makes it confusing, but LOGICAL expressions are used to tell the controller exactly what to do. Fortran instructions are precise, *not "maybe do this" or "maybe do that," so* LOGICAL *values are always either* .TRUE. *or* .FALSE., *never both.*

Fortran uses a pattern of 1's and 0's to represent the LOGICAL *values* .TRUE. *and* .FALSE., *but there is no range limitation as with the numeric data types, since there are only two* LOGICAL *values.*

The third type of basic LOGICAL element, the **relational expression**, states a relation between two arithmetic expressions. The value of a relational expression is .TRUE. if the stated relation is true.

As you may recall from Chapter 3, relations are stated using the six relational operators.

.EQ.	meaning equals
.NE.	meaning not equal to
.LT.	meaning less than
.LE.	meaning less than or equal to
.GE.	meaning greater than or equal to
.GT.	meaning greater than

The results of the comparisons (relational expressions) we used in Chapter 3, then, are LOGICAL values. For example, the relational expression

```
(A**2) + (B**2) .EQ. C**2
```

has the value .TRUE. if the square of the value of C is the same as the sum of the squares of the values of A and B; otherwise, its value is .FALSE..

The six operators above are the *only* relational operators that are defined in Fortran. Other natural relations like .EG. ("equal to or greater than") or .SGT. ("slightly greater than") will not be accepted. However, you can use LOGICAL operators to make combinations of relational expressions.

Any of the basic LOGICAL elements may be used to construct a more involved LOGICAL expression by using the LOGICAL operators .AND., .OR., or .NOT.. Fortran arithmetic expressions are pretty easy to understand because most everybody is familiar with the arithmetic operators (+, −, *, /, and **). Probably you tend to use LOGICAL operators when you speak and think without being too familiar with their formal definitions.

If P and Q are names of LOGICAL memory cells, then

P .AND. Q

is a LOGICAL expression which has the value .TRUE. if both P *and* Q have the value .TRUE.; otherwise, the expression has the value .FALSE..

The expression

P .OR. Q

has the value .TRUE. if either P *or* Q (or both) has the value .TRUE.; otherwise, the expression has the value .FALSE..

The expression

.NOT. P

has a value just the opposite of P. That is, if P has the value .TRUE., then .NOT. P has the value .FALSE.; if P has the value .FALSE., then .NOT. P has the value .TRUE..

Examples

.AND.

"[It is raining] and [the sun is shining.]"
A   B

The statement is true if both A *and* B are true.

.OR.

"[He is heavy] or [he's wearing a pillow around his waist.]"
A   B

The statement is true if either A *or* B (or both) is true.

.NOT.

"He is not [pregnant]."
A

The statement is true if A is *not* true.

The above examples are, of course, not Fortran but English. The "basic logical elements" in the sentences are bracketed. Two of the logical operators, *and* and *or*, are *conjunctions*; they connect two statements (or "basic logical elements," as we have called them). In Fortran the LOGICAL operators .AND. and .OR. are also conjunctions—they connect two basic LOGICAL elements. The third LOGICAL operator, .NOT., is different. In the English example, the word *not* applies only to *pregnant* rather than to two parts of a sentence. Similarly, .NOT. operates on *one* basic LOGICAL element. For this reason .AND. and .OR. are called **binary operators** (operating on two things), and .NOT. is called a **unary operator** (operating on *one* thing).

Notice the difference between *relations* (like .EQ. or .GT.) and LOGICAL *operators* (like .AND. or .NOT.). Relations compare two *arithmetic* expressions and the result of the comparison is either .TRUE. or .FALSE. LOGICAL operators operate on *LOGICAL* expressions, and again the result is .TRUE. or .FALSE. Since a relational expression results in a LOGICAL value, it is a special case of the general class of LOGICAL expressions.

There are several ways in which LOGICAL expressions can be used. You have already seen their use in IF statements. Another use is as the right-hand side of an assignment statement. For example, the program below assigns a LOGICAL

```
      LOGICAL TRI1, TRI2, TRI3
      INTEGER SIDE1, SIDE2, SIDE3
      SIDE1=3
      SIDE2=4
      SIDE3=5
      TRI1=SIDE1 .LE. SIDE2+SIDE3
      TRI2=SIDE2 .LE. SIDE1+SIDE3
      TRI3=SIDE3 .LE. SIDE1+SIDE2
      IF (TRI1 .AND. TRI2 .AND. TRI3) GO TO 100
      WRITE(6,1000)
1000  FORMAT(' NO')
      STOP
100   WRITE(6,1010)
1010  FORMAT(' YES')
      STOP
      END
```

value to each of the three memory cells TRI1, TRI2, and TRI3, and then uses an IF statement to see if all three are .TRUE. What will be printed? Remember! a LOGICAL variable can take only one value at a time.

The most common use of LOGICAL expressions is in IF statements. You already know how to write IF tests like

```
IF (I .GT. 2)  WRITE(6,1000) I
```

Now, using the LOGICAL operators, you can write all sorts of elaborate tests. For example,

```
IF ((X .GT. 0.0) .AND. (X .LT. 10.0))  STOP
```

will cause the program to STOP if X lies between 0 and 10.

Like arithmetic operators, LOGICAL operators have a hierarchy of precedence: .NOT. is performed first, then .AND., and finally .OR. operations are performed. Of course, parentheses may be used to override this hierarchy.

IF statement

form

    IF (*b*) *stmt*

    b is a LOGICAL expression

    stmt is an executable statement other than an IF or DO (DO statements are covered in Chapter 8)

meaning

    executes statement *stmt* if the expression *b* has the value .TRUE. In any case, proceed from the next statement unless the execution of statement *stmt* transfers control to another part of the program (as in a GO TO).

examples

```
IF (X .LE. 0.0)  GO TO 27
IF (A*B .GT. C**2)  WRITE(6,1000)A,B,C
IF (Q1 .AND. (.NOT. Q2))  A=B+2
IF (N .EQ. 0 .OR. Q)  STOP
```

One common use of LOGICAL values is in creating and using **decision tables**. Here's a program that uses LOGICAL values to implement a simple decision table.

Each year, pro football teams go through data on a huge number of players they want to consider hiring, recruiting, or making trades for. Most of the players don't fit a given team's needs, so to save time, one team has developed a computer program to scan the data. Since the team's needs change from year to year, the program must be flexible. Each year the team fills in a decision table to describe its needs. The one for this year looks like this and says that the team needs experienced offensive players and young defensive players. A player is assumed to be experienced if he has played at least four years of pro ball.

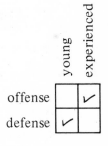

Each card for our program will contain an identification number, the number of years the player has been in the pros, and a number which tells whether he plays offense (1) or defense (2). The decision table information is given by assignment statements 10, 11, 12, and 13. Next year, if the team's needs change, all it has to do is alter the assignments appropriately. Look carefully at the way the LOGICAL values are used to control which players' names are printed out.

```
        LOGICAL EXPOFF, EXPDEF, YNGOFF, YNGDEF
        INTEGER ID, YRS, POS
COMMENT:  THIS PROGRAM FILTERS OUT THOSE PLAYERS WHICH MEET
C         THE TEAM'S NEEDS
C         HERE'S THE DECISION TABLE INFORMATION
  10    EXPOFF = .TRUE.
  11    EXPDEF = .FALSE.
  12    YNGOFF = .FALSE.
  13    YNGDEF = .TRUE.
        WRITE(6,1000)
1000    FORMAT(' HERE ARE SOME PLAYERS TO LOOK AT.')
 100    READ(5,1100) ID, YRS, POS
1100    FORMAT(I4,I3,I2)
        IF (ID .LT. 0)  STOP
          IF (YRS .GT. 4)  GO TO 300
            IF (POS .NE. 1)  GO TO 200
C               THIS IS A YOUNG OFFENSIVE PLAYER.  WANT HIM?
                IF (YNGOFF) WRITE(6,5000) ID,YRS,POS
                GO TO 100
C
C               THIS IS A YOUNG DEFENSIVE PLAYER.  WANT HIM?
 200            IF (YNGDEF) WRITE(6,5000) ID,YRS,POS
                GO TO 100
C
 300          IF (POS .NE. 1)  GO TO 400
C               THIS IS AN EXPERIENCED, OFFENSIVE PLAYER.
                IF (EXPOFF) WRITE(6,5000) ID,YRS,POS
                GO TO 100
C
C               THIS IS AN EXPERIENCED DEFENSIVE PLAYER.
 400            IF (EXPDEF) WRITE(6,5000) ID,YRS,POS
                GO TO 100
5000    FORMAT(' ID:',I4,'    YEARS:',I3,'    POSITION:',I2)
        END
```

data

```
    12  1 1
   984 12 1
    32  6 1
   101  2 2
    66  9 2
    86  2 1
   682  0 1
    29  6 1
   472  3 2
   -1
```

output

```
HERE ARE SOME PLAYERS TO LOOK AT.
ID: 984    YEARS: 12    POSITION: 1
ID:  32    YEARS:  6    POSITION: 1
ID: 101    YEARS:  2    POSITION: 2
ID:  29    YEARS:  6    POSITION: 1
ID: 472    YEARS:  3    POSITION: 2
```

> *There are two common errors that people tend to make when using* LOGICAL *expressions. First, people tend to write things like*
>
> ```
> IF (A .GT. 0 .AND. .LT. 100) STOP
> ```
> *when they should have written*
> ```
> IF (A .GT. 0 .AND. A .LT. 100) STOP
> ```
> *Remember that* LOGICAL *operators can operate only on* LOGICAL *values, and*
> ```
>         .LT. 100
> ```
> *is not a* LOGICAL *value.*

> *Another common error is writing a statement which tries to compare two* LOGICAL *values using a relational operator. A relational operator cannot compare* LOGICAL *values*

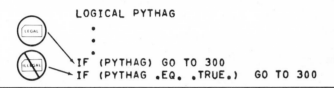

```
        LOGICAL PYTHAG
           .
           .
           .
        IF (PYTHAG) GO TO 300
        IF (PYTHAG .EQ. .TRUE.) GO TO 300
```

EXERCISES 4 8

1 If

```
LOGICAL A, B, C
A = .TRUE.
B = .TRUE.
C = .FALSE.
```

then what values do these expressions have:

```
A .OR. B
.NOT. C
(A .OR. B) .AND. C
.TRUE. .OR. C
.TRUE. .AND. C
(.NOT. C) .OR. B
```

2 Write one IF statement which will have the same effect as the statements below:

```
        IF (X .GT. 0) GO TO 20
        GO TO 30
20      IF (X .LT. 10) STOP
30      ...
```

3 Again, as in problem 2 above:

```
        IF (X .GT. 10) GO TO 20
        IF (X .LT. 0) GO TO 20
        GO TO 30
20      STOP
```

4 Write a LOGICAL expression involving two LOGICAL variables A and B which has the value .TRUE. if only A is .TRUE. or if only B is .TRUE.; and is .FALSE. if both A and B are .TRUE. or both are .FALSE. (This expression is called the **exclusive-or**.)

5 Alter the football team's program so that it implements this decision table:

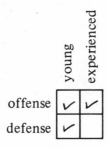

Section 4 9

Characters

If Fortran could handle nothing but numeric and logical values, only dyed-in-the-wool technical people would use it. Fortunately, Fortran can be used to manipulate most of the symbols we ordinarily use in writing. Unfortunately, the current ANSI standards do not provide a separate data type for values which are neither numeric nor LOGICAL, and we must sneak in through the back door.

The data descriptors (so far we've seen just I*w* and F*w.d*) which appear in a FORMAT associated with a READ statement specify how the symbols which appear on the data card are to be interpreted. Thus, symbols interpreted under an I*w* data descriptor are converted into the pattern appropriate for storing INTE-GERs, and symbols interpreted under an F*w.d* data descriptor are converted into REALs. By altering the data descriptor, we can alter the interpretation of the symbols appearing on the data card.

To specify that we wish the symbols interpreted as **characters** (i.e., letters of the alphabet, parentheses, punctuation marks, digits, etc.) we use the A*w* data descriptor. The A stands for **alphameric**, which for our purposes means any character you can find on the keyboard.

We can also use the A*w* descriptor for output. In that case the value in the memory cell named in the WRITE statement is interpreted as a sequence of *characters* to be printed.

Just as the size of the memory cells limits the size of allowable INTEGERs and REALs, so it determines the number of characters which will fit in one memory cell. In our examples, we'll assume that this is four. Usually we'll want to deal with words containing more than four letters. In that case we'll just use more than one memory cell. Here's a simple program that reads one person's name (or the first 16 characters of the name) and then prints it.

```
      INTEGER NAME1, NAME2, NAME3, NAME4
      READ(5,1000) NAME1, NAME2, NAME3, NAME4
 1000 FORMAT(A4,A4,A4,A4)
      WRITE(6,2000) NAME1, NAME2, NAME3, NAME4
 2000 FORMAT(' THE PERSON IS ', A4, A4, A4, A4)
      STOP
      END
```

data

   HEINRICH HAMKER

output

   THE PERSON IS HEINRICH HAMKER

After the READ is performed, the memory cells look like this:

NAME1 | HEIN |

NAME2 | RICH |

NAME3 | HAM |

NAME4 | KER |

---

character data descriptor

form

   A*w*

   w is an unsigned INTEGER constant

meaning

   describes a field of width *w* whose contents are interpreted as characters. On input, if *w* is greater than the number of characters which can fit in one memory cell, only the rightmost part of the field will be stored, while if *w* is less than the number of characters that can fit, blanks will be inserted on the right to fill up the cell. On output, if *w* is greater than the number of characters in a memory cell, blanks will fill up the left part of the field, while if *w* is less than the number of characters that fit, only the leftmost characters will appear.

examples

   Assume that four characters can be stored per memory cell.

input	data descriptor	memory cell
ABCDEF	A6	C D E F
FM	A2	F M
ECHH	A4	E C H H

memory cell	data descriptor	output
D U C K	A2	DU
$ 1 0 0	A6	$100

Remember that the content of a memory cell is a pattern of 1's and 0's. Since we told the compiler that NAME1, NAME2, and so on, contain INTEGERs, the controller doesn't know (or care) that we're thinking of the bit patterns in the memory cells as a person's name. This has an important implication: we can *compare* characters by using relational expressions. The bit patterns corresponding to characters are deliberately chosen so that we can tell if one group of characters is in alphabetical order with respect to another by using the .LE. relation. Suppose that the memory cells NAME1 and NAME2 contain these characters:

NAME 1   ATOM

NAME2   BONG

Then the relational expression

```
NAME1 .LT. NAME2
```

has the value .TRUE. because ATOM comes before BONG alphabetically. Later we will see how to use this property to put lists of people's names in alphabetical order.

---

collating sequence: The ANSI standards don't require that letters be represented so that they'll be in alphabetical order when compared as INTEGERs, but we don't know of any system where they're in a different order.

Suppose that we want to write a program which will READ a number of people's last names and count the number of times the common last names Brown, Smith, and Nerdly appear. Since we know how to READ the names, and we know how to make comparisons, we might plunge right in. But wait! We need to check each name to see if it is Brown, Smith, or Nerdly. How do we do that? The answer is a little unpleasant, but it can be done. To ease our way in, first we'll show a method which, while not conforming to the ANSI standard, is allowed by many versions of Fortran. This involves using the Hollerith constant notation, as in these statements.

```
IF (NAME1 .EQ. 4HBROW .AND. NAME2 .EQ. 1HN) B=B+1
IF (NAME1 .EQ. 4HSMIT .AND. NAME2 .EQ. 1HH) S=S+1
IF (NAME1 .EQ. 4HNERD .AND. NAME2 .EQ. 2HLY) N=N+1
```

While this may be awkward and hard to read (especially if there are any very long names to be checked) at least it is fairly similar to the sorts of tests we've made many times before.

To make the test using only ANSI standard statements, we must introduce a restricted form of a new statement, the DATA statement. The DATA statement is a nonexecutable statement, that is, an instruction to the compiler. It tells the compiler to place values in memory cells before execution of the program begins, thus allowing us to give memory cells initial values. The standards allow these initial values to be Hollerith constants.

At last we can write our program to count common last names.

```
COMMENT: THIS PROGRAM READS A LIST OF LAST NAMES AND COUNTS
C        THE NUMBER OF OCCURRENCES OF THE NAMES "SMITH,"
C        "BROWN," AND "NERDLY."
C        THE LAST CARD CONTAINS "****"
         INTEGER B, S, N,  W1,W2,  NAMEB1,NAMEB2,NAMES1,NAMES2,
        +                          NAMEN1,NAMEN2,  FINIS
C     STORE THE NAMES WE SEEK
      DATA NAMEB1/4HBROW/, NAMEB2/1HN/
      DATA NAMES1/4HSMIT/, NAMES2/1HH/
      DATA NAMEN1/4HNERD/, NAMEN2/2HLY/
      DATA FINIS/4H****/
C     INITIALIZE
      B=0
      S=0
      N=0
C     READ DATA AND ACCUMULATE SUMS
   10 READ(5,1000) W1,W2
 1000 FORMAT(A4,A4)
         IF (W1 .EQ. FINIS)  GO TO 20
         IF (W1 .EQ. NAMEB1  .AND.  W2 .EQ. NAMEB2)  B=B+1
         IF (W1 .EQ. NAMES1  .AND.  W2 .EQ. NAMES2)  S=S+1
         IF (W1 .EQ. NAMEN1  .AND.  W2 .EQ. NAMEN2)  N=N+1
         GO TO 10
C     REACHED END OF LIST
   20 WRITE(6,2000) B, S, N
 2000 FORMAT(' THERE WERE', I3, ' BROWNS,',
        +        I3, ' SMITHS, AND ', I3, ' NERDLYS')
      STOP
      END
```

data
```
   JIMENEZ
   DEREMER
   BROWN
   BROWNING
   NERDLY
   VALTEAU
   DROVOS
   SMITH
   BROWN
   RODRIGEZ
   NERDLY
   ****
```

output

```
THERE WERE  2 BROWNS,  1 SMITHS, AND   2 NERDLYS
```

With a little more effort, we could alter our program so that it accepts full names and searches for BROWN, SMITH, and NERDLY, ignoring the rest of the name. Problem 7 24 gives hints for how to proceed when the data is given in the classical "Nerdly, Phillip R." style. The program we showed here won't work for that case because if the name is

NERDLY, PHILLIP R.

then memory cell W2 will contain the characters LY, P. which is not equal to the string stored in NAMEN2, even though the last name is NERDLY.

> *Although it is legal to use memory cells of any numeric type (INTEGER or REAL) to store characters, it is far safer to use INTEGERs. Since manipulation of REALs is not an exact process, some odd conditions can arise which can cause unexpected results when values are stored in REAL memory cells.*

EXERCISES 4 9

1 What would we have to change in the last name counting program to make it look for JONES instead of SMITH?

2 Write Fortran statements which will READ a data card and search for a dollar sign anywhere in the first five columns.

Section 4 10

More about FORMATs

So far we've seen two kinds of FORMAT descriptors: literal descriptors, as in

```
1000 FORMAT(* RESULT=*)
```
     a literal descriptor

and data descriptors for INTEGERs, REALs, and character information, as in

```
2000 FORMAT(I5,F7.2,A4)
```
        data descriptors

This section covers a number of additional constructs which may be used in FORMATs, and which give a very general (if sometimes clumsy) control capability over the processing of input and output records. These include data descriptors for all the data types we've seen, spacing descriptors for controlling the positioning of values, and repetition and grouping specifications which allow FORMATs to be specified more concisely.

> *In order to keep the material on FORMATs in one place for easier reference, we've included some features which are not strictly necessary at this point. If some of the topics don't seem useful to you right now, just skim the material and come back later if and when you find a use for them.*

As you try to decipher FORMAT statements or construct your own, keep in mind that a FORMAT statement is always associated with an input or output statement (READ or WRITE), and that the FORMAT describes the *appearance* of the input or output record (card or printed line). The associated input or output statement (READ or WRITE) designates the memory cells whose values will be changed (in a READ) or used (in a WRITE).

Let's recap the data descriptors we've seen so far and then move on to new territory.

In the descriptions which follow, the term **external** refers to the pattern which appears on the output record (printed line) or input record (card) while **internal** refers to the value in memory. Thus a READ statement causes external symbols to be processed and stored as internal values in memory cells. The associated FORMAT specifies details of the transformation.

Fortran Charlie prepares to learn FORMATs (It's a whole 'nother language)

> *b: In picturing printed lines or punched cards where spacing is critical, we'll use the symbol b for the blank character.*

> *right-justified: A string of characters is right-justified in a field if the last character is in the rightmost position in the field.*

I*w* (INTEGER)

input

An external string of *w* or fewer digits which may include a preceding sign (+ or −) is converted to an INTEGER constant. No characters other than blanks, digits, or a sign are legal. Any blanks in the field will be interpreted as zero digits.

external	I6	internal
bb1042		1042
bbb−27		−27
−27bbb		−27000
bb+bb6		6
−3bb4b		−30040
bbbbbb		0
b−3+44		illegal
bb3.14		illegal

output

An internal INTEGER value is converted to a string of *w* characters. If the value is negative, the digits will be preceded by a minus sign. If the value does not use up all *w* characters in the field, the number is right-justified in the field with blanks to the left. If the value is too large to fit in a field of width *w*, most systems issue an error indicator.

internal	I6	*external*
1042		*bb*1042
−27		*bbb*−27
−27000		−27000
6		*bbbbb*6
−30040		−30040
0		*bbbbb*0
−300400		illegal
3.14		illegal

F*w*.*d* (REAL)

input

The external character string in the field of width *w* is interpreted as a REAL constant. As such it may be preceded by a plus or a minus sign and may contain a decimal point. If the decimal point is not present, it is assumed to precede the *d* rightmost characters in the field (*d* must be smaller than *w*). The number may be written in scientific notation (E-notation). All blank characters are interpreted as zeros.

external	F6.2	*internal*
*bb*3.14		3.14
b−2.79		−2.79
+*b*90.1		90.1
0.1234		0.1234
*bbb*372		3.72
*bb*372*b*		37.20
9001+1		900.1
2.1E−3		0.0021

output

An internal REAL value is converted to a character string of length *w*. The value is rounded (not truncated) to *d* decimal places (digits beyond the decimal point). If the external value has fewer than *w* characters, including the decimal point and a possible minus sign, then the number is right-justified and the field is filled with blanks to the left. If the number is too large to fit into *w* character positions, most systems issue an error indicator.

internal	F6.2	external
3.14		b3.14
−2.79		b−2.79
90.1		b90.10
$49.2*10^{-3}$		bb0.05
$49.2*10^{-6}$		bb0.00
0.0000		bb0.00
$49.2*10^{6}$		******
3927		illegal

Ew.d (REAL)

input

The effect is the same as Fw.d if the external value isn't written in scientific notation. If it is written in scientific notation, then the decimal point shift factor must be right-justified in the field; otherwise, the blanks following it will be interpreted as zeros, thus increasing the shift by factors of ten. If a sign is included with the decimal point shift factors, as in 1.7E−6, and 4.932E+8, then the E may be omitted to save room in the data field. In addition, the decimal point may be omitted from the number, but if so, it is implicitly placed d places to the left of the decimal point shift factor. The following examples should clarify the myriad cases.

external	E7.2	internal
bb3.141		3.141
bbb3.14		3.14
$bbbb$314		3.14
3.14E00		3.14
3.14E−2		.0314
b314E−2		.0314
bb314−2		.0314
314b+2b		$31.40*10^{20}$

output

The REAL value in the corresponding memory cell is output in scientific notation, rounded to d significant digits. The rightmost four spaces in the output field of width w are used for the decimal point shift factor printed in the form E+xx or E−xx, where each x is a single digit. The number is printed in the $d + 3$ spaces to the left of the decimal point shift factor in the form b0.f or −0.f where f is a d digit unsigned INTEGER. The leftmost $w − (d + 7)$ spaces are left blank. As you can see, w should be at least as large as $d + 7$ to allow enough room for the number.

internal	E10.2	external
3.168		bb0.32E+01
$492.1*10^{-23}$		bb0.49E−21
−3987.12		b−0.40E+04
3749		illegal

Gw.d (generalized REAL)

Fw.d and Ew.d specifications are particularly useful when you wish to print out values to a certain number of decimal places, but there are also times when you wish to print out values with a certain number of significant digits. The G specification is designed for that purpose. Its form is

$$Gw.d$$

where w is the field width and d is the number of significant digits to be printed rather than the number of decimal places. The Gw.d specification has the pleasant feature that the value will be printed in an F style if that is possible in a field width of $w - 4$. Otherwise, it is printed in the E style. E-style numbers are right-justified, and F-style numbers are justified to the fifth from the right space of the field, leaving four spaces to the right of the number. Thus, if the same FORMAT is used repeatedly, the digits of the numbers will line up in a column, and the exponents will line up in the rightmost four spaces of the field.

input

Same as Fw.d.

output.

The rightmost four spaces in the field of width w are reserved for a decimal point shift of the form E+xx or E–xx (each x is a single digit). If the number rounded to d significant digits will fit in the remaining $w - 4$ leftmost spaces in the field, then the rightmost four spaces are left blank. On the other hand, if the number won't fit into $w - 4$ spaces, then it is written with a decimal point shift factor. In this case the number itself is rounded to d significant digits and is written in the form $bx.y$ or $-x.y$, where x is a single digit and y is a string of $d - 1$ digits.

internal	**G11.4**	*external*
–1.7526843		b–1.753bbbb
–175268.43		b–1.753E+05
3.1416		bb3.142bbbb
0.000031416		bb3.142E–05

Dw.d (DOUBLE PRECISION)

input

The input field is interpreted as in the E data descriptor except that E's in the data field may be D's instead, and the corresponding memory cell in the input list should be of type DOUBLE PRECISION.

external	**D16.9**	*internal*
1.7bbbbbbbbbbbbb		1.700000000000000
1.23456789012345		1.234567890123450
bbbbbbbb4.92D–3		.004920000000000000
bbbbbb5123456789		5.123456789000000

The output form of a DOUBLE PRECISION value under a D data descriptor is like that of a REAL under an E descriptor except that a D instead of an E separates the number from the decimal point shift factor.

COMPLEX

There is no data descriptor specifically for COMPLEX values. A COMPLEX memory cell is treated, in FORMATs, as if it were two REAL memory cells. That is, a COMPLEX memory cell in an I/O list is matched with *two* corresponding data descriptors in the FORMAT. In the program fragment below, the real part of ZETA is input under the F10.3 descriptor, and the imaginary part is matched with the E10.3 descriptor.

```
      INTFGER A, B
      COMPLEX ZETA
      READ(5,1000) A, ZETA, B
 1000 FORMAT(I10, F10.3, E10.3, I4)
```

data

    *bbbbbbbb*10*bbbbbbb*0.0*bbbbbbb*1.0*bb*20

Lw (LOGICAL)

input

The corresponding LOGICAL memory cell in the input list is given the value .TRUE. if the first nonblank character in the data field is a T. If the first nonblank character in the field is F, the cell is given the value .FALSE.

external	L6	internal
*bb*T*bbb*		.TRUE.
TURF*bb*		.TRUE.
*bbbbb*F		.FALSE.
F*bbbbb*		.FALSE.
*b*TRUE*b*		.TRUE.
FALSE*b*		.FALSE.

output

The letter T or F is right-justified with blank fill to the left if the value of the corresponding memory cell in the output list is .TRUE. or .FALSE. respectively.

internal	L6	external
.TRUE.		*bbbbb*T
.FALSE.		*bbbbb*F

FORMAT Fatigue Sets In

Aw (character)

The A stands for *alphameric*, another name for character strings. It is safest to store characters in INTEGER memory cells, but it's legal to use the A*w* descriptor in conjunction with memory cells of any type.

> *In character fields blanks are legitimate characters and stand for blanks, not zeros.*

input

The *w* characters in the data field are placed into the corresponding memory cell in the input list. All characters in the field, blanks and single quotes included, are part of the character string placed into the cell. If the cell isn't large enough to hold all *w* characters, then only the rightmost *w* characters in the data field are placed in the cell. On the other hand, if the cell is large enough to hold more than *w* characters, then the *w* characters are placed into the leftmost part of the cell and blank characters are put into the remainder of the cell.

> *The number of characters a memory cell can store varies from system to system. In this book we assume that four characters will fit in an INTEGER memory cell.*
>
> | external | descriptor | internal |
> |----------|------------|----------|
> | ABCD | A4 | ABCD |
> | ABCDEF | A6 | CDEF |
> | AB | A2 | AB*bb* |

output

The *w* characters in the corresponding memory cell in the output list are written in the *w*-space output field. If the memory cell has more than *w* characters, then only the leftmost *w* characters in the cell are written in the output field. On the other hand, if the cell has fewer than *w* characters, then its characters are right-justified in the output field with blank fill to the left.

internal	descriptor	external
ABCD	A4	ABCD
ABCD	A2	AB
ABCD	A6	*bb*ABCD

sP (scaling factor)

s is an unsigned INTEGER constant or a negative INTEGER constant.

The P scaling factor is not really a data descriptor in the sense we have been using the term. Instead of matching with an element of the I/O list and serving to describe the corresponding data item, it changes the effect of all succeeding REAL and DOUBLE PRECISION data descriptors in the FORMAT (that is, it alters the effect of F, E, D, and G data descriptors).

A P scaling factor is written immediately before an F, E, G, or D data descriptor (with no comma), e.g., −2PF10.1 or 3PD11.3. If the data descriptor is modified by a repeat specification (p. 101), the P scaling factor must precede it. To remove the effects of a previous P scaling factor in a FORMAT, a new scaling factor can be included. The scaling factor 0P returns REAL and DOUBLE PRECISION data descriptors to their normal meanings.

input

REAL or DOUBLE PRECISION numbers written in an input field without decimal point shift factors (i.e., without E or D) are rescaled by a factor of 10^{-s}. Thus, the relationship between the number in the data field and the stored value is

$$\text{internal value} = 10^{-s} * \text{external value.}$$

Numbers written in the input field *with* decimal point shift factors are not affected.

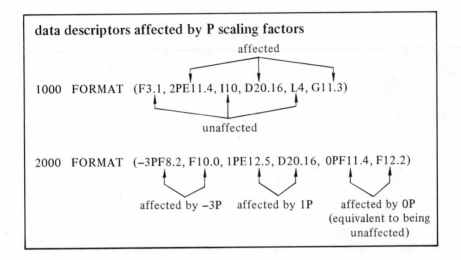

external	−2P	internal
1.952		195.2
397489.55		39748955.00000000
0.47		47.
3.72E−2		0.0372
4.951D01		49.51000000000000

external	2P	internal
492.1		4.921
3.72E−4		0.000372
4.951D01		49.51000000000000
397489.55		3974.8955

output

The *s*P scaling factor affects the meanings of different data descriptors in different ways.

effect on F: *external value = 10^s * internal value*

internal	3PF8.2	*external*
1.9873		*b*1987.30
−0.00314		*bbb*−3.14

effect on E and D: the decimal point is shifted *s* places (right for positive *s*, left for negative *s*) and the decimal point shift factor is reduced by *s*

internal	2PE10.3	*external*
1.9873		*bb*19.9E−01
−0.00314		*b*−31.4E−04

effect on G: no effect unless the number must be written with a decimal point shift factor in which case the result is like that with E or D output

Literal descriptors and data descriptors provide enough flexibility to allow you to do any sort of input or output processing that is possible using Fortran FORMATted I/O.

The rest of the options in FORMATs are concerned with making them easier to use, less lengthy, and so on.

One way to space over ten columns from the margin is to begin your FORMAT specification with a literal descriptor which consists of ten blanks.

```
1000 FORMAT('0 bbbbbbbbbb ', I2)
```

Since this can be inconvenient (you have to count how many blanks you've punched; it's boring to space long distances), Fortran provides a **spacing descriptor**. The *n*X descriptor tells the controller to skip the next *n* character positions on a data card or output line.

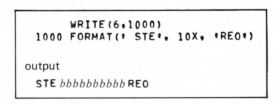

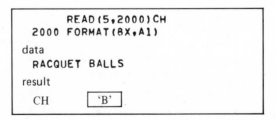

Formatted records, whether they are lines or cards, often have a very regular structure. In a number of examples we've had several *identical* data descriptors in a row. For example, suppose our data cards contain ten numbers in fields of width eight. One way to describe such a card is with FORMAT 1000 below:

```
1000 FORMAT(F8.0,F8.0,F8.0,F8.0,F8.0,
   +         F8.0,F8.0,F8.0,F8.0,F8.0)
```

Fortunately, we don't need to write so many identical descriptors. Instead, we can place a **repeat specification** in front of one descriptor. The effect is then the same as if the data descriptor is repeated the number of times indicated by the repeat specification. Thus, FORMAT 2000 below is equivalent to FORMAT 1000 above.

```
2000 FORMAT(10F8.0)
```

The repeat specification is an unsigned INTEGER constant *r* which appears in front of a FORMAT descriptor.

---

repeat specification: an unsigned nonzero INTEGER constant r placed in front of data descriptor or group to indicate that the group is to be repeated r times

---

If the same pattern of FORMAT descriptors is repeated several times, as in FORMAT 3000 below, then that *pattern* may be grouped by parentheses and a repeat specification placed in front of the group, as in the equivalent FORMAT 4000 below.

```
3000 FORMAT(' ',F11.4,' AND',I10,20X,
   +              F11.4,' AND',I10,20X,I15)

4000 FORMAT(' ',2(F11.4,' AND',I10,20X),I15)
```

---

group: a parenthesized sublist of FORMAT descriptors. It may be preceded by an explicit repeat specification. Groups may be nested to a depth of two.

Any list of FORMAT descriptors can become a group, and groups may be nested two deep, but no deeper. Usually a group is preceded by a repeat specification, but it doesn't have to be. If the repeat specification is omitted, it is taken to be one. Even a group with no explicit repeat factor affects the meaning of a FORMAT in the aberrant (but legal) case when a READ or WRITE list includes more values than the FORMAT appears equipped to handle. We'll ignore that possibility for a while. Then these two FORMATs are equivalent:

```
5000 FORMAT(A5, A5, I3, I3, 1X, A1, 1X, A1,
   +               I3, I3, 1X, A1, 1X, A1,
   +               I3, I3, 1X, A1, 1X, A1, A8, A8, A8)

6000 FORMAT(2A5, 3(2I3,2(1X,A1)), 3A8)
```

Most FORMATs describe a single line or a single card. In other words, they describe one I/O **record**. The length of a formatted I/O record is measured in characters. For example, the length of a record for the 80-column card reader is 80

> *record: the basic unit of I/O. Different I/O devices have different types of records. The card reader record is one card (usually 80 characters). The printer record is one line. Different printers have different line lengths; 132 is the line length for many printers.*

characters. No FORMAT should describe a record longer than the record length for the intended I/O device. However, it is possible for a FORMAT to describe more than one record. For example, the following statement prints two records (i.e., two lines) as a heading on a page.

```
        WRITE(6,1000)
   1000 FORMAT('1', 5X, 'SCREWS'/ ' ', 'SIZE', 4X, 'PRICE')
```

carriage control character

The slash (/) in the FORMAT separates the descriptions of the two records. (Note that each record, being a printed line, has a carriage control character.) In general, a FORMAT may describe many records, with each record separated from the next by a slash. For example, the following READ statement will read three cards. Two values will be taken from the first card, one value from the second, and two from the third.

```
        READ(5,2000)
   2000 FORMAT(2F20.0/F30.0/2F15.0)
```

Two consecutive slashes imply a blank record in between. The printer will skip a line because the implied blank line includes a blank character for carriage control. The reader will skip a card when given a // specification.

An I/O statement may process several records even if the FORMAT describes only one. Here's how that can happen. The WRITE statement below has more values in its list than there are data descriptors in the FORMAT. The computer must print all the values listed, so it simply uses the FORMAT over again, starting a new record when it comes to the end of the specification.

```
        INTEGER A, BEE, SEA, D
        A = 110
        B = 60
        SEA = 950
        D = SEA - 5*A
        WRITE(6,1000) A, BEE, SEA, D
   1000 FORMAT(' ', 2I6)
```

results

```
   bbb110bbbb60
   bbb950bbb400
```

In general, if an I/O statement is not completed when it runs out of data descriptors in the FORMAT, it starts a new record and uses the FORMAT over again. This is a relatively simple and useful idea. It lets you describe one record or even several records that you're thinking of as one logical unit and lets you use that description over and over to input or ouptut several sets of data. The following FORMAT describes a pair of data cards, one containing a car name and the other a REAL and an INTEGER. The READ statement READs three pairs of cards, using the FORMAT three times.

```
      INTEGER CAR1A, CAR1B
      INTEGER CAR2A, CAR2B
      INTEGER CAR3A, CAR3B
      INTEGER M1, M2, M3
      REAL PRICE1, PRICE2, PRICE3
      READ(5,1000) CAR1A,CAR1B,PRICE1,M1,
     +             CAR2A,CAR2B,PRICE2,M2,
     +             CAR3A,CAR3B,PRICE3,M3
 1000 FORMAT(2A4/F7.0,I7)
```

data

RABBIT*bb*
3300.00*bbbb*41
FOX*bbbbb*
5000.00*bbbb*37
DASHER*bb*
4500.00*bbbb*38

The repeated use of the FORMAT gets a little more complicated if the FORMAT contains groups of descriptors. In this case, the repetition starts from the last top-level group or from the repeat factor preceding it, if it has one. The following WRITE statement illustrates this feature. It assumes the memory cells have the values they were given by the READ statement above.

```
      WRITE(6,2000) CAR1A,CAR1B, PRICE1, M1,
     +              CAR2A,CAR2B, PRICE2, M2
     +              CAR3A,CAR3B, PRICE3, M3
 2000 FORMAT(' CAR          PRICE    EPA MILEAGE'/
     +        (1X,2A4, F9.2, I8))
```

output

```
   CAR        PRICE   EPA MILEAGE
   RABBIT    3300.00      41
   FOX       5000.00      37
   DASHER    4500.00      38
```

> *last top-level group: the group in a* FORMAT *which is terminated by the first right parenthesis to the left of the right parenthesis which closes the* FORMAT. *Got that?*

Now you know what happens if an I/O list includes more memory cell names than the associated FORMAT has data descriptors. There is yet another possibility, believe it or not. What if there are fewer memory cells to be dealt with than there are data descriptors left in the FORMAT? Perhaps the answer "the remaining data descriptors are ignored" is obvious. But what's *not* obvious is what happens if there is a slash or a literal descriptor after the last data descriptor that was used but before a data descriptor which is not needed. Do we ignore those too, or not? Well, it's not hard to imagine cases in which you would want them to be used, nor is it difficult to imagine cases in which you wouldn't want them. Verbosity won out, as illustrated below:

```
      INTEGER X, WN1,WN2
      DATA WN1/4HMILL/, WN2/2HER/
      X=2
      WRITE(6,1200) X, WN1,WN2
      X=0
      WRITE(6,1200) X
 1200 FORMAT(' THERE WERE', I2, ' PRIZE WINNERS.  ',
     +         2A4, ' CAME IN FIRST')
      STOP
      END
```

output
```
THERE WERE 2 PRIZE WINNERS.  MILLER   CAME IN FIRST
THERE WERE 0 PRIZE WINNERS.
```

The second WRITE statement doesn't have list elements to match with the 2A4 data descriptor. Hence, all the literal descriptors in the FORMAT, up to the 2A4 data descriptor, are printed; everything else is ignored.

FORMAT

form
> FORMAT (*spec*)
>
> *spec* is a list of FORMAT descriptors (i.e., data descriptors, literal descriptors, spacing descriptors, slashes, or groups of these) separated by commas. Slashes serve as delimiters, so commas should be omitted around slashes. Every FORMAT must have a statement label.

meaning
> A FORMAT describes the layout of an I/O record or records.

examples
```
1000 FORMAT(I10,A20,G11.4)
2000 FORMAT(5G10.0)
3000 FORMAT(' ',20('*****',F5.2))
4000 FORMAT('1',3F4.2//' ',6(3F5.2,I5))
```

> *group: A group of FORMAT descriptors is a parenthesized sublist of descriptors in **spec**. It may be preceded by an explicit repeat specification. FORMAT 4000 above contains the group 6(3F5.2,I5).*

Let's face it. This has been a hard, unpleasant section. You might feel that just as you were starting to learn Fortran, all of a sudden an entirely foreign language called FORMATs was pushed on you. You'd be right. Unless you are using a version of Fortran which allows some form of format-free I/O (for which there are no standards), you simply have to put up with the baroque details of FORMATs.

Now that you've learned the language for controlling the interaction of your program with input and output devices, we can get back to the more interesting (to us at least) parts of computing.

EXERCISES 4 10

1 Which data type and corresponding data descriptor would be most appropriate if you were printing out
    a baseball batting averages
    b the number of olives in a martini
    c a list of people's names
    d the national debt

2 Below are some pairs of FORMAT statements. Which have the same effect? Which are different?

```
1000 FORMAT(' ', I3, I3, I3, F12.2)
1001 FORMAT(' ', 3(I3,F12.2))

2000 FORMAT(' ', I3, I3, A2, I3, I3, A2)
2001 FORMAT(' ', 2(2I3, A2))

3000 FORMAT('0', F10.2)
3001 FORMAT(/' ', F10.2)

4000 FORMAT(13(' '), I10)
4001 FORMAT(13X, I10)

5000 FORMAT(' ', 10X, ' A=', I5)
5001 FORMAT(12X, 'A=', I5)
```

3 If the following READ FORMAT is used, where should the REAL number be put on the data card?

```
1000 FORMAT(F80.0)
```

4 What is wrong with the following FORMAT?

```
      READ(5,1000) A,B,C,D,E,F
1000 FORMAT(6F20.0)
```

5 How should the data be punched on cards for the following READ statement?

```
      READ(5,2000) A,B,C,D,E,F
2000 FORMAT(2F10.0)
```

6 Write a FORMAT describing a card with the following layout:

    col 1–2, alphameric
    col 21–30, REAL
    col 41–50, REAL
    col 61–70, REAL

7 What values will be placed in A and B?

```
      REAL A, B
      READ(5,1000) A,B
 1000 FORMAT(2E9.1)
            .
            .
            .
```

data

```
 +6.02E+23+602E+23
```

8 What will be printed?

```
      REAL A
      A = 1.234E+5
      WRITE(6,1000) A,A,A
 1000 FORMAT('bbA=',    F10.1, 'bbA=', E9.3, 'bbA=', E9.1)
      WRITE(6,2000) A,A,A
 2000 FORMAT('bbA=', 1PF10.1, 'bbA=', E9.3, 'bbA=', E9.1)
      WRITE(6,3000) A,A,A
 3000 FORMAT('bbA=',-1PF10.1, 'bbA=', E9.3, 'bbA=', E9.1)
      STOP
      END
```

9 Write one WRITE and one FORMAT statement which will print the line FORMAT IS A TRICKY LANGUAGE 100 times, starting at the top of a page.

10 What will be produced by

```
      INTEGER X, WN1,WN2
      DATA WN1/2HBO/, WN2/2HMO/
      X = 2
      WRITE(6,1350) WN1, X, WN2
 1350 FORMAT('0IN FIRST PLACE WAS ',A2/
     +        ' THERE WERE', I2, ' TIED FOR IT')
      STOP
      END
```

PROBLEMS 4

1 If 1.0/3.0 + 1.0/3.0 + 1.0/3.0 doesn't quite equal 1.0, how far off is it? How about 1.0/4.0 + 1.0/4.0 + 1.0/4.0 + 1.0/4.0? Answer these questions by computing these sums (and others with larger denominators) and printing the difference between the sums and 1.0. Use an E or G data descriptor to print the difference.

2 Design a program which READs pairs of INTEGERs from data cards. Each pair represents a fraction, with the first value being the numerator, the second the denominator. Print out each fraction as a whole number with a proper fraction.

Examples:

input	output
2 3	0 2/3
7 3	2 1/3
22 7	3 1/7
19 10	1 9/10

If the denominator on a card is 0, STOP.

3 Write a program which reverses the effect of Problem 2. Each data card should contain three INTEGER values which represent a number and a proper fraction. Print the equivalent improper fraction.

Examples:

input	output
2 1 3	7/3
2 5 7	19/7
0 1 3	1/3

4 The truncation that occurs when a REAL value is converted to an INTE-GER value is useful for getting rid of unwanted fractional parts. But what if you want to print out a value in dollars and cents? You don't want to get rid of all the fractional part—just everything past two digits to the right of the decimal place. Write a program which accepts REAL values and prints them out after removing the unwanted fractional digits.

5 Do problem 4 over again but accept two values per data card, one a REAL value and the other an INTEGER which tells how many digits to the right of the decimal point to retain. (Hint: It requires only a minor change to the solution to problem 4.)

Examples:

input		output
1.2345	1	1.2000
327.1039	3	327.1030
98.7219	0	98.0000
123.3217	−1	120.0000

6 Use a series of WRITE statements to print a giant version of the letter(s) of your choice in the middle of the page.

```
Z Z Z Z Z
Z Z Z Z Z
        Z Z
       Z Z
      Z Z
     Z Z
Z Z Z Z Z
Z Z Z Z Z
```

7   Write a program to count the votes in an election. There are three candidates: Milton P. Waxley (incumbent), Patricia Rhoder (progressive liberal), and Frederick "Red" Kemmeny (a reluctant candidate who filed at the last minute). Each voter makes his vote by punching a card with a digit in the first column: 1 for Waxley, 2 for Rhoder, or 3 for Kemmeny.

   At 7:30 p.m. an election official places a card with an X in column 80 at the end of all the ballot cards in the box and submits them as data for your program. Your program should print the election results. (Note: be sure to reject all mismarked ballots.)

This man has supported Milton P. Waxley
in the last seventeen elections

8   Do problem 7 and include the number of mismarked ballots in the output. Also print a brief victory statement by the winner which includes the names of his or her worthy opponents.

9   Write a program which READs INTEGERs, one from each card, and which prints the value of a LOGICAL variable which is .TRUE. only if the latest number is larger than the one immediately before. When a card is READ which has a value greater than 1000000 on it, print a LOGICAL value telling whether all the numbers were in increasing order.

10 READ a person's name (character data) from the first 20 columns of each card. Print the name unless it is your own. In that case, print an alias (to protect your real identity). Keep READing cards until you find one with FINISH in the first 6 columns.

11 You are given eight sets of three values each.

23.37	19.51	8.37
57.46	40.06	27.57
42.09	35.78	61.65
8.63	15.74	12.38
61.94	78.07	10.87
19.56	23.54	33.28
84.37	61.98	15.93
37.80	49.24	23.51

Write a program to determine whether or not the three values of a set could represent the lengths of the sides of a triangle. If the three sides could make a triangle, calculate its area and print a message like:

```
WHEN AB=3.00 AND BC=4.00 AND CA=5.00,
THE AREA OF TRIANGLE ABC IS 6.00
```

If a, b, and c are three side lengths, then the area is $\sqrt{[s(s-a)(s-b)(s-c)]}$, where s is the half perimeter $(a+b+c)/2$. (The formula is due to Hero, a mathematician of ancient times.)

   If the three values in a set couldn't represent the sides of a triangle, print a message like

```
23.37,  19.51, AND    9.37 COULD NOT POSSIBLY BE
                      THE SIDES OF A TRINGLE.
```

> *a property of Hero's formula: If s(s−a)(s−b)(s−c) is negative, then a, b, and c can't make a triangle.*

(Thanks to Rob Kelman for his help with this problem.)

12 Find the number of half-dollars, quarters, dimes, nickels, and pennies returned as change from one dollar. READ a purchase price (in pennies), and print out how many of each coin go into the change. Continue until you come to a negative purchase price. If a purchase price is greater than one dollar, issue an appropriate message.

13 Write a program which simulates fleas on a dog, using the equations on p. 110. Perform the simulation for several different values of the parameters and see what happens (for some values, the fleas die out, for some they overwhelm the poor dog, for some they reach an uncomfortable compromise with the dog). For each set of parameter values, print out the flea population each minute for a total of 60 simulated minutes.

memory cell	meaning	typical value
FLEAS	The total number of fleas on the dog this minute.	50
SCRACH	The number of scratches the dog makes this minute.	10
SCRATE	The number of scratches the dog makes per minute per flea.	.1
TIRED	The maximum number of scratches the dog can make each minute.	20
NEWFLE	The fraction of fleas born or hopping on the dog each minute.	.2
DEATHF	The fraction of fleas which die or jump off the dog each minute.	.1

Equations:

SCRACH = (SCRATE * FLEAS) or TIRED, whichever is less

FLEAS (next minute) = FLEAS + NEWFLE * FLEAS − DEATHF * FLEAS − SCRATCH

14 Write a program which uses the trapezoidal rule to approximate the area under the curve $f(x) = x^3$ from $x = 0$ to $x = 1$. The formula is

$$\text{area} = (h/2)[f(0) + 2f(h) + 2f(2h) + \ldots + 2f(1 - h) + f(1)]$$

The stepsize h should be chosen so that $1/h$ is a whole number (integer). What this formula does is to divide the area into strips of width h and to sum up estimates of the area of each strip.

Optional: Use a loop to compute the area for several values of h, say .1, .01, and .001, and compare the results.

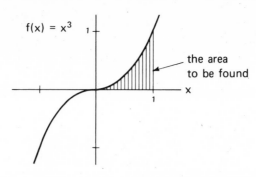

$f(x) = x^3$

the area to be found

15 Write a program to compute the mean and variance of a set of numbers. READ the numbers from data cards one to a card. Design the READ statement and FORMAT so that each card contains two values, one REAL and one LOGICAL. The program can test for the LOGICAL value .TRUE. to determine when it has reached the last card. You will need a memory cell in which to accumulate the sum of the numbers, a second memory cell for the sum of the squares of the numbers, and a third to accumulate the number of terms in the sum. Compute the mean and variance by

$$\text{mean} = \text{sum of numbers}/n$$
$$\text{variance} = (\text{sum of squares}/n) - \text{mean}^2$$

where n is the number of terms in the sum.

16 Write a program to make daily weather reports. Each data card should contain nine INTEGER values giving the following information: current month, day, and year; high temperature for the day, low temperature for the day; year in which the record high for this day was set; record high temperature; year of record low; and record low temperature. After READing a data card, print a message of one of the following four types, depending on the data.

1	10/23/77	HIGH TODAY	52
		LOW TODAY	23
2	10/24/77	HIGH TODAY	71*
		LOW TODAY	38

*(BEATS RECORD OF 70 SET IN 1906)

| 3 | 10/25/77 | HIGH TODAY | 73* |
| | | LOW TODAY | −10** |

*(BEATS RECORD OF 68 SET IN 1932)
**(BEATS RECORD OF −8 SET IN 1918)

| 4 | 10/26/77 | HIGH TODAY | 22 |
| | | LOW TODAY | −18* |

*(BEATS RECORD OF −12 SET IN 1892)

Stop READing data cards when you come to one whose month number is 0.

17 An electric guitar whose A string is plucked puts out this signal

$$11\underbrace{\sin(2\pi \times 220t)}_{\text{fundamental}} + 3(1 + s)\sin(2\pi \times 440t) + (1/2 + s)\sin(2\pi \times 880t)$$

where $s = 1$ if the switch is set to select the pickup nearest the bridge and $s = 0$ if the other pickup is selected.

One way to make the guitar sound less "pure" is to run the signal through a fuzz box. The fuzz box works by clipping its input signal.

$$\text{fuzz output} = \begin{cases} \text{input if } |\text{input}| \leqslant F \\ +F \text{ if input} \geqslant F \\ -F \text{ if input} \leqslant -F \end{cases}$$

where F is the fuzz setting on the fuzz box.

Write a program which prints out the signal every $1.0/4400.0$ of a second for a total of $1.0/110.0$ of a second (two cycles of the fundamental). Run the program and draw a graph of the results for each of the four combinations of the two switch settings and the two settings of the fuzz box at $F = 11$ and $F = 15$.

18 There are many infinite series whose sums are equal to π. Leibnitz's formula (1674) is one with a nice property.

$$\pi = 4 - 4/3 + 4/5 - 4/7 + 4/9 - 4/11 + \ldots$$

It consists of alternating positive and negative terms. If we stop adding after a positive term, the sum is a little larger than π, and if we stop after a negative term, it's a little smaller. Thus we can get upper and lower bounds on π. Write a program to estimate π using Leibnitz's formula. Print the estimate after 99 terms and after 100 terms. Use the fact that ATAN(1.0) = $\pi/4$ to determine whether the 99-term sum or the 100-term sum is closer to π.

19 A well-known dare-devil stunt man plans to jump a canyon on his motorcycle. Assuming that the air drag is proportional to his velocity (k is the proportionality constant), his position after t seconds is given by the equations below.

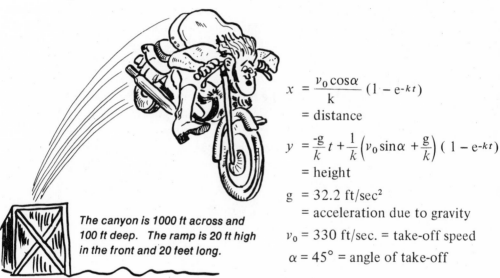

$$x = \frac{v_0 \cos\alpha}{k}(1 - e^{-kt})$$
$$= \text{distance}$$

$$y = \frac{-g}{k}t + \frac{1}{k}\left(v_0 \sin\alpha + \frac{g}{k}\right)(1 - e^{-kt})$$
$$= \text{height}$$

$g = 32.2$ ft/sec² = acceleration due to gravity

$v_0 = 330$ ft/sec. = take-off speed

$\alpha = 45°$ = angle of take-off

The canyon is 1000 ft across and 100 ft deep. The ramp is 20 ft high in the front and 20 feet long.

Write a program that writes out his path (x, y, and t) for the cases when k is .05, .15, and .25. Draw the trajectories your program predicts. If he lands on the other side, assume he stops immediately (in a heap).

20 The motorcyclist in problem 19 has a parachute to ease his fall, but the release mechanism is somewhat unstable. When the parachute releases, its effect is to increase the wind resistance factor k.

Do problem 19 using $k = .05$ in the equations before the parachute opens and $k = .5$ after. Print his path (x, y, and t) for these three cases:

case	parachute opens after
1	1 second
2	5 seconds
3	20 seconds

21　The thermostat in a heating system generates a command to the furnace on the basis of the difference between the setting on the thermostat dial and the current room temperature.

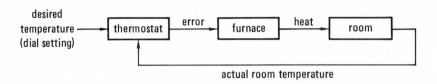

desired temperature (dial setting) → thermostat — error → furnace — heat → room

actual room temperature

In the particular heating system we're dealing with here, the command to the furnace is proportional to the difference between the desired temperature and the actual temperature. (Most thermostats just send one of two commands to the furnace—"all the way on" or "all the way off.")

Convert the flowchart on the facing page into a program and run it to study the effects of changing the proportionality constant k. Try $k = 0.5$, 0.95, 1.0, and 1.5 (and others if you like). The assumption in the flowchart is that the room temperature starts at 65°F and that the thermostat is set to 72°F. It also includes a term which corresponds to the time delay while the room heats up. Use the output to draw graphs of the various cases. Choose a value that you would like k to have if the system were controlling the heating of *your* house.

Take care to print appropriate messages if strange things happen—like temperatures below freezing or above 120°F. In such cases the setting of k must be poor. Stop the loop and try another setting.

VERBAL DESCRIPTION

Get proportionality constant k.

Chart temperature behavior for this value of k.

Repeat.

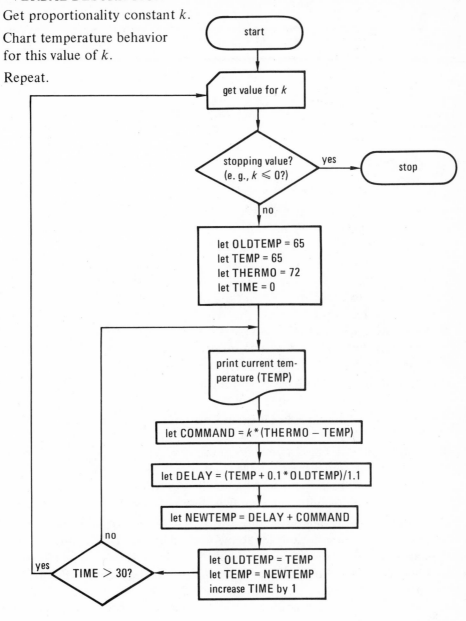

start

get value for k

stopping value?
(e. g., $k \leq 0$?)

yes → stop

no

let OLDTEMP = 65
let TEMP = 65
let THERMO = 72
let TIME = 0

print current temperature (TEMP)

let COMMAND = k * (THERMO − TEMP)

let DELAY = (TEMP + 0.1 * OLDTEMP)/1.1

let NEWTEMP = DELAY + COMMAND

let OLDTEMP = TEMP
let TEMP = NEWTEMP
increase TIME by 1

TIME > 30?

yes

no

5 DEBUGGING YOUR PROGRAMS

Section 5 1

Introduction

So far it must seem that we think if you read this book you'll be able to write programs that contain no errors. After all, all our examples have involved programs that work properly. Probably you are spending most of your time rewriting programs that *don't* work. As you know, the often laborious task of getting a program to run the way you want is called **debugging**. This chapter gives hints about how to proceed.

The best course, obviously, would be to avoid errors in the first place. By using verbal descriptions and flowcharts, and by designing your program carefully before you write down anything in Fortran, you can avoid an amazing number of bugs. By using comment statements in your program, you can make it much easier to follow the logic of the troublesome parts of your program. By taking your

> **debug:** *to remove the errors (bugs) from a program*

time and checking each card carefully after you punch it, you can eliminate a number of typing errors. Even if you do all these things, however, you will, no doubt, still have bugs in your programs. Everybody does, and everybody *will* for a long time, although some people think that new proof-based techniques of writing programs can be developed which will help enormously. We'll discuss some of the techniques more fully in Chapter 9. For now we'll just hit the salient points. Try to think of designing programs as a four-step process: (1) problem statement, (2) input/output description, (3) stepwise refinement of the solution, and (4) Fortran coding. It won't always be possible to keep these steps completely separate. Sometimes you'll have to repeat parts of the process (see the Big Picture, Section 1 2), but using this general approach can be very helpful.

Let's assume that you've done all you can beforehand, you've run your program, and it doesn't work right. There are three main ways your program can fail. First, it might be that you have written some illegal statements and the compiler couldn't figure out what you meant. We'll call such errors **compile-time errors** because they are detected in the process of translating your Fortran statements into machine language. Another possibility is that even though you've written a legal Fortran program, it has illegal consequences; for example, it might wind up dividing by a variable which has the value zero. We'll call such errors **execution-time errors** because they are detected while the machine language instructions corresponding to your program are being performed (executed). The third possibility is that while your program produces results, the results are wrong. For example, if your program was supposed to compute the area of a basketball court and it gave a negative number as the answer, you'd know right away that something was wrong. We'll call these kinds of errors **logic errors** because they are caused by flaws in the way you wrote your program, errors in your logic. Often, logic errors cause execution-time· errors, and we'll tend to lump the two together for that reason.

Section 5 2

Compile-time Errors

Compile-time errors are easy to find—the compiler itself will carefully mark where they occur and will supply an error message that usually has something to do with the problem. Keypunching mistakes often cause this sort of error. Things like accidentally leaving out the replacement operator (=), forgetting to mark column 6 on continuation cards, leaving out an asterisk (*), using too many letters in a memory cell name, and not balancing parentheses are typical compile-time errors. If you're not absolutely certain of the form of a statement you want to use, look it up.

Sometimes one error can lead to lots of error messages. For example, an error in a type statement which was supposed to declare a LOGICAL variable

```
LOGICUL P
```

will result in an error message each time you try to use the variable, as in P = .TRUE. or IF(P) STOP, because the compiler won't know that P is of type LOGICAL (it will assume P is REAL). The mistake in your declaration (misspelling LOGICAL) causes this cascade of errors. Fortunately, it is likely that some error messages in this cascade caused by the erroneous declaration will suggest the possibility that a memory cell of the wrong type is being used, a good hint toward what went wrong.

> *error cascade: Each compile-time error leaves the compiler with less information than it needs to properly compile the program. Often this lack of information causes the compiler to flag errors in statements which are actually correct. This is an error cascade.*

Another thing to watch for is this: if you have *two* errors in one expression, e.g.,

```
A = 2(1+AARDOR))
```

sometimes only the *first* error is discovered by the compiler. If you don't look closely, you might correct the statement to read

```
A = 2*(1+AARDOR))
```

only to discover another error message staring at you after your next run. There are too many right parentheses. Look over your statements carefully to find all the errors at once.

> *multiple errors: Because people tend to make errors in groups, it is quite common for one statement to have several errors. When this happens, the compiler often fails to catch some of them. Check each erroneous statement carefully for multiple errors.*

Compile-time Errors

Section 5 3

Execution-time Errors

We face a problem in writing this section—many errors that will occur are errors which are detected by the actual machine hardware, when the Fortran compiler isn't around to help you. This means that the details of the errors are machine-dependent and vary widely from one model to another (let alone the variations from manufacturer to manufacturer). What we'll do is go through an example and indicate the nature of the errors. Your instructor should be able to tell you exactly what the error messages will look like on your system.

To correct an error you need to know (1) where in your program the error occurred and (2) what caused it. To help locate the error, we'll describe three (increasingly difficult) ways to proceed. First, you may be fortunate and be provided with a message that tells you which line of your program the error occurred in or at least at which memory location in the machine it occurred. Second, by studying which of your WRITE statements were printed before the error occurred, you may be able to deduce in what part of your program the error occurred. This is a reason to put extra WRITE statements in programs you are debugging. (On some systems, with some types of errors, the last few WRITE statements' results may not appear even though they were executed, however.) Third, you may be able to infer where the error occurred from the nature of the error. For example, if your program exceeded its time limit, then it probably was in a loop at the time. If it tried to divide by zero, then obviously it was carrying out some statement which involved a division. If you absolutely cannot locate the error, you will have to insert additional WRITE statements in suspicious spots of your program and run it again.

> *The precise nature of an execution-time error, that is, the error mentioned in the resulting error message, is often only the tip of the iceberg. You must deduce the underlying cause.*

To fix the error once it's located, you must determine its cause. If the error is for time limit, then the conditions for stopping a loop must not have been met for some reason. If it is an arithmetic sort of error (overflow, underflow, division by zero), then some variable is getting a value you didn't expect. If it is an "address out of range," that means your program attempted to use a memory cell it shouldn't have—this is almost always caused by an array subscript which has an improper value (see Chapter 6).

Many errors result from bad logic in the program which ultimately makes the instructions in your program impossible to perform, thus helping you detect the errors. However, some logic errors simply cause your program to produce incorrect results without asking the computer to perform impossible operations. These errors are often more difficult to fix—you simply may not notice that there is anything wrong. Just because something comes out of a computer doesn't mean it's right! It's a good idea to run a small test case in order to verify that your program really is working properly. If the small test doesn't work as you expect,

> *Test your program on simple data where you know the results before you assume it is producing correct results on more complicated data.*

you may be able to locate the trouble, or you may be forced to get more information by sprinkling your program with WRITE statements to give you partial results. Once the error is located and you know what caused it, alter the program and run it again. It is an *extremely* bad bet ever to assume that the error was a fluke and to run the program again hoping the error will go away by itself!

> *Print partial results to trace the execution of the program and find errors.*

Once you get the hang of it, debugging is almost fun. There's a Sherlock Holmes flavor to it. To illustrate, we'll run through an actual case from our programming diary.

Debugging Example

Recall the program we wrote in Section 3 3 which computed the average cost of laundry detergents. Look at the flowchart in Figure 3 3 1 to refresh your memory about how the program was organized. The program, in a prior, undebugged form, appears below.

Here's what we started with after drawing a flowchart, converting it to Fortran, punching up the deck, and removing the compile-time errors.

```
COMMENT:  FIND THE AVERAGE COST OF LAUNDRY DETERGENT
          REAL PRICE, WGT, SUM, N, AVG
C
C         GET PRICES AND WEIGHTS, KEEPING TRACK OF TOTAL UNIT
C         COSTS AND NUMBER OF BRANDS SAMPLED.
          N = 0.0
          SUM = 0.00
   10     READ(5,1000) PRICE,WGT
 1000 FORMAT(F5.0,F5.0)
C         ANOTHER BRAND TO AVERAGE IN
          N = N+1.0
C         IF PRICE IS NEGATIVE, WE'RE DONE
          IF (PRICE .LT. 0.00)  GO TO 20
C         ADD IN UNIT PRICE OF THIS BRAND
          SUM = SUM + (PRICE/WGT)
          GO TO 10
C
C         WE'VE GOT THE TOTAL UNIT COST.  NOW COMPUTE AVERAGE.
   20     AVG = SUM/N
          WRITE(6,2000) AVG
 2000 FORMAT(' THE AVERAGE PRICE PER POUND IS  $',F6.2)
          STOP
          END
```

We made up some data cards with a few easily computed values on them to test our program before turning it loose on our real data.

```
 2.00    2.0
10.00    5.0
```

If our program had worked the way we wanted, it would have gotten the result (2./2. + 10./5.)/2. = 1.5. We ran it and, not only didn't we get 1.5, we didn't get anything at all except an error message telling us that an "end of file" had been reached on "unit 5." Needless to say, we were a little disappointed. The error message seemed a bit obscure, but since statement 10 is the only READ statement, and it, of course, refers to unit 5, we realized that the error must have occurred while the controller was carrying out statement 10. This set us to thinking . . . The program must not have stopped READing soon enough and must have gone on past what we intended to be our last card, looking for another card, finally READing the job control card at the end of our deck.

> *When eliminating complicated errors, especially in large programs, it helps to form a* hypothesis, *keeping notes on the hypotheses you have checked. Eventually you can deduce the roots of the problems.*

We checked our data and, sure enough, we'd forgotten to put a trailer card at the end of the data. We added a final card with −1.0 in the first field and tossed our program in to be run again. This, by the way, is a *mistake*. You should *never* correct just one error and assume there aren't others. If we had taken a little more time to go over our program carefully, we could have avoided the next round of errors.

This time we got no error messages, but the result was

```
THE AVERAGE PRICE PER POUND IS  $    1.00
```

"What?" we said. "We expected a much higher average!" We stared at the statements for a while but didn't see anything wrong. We looked at the data cards carefully to see if we had mispunched any (wishing all the time that we had placed statements like

```
      WRITE(6,1100) PRICE,WGT
 1100 FORMAT(' PRICE=',F6.2,' AND WEIGHT=',F6.2)
```

after the READ statement). Since we didn't find anything wrong, we began a time-honored process. We wrote down the names of all the memory cells we used in the program and drew a box beside each. Then we put one finger beside the first statement of the program, keeping one hand free to write values into the 'memory cells' as necessary. We analyzed the effect of the statement our finger

> *mirror printing: It is usually a good idea, especially in the debugging stage of writing a program, to print values obtained by READ statements immediately after READing. This is called mirror printing. It helps discover errors in the program which cause the data to be misinterpreted.*

was on. If it altered a memory cell value, we crossed out any old value we had for that cell and wrote in the new one. If it was a control statement like

```
GO TO 10
```

we moved our finger appropriately. After a while we found the problem. By the time we got to statement 20, N had the value 3.0. even though there were only two brands of detergent in the data. Our program was counting the end-of-data card!

Tracking Down Errors

Now that our attention was drawn to it, we were embarrassed to discover that our loop wasn't even one of the recommended forms (pre-test or post-test). We made the loop a pre-test READ loop by moving the statement

```
N = N+1.0
```

and its associated comment so that they appeared immediately *after* the IF test, not before. This had the twin benefits of making the loop into a pre-test form and of allowing 1.0 to be added to N only when the data represented a legitimate detergent price and weight.

We looked our program over carefully, decided to add another WRITE statement

```
      WRITE(6,3000) N
3000 FORMAT(' ', F5.0,' BRANDS WERE IN THE SURVEY')
```

and ran it again. Notice that if we'd been awake enough to use this more informative WRITE statement to begin with, we would have been able to find the problem more quickly.

The computer is a "great humbler". It seems that no matter how careful you are, there will always be bugs in your programs. Learning to avoid them requires great patience and great self-control. Like a master craftsman, a good programmer produces well-thought-out, finely finished work.

> *For a number of good ideas about how to improve your programs, make them more readable, more easily debugged, more efficient, and so forth, see the little book* **Elements of Programming Style** *by B. W. Kernighan and P. J. Plauger, McGraw-Hill, 1974.*

6 ARRAYS

Section 6 1

Using Arrays

You already have a repertoire of Fortran instructions sufficient to describe all possible computations. Many computations, however, would require programs of unmanageable size if you used only your present stock of instructions. For this reason, all programming languages incorporate some way of referring to a large number of memory cells simply and concisely. In Fortran, **arrays** are provided for this purpose. The following problem is one in which the use of arrays leads to great simplification.

Let's suppose we have written to the governors of 11 western states inquiring about sales tax. While we are waiting for replies, we will prepare a program to analyze the data we hope to receive. Given 11 data cards, each of which contains the name of a state and its sales tax rate, we want our program to list those states where the sales tax is below average.

We can compute the average from the data easily enough. The problem arises from the necessity to print certain parts of the data after the average is computed and, therefore, after the data cards have all been read. Since there is no way to reread the cards, we must save the information in memory cells. Figure 6 1 1 describes our general strategy. Our program appears below.

VERBAL DESCRIPTION

Get sales tax data.

Compute average.

Print states with below average sales tax.

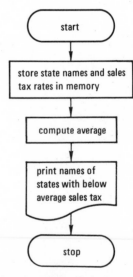

Figure 6 1 1

```
COMMENT--PROGRAM TO LIST THE WESTERN STATES WITH
C          BELOW AVERAGE SALES TAX RATES.
      INTEGER S1,S2,S3,S4,S5,S6,S7,S8,S9,S10,S11
      REAL T1,T2,T3,T4,T5,T6,T7,T8,T9,T10,T11,AVE
C     STORE DATA
      READ(5,1000) S1 ,T1
      READ(5,1000) S2 ,T2
      READ(5,1000) S3 ,T3
      READ(5,1000) S4 ,T4
      READ(5,1000) S5 ,T5
      READ(5,1000) S6 ,T6
      READ(5,1000) S7 ,T7
      READ(5,1000) S8 ,T8
      READ(5,1000) S9 ,T9
      READ(5,1000) S10,T10
      READ(5,1000) S11,T11
 1000 FORMAT(A2,F7.0)
C
      AVE=(T1+T2+T3+T4+T5+T6+T7+T8+T10+T11)/11.0
C
      WRITE(6,2000)
 2000 FORMAT('1STATES WITH BELOW AVERAGE SALES TAX'/)
      IF (T1  .LE. AVE) WRITE(6,3000) S1
      IF (T2  .LE. AVE) WRITE(6,3000) S2
      IF (T3  .LE. AVE) WRITE(6,3000) S3
      IF (T4  .LE. AVE) WRITE(6,3000) S4
      IF (T5  .LE. AVE) WRITE(6,3000) S5
      IF (T6  .LE. AVE) WRITE(6,3000) S6
      IF (T7  .LE. AVE) WRITE(6,3000) S7
      IF (T8  .LE. AVE) WRITE(6,3000) S8
      IF (T9  .LE. AVE) WRITE(6,3000) S9
      IF (T10 .LE. AVE) WRITE(6,3000) S10
      IF (T11 .LE. AVE) WRITE(6,3000) S11
 3000 FORMAT(' ',A2)
      STOP
      END
```

data

```
WA 0.045
ID 0.03
MT 0.00
OR 0.04
WY 0.03
CA 0.06
NV 0.03
UT 0.04
CO 0.03
AZ 0.04
NM 0.04
```

output

```
STATES WITH BELOW AVERAGE SALES TAX

ID
MT
WY
NV
CO
```

As you can see, the program's input section has 11 almost identical statements. So does the output section. Normally we'd like to make a loop out of such a section, but in this case we have no way of making the statements identical so that we can replace them with a loop. To do so, we'd have to refer to the same memory cells in each READ, and this would continually wipe out previously recorded information. We'd wind up with only one state's sales tax rate in memory. What we need is some way to change the memory cell used by the READ statement without changing the READ statement itself. We can do this by using arrays.

An **array** is a group of memory cells which all have the same name. They are distinguished by a **subscript** or **index** which is associated with the name. In a program the name and the subscript are associated by enclosing the subscript in parentheses to the right of the name. In our example we will need two arrays, each of which is a group of 11 memory cells, one group for the names of the states, and the other for the taxes. Then, instead of dealing with the 11 separate memory cells S1, S2, S3 and so on, we will use the array S and refer to S(1), S(2), S(3), and so on.

Of course, if our only option were to write S(5) instead of S5 or S(7) instead of S7, nothing would be gained. The advantage is that we can write the subscript as an *arithmetic expression* whose value can change from time to time as the program runs. Instead of writing

    READ(5,1000) S1,T1

we will write

    READ(5,1000) S(N),T(N)

where N is an INTEGER memory cell whose value will be 1 the first time the computer executes the READ statement, 2 the second time, and so on.

Arrays used in a program must be declared at the beginning. Like memory cell declarations, **array declarations** establish the name and the type of information the array will contain—INTEGER, REAL, or whatever. (An array may contain only one type of data; no single array can contain both INTEGER and REAL numbers, for example.) In addition, an array declaration must specify the number of memory cells in the array by placing that number in parentheses after the array name. This part of an array declaration is known as the **length declarator** and should not be confused with a subscript. A subscript designates a particular memory cell in an array. A length declarator establishes the *number* of memory cells in the entire array.

---

array declarator

form
> *name* (*len*)
>
> *name* is a Fortran identifier (up to six characters)
> *len* is an unsigned INTEGER constant

meaning
> establishes an array named *name* with *len* memory cells

example
```
INTEGER A, B(12), ARA(103)
REAL QUZNT(27), RAG, RAGGY
LOGICAL P, Q(32), G
```
These statements establish four arrays to contain various kinds of information. In addition, the types of five simple memory cells are established. Array declarators and memory cell declarators may be mixed in the same declaration statement.

Together, the name and length declarator make up an **array declarator**. Array declarators are placed in type statements (INTEGER statements, REAL statements, and the like) either interspersed with ordinary memory cell declarations or alone.

An **array element** (a memory cell in an array) is used in the same ways that other memory cells are used, but each reference to an array element must include both the array name and the subscript. The elements are always numbered starting from 1. The last element's subscript, therefore, is the same as the number of elements in the array.

> *array element: a memory cell in an array*

---

array reference

form
> *name*(*e*)
>
> *name* is an array name
> *e* is an expression whose value is an INTEGER in the range 1 to *len* where *len* is the number of elements in *name*

meaning
> designates the *e*th element of *name*

examples
```
A(3)=47.0*Q
WRITE(6,1000) B(3*J-1)
IF (4.0*RT(L-2) .LT. T(4)+1) STOP
B(L)=B(L-1) + 1.0
A(I+2)=A(J)+A(I)
```

Using arrays, we can rewrite our sales tax program in a simpler way still following the plan of Figure 6 1 1.

```
COMMENT--PROGRAM TO LIST THE WESTERN STATES WITH
C       BELOW AVERAGE SALES TAX RATES.
        INTEGER S(11)
        REAL T(11), AVE
        INTEGER N
C
C       STORE DATA
        N=1
 100    READ(5,1000) S(N),T(N)
 1000   FORMAT(A2,F7.0)
         N=N+1
         IF (N .LE. 11) GO TO 100
C
        AVE=(T(1) + T(2) + T(3) + T(4) + T(5) + T(6) +
     +       T(7) + T(8) + T(9) + T(10) + T(11))/11.0
C
        WRITE(6,2000)
 2000   FORMAT('1STATES WITH BELOW AVERAGE SALES TAX'/)
        N=1
 300    IF (T(N) .LE. AVE) WRITE(6,3000) S(N)
 3000    FORMAT(' ',A2)
         N = N+1
         IF (N .LE. 11) GO TO 300
        STOP
        END
```

data

```
WA 0.045
ID 0.03
MT 0.00
OR 0.04
WY 0.03
CA 0.06
NV 0.03
UT 0.04
CO 0.03
AZ 0.04
NM 0.04
```

output

```
STATES WITH BELOW AVERAGE SALES TAX

ID
MT
WY
NV
CO
```

EXERCISES 6 1

1 Under what conditions would B(I) and B(J) refer to the same element of array B?

2 What would the following program print?

```
       INTEGER A(10),I
       A(1)=0
       A(2)=1
       I=3
100    A(I)=A(I-1) + A(I-2)
       I=I+1
       IF (I .LE. 10) GO TO 100
       WRITE(6,1000) A(1), A(2), A(3), A(4), A(5)
       WRITE(6,1000) A(6), A(7), A(8), A(9), A(10)
1000   FORMAT(5I4)
       STOP
       END
```

3 Assuming that B is an array of ten elements and I and J are memory cells with the values 3 and 7 respectively, which of the following statements are legal? If not, why not?

```
B(3) = B(I)
B(I) = B(I-1)
B(J) = B(2*I)
B(4) = B(J-1) + B(I*J-21)
B(2*I) = B(J+4)
B(1.7) = 0
```

4 Suppose that, instead of wanting to list only the states whose sales tax is below average, we had wanted to make a list of the states and their sales taxes and print the average sales tax at the end of the listings. If the data provided were the same as that of this section, would we need to use arrays to write the program?

5 Which of the following are legal declarations?

```
REAL A(10)
INTEGER A(13-2)
INTEGER A(I)
REAL A(150) , BOK(3472)
REAL X(15.0)
LOGICAL QS(23), PS(47)
```

Section 6 2

A More Useful Solution

We were probably not being realistic when we wrote the program of Section 6 1 because we assumed that all 11 governors would reply to our letter. A program which would still work with only a partial response would be more useful. Fortunately, such a program is easy to write now that we know about arrays. (Without arrays the program becomes much more difficult—see the exercises.)

The main problem we face is that we can no longer compute the average by summing and dividing by 11.0. The program itself will have to keep track of the number of responses so that it can divide the sum by the appropriate number. So the program can recognize the end of the input loop, we'll add a special data card containing the characters **.

Figure 6 2 1 depicts the general plan of our revised program. With the exception that it keeps track of the number of data items, our new plan doesn't differ much from the old one in Figure 6 1 1.

VERBAL DESCRIPTION

Store data in memory, keeping track of the number of data items.

Compute average.

Print states with below average sales tax.

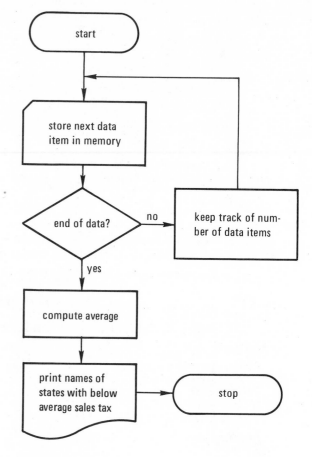

Figure 6 2 1

Study the new program carefully; it is typical of many that you will write in the future. An important point to notice is that the memory cell N is used to count the number of state governors who responded to our question. The computer performs the READ statement (statement 100) many times, but it is always true that just prior to a time when the READ statement is performed, the value of N is the number of governors' responses which have been read. In addition, since N is not increased until after the test for the end of the data, the value of N when the computer reaches statement 200 is the total number of governors' responses. Thus the count N does not include the special "**" card; it counts only response cards. This section's exercises help explain other details of the program.

```
COMMENT--PROGRAM TO LIST STATES WITH BELOW AVERAGE SALES TAX
      INTEGER S(12),N,K,FIN
      REAL T(12),AVE,SUM
      DATA FIN/2H**/
C
C     STORE DATA
      N=0
 100  READ(5,1000) S(N+1),T(N+1)
 1000   FORMAT(A2,F7.0)
        IF (S(N+1) .EQ. FIN) GO TO 200
        N=N+1
        GO TO 100
C
C     COMPUTE AVERAGE
 200  SUM=0.0
      K=1
 210  SUM=SUM+T(K)
        K=K+1
        IF (K .LE. N) GO TO 210
      AVE=SUM/N
C
      WRITE(6,2000)
 2000 FORMAT('1STATES WITH BELOW AVERAGE SALES TAX'/)
      K=1
 310  IF (T(K) .LE. AVE) WRITE(6,3100) S(K),T(K)
 3100 FORMAT(' ',A2,F7.3)
        K=K+1
        IF (K .LE. N) GO TO 310
      STOP
      END
```

data

```
 WA 0.045
 ID 0.03
 MT 0.00
 OR 0.04
 WY 0.03
 CA 0.06
 NV 0.03
 UT 0.04
 CO 0.03
 AZ 0.04
 NM 0.04
 **
```

output

```
STATES WITH BELOW AVERAGE SALES TAX

 ID    .030
 MT   0.000
 WY    .030
 NV    .030
 CO    .030
```

EXERCISES 6 2

1 Why did we allocate 12 memory cells to the arrays instead of 11?

2 Show how the running sum could be incorporated into the input loop to avoid the loop in the section where the average is computed.

3 If none of the governors respond and we run our program with only the "**" card, something bad will happen. What?

4 What changes need to be made in the program to allow all 50 states to be included in the data?

5 Suppose, by some fluke, we give the program more than 11 response cards. What will happen? How can we change the program to avoid this problem? (This is a very important way of making the program more robust.)

> robust: a program is more robust if it functions properly given a wider range of input values

6 Write a program which does the same thing as the one in this section without using arrays. (Note: This is a lot of work. Why not just look at the answer?)

7 Rewrite the program of Section 4 5 so that it uses an array in place of the memory cells BAR0, BAR1, BAR2, BAR3, BAR4, and BAR5.

Section 6 3*

Some Misconceptions to Avoid

> This section may be skipped without loss of continuity.

Arrays confuse many novice programmers. The following list may help you avoid some common mistakes.

1 Don't confuse the subscript value with the array element value. The value of the element A(5) usually has nothing to do with the number 5.

	A
A(1)	−4.7
A(2)	192.1
A(3)	3.9
A(4)	485.3
A(5)	−19.1
A(6)	0.00

2 When a memory cell name is used in a subscript, it is only the *value* of that memory cell which is important; its name is irrelevant. At one point in a program, we may refer to A(I), and at another point in the same program we may refer to A(J). In each case we are dealing with the same array. In fact, we may even be referencing the same element of the array depending on what values I and J have at the times of the array references.

3 For the same reason, a program may reference both A(I) and B(I). That is, the same memory cell may be used as a subscript in referencing two (or more) different arrays. Again it is the value of the subscript which counts, not its name.

4 Don't use arrays when you don't need them. Profligate use often results in unclear, inefficient programs (see exercise 6 1 4).

5 In general, Fortran can deal with only one element of an array at a time. For example if A is an array of ten elements, then the statement
```
IF ( A .NE. 0 )  GO TO 100
```
does not test all ten elements of A. In fact, it isn't even a legal statement. If the intention is to transfer to statement 100 in case some element of A is nonzero, then each element must be tested individually as in the loop below.

```
        I = 1
10      IF (A(I) .NE. 0)  GO TO 100
        I = I+1
        IF (I .LE. 10)  GO TO 10
```

6 Remember: In Fortran, the number of memory cells in an array may not be changed in your program. If you don't know exactly how much room you will need (as we didn't in Section 6 2), you must declare the array larger than you will actually need, and let your program keep track of how many memory cells it is using.

Section 6 4

Arrays with Two Subscripts

t	w	o								a	y
									r		
d	i	m	e	n	s			r			
					i		a				
					o						
					n	a	l				

There are situations in which it would be convenient to have arrays with more than one subscript. For instance, imagine that you work for a politician and you want to analyze patterns of support for your candidate. You have block-by-block results of preliminary polls taken by your volunteers and would like to store your data in a convenient form. An array with two subscripts works beautifully here since you can let the value of the first subscript represent the north-south position of the block, the second subscript represent the east-west position, and the value stored in each memory cell be the percent of positive responses in that block (see Figure 6 4 1).

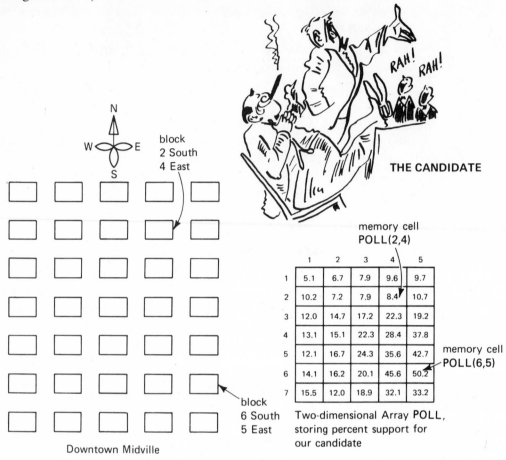

THE CANDIDATE

memory cell POLL(2,4)

	1	2	3	4	5
1	5.1	6.7	7.9	9.6	9.7
2	10.2	7.2	7.9	8.4	10.7
3	12.0	14.7	17.2	22.3	19.2
4	13.1	15.1	22.3	28.4	37.8
5	12.1	16.7	24.3	35.6	42.7
6	14.1	16.2	20.1	45.6	50.2
7	15.5	12.0	18.9	32.1	33.2

memory cell POLL(6,5)

block 2 South 4 East

block 6 South 5 East

Downtown Midville

Two-dimensional Array POLL, storing percent support for our candidate

Figure 6 4 1

An array with two subscripts is usually called a **two-dimensional array**. The name of a memory cell in a two-dimensional array is simply the array name followed by a parenthesized list of two subscripts separated by a comma. The memory cells with the names POLL(2,4) and POLL(6,5) are indicated in Figure 6 4 1. Just as with one-dimensional arrays, dimensions must be given at the beginning of our program. The lowest legal value of a subscript is 1, so all we need in the declaration is the maximum subscript value. In our case the declaration

```
REAL POLL(7,5)
```

would be appropriate since we want to be able to use all memory cells from POLL(1,1) (the top left memory cell in Figure 6 4 1) to POLL(7,5) (the bottom right memory cell). We'll give a precise summary of all types of array declarations in Section 6 5. Until then, we will make do with this informal description.

It is often convenient to think of a two-dimensional array as a grid of boxes arranged in rows and columns, as we have pictured the array POLL in Figure 6 4 1. The first subscript is customarily thought of as the row number and the second as the column number. Thus the declaration says how many rows and columns the array has. (We should emphasize, however, that this is only a custom. You can think of subscripts in any arrangement you like.) Arrays in which the number of rows is the same as the number of columns are thought of as **square arrays**. Those like the one we're using here in our polling problem, in which the numbers of rows and columns are different, can be visualized as **rectangular arrays**.

Storing our poll data in a two-dimensional array makes it easy to analyze the data in a number of different ways. For instance, let's compute the average support for our candidate in the eastern blocks as opposed to his support in the west. This amounts to looking at the average of the numbers in each column of the array. To compute these averages, we will use a loop which cycles across the columns. For each column we have to sum the elements, and to do this we'll use another loop nested inside the column loop which scans down a column. Figure 6 4 2 shows the overall plan. We've left out the details of computing the sum for two reasons: it makes the plan easier to follow, and you are already familiar with the process of computing sums. The program follows.

VERBAL DESCRIPTION
Store results of poll in memory.

Compute and print average along each north-south street.

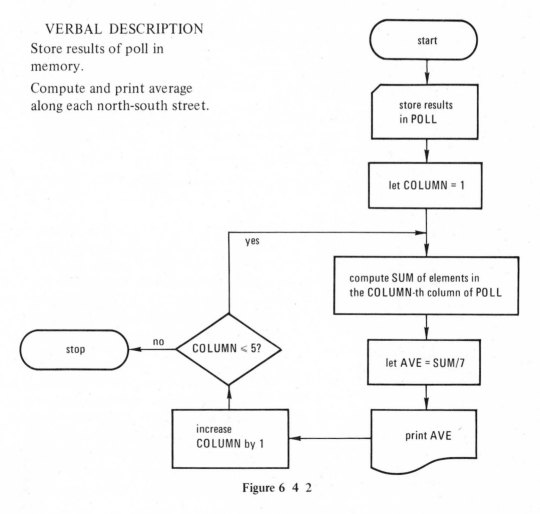

Figure 6 4 2

If an array has ROW rows and COLUMN columns, then the number of elements in each row is COLUMN and the number of elements in each column is ROW.

```
COMMENT--PROGRAM TO PRINT POLITICAL POLL SUMMARIES.
       REAL POLL(7,5),AVERGE,SUM
       INTEGER COLUMN,ROW,I
C      STORE DATA
       I=1
  100  READ(5,1000) ROW,COLUMN,POLL(ROW,COLUMN)
 1000    FORMAT(2I4,F7.0)
         I=I+1
         IF (I .LE. 35) GO TO 100
C
C      COMPUTE AVERAGE SUPPORT IN NORTH-SOUTH SLICES OF AREA
C
C      START WITH COLUMN 1 AND AVERAGE ONE COLUMN AT A TIME
       COLUMN=1
  200  SUM=0.0
       ROW=1
  250    SUM=SUM+POLL(ROW,COLUMN)
         ROW=ROW+1
         IF (ROW .LE. 7) GO TO 250
C        FINISHED SUMMING COLUMN--COMPUTE AVERAGE
       AVERGE=SUM/7.0
       WRITE(6,2000) COLUMN
 2000  FORMAT(' THE AVERAGE SUPPORT IN SLICE ',I3)
       WRITE(6,3000) AVERGE
 3000  FORMAT(' FROM THE WEST IS',F7.3,' PER CENT'//)
       COLUMN=COLUMN+1
       IF (COLUMN .LE. 5) GO TO 200
       STOP
       END
```

data
```
    1   1      7.
    1   2     40.
    1   3     91.
    1   4     18.
    5   4     25.
    5   5     24.
    2   3     44.
    3   4     75.
    3   5     28.
    6   1     93.
    6   2     94.
    2   4     99.
    4   1     27.
    4   2     12.
    6   3     45.
    6   4     40.
    6   5     57.
    4   5      1.
    4   3     88.
    4   4     79.
    1   5     81.
```

```
2    5    52.
7    1    33.
2    1    88.
3    1    44.
5    1    24.
3    2    79.
5    2    82.
3    3    31.
7    2    90.
5    3    52.
2    2    68.
7    3    74.
7    4    86.
7    5    37.
```

output
```
THE AVERAGE SUPPORT IN SLICE   1
FROM THE WEST IS 45.143 PER CENT


THE AVERAGE SUPPORT IN SLICE   2
FROM THE WEST IS 66.429 PER CENT


THE AVERAGE SUPPORT IN SLICE   3
FROM THE WEST IS 60.714 PER CENT


THE AVERAGE SUPPORT IN SLICE   4
FROM THE WEST IS 60.286 PER CENT


THE AVERAGE SUPPORT IN SLICE   5
FROM THE WEST IS 40.000 PER CENT
```

As you can see, the way the results are organized in the two-dimensional array POLL makes all kinds of regional analysis of the data easy.

EXERCISES 6 4

1   Which of the following are legal declarations?

```
INTEGER A(100,3), B(3,100), I
REAL QRT(3,49)
LOGICAL P(10), Q(4,2)
REAL X(N,100)
```

2   Assuming the declarations of exercise 1 have been made, mark the statements below which are not legal.

```
A(4,2) = 0
B(4,2) = 0
A(3,50) = 0
I = 10
Q(I/3,I-8) = .TRUE.
P(8) = Q(3,2)
```

3 Add a section to the political poll analysis program which computes the average support for our candidate in each of the east-west slices across the region.

4 Add a section which computes the average support for our candidate in the southwest quarter of the region.

5 Change the input section of the poll analysis program so that it accepts raw data from the pollsters; each card will contain a north-south block number of 2100, 2200, 2300, . . ., or 2700; an east-west block number of 4800, 4900, . . . , or 5200; the number of votes for our candidate; and the number for the other candidate.

Section 6 5

Three-D Arrays*

ANSI Fortran arrays may have one, two, or three subscripts. Some versions of Fortran allow more. Problems where arrays with several subscripts are handy come up occasionally, but since you are already familiar with one- and two-dimensional arrays, you should have no problem applying your knowledge to arrays with higher dimensions. Just for fun, we include the following example where a three-dimensional array is useful.

Rumor has it that one agency of a large Western government kept careful records on the habits of some of its citizens during the sixties. The citizens of interest

---

array declarator

form
> a (size)
>
> a is an array name
> size is a list of up to three unsigned INTEGER constants separated by commas. The declarator appears as an element in the list of a type statement.

meaning
> Used in a type statement, it declares an array a. The array will have as many subscripts as there are elements in the list size; each subscript will have a range starting at 1 and running up to the corresponding element of size.

examples

```
INTEGER A(4),B(10,40),C(22)
REAL X(4,10,8),Y(32)
LOGICAL P(2,2),Q(3,7,4)
```

---

to this agency were those belonging to certain organizations which will remain unnamed. Many records were kept on each of these citizens, but the ones of greatest interest had to do with their age, political affiliation, and hair length.

Let's suppose the agency has hired us to organize the data in such a way as to make it easy to obtain facts like the number of organization members who have long hair and are Republicans, or the proportion who are between ages 20 and 25 and are neither Republicans nor Democrats.

The approach we will take is to produce a three-dimensional array of **class counts**. Each **class** will consist of those organization members of a given age, political affiliation, and hair length. The raw data consists of one punched card for each member containing his age (in the range 18 to 29), his political affiliation (Republican, Democrat, or other), and his hair length (long or short). Thus, one class is composed of those members who are age 18, Republican, and have long hair; another class contains members who are age 28, Democrat, and have long hair; and a third class contains those who are age 21, Republican, and have short hair. There are $12*3*2 = 72$ different classes because there are 12 possible ages, 3 possible political affiliations, and 2 possible hair lengths. Therefore, our array C of class counts will have three subscripts used as follows.

> *subscript 1* indicates age: 1 for age 18
> 2 for age 19
>
> .
>
> .
>
> .
>
> 12 for age 29
>
> *subscript 2* indicates affiliation: 1 for Republican
> 2 for Democrat
> 3 for other
>
> *subscript 3* indicates hair length: 1 for short
> 2 for long

After we organize the raw data, C(9,3,1) will contain the number of short-haired 26-year-olds who are neither Republicans nor Democrats. What will C(1,2,2) contain?

The following program organizes the raw data according to this scheme and computes the number of long-haired members of the organizations of interest who are between ages 21 and 26. The exercises at the end of this section involve adding other summary calculations to the program.

```
COMMENT--THIS PROGRAM ORGANIZES RAW DATA CONSISTING OF THE
C         AGES, POLITICAL AFFILIATIONS, AND HAIR LENGTHS
C         INTO A TABLE OF CLASS COUNTS.
          INTEGER C(12,3,2)
          INTEGER AGE,AFIL,HAIR,REPUB,DEMOC,LONG
          INTEGER AGECD,AFILCD,HAIRCD,S
          DATA REPUB/3HREP/,DEMOC/3HDEM/,LONG/4HLONG/
C
C         INITIALIZE COUNTERS
          AGECD=0
  100     AGECD=AGECD+1
          C(AGECD,1,1)=0
          C(AGECD,2,1)=0
          C(AGECD,3,1)=0
          C(AGECD,1,2)=0
          C(AGECD,2,2)=0
          C(AGECD,3,2)=0
          IF (AGECD .LT. 12)  GO TO 100
C
C         GET DATA AND COMPUTE CLASS COUNTS
  200     READ(5,2000) AGE,AFIL,HAIR
  2000    FORMAT(I2,6X,A3,14X,A4)
          IF (AGE .EQ. 0) GO TO 300
          AGECD=AGE-17
          AFILCD=3
          IF (AFIL .EQ. REPUB) AFILCD=1
          IF (AFIL .EQ. DEMOC) AFILCD=2
          HAIRCD=1
          IF (HAIR .EQ. LONG) HAIRCD=2
          C(AGECD,AFILCD,HAIRCD)=C(AGECD,AFILCD,HAIRCD)+1
          GO TO 200
C
C         PRINT SUMMARY
  300     S=0
          AGE=21
  310     AGECD=AGE-17
          S=S+C(AGECD,1,2)+C(AGECD,2,2)+C(AGECD,3,2)
          AGE=AGE+1
          IF (AGE .LE. 26) GO TO 310
C
          WRITE(6,3000) S
  3000 FORMAT(' THERE ARE',I5,' LONG-HAIRED MEMBERS OF',/
      +        ' THE SUSPECT GROUP BETWEEN AGES 21 AND 26')
          STOP
          END
```

data

18	DEMOCRAT	LONG
20	OTHER	LONG
26	DEMOCRAT	LONG
24	DEMOCRAT	LONG
21	OTHER	SHORT
21	REPUBLICAN	LONG
27	REPUBLICAN	SHORT
27	DEMOCRAT	SHORT
20	OTHER	LONG
23	DEMOCRAT	LONG
22	OTHER	LONG
28	DEMOCRAT	LONG
22	DEMOCRAT	SHORT
27	REPUBLICAN	SHORT
18	DEMOCRAT	SHORT
22	DEMOCRAT	SHORT

```
29        DEMOCRAT          LONG
25        REPUBLICAN        LONG
26        OTHER             SHORT
24        DEMOCRAT          LONG
18        OTHER             LONG
28        DEMOCRAT          SHORT
18        DEMOCRAT          LONG
29        REPUBLICAN        LONG
24        DEMOCRAT          LONG
0
```

output
THERE ARE *bbbb* **8 LONG-HAIRED MEMBERS OF**
THE SUSPECT GROUP BETWEEN AGES 21 AND 26

EXERCISES 6 5

1 Add a section to the program which will compute the number of 29-year-old longhairs.

2 Add a section to the program which will compute the number of 21-year-olds.

3 What does the man-with-the-dog's sign say?

4 Who is looking through the grating with the periscope?

5 Why is the agent wearing wing-tipped shoes and a wig?

Section 6 6

Input and Output of Arrays

By now you have had a fair amount of experience printing out arrays. Perhaps you have noticed that in each WRITE statement, you had to know, while writing the program, exactly how many elements of an array you wanted to print. If the number of array elements you wanted to print depended on a computation in the program, you had to write a loop and print one element at a time until you had printed all the appropriate elements (as in the example in Section 6 2). This doesn't cause any particular problems if you want each element on a separate line, but if you want them on the same line, you're in for a lot of work. To eliminate this extra effort, there is an alternative form of the I/O list.

Previously we said that the list in a READ or WRITE statement must be made up of variable names separated by commas. Until now we haven't really needed anything else. However, the list can be slightly more complicated. In addition to variable names, it can also contain repetitive lists called **implied do lists**.

An implied do list is a list of variable names (possibly subscripted) followed by indexing information which specifies how many times to repeat the variables in the implied do list (that is, how many times to "do" the list) and what values of the index to use in these repetitions. Before we describe the exact form of an implied do list, let's look at an example or two.

Suppose we want to print out all the values in the array A from A(1) to A(N), where N is a memory cell containing some INTEGER. Instead of writing a loop:

```
      I=1
50    WRITE(5,1000) A(I)
      I=I+1
      IF (I .LE. N) GO TO 50
```

we can simply put

```
WRITE(5,1000) (A(I), I=1,N)
```

This is not only shorter to write and easier to read but has the added benefit of commanding the computer to try to put all the values on one line. If there are too many to fit on one line, the computer will automatically go on to the next. In the case of the loop, each value goes on a separate line because each time the computer performs a WRITE statement, it begins on a new line.

An implied do list doesn't have to be exactly like the one we have written above. The list section can contain more than one element and the indexing section doesn't have to start the index at 1 and increase by 1 each time; it can start at any positive INTEGER value and increase at each stage by any positive INTEGER value. What's more, these starting and increment values can be specified by variables instead of constants. For example, the following WRITE statement's implied do list is legal.

```
WRITE(5,7000) (L,A(L),B(L), L=M,N,K)
```

It says to set L equal to M, print out the value of L, then the value of A(L), then

B(L), and then to increase L by K and print L, A(L), B(L), and so on. It keeps repeating as long as L isn't larger than N. If we had known while writing the program that M would be 2, N would be 7, and K would be 3, we could have gotten the same result by writing

```
I1=2
I2=5
WRITE(5,7000) I1,A(2),B(2),I2,A(5),B(5)
```

What happens if the upper bound in the indexing section is smaller than the starting value? The ANSI standards simply call it illegal and leave it at that. Most versions of Fortran will accept it and do this: print the list section for the starting value of the index, and that's all. This isn't a case you should worry about excessively, but it might happen and it pays to be vaguely aware of the consequences.

Note that the general form allows **nesting** of implied do lists. That is, one implied do list can be inside another. The effect of nesting is to cause the inside

---

implied do list

forms

$(list, v = s, b)$
$(list, v = s, b, i)$

list is any legal I/O list
v is an unsubscripted INTEGER memory cell name
s, *b*, and *i* are nonzero unsigned INTEGER constants or unsubscripted INTEGER memory cell names (with positive values)

meaning

describes an I/O list consisting of consecutive repetitions of *list* for each value of *v* starting at *s* and incrementing by *i* as long as *v* doesn't exceed *b* (the increment is 1 if *i* is omitted)

examples

```
READ(5,1000) (A(I), I=1,10,3)
WRITE(6,3050) (A(K-1), K=2,N)
WRITE(6,2000) (NXT,A(NXT),FX , NXT=L,M,INC)
```

---

array transmission: Entire arrays may be transmitted to output or filled from data cards by placing the array name alone, without subscripts, in an I/O list. The order of transmission is the order in which the array's memory cells are stored in the machine.

```
REAL A, B, C(3)
READ(5,3000) A, C, B
```

is equivalent to

```
REAL A, B, C(3)
READ(5,3000) A, C(1),C(2),C(3), B
```

---

implied do list to be completely repeated with every repetition of the outside implied do list. The following examples should help clarify the effects of this nesting.

```
WRITE(6,1000) C, (B, (A, I=1,3), J=1,2), D
                     is equivalent to
WRITE(6,1000) C,  B, A,A,A,   B, A,A,A,  D


WRITE(6,2000) ((A(I,J),J=1,3),I=1,2)
                     is equivalent to
WRITE(6,2000)A(1,1),A(1,2),A(1,3),A(2,1),A(2,2),A(2,3)
```

As you can see in the first example, the *list* section of an implied do list does not need to involve the index. It may or it may not, at your option.

> **nesting:** *placing a certain program construct inside a program construct of the same form*

Implied do lists may also be used in READ statements. They order input variables in the same way that they order output variables. You will get a chance to use some implied do lists in READ statements in the exercises. Here's one last example using implied do lists.

In the bar graph example (Section 4 5) our program printed out the size of each bar, but didn't print the bar graph itself. Implied do lists make it very easy to print bar graphs with the bars going across the page because a bar can be "drawn" by repeatedly printing some character.

The program in Section 4 5 READs in distances, figures out which bar to record the occurrence of each distance in, and eventually leaves the totals for each bar in memory cells BAR0, BAR1, BAR2, . . ., BAR5. These statements:

```
      INTEGER COUNT, XCH
      DATA XCH/1HX/
           .
           .
           .
      WRITE(6,5000) (XCH,COUNT=1,BAR0)
 5000 FORMAT(' BAR0:', 100A1)
```

will print BAR0 (the number of distances assigned to that bar) copies of X across the page. However, we will have a problem if BAR0 has no entries in it. Then, because of the way implied do lists work, the WRITE statement would be illegal and the results unpredictable. (On most Fortran systems exactly one X would be printed.) We'll have to test for the missing bar case separately and execute a different WRITE statement in that case.

```
      IF (BAR0 .LE. 0)  GO TO 510
      WRITE(6,5000) (XCH, COUNT=1,BAR0)
 5000 FORMAT(' BAR0:',100A1)
      GO TO 600
 510  WRITE(6,5000)
 600     .
         .
         .
```

We could insert a sequence of such statements for each of BAR0, BAR1, BAR2, . . ., BAR 5 in the program of Section 4 5, but that would require a lot of work. Instead we'll alter the much shorter bar graph program which uses arrays (see exercise 6 2 7 and answer).

```
      COMMENT: MAKE A BAR GRAPH FROM DISTANCE DATA.
           INTEGER BAR(6),NUMB
           REAL DIST
           INTEGER COUNT,XCH,THISB
           DATA XCH/1HX/
      C    INITIALIZE BAR HEIGHTS.
           NUMB=1
      10   BAR(NUMB)=0
             NUMB=NUMB+1
             IF (NUMB .LE. 6) GO TO 10
      C    READ IN A DISTANCE.  IF IT'S NEGATIVE, THEN
      C    THERE ARE NO MORE DISTANCES IN THE DATA.
      20   READ(5,2000) DIST
      2000 FORMAT(F7.0)
             IF (DIST .LT. 0.0) GO TO 200
      C    CONVERT THE DISTANCE INTO AN INTEGER (DROP FRACTION)
           NUMB=DIST
      C    INCREMENT BAR COUNTER.
           IF (NUMB .LE. 5) GO TO 30
             WRITE(6,2010) DIST
      2010   FORMAT(' DISTANCE ',F7.1,' IS OUT OF RANGE.')
             GO TO 20
      30     BAR(NUMB+1)=BAR(NUMB+1) + 1
             GO TO 20
      C
      C    PLOT A BAR GRAPH.
      200  NUMB=0
      300  THISB=BAR(NUMB+1)
             IF (THISB .LE. 0) GO TO 310
             WRITE(6,3000) NUMB,(XCH,COUNT=1,THISB)
      3000   FORMAT(' BAR',I1,':',100A1)
             GO TO 400
      310    WRITE(6,3000) NUMB
      400    NUMB=NUMB+1
             IF (NUMB .LE. 5) GO TO 300
           STOP
           END
```

data
```
      3.9
      0.4
      5.4
      0.9
      3.9
      17.5
      5.6
      2.8
      4.5
      5.8
      3.2
      5.8
      6.9
      4.5
      3.7
      2.9
      5.2
      -1.0
```

output

```
DISTANCE    17.5 IS OUT OF RANGE.
DISTANCE     6.9 IS OUT OF RANGE.
BARO:XX
BAR1:
BAR2:XX
BAR3:XXXX
BAR4:XX
BAR5:XXXXX
```

EXERCISES 6 6

1   Without using implied do lists, write I/O statements equivalent to the following ones, assuming that M, N, and K have the values 4, 12, and 2 respectively.

```
READ(5,5000)  (A(J), J=1,4)
WRITE(6,1000)  (A(J), J=M,N,K)
WRITE(6,3000)  (A(J), J=K,N,M)
READ(5,2000)  ( (B(I,J),I=1,M), J=1,K )
WRITE(6,4000)Q,R,(S,B(3,J),A(J),J=1,K),BC,(A(J),J=1,4)
```

2   Using implied do lists, write I/O statements equivalent to the following ones.

```
WRITE(6,1000) A(1), A(2), A(3), A(4), A(5)
WRITE(6,1000) A(2), A(4), A(6), A(8), A(10)
READ(5,2000) B(2,1),B(3,1),B(2,2),B(3,2),B(2,3),B(3,3)
```

3   What is illegal in the following I/O statements?

```
WRITE(6,2000)  (A(J), J=1,N-1)
READ(5,7000)  (J, A(J), J=1,N)
WRITE(6,1000)  (A(J), J=1,C(N))
```

4   What will happen in the bar graph routine if there are more than 100 items in a bar?

5   Suppose that instead of using X's to make bars, you wanted to use numbers—0's for bar 0, 1's for bar 1, etc. What would you change?

PROBLEMS 6

1   The Boss Tweed clothing store has computerized its inventory operations. It sells ten different styles of suits referred to by number. Initially, it has five of each in stock. Each time a salesperson unloads a suit on a customer, a card is punched with the word SOLD followed by the style number. Each time the manager wants to check on supplies, she inserts a card which reads WELL? and the computer prints out the number of suits in stock of each style.

Write a program to handle Boss Tweed's inventory procedure. Your program should READ cards like those described above and update the inventory appropriately or print the inventory depending on the type of card. If the number of suits of a particular style becomes less than two, print a message warning the manager to restock that style. Keep READing cards until one with END on it comes in. Use these data cards:

```
SOLD   3
SOLD   2
WELL?
SOLD   5
SOLD   5
SOLD   4
SOLD   5
SOLD   3
WELL?
END
```

2   Expand the capabilities of the Boss Tweed clothing store's inventory program (problem 1). If a salesperson sells a style of suit that the store is out of, print a message. (Depending on how you think the store should run, either tell the salesperson that there has been some mistake or else that he or she will be considered for a raise.)

Also, allow for a fourth type of card for restocking:

RESTOCK STYLE 3 5

Such a card will indicate the number of suits of a given style purchased by the store. Make up 15 or 20 data cards which demonstrate the capabilities of your program.

3   Here are instructions for knitting a scarf:

Using No. 9 needles, cast on 76 sts.
row 1 and all odd rows up to 19: k across
row 2 and all even rows up to 20: p across
rows 21–100: k4, p2 across, end k4
row 101 and all odd rows up to 119: p across
row 102 and all even rows up to 120: k across

Write a program which carries out the knitting instructions by

a   printing a + for every "knit"
b   printing a – for every "purl"
c   going to a new line for each new row

Use an array of 76 characters to store each "row" as it is "knitted," then print the entire array each time a row is finished.

4   Write a program to compute the sales price of an automobile given its base price and the prices of its optional equipment, if any. The data cards for the program will be in groups. Each group will describe one car and will be organized as follows.

Typical group of cards describing a car:

card 1:	car name (up to 24 characters)	base price (INTEGER)
0 to 25 more cards:	name of option (up to 24 characters)	price (INTEGER)
termination card:	NO MORE OPTIONS	

There may be from 0 to 25 option cards, making a group consisting of anywhere from 2 to 27 cards. Following all the groups of cards will be the termination card shown below.

NO MORE CARS

For each automobile described in the data cards, store the information about the car in memory, compute its total price by adding its base price, all its option prices, a $150 dealer preparation charge, and 6 percent sales tax, and print the results in the following order:

line 1:	car name	base price	total price (including tax and dealer prep)
0 to 25 more lines:	name of option	price	
last line:	blank		

Your program should make *no* assumptions about the number of cars described in the data cards.

5 Write a program to produce a list of students, an honor roll, and a list of suspended students. Each data card will contain a student's name (up to 40 characters) and his grade point on a scale from 0.000 to 4.000 (REAL). The terminating data card will read

NO MORE STUDENTS

Your program should print the heading CLASS ROLL followed by a list of all students and their grade points, the heading HONOR ROLL followed by a list of those students whose grade points exceed 3.299, and finally the heading SUSPENDED followed by a list of students whose grade points are less than 1.7. Your program may assume that there are no more than 100 students.

6 Write a program using the same data cards as those in problem 5 but which prints the list of all students with an asterisk (*) beside each student whose grade point is above the average grade point for all the students. After the list, print the percentage of students whose grade point is above average.

7
> *palindrome: a word or phrase which reads the same forward as backward.*
>
> *A palindrome: "Madam, I'm Adam."*
>
> *Not a palindrome: "Able was I ere I saw Chicago."*

Write a program which detects palindromes. Assume that there won't be more than 50 characters. Remember that blanks, punctuation marks, and CapiTaliZations don't count in determining palindromes, so don't enter anything but letters on your data cards. Print the input phrase and follow it by the phrase IS PALINDROMIC or IS NOT, IN FACT, PALINDROMIC, whichever is appropriate. Keep going until a card with an * in column 1 is read.

Use these data and any others you think up.

```
RADAR
TOOHOTTOHOOT
ARSMITHIII
*
```

8 Write a program to READ a card containing a sentence. Assume that no punctuation is used other than blanks and commas in the sentence and a period at the end of the sentence.

Your program should print the sentence, then compute and print the number of words in the sentence. To do this, you'll have to READ the card in 80A1 FORMAT so that you can examine each character separately to look for symbols like commas, which indicate separations between words.

9 Write a program to READ a word up to ten characters long from one card, and a sentence from the next card (up to 80 characters, including blanks and other punctuation), then print the word, the sentence, and the number of occurrences of the word in the sentence. You may assume that there is no punctuation other than blanks and commas, with a period at the end.

10 As part of a certification test, scientists record the potentials induced in a 10-by-10 sheet of polystyrene by the meditations of candidate gurus. If a candidate is able to cause some point on the sheet to have a voltage more than ten times the average voltage, he passes this phase of the test. Otherwise he is labeled a sham and sent away in disgrace.

Write a program which carries out the certification test on the voltages and issues an appropriate message. Make up some data, or make the measurements yourself on a guru of your acquaintance. (Hint: Finding the average of the values in a 10-by-10 two-dimensional array is similar to what was done in the political poll problem of Section 6 4.)

Aging Guru Radiates Potential

11 Write a program which prints out a multiplication table. The size of the table should be determined by an INTEGER between 2 and 9 written on a data card. Your program should print a table of products up to that number. For example, if the number is 3, your output should look like that below.

```
*   1   2   3
1   1   2   3
2   2   4   6
3   3   6   9
```

12 Write a program that accepts data cards containing names of states or abbreviations of names of states and that returns the official U.S. Post Office abbreviations for each state named. If an abbreviation is undecipherable, print an appropriate message. Unless you feel like doing more, just have your program deal with the 11 western states whose official abbreviations are listed in Section 6 1.

Sample:

input	output
NEV.	THE OFFICIAL USPO ABBREVIATION IS NV
MONT.	THE OFFICIAL USPO ABBREVIATION IS MT
C.	SORRY. I DON'T KNOW WHAT STATE YOU MEAN

13 Write a program which prints beef price differences in a group of up to 100 cities. Each data card will contain the name of a city (up to 40 characters) followed by the price of a pound of hamburger at a local supermarket. The last data card will be

NO MORE CITIES

Your program should compute the average price of hamburger over all the cities and print a table of cities, hamburger prices and the amounts above or below the average price. Thus, each line of the table should contain the name of a city, the price of hamburger there, and the difference between that price and the average price of hamburger (a positive number if the price is above average and a negative number if it's below average).

14 Add a section to the program of problem 13 to print the lowest and highest of the hamburger prices surveyed along with the corresponding cities.

NOTICE: *Problems 15 through 23 require a background in several areas of mathematics.*

---

15 The year is 1811 and the fame of the pirate Lafitte has spread throughout the islands of the Caribbean and the Gulf. In Havana there resides a wealthy soldier of fortune, Captain Hawkbill, who owns a fast gunship and can hire a large crew of tough sailors. He reasons that he can make a fortune if he can capture Lafitte and take his loot. His enterprise would bring him both fortune and favor because Lafitte is universally hated by honest, law-abiding people.

The Captain sails his ship into the Gulf of Mexico to a point 5 nautical miles south and 5 nautical miles east of New Orleans. Then, from his position, he sees Lafitte's ship 5 nautical miles due west. Fortunately for Hawkbill, Lafitte's crew has just finished robbing a large cargo of

> knot: a measure of speed, one nautical mile per hour

gold and furs from a British ship. Lafitte's ship is sailing straight north toward New Orleans at 9 knots. Hawkbill gives chase immediately. In today's wind his ship can travel at 13 knots, and he orders his crew to keep the ship at top speed and pointed directly at Lafitte's ship.

Write a program that computes each ship's position at one-minute intervals in terms of nautical miles south and east of New Orleans. Assume that the chase is ended if Lafitte reaches New Orleans or is overtaken by Captain Hawkbill. Print out on the line printer a graphic display of the chase in a format similar to the following:

```
New Orleans
X . . . . . . . . . . . . . . . . . . . . . . .
.
.
.
H
.
L
.
.
.
.
L
.
.
.
L       H
.
L                 H
.                     H
.
L                         H       H
```

Note that the chase is over if either Hawkbill's distance east of New Orleans or Lafitte's distance south of New Orleans becomes negative.

16 Write a program which evaluates polynomials. The data should consist of two groups of cards. Group 1 describes the polynomial by giving the coefficients and corresponding powers. That is, each card in group 1 contains a coefficient (REAL) and a power (INTEGER). This group is followed by a termination card with coefficient 0.0 and power -1. The following group of data cards would describe the polynomial $3x^4 + 2x^2 + 4.7x + 1$.

```
3.0    4
2.0    2
4.7    1
1.0    0
0.0   -1
```

You may assume that there are no more than 51 cards in group 1.

Group 2 is a list of points at which the polynomial is to be evaluated. That is, each card in group 2 will contain a REAL value for the independent variable in the polynomial. The termination card for group 2 will contain 999999.9 (which shouldn't be taken as a value at which to evaluate the polynomial). Your program should print a description of the polynomial and a table of values of the polynomial at the points listed in the group 2 data cards.

17 Horner's scheme for evaluating polynomials is quicker and more accurate than the straightforward scheme. Write the program of problem 16 so that it uses Horner's evaluation scheme.

Horner's scheme:

$$a_n x^n + a_{n-1} x^{n-1} + \ldots + a_1 x + a_0 =$$

$$(((a_n x + a_{n-1})x + a_{n-2})x + \ldots + a_1)x + a_0$$

e.g., $3x^4 + 2x^2 + 4.7x + 1 = (((3x + 0)x + 2)x + 4.7)x + 1$

18 For people who really like factorials: Write a program that can compute $n! = n*(n-1)*(n-2)* \ldots *2*1$ for values of n that are so large that the answer can't fit in a single INTEGER memory cell.

$$\boxed{25! = 15{,}511{,}210{,}043{,}330{,}985{,}984{,}000{,}000}$$

One way to do this is to use an array to store the answer (and partial results) using one memory cell in the array per digit. Thus, $12! = 479{,}001{,}600$ would be stored like this:

	9	8	7	6	5	4	3	2	1
...	4	7	9	0	0	1	6	0	0

Now to find $13!$, multiply each memory cell by 13 (taking care to move carries) to get

	11	10	9	8	7	6	5	4	3	2	1
...		6	2	2	7	0	2	0	8	0	0

If you feel like going to a little extra effort, print the answer out in the way we usually write big numbers—in groups of three digits separated by commas.

19 Write a program to list all the prime numbers between 1 and 1000. To compute these numbers, use the algorithm below, which is known as **Eratosthenes' sieve**.

    a Make a list of all the consecutive integers you are interested in, starting from 2.

    b Mark off all the multiples of 2 (they can't be primes).

    c Find the next integer remaining in the list beyond the one whose multiples you just marked off, and mark off *its* multiples (they can't be primes).

    d Repeat step c unless the integer whose multiple you just marked off is the square root of the largest integer in the list; that is, the square root without its fractional part. (This termination condition depends on the fact that the two factors in a product can't both exceed the square root of the product.)

One way to keep track of which numbers are still on the list is to initialize a logical array of 1000 elements to .TRUE. (for "on the list") and cross the number n off the list by changing the nth element of the array to .FALSE.

20 If you are familiar with vectors, write a program to convert a given vector to a unit vector in the same direction. Assume each card contains the dimension (i.e., number of components) of the vector (INTEGER) followed by the components of the vector (REALs). You may assume the dimension is less than 100. The termination card will contain the vector 0.0 of dimension 1. (Don't try to convert it to a unit vector!)

The unit vector in the same direction as $(x_1, x_2, \ldots, x_n)$ is $(u_1, u_2, \ldots, u_n)$, where

$$u_k = x_k/r$$

and $r = \sqrt{(x_1{}^2 + x_2{}^2 + \ldots + x_n{}^2)}$

Print the vector and the corresponding unit vector.

21 Write a program to compute the cosine of the angle between two given vectors. Assume each data card will contain the dimension of the two vectors involved (INTEGER) followed by the components of the one, and finally the components of the other. Assume the dimension is less than 100. The termination card will contain 1,0.0,0.0. If $(u_1, \ldots, u_n)$ and $(v_1, \ldots, v_n)$ are the unit vectors in the same direction as the given vectors x and y, respectively, then the cosine of the angle between the two given vectors is $u_1 v_1 + u_2 v_2 + \ldots + u_n v_n$. A formula in problem 20 shows the relation between a given vector and the corresponding unit vector.

22 Write a program to do the matching for a computer dating service. The dating service's questionnaires have statements and the applicant indicates his degree of agreement with each question on a scale of one to five. Thus each data card will contain the name of an applicant (up to 28 characters), sex (M or F), and responses to the questionnaire (20 INTEGERs). The last data card will contain the phrase NO MORE APPLICANTS. You may assume there are no more than 100 applicants.

Match each person with the two most compatible people of the opposite sex. As a measure of compatibility, use the cosine of the angle between their two response vectors; the larger the cosine, the more compatible the couple (see problem 21 for a way to compute the cosine). Your program's output should be a list of the applicants along with the names of their two guaranteed dates, e.g.,

```
JOHN DOE        DATES MARY SLATE
                AND ALICE HILL

JANE FLUG       DATES ROGER WHIMSBY
                AND JOE THORNTOR
```

23 Problem 22 has a feature which wouldn't be acceptable to a real computer dating service. If one person is particularly compatible, he or she will receive the names of two dates, but may be listed as a good date on *many* people's lists. The whole thing could get out of balance with almost everybody trying to date a few highly compatible people. Do problem 22 so that no one person is listed for more than six other people. Print *all*

the dates a person is involved in, not just his own two optimal matches as before. Now another problem arises. You may have to refund some participants' money because in some cases there may not be enough suitable matches to go around. Print a polite apology to those who come up short.

> WARNING: *While the following problems do not require any special background, they are more difficult than those preceding problem 15.*

24 Write a program which, given a tic-tac-toe board situation, decides on a nonlosing next move, or, if there is none, prints a snide concession of defeat.

25 Write a program to compute unemployment statistics. Assume each data card contains the name of a city (up to 24 characters) followed by the unemployment percentages (INTEGERs) for each month of the fiscal year, from July through the following June. The termination card will contain the phrase NO MORE STATISTICS. For each month, print out the cities with the lowest and highest unemployment rates and the average unemployment rate over all the cities for the entire year. You may assume that there are no more than 50 cities.

26 Suppose you own a travel service and your policy is to book your customers with a direct flight if possible. You have a stack of punched cards describing the direct flights for which you may schedule passengers. That is, each card contains a departure point and time, an arrival point and time, and the name of an airline, e.g.,

flight description card:

KANSAS CITY   10:00AM   DENVER   11:00AM   TWA

You have a second stack of cards each of which contains the name of a customer, his point of departure and his destination, e.g.,

customer request card:

CLIFFORD TREASE   CHICAGO   SAN FRANCISCO

You are to write a program which stores the flight descriptions in memory then tries to find a direct flight to fill each customer request. If the program finds a direct flight, it should print out the customer's name, departure point and time, arrival point and time, and airline. Otherwise print the customer's name and a message to the effect that there is no direct flight available for the customer between his requested departure and arrival points.

Your program may *not* assume that the cards have been counted, so you will need some sort of termination card at the end of each of the two stacks so that it can test to see when it has stored all the flight descriptions and when it has taken care of all the customers. You may assume that there are no more than 100 flight descriptions, but your program should not depend *in any way* upon the number of customers.

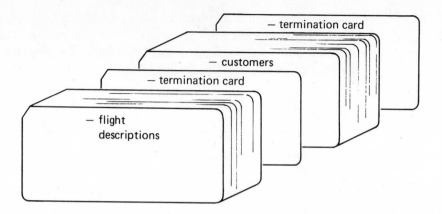

- termination card
- customers
- termination card
- flight descriptions

27 Write a program to make airline reservations. Assume that the airline you work for has seven flights with the number of seats given in the table below.

flight	seats available
101A	147
237	83
208	6
505	21
110	122
650	62
810B	3

Your program should reserve seats on these flights on a first come, first served basis. Each data card will contain a customer's name (up to 40 characters) and the number of the flight he wants (4 characters). The termination card will contain the phrase NO MORE CUSTOMERS in place of the name. Make no assumptions about the number of customers.

For each request, print the name of the customer and a message indicating whether or not his reservation is confirmed.

28 Write a program to solve a more general version of the previous problem. The program should first READ the flight information from data cards. Each flight description will be on a separate card with the flight number (4 characters) followed by the number of seats available (INTEGER). The termination card for the flight descriptions will be

♦♦♦♦   0

The rest of the data cards will be customer requests as in problem 26. As before, make no assumptions about the number of customers, but assume that the airline has no more than 100 flights.

The advantage of this version is that the airline can still use the program if it adds or deletes flights or changes to planes of different capacities.

29 Design a program which converts kitchen measures. Data cards will look like this:

```
            col. 14        col. 26  col. 29
              |              |      /
              ↓              ↓    /
CONVERT    3?  TABLESPOONS  TO  GALLONS
CONVERT    2   QUARTS           TO  TEASPOONS
```

The output should look like this:

```
32 TABLESPOONS MAKE    0.1250 GALLONS
 2 QUARTS         MAKE 384.0000 TEASPOONS
```

Here are some hints on how to proceed. First, create an array which stores the names of the measures you want to deal with, and which will allow you to associate an INTEGER with each measure. Suppose this array is a two-dimensional array called NAMES with values as shown below.

NAMES

	1	2	3	4	5	6	7	8	9	10	11
1	G	A	L	L	O	N	S				
2	Q	U	A	R	T	S					
3	P	I	N	T	S						
4	C	U	P	S							
5	T	A	B	L	E	S	P	O	O	N	S
6	T	E	A	S	P	O	O	N	S		

Then the INTEGER 1 will denote gallons; the INTEGER 2, quarts; etc.

Suppose the second sample data card above is the one we are working on. We find QUARTS in the array NAMES on the second row and associate QUARTS with 2. We'll call the INTEGER associated with this input measuring unit the **source**. We find that TEASPOONS is associated with 6, and we'll call this INTEGER the **destination**.

We need one more collection of information before we can carry out the conversion. We need to know the number of cups per pint, pints per quart, and so on. We'll put this information in an array called CONV.

```
            1   2   3   4   5   6
CONV      | ₹ | 4 | 2 | 2 | 16| 3 |
```

CONV(i) tells how many units of measure i make one unit of measure $i - 1$. Thus CONV(2) = 4 because there are 4 QUARTS in a GALLON. The value stored in CONV(1) doesn't matter since we can't handle any units larger than gallons. The flowchart on p. 158 shows how to put all the parts together.

VERBAL DESCRIPTION

Initialize NAMES array. Initialize CONVersion array.

Get a conversion problem from input.

Convert symbolic names to integers (e.g., GALLONS to 1) using the NAMES array.

Convert source units to destination units and print results.

Repeat.

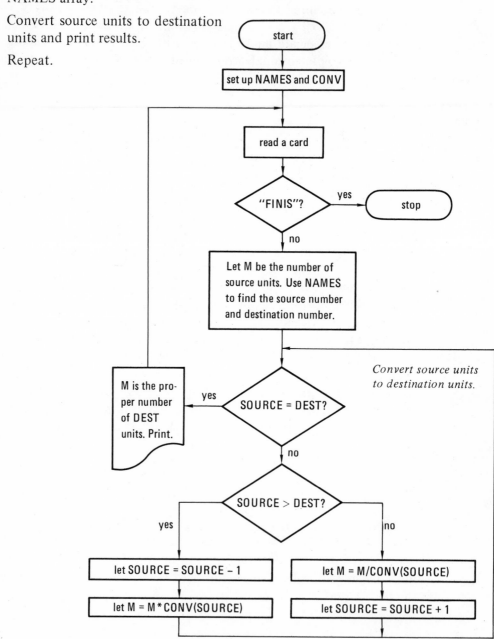

30   The 55th Street Whiz Kids (a tough gang) have found it necessary to send messages to one another in secret code. In order to write a message in this secret code, a member must write down the message on a piece of scrap paper. Then under each character (including spaces and punctuation marks), he places an integer between 0 and 42 according to the following scheme: 0 through 25 for A through Z respectively; 26 through 42 for the characters blank . , – ( ) ' 0 1 2 3 4 5 6 7 8 9 respectively. Then he adds each pair of numbers and writes the result below the pair with the convention that if the sum is 43 or more, he subtracts 43 from it before writing it down, so that each number written will be between 0 and 42. He then decodes the numbers into characters, again using the above scheme.

Example:

1	written message:	MEET JIM 10 P.M.

2 integers:	12	04	04	19	26	09	08	12
	26	34	33	26	15	27	12	27

3 added integers:	16	08	23	02	35	17	20	38
	17	24	16	41	42	39	39	

4	coded message:	QIXC2RU5RYQ8966

Note that the coded message has only 15 characters, whereas the original message has 16. It will always be the case with this code system that the original message has one more character than the coded message. To make it possible to decode their message, the Whiz Kids made an agreement that the original message should always end with a period.

Write a program which will read coded messages from cards in the FORMAT 80A1 and print out the decoded message. You may assume the coded message has fewer than 500 characters and that the end of the coded message will be marked with a slash (/). The slash will be used for no other purpose than to mark the end of the coded message and therefore should not be used in decoding the message. You may use the above message to test your program.

7 SUBPROGRAMS

Section 7 1

Introduction

"I'm learning to program."
"What's that mean?"
"I'm learning to write instructions for computers."
"Oh yeah? What's a computer?"
"You're kidding."
"No, what's a computer?"
"A computer is, uh, a machine that manipulates symbols."
"Oh yeah? What's a symbol?"
". . . . !"

All human languages encourage the use of short, simple words and phrases to refer to complex ideas. The meaning of a sentence depends on its words, many of whose meanings might be quite complicated and difficult to explain. Sometimes it's necessary to clarify the meaning of a sentence to the listener by defining some of its words or phrases. The definitions, of course, are given in other sentences whose words may be unfamiliar, and so on down the hierarchy of clarification until the meaning of the original sentence is couched in terms the listener understands. This process can be time-consuming and difficult. We'd rather not do it at all, or at least keep the layers of definitions at a minimum. In fact many concepts are virtually impossible to explain in detail without assuming a considerable amount of specialized life experience on the part of the listener. Think, for example, of trying to explain to your friends about learning to program. You'd never get all the details across, but you could probably explain enough to leave them feeling that they had some idea of what you're doing.

Writing a program is a problem in communication. It should come as no surprise that people have found that the most effective way to program is not to lay all the details out in linear order but to break the program up hierarchically, using simple expressions to refer to complex subparts which are expanded elsewhere.

There are several convenient ways to give a sequence of statements a simple name. We'll cover two of them, SUBROUTINEs and FUNCTIONs, in this chapter. Both are lumped under the term **subprograms** because they play a *subordinate* role, giving details of computations referred to elsewhere.

FUNCTIONs are appropriate when a single value is returned from the subprogram, and SUBROUTINEs are a better choice when the subprogram returns a number of values each time it is referenced. We'll deal with SUBROUTINEs first.

> **subprogram:** *a complete and separate program which may be referred to by another program*

> **program unit:** *the main program or a subprogram. Every Fortran program has at least one program unit. All our programs up to now have had exactly one unit, the main program.*

Section 7 2

SUBROUTINEs

One important use of SUBROUTINEs is to avoid having to write the same sequence of statements over and over again. For example, if you are writing a program that generates a long report, you'd probably want to number the pages. To do this your program needs to keep track of the number of pages printed. Each time a new page is printed, the page counter needs to be updated and its value printed at the upper right-hand corner of the next page of output. In addition, it would be nice to print the title of the report under the page number to insure that different reports don't get scrambled after the pages are burst. This is not a complicated process, but there are several Fortran statements involved, and by putting these statements in a SUBROUTINE we can avoid having to write them at every point in the program where we want to start a new page of output.

> *burst: to separate continuous form paper into separate sheets*

A SUBROUTINE is a separate program. It has its own declarations, memory cells, statement numbers, FORMATs, END statement, and so forth. All of these things are **local** to the SUBROUTINE. That is, they are automatically kept separate from their counterparts in other program units. Even if your main program and a SUBROUTINE both have statements labeled 100, the two labels won't be confused. They are local to their own program units. The same goes for memory cells and the other constructs.

In our example, we need some way to tell the page-numbering SUBROUTINE what the current page number is so that the SUBROUTINE can update the number and print it. Thus, we need some communication between the main program and the SUBROUTINE. We can transmit a memory cell to the SUBROUTINE via an **argument** in a **CALL statement**, the statement which gets the SUBROUTINE into action. Let's take a look at a typical CALL statement.

A CALL statement has three parts: (1) the key word CALL, indicating that a SUBROUTINE is to be invoked; (2) the name of the SUBROUTINE to be brought into action (NEWPGE in our example); and (3) the argument list (there is

---

CALL statement

forms
    CALL $s(a_1, a_2, \ldots, a_n)$
    CALL s
    s is a SUBROUTINE name
    a_i is an argument (i.e., a memory cell name, array name, constant, or expression)

meaning
    performs the computation described by SUBROUTINE s using the information and/or memory cells specified in the arguments

examples
```
CALL SORT (NAMES, N)
CALL AVG(GRD, N, AV)
CALL PRMESS
CALL CMPT(A, 32.0*CAB+1.0, SQRT(C))
```

---

only one argument, the INTEGER memory cell PGENUM, in our example, but other SUBROUTINEs may have several arguments).

To perform a CALL statement, the controller does three things: (1) it sets up a linkage so that control can return to the statement following the CALL, (2) it sets up the arguments to be transmitted to the SUBROUTINE, and (3) it transfers to the beginning of the SUBROUTINE to get its next instruction.

> *argument*: an "input" to a computation. One very old meaning was related to the word refashioning. *We could say that in SQRT (2.0), the argument 2.0 is "refashioned" into 1.4142 . . .*

Now let's take a look at the SUBROUTINE itself.

```
      SUBROUTINE NEWPGE (PAGE)
      INTEGER PAGE
      PAGE = PAGE+1
      WRITE(6,1000) PAGE
 1000 FORMAT('1', 51X, 'PAGE', I5)
      WRITE(6,1001)
 1001 FORMAT(32X, 'BOOK REPORT--E100'/
     +        32X, 'SILAS MARNER, BY GEORGE ELIOT')
      RETURN
      END
```

The first line of a SUBROUTINE, known as the **header** statement, gives the name of the SUBROUTINE and a list of **formal parameters**. Formal parameters are symbols which will be used in the **body** of the SUBROUTINE (the part between the header statement and the END) to stand for the arguments which will be transmitted via a CALL statement.

The name (NEWPGE) of the SUBROUTINE is placed after the key word SUBROUTINE and followed by the parenthesized list of formal parameters (PAGE).

SUBROUTINE statement

forms

SUBROUTINE s $(p_1, p_2, \ldots, p_n)$
SUBROUTINE s

s (the SUBROUTINE name) is an identifier

$p_1, \ldots, p_n$ (the parameter names) are identifiers

The **body** of the SUBROUTINE, that is, the part between the SUBROUTINE statement and corresponding END, must contain at least one RETURN statement. (The parenthesized list of parameters may be omitted if the SUBROUTINE neither needs nor delivers outside information.)

meaning

describes an algorithm which may be invoked by a CALL statement

examples

```
SUBROUTINE SORT (A,N)
SUBROUTINE X(U)
SUBROUTINE BUILD(A, C, ROUND)
```

After the header statement come the formal parameter declarations (INTEGER PAGE). Even though these look like normal declaration statements, their effect is quite different. Instead of instructing the compiler to attach names to memory cells or arrays, they tell the compiler what kind of values or structures to expect the formal parameters to be attached to when the SUBROUTINE is called. The first thing the controller does when it begins to perform the statements in a SUBROUTINE is to attach the formal parameter names to the arguments transmitted by the CALL statement. Once that is done, the controller begins to perform the executable statements in the body of the SUBROUTINE. In our example, this amounts to increasing the value of the memory cell attached to the

Subprograms help you break your program into smaller logical chunks. Then you can work on each chunk separately.

formal parameter PAGE. Our CALL would have transmitted the memory cell PGENUM from the main program, hence the first statement would increase the value of PGENUM. Next come the WRITE statements, which put the page number in the upper right-hand corner of the next page and the report title underneath. Finally, the controller encounters the **RETURN instruction**. At this point it uses the linkage established by the CALL to return to the statement following the CALL in the main program. Since every SUBROUTINE is a separate program unit, the compiler must be instructed when to wrap up the compilation of a SUBROUTINE. The END statement is used for this purpose. It must be the last

---

RETURN statement

form
    RETURN

meaning
    instructs the controller to go back to the point in the calling
    program where this subprogram was called

examples
    RETURN
    IF (X .EQ. Y)   RETURN

---

statement in every program unit. In the deck setup, program units are simply placed in sequence, one behind the other (as in Figure 7 2 1).

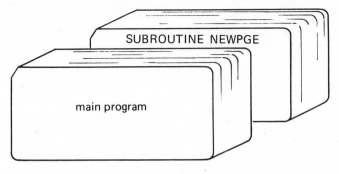

Figure 7 2 1

The following program uses the SUBROUTINE NEWPGE.

```
COMMENT:  PROGRAM TO PRINT SILAS MARNER BOOK REPORT
C   VARIABLES:
C      PGENUM--CURRENT PAGE NUMBER
C               (UPDATED BY SUBROUTINE NEWPGE)
C      REPORT--ARRAY TO STORE CURRENT LINE
C      LINE--NUMBER OF LINES PRINTED SO FAR ON CURRENT PAGE
C      PGLEN--NUMBER OF LINES ALLOWED PER PAGE
       INTEGER PGENUM, REPORT(15), LINE, PGELEN, FINIS
       DATA PGELEN/35/,  FINIS/4H*END/
C   TITLE PAGE
       PGENUM = 0
       CALL NEWPGE(PGENUM)
       WRITE(6,1000)
 1000 FORMAT(4('0'/),10X,'REVIEW OF'/
      +        8X,'SILAS MARNER'/
      +        '0   A NOVEL BY GEORGE ELIOT'/
      +        '0   REVIEW BY RODNEY BOTTOMS')
C   DEDICATION PAGE:
       CALL NEWPGE(PGENUM)
       WRITE(6,1010)
 1010 FORMAT(4('0'/),8X,'THIS REVIEW IS'/
      +        5X,'GRATEFULLY DEDICATED'/
      +        10X,'TO MY MOTHER'/
      +        9X,'AND MY DOG, SPOT')
C   BODY OF REPORT
       LINE = PGELEN+1
 200  READ(5,2000) REPORT
 2000 FORMAT(15A4)
       IF (REPORT(1) .EQ. FINIS)  STOP
       LINE = LINE +1
       IF (LINE .LE. PGELEN)  GO TO 210
          LINE = 1
          CALL NEWPGE(PGENUM)
 210     WRITE(6,2100) REPORT
 2100    FORMAT(1X, 15A4)
       GO TO 200
       END
```

da

```
       SILAS MARNER WAS A MISER.
DUNSTAN CASS STOLE HIS GOLD.
EPPIE WAS THE LITTLE BABY.
SHE GREW UP AND WAS HAPPY.
SO WAS SILAS.

       GEORGE ELIOT WILL GO IN
THE ANNALS OF LITERATURE.
HE WAS A REAL GOOD WRITER.

              THE END
*END
```

output

```
                                    PAGE    1
              BOOK REPORT--E100
              SILAS MARNER, BY GEORGE ELIOT



          REVIEW OF
          SILAS MARNER

     A NOVEL BY GEORGE ELIOT

     REVIEW BY RODNEY BOTTOMS


                                    PAGE    2
              BOOK REPORT--E100
              SILAS MARNER, BY GEORGE ELIOT


          THIS REVIEW IS
        GRATEFULLY DEDICATED
           TO MY MOTHER
        AND MY DOG, SPOT


                                    PAGE    3
              BOOK REPORT--E100
              SILAS MARNER, BY GEORGE ELIOT


       SILAS MARNER WAS A MISER.
DUNSTAN CASS STOLE HIS GOLD.
EPPIE WAS THE LITTLE BABY.
SHE GREW UP AND WAS HAPPY.
SO WAS SILAS.

       GEORGE ELIOT WILL GO IN
THE ANNALS OF LITERATURE.
HE WAS A REAL GOOD WRITER.

              THE END
```

Because SUBROUTINEs are completely separate program units, they are often called **externals**. The consequences of this subprogram independence can be confusing at first. Suppose, for example, that you write a SUBROUTINE AREA which has two REAL parameters, but when you CALL AREA you accidentally use an INTEGER argument.

```
CALL AREA(2, S)



SUBROUTINE AREA(R, A)
REAL R, A
    .
    .       the constant 2 takes on the name R (error! wrong type!)
    .
    .
    .
    .
    .       the cell S takes on the name A
    .
    .
    .
    .
END
```

```
                          error!
      REAL S
      CALL AREA(2, S)
      WRITE(6,1000) S
 1000 FORMAT(' AREA IS', F5.2)
      STOP
      END

      SUBROUTINE AREA(R, A)
      REAL R, A
      A = 3.14*R**2
      RETURN
      END
```

> *Caution—data type: The data type of each argument in a CALL statement must match that of the corresponding parameter in the SUBROUTINE.*

This will cause an error when the computer tries to do the computation in AREA because the INTEGER 2 and the REAL 2.0 are not the same. On most Fortran systems the pattern of 1's and 0's that represents the INTEGER 2 is very close to the pattern that represents the REAL number 0.0. This information might help you track down errors of this nature in case your Fortran system doesn't detect them (most don't). Even so, this kind of error can be exceedingly difficult to find. The moral is to make sure the arguments in CALL statements match the corresponding parameter declarations in the SUBROUTINE.

To illustrate this point further, let's consider a second case. As you know, the arguments in CALL statements may be values (that is, arithmetic or LOGICAL expressions or constants like 2 in the CALL AREA(2,S) above, or they may be memory cell names, or array names. But you must be careful when you write CALL statements: Don't give the SUBROUTINE arguments that it will try to use in illegitimate ways. For example, suppose we had gotten the data types right in our CALL statement above, but had accidentally switched the order of the arguments, as shown below.

```
CALL  AREA(S,  2.0)




SUBROUTINE  AREA(R,  A)
   .
   .     the cell S takes on the name R
   .     the constant 2.0 takes on the name A
   .
   .
   .
   .
   .     A  =  3.14*R**2   (error! constants can't be changed!)
   .

END
```

```
        REAL  S                    error!
        CALL  AREA(S,  2.0)
        WRITE(6,1000)  S
  1000  FORMAT(' AREA IS', F5.2)
        STOP
        END

        SUBROUTINE  AREA(R,  A)
        REAL  R,  A
        A  =  3.14*R**2
        RETURN
        END
```

Then the A in the SUBROUTINE gets linked to the 2.0 in the CALL. But when the SUBROUTINE tries to perform the assignment statement A = 3.14 * R**2, it is actually trying to assign a new value to the constant 2.0. Clearly a mistake! The results of such an error vary from one Fortran system to another, but many systems don't give you any warning when this happens, making the mistake very hard to find.

> *Caution—constant arguments: A* SUBROUTINE *must not try to change the value of a parameter which is linked to a constant in a* CALL *statement.*

A third way in which CALL arguments and SUBROUTINE parameters must match is in structure. If a SUBROUTINE parameter is declared as an array, the corresponding argument in a CALL must be an array. The two examples in Figure 7 2 2 illustrate the point. In the program on the left, the SUBROUTINE expects the CALL statement to give it access to a memory cell, and it gets one—the third element in the array A. All is well. In the example on the right, the SUBROUTINE is expecting an array but gets a memory cell instead. Things will go badly there, possibly without warning—again, a difficult error to eliminate from the program once it creeps in. Be careful when CALLing SUBROUTINEs!

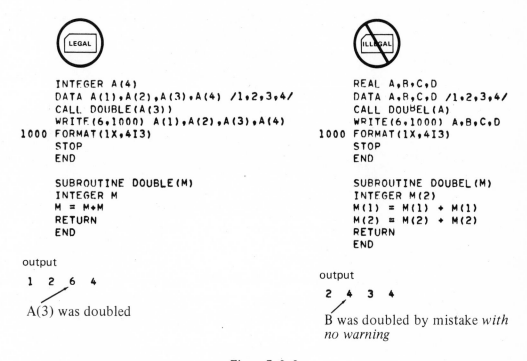

```
          INTEGER A(4)
          DATA A(1),A(2),A(3),A(4) /1,2,3,4/
          CALL DOUBLE(A(3))
          WRITE(6,1000) A(1),A(2),A(3),A(4)
1000      FORMAT(1X,4I3)
          STOP
          END

          SUBROUTINE DOUBLE(M)
          INTEGER M
          M = M+M
          RETURN
          END
```

output

1   2   6   4

A(3) was doubled

```
          REAL A,B,C,D
          DATA A,B,C,D /1,2,3,4/
          CALL DOUBEL(A)
          WRITE(6,1000) A,B,C,D
1000      FORMAT(1X,4I3)
          STOP
          END

          SUBROUTINE DOUBEL(M)
          INTEGER M(2)
          M(1) = M(1) + M(1)
          M(2) = M(2) + M(2)
          RETURN
          END
```

output

2   4   3   4

B was doubled by mistake *with no warning*

Figure 7 2 2

Caution—array parameters: If a SUBROUTINE *parameter is declared to be an array, make sure the* CALL *statement supplies an array for the* SUBROUTINE *to use.*

The matching correspondence between CALL arguments and SUBROUTINE parameters is so crucial that we think one final cautionary example will be helpful. When a SUBROUTINE parameter is declared to be a multidimensional array, the corresponding argument in the CALL statement must be an array of the same shape. If it isn't, problems will ensue. You'll learn more about these problems in Chapter 11. Until then, avoid problems by being careful in CALL statements.

The two CALL statements in Figure 7 2 3 illustrate what can happen. In the first CALL statement, the array R has a 3-by-3 arrangement, and the corresponding parameter in the SUBROUTINE is declared to be a 3-by-3 array, consistent with the argument. The SUBROUTINE puts zeros across the bottom row as it was intended to do. In the second CALL, the argument W is again a 3-by-3 array, but the SUBROUTINE is led to believe its parameter will be a 2-by-2 array. Instead of getting a row of zeros, as expected, we get strange results and no clue as to what went wrong.

The moral is to be careful when CALLing SUBROUTINEs. Know what assumptions the SUBROUTINE will make about its parameters, and make your CALL statements consistent with those assumptions.

```
        INTEGER R(3,3), W(3,3)
        DATA R(1,1),R(1,2),R(1,3) /11,12,13/
        DATA R(2,1),R(2,2),R(2,3) /21,22,23/
        DATA R(3,1),R(3,2),R(3,3) /31,32,33/
        DATA W(1,1),W(1,2) /11,12/
        DATA W(2,1),W(2,2) /21,22/
        CALL ZAPROW(R,3)
        CALL ZAPROW(W,2)
        WRITE(6,1000) R(1,1),R(1,2),R(1,3), W(1,1),W(1,2),
     +                R(2,1),R(2,2),R(2,3), W(2,1),W(2,2),
     +                R(3,1),R(3,2),R(3,3)
1000    FORMAT(1X,3I3,10X,2I3)
        STOP
        END

        SUBROUTINE ZAPROW(A,N)
        INTEGER N, A(N,N)
        INTEGER C
        C=1
100     A(N,C) = 0
        C = C+1
        IF (C .LE. N)  GO TO 100
        RETURN
        END
```

output

```
11 12 13          11  0
21 22 23           0 22
 0  0  0
```

Figure 7 2 3   Right and Wrong Ways to CALL

Caution—multidimensional array arguments: When you put a multidimensional array in a CALL statement's argument list, make sure its dimensions are the same as those declared for the corresponding parameter in the SUBROUTINE.

In spite of the difficulties they sometimes cause, SUBROUTINEs are one of the most important and useful features of Fortran. Over the years, people have written programs to do many things. Those that may be applied to many common problems are often written in the form of SUBROUTINEs and saved. At your computer center, no doubt, there is a large collection of SUBROUTINEs already written and available for you to use. Since the means of access to the collection differs from place to place, you will have to consult a local expert. Once you know how to attach these SUBROUTINEs to your program, you can use them simply by writing CALL statements with appropriate arguments. The availability of prepackaged SUBROUTINEs, by itself, would be a good reason to learn how to use SUBROUTINEs. This, along with their use as time-savers in coding, as in the book report example, should motivate you to become proficient with SUBROUTINEs.

> *Fortran subprograms are said to be **externals**. As a consequence of this organization, the compiler treats each program unit (i.e., your main program and your subprograms) independently. The END card, which must be the last card of every program unit, tells the compiler to stop compiling one program and to get ready to compile another.*
>
> #### Things to remember about subprograms
>
> *Variable names and statement numbers are not confused between programs.*
>
> *It is very easy to use subprograms written by someone else.*
>
> *They can make your program more readable.*
>
> *You cannot use variables from the calling program merely by using the same names in the subprogram.*

EXERCISES 7 2

1 Which of the following are legal SUBROUTINE statements? If not, explain why not.

```
SUBROUTINE APPLE(RED,GREEN)
SUBROUTINE PEAR
SUBROUTINE POMEGRANATE(SEED)
SUBROUTINE PIZZA(SMALL, OR, LARGE(ONE))
```

2 Which of the following are legal CALL statements? If not, explain why not.

```
CALL APPLE(1,3HRED)
CALL PEAR
CALL POMEG(RANATE)
CALL PIZZA(SMALL,OR,LARGE(ONE))
```

3 What would the following program print?

```
      INTEGER A, B, C
      CALL SQUARE(3,A)
      CALL SQUARE(4,B)
      CALL SQUARE(5,C)
      WRITE(6,1000) A,B,C
1000  FORMAT(1X,3I3)
      STOP
      END
```

```
SUBROUTINE SQUARE(NUMBER,SQ)
INTEGER NUMBER, SQ
SQ = NUMBER*NUMBER
RETURN
END
```

4 What would the following program print?

```
      INTEGER A(3)
      DATA A(1)/3HDOG/, A(2)/3HCAT/, A(3)/3HBAT/
      CALL CHANGE(A,2)
      WRITE(6,1000) A
 1000 FORMAT(' A=',3(1X,A4))
      STOP
      END

      SUBROUTINE CHANGE(ARRAY, INDEX)
      INTEGER ARRAY(3), INDEX
      INTEGER NONE
      DATA NONE/4HNONE/
      ARRAY(INDEX) = NONE
      RETURN
      END
```

Section 7 3

Plotting—An Example Using SUBROUTINEs

It wasn't long after the first printed pages came zooming out of computer line printers that people, perhaps initially attracted by the moving, shifting patterns of program listings, began writing programs which produce two-dimensional patterns for their own sake. One example of the sorts of patterns that can be produced fairly easily is the map of the United States in Figure 8 3 1. Practitioners of **computer graphics** have developed elaborate techniques and can produce a fantastic range of visual effects.

In this section we'll point out a few of the mechanics of plotting—specifically, how to go from an internally stored or generated image to a properly scaled image on the printed page. There are numerous ways of creating images to plot. For the plot in Figure 8 3 1 we just laid a piece of graph paper over a map, marked all the squares that were outside the United States, and punched cards with the coordinates of each point. For the plot on the cover, we used the SUBROUTINE given in Problem 20 at the end of this chapter to compute the locations and superimposed a number of boxes at each of those spots. Other ideas include generating lines and boxes with random orientations, generating random subpatterns and sprinkling them around, storing subpatterns (circles, squares, or whatever) and expanding or shrinking and shifting copies of them. It is also fairly simple to write subprograms which will make mirror images of already created subpatterns.

Your computer center may well have more elaborate devices for plotting which will make it possible to create more elaborate, more finely detailed drawings. For instance, we used a microfilm plotter to make the cover drawing for this book. Fancy gadgetry is no substitute for imagination, though.

The basic idea we will use to draw pictures on the line printer is **discretization,** which means representing something which is continuously, smoothly changing in terms of a small number of specific values. This is necessary because the printer can't print symbols just anywhere on the page; it is neatly organized to print in columns and rows. We must convert any other sort of image into one which has symbols in column and row positions. Conceptually we lay a grid over our image and let each grid square correspond to a character position on the printed page (i.e., some specific row and column). Then we place a symbol on the page for each grid which covers any dark part of the image. Figure 7 3 1 shows a continuous image and three discrete versions of it at different levels of discretization.

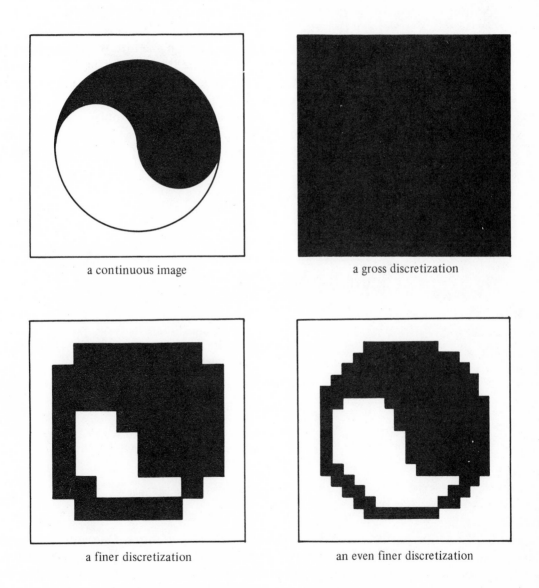

a continuous image   a gross discretization

a finer discretization   an even finer discretization

Figure 7 3 1   Discretization

Probably the most convenient way to deal with the print grid is to use a two-dimensional array. If the image grid has H rows and W columns, then we use a W-by-H two-dimensional INTEGER array to represent the printed page. To begin, we fill the array with blanks. Then we store nonblank symbols (e.g., asterisks) in array positions which correspond to dark spots in the image. The hard part is setting up this correspondence between the image plane and the two-dimensional array. What we need is a way to convert a pair of REAL coordinates (X, Y) in the image plane to a pair of INTEGER subscripts (I, J) in the ranges 1 to H and 1 to W respectively.

First we'll convert X to 1. If the left boundary of the image plane corresponds to X = XMIN and the right boundary to X = XMAX, then (X − XMIN)/(XMAX − XMIN) is a number between 0.0 and 1.0. Consequently, INT(W*(X − XMIN)/(XMAX − XMIN)) + 1 is an INTEGER between 1 and W. This is the conversion formula we wanted. Essentially it divides the image plane into W vertical strips of equal width and takes the value I when X is in the Ith strip. Similarly we convert Y to INT(H*(Y − YMIN)/(YMAX − YMIN)) + 1 where YMIN and YMAX correspond to the bottom and top boundaries of the image plane. Actually, if an image point lies exactly on the top or right boundary, we'll have problems, so we won't allow image points on the top or right boundary. This is easy to do—if there are any troublesome points, just shift the grid a tiny amount by increasing XMAX and YMAX.

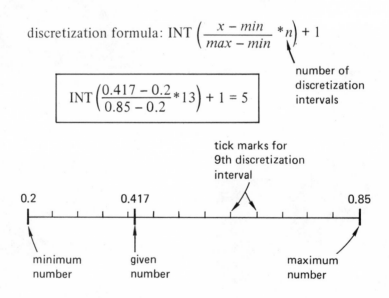

Figure 7 3 2   Discretizing a Given Number

We will write three SUBROUTINEs to help plot pictures. One will put blanks in the two-dimensional plotting array; another will put a symbol into the array at a point corresponding to a given point in the image plane; and the third will print the contents of the array. Thus, plotting a picture amounts to CALLing the blank-out routine, then CALLing the point-plotting routine once for each dark spot in the image, and finally, CALLing the printing routine. These SUBROUTINEs are written below. The only tricky part is the discretization, that is, converting X to I and Y to J, which we've already discussed.

```
          SUBROUTINE BLKOUT (GRAPH, W,H)
          INTEGER W,H, GRAPH(W,H)
COMMENT:  THIS SUBROUTINE FILLS THE PLOTTING ARRAY "GRAPH"
C              WITH BLANKS
          INTEGER I,J, BLANK
          DATA BLANK/1H /
          J=H
  100     I=1
  200       GRAPH(I,J) = BLANK
            I = I+1
            IF (I .LE. W)  GO TO 200
          J = J-1
          IF (J .GE. 1)  GO TO 100
          RETURN
          END


          SUBROUTINE PLOT (X,Y, XMIN,XMAX, YMIN,YMAX,
         +                 SYMBOL, GRAPH,W,H)
          REAL X,Y, XMIN,XMAX, YMIN,YMAX
          INTEGER SYMBOL, W,H,GRAPH(W,H)
COMMENT:  THIS SUBROUTINE PUTS "SYMBOL" INTO THE PLOTTING
C              ARRAY "GRAPH" AT A POINT CORRESPONDING TO
C              (X,Y) IN THE IMAGE PLANE
C              THE RANGE OF COORDINATES IS ASSUMED TO BE
C                 (XMIN TO XMAX , YMIN TO YMAX)
C              COORDINATES OUTSIDE THIS RANGE WILL NOT BE PLOTTED
          INTEGER I,J
C         DISCRETIZE X AND Y
          I = INT( ((X-XMIN)/(XMAX-XMIN)) * FLOAT(W) ) +1
          J = INT( ((Y-YMIN)/(YMAX-YMIN)) * FLOAT(H) ) +1
C         PUT (X,Y) INTO "GRAPH" (IF IN RANGE)
          IF (I .GE. 1   .AND.
         +    I .LE. W   .AND.
         +    J .GE. 1   .AND.
         +    J .LE. H          ) GRAPH(I,J) = SYMBOL
          RETURN
          END


          SUBROUTINE PRGRPH (GRAPH,W,H)
          INTEGER W,H, GRAPH(W,H)
COMMENT:  THIS SUBROUTINE PRINTS THE PLOTTING ARRAY "GRAPH"
          INTEGER I,J
          J = H
  100     WRITE(6,1000) (GRAPH(I,J), I=1,W)
            J = J-1
            IF (J .GE. 1)  GO TO 100
          RETURN
 1000     FORMAT(1X, 120A1)
          END
```

> J steps "backwards" here because high values of J correspond to points at the top of the figure, and the top of the figure must be sent to the printer first if we want things right-side up.

```
COMMENT:  PLOT THE EXPONENTIAL CURVE
        REAL X, EXP
        INTEGER G(25,15)
        CALL BLKOUT(G,25,15)
        X = -1.0
100     CALL PLOT (X,EXP(X), -1.0,1.0, 0.0,2.0, 1H*, G,25,15)
        X = X + 0.05
        IF (X .LE. 1.0)  GO TO 100
        CALL PRGRPH (G,25,15)
        STOP
        END
```

output

When plotting with the line printer, you will get better results if you keep in mind that the distance between characters on a line is less than the distance between lines. That is, the plotting device you are using has sharper resolution in the horizontal direction than in the vertical direction. The ratio of these resolutions is about five to three for most line printers. Therefore, in order to avoid distorting your picture, you should divide the image plane into about five parts in the horizontal direction for every three parts in the vertical direction. In other words, the ratio w/h of the width to the height of your plotting array should be about 5/3.

Some of the problems at the end of this chapter will give you a chance to use this plotting package we have developed. In addition, problem 7 18 illustrates a way to plot a single line at a time without using a big two-dimensional array. This technique saves memory at the expense of time.

EXERCISES 7 3

1 What would you have to change in SUBROUTINE PRGRPH to make it plot the curve x^2 instead of the exponential growth curve?

Section 7 4

FUNCTIONs

If you want to describe the warranty on your new car, you might say something like "it's good for 24,000 miles, two years, or when something goes wrong, *whichever comes first*." That is, the warranty period is equal to the minimum of the three time periods.

As you know, Fortran gives us a way of using a simple word like *minimum* to refer to more detailed computations right in the midst of an expression. This clarifies the program by eliminating clutter. The built-in FUNCTION MIN0 is made to order for the problem of computing the actual warranty period of the car we were talking about. If it took us 57 weeks to drive 24,000 miles, and it took 7 weeks before something went wrong with our car, then these Fortran statements tell us how long our warranty period was:

```
      INTEGER WARPER
      WARPER = MIN0(57, 2*52, 7)
      WRITE(6,3000) WARPER
 3000 FORMAT(' WARRANTY LASTED', I4, ' WEEKS')
      STOP
      END
```

output

```
WARRANTY LASTED    7 WEEKS
```

We are not limited to using just the built-in FUNCTIONs—we can define our own, suiting them to our exact needs. But before plunging into the details of defining our own, let's make clear where and how references to FUNCTIONs are used.

When we write MIN0(57, 2*52, 7) or SQRT(2.0) or ABS(-3.14159), we are referring to the FUNCTIONs MIN0, SQRT, and ABS, but more importantly, we are specifying numbers. For example, MIN0(57, 2*52, 7) may be viewed as specifying the INTEGER value 7. Since FUNCTION references are values, you may use a FUNCTION reference anywhere that an expression may appear. Thus,

```
  WARPER = MIN0(57, 2*52, 7)
```

contains a legitimate FUNCTION reference—it makes sense to assign the value of the FUNCTION reference to memory cell WARPER. However,

```
   MIN0(57, 2*52, 7) = 7
```

is not legitimate—MIN0(57, 2*52, 7) is not a memory cell, it is a value.

```
FUNCTION-value
(FUNCTION reference)

form
    f(e₁, e₂, . . . , eₙ)
    f is the name of a FUNCTION taking n arguments (n ⩾ 1)
    e is a constant, expression, memory cell, array, FUNCTION
    name, or SUBROUTINE name (special arrangements are
    needed for the last two—see EXTERNAL in the index)

meaning
    A FUNCTION-value is a single value of numeric or LOGICAL
    type and may be used in any arithmetic or LOGICAL expres-
    sion where a constant of that data type may be used

examples
    Z = SQRT(173.7*R)
    X = F(Y**2)
    J = LOCSM(A,N) +12
```

Notice that since a FUNCTION-value may be used in any expression, it is possible for a FUNCTION-value to appear as one of the arguments of another FUNCTION-value. Thus,

```
WARPER = MINO (MINO(24,57), MINO(104,48), 7)
```

is a legal form which, like the examples above, assigns the value 7 to memory cell WARPER.

In Fortran, FUNCTION-values may be of any numeric type or they may be LOGICAL, but they can produce only one value. If you want a subprogram which returns an array of values, use a SUBROUTINE.

Now let's go through an example which shows why and how we might use a FUNCTION that's not built-in. Suppose you are involved in writing a program which needs to compute the sales tax of a given dollar amount. Sales tax computations aren't difficult, and you could put the statements for computing the sales tax right in the program wherever you needed them. But since there are several statements involved in the sales tax computation, it would be more convenient to have a FUNCTION designed to do it and to use the FUNCTION when the sales tax is needed.

The following program computes the price of two automobiles, including tax and license.

```
      REAL TAX
      REAL AUTO1, PAINT, TIRES, LIC1, PRICE1
      REAL AUTO2, TRIM, LIC2, PRICE2
      READ(5,1000) AUTO1, PAINT, TIRES, LIC1
 1000 FORMAT(4F10.0)
      PRICE1 = AUTO1 + PAINT + TIRES +
     +         TAX(AUTO1+PAINT+TIRES) + LIC1
      READ(5,1000) AUTO2, TRIM, LIC2
      PRICE2 = AUTO2 + TRIM + TAX(AUTO2+TRIM) + LIC2
      WRITE(6,2000) PRICE1, PRICE2
 2000 FORMAT(' PRICE OF FIRST AUTO IS', F8.2/
     +        ' PRICE OF SECOND IS', F8.2)
      STOP
      END
```

data

```
7685.65    287.00     259.46     109.00
5400.27     56.95      86.50
```

output

```
PRICE OF FIRST AUTO IS 8835.04
PRICE OF SECOND IS 5871.15
```

As you can see, the FUNCTION TAX is used at two points in the program to compute the sales tax on the taxable portions of the total price (the license fee is not taxable). This is a typical situation in which we write FUNCTIONs. The important point is that the same computation must be performed at several points, but on different input values. Thus FUNCTIONs, like SUBROUTINEs, can be used to break the program into manageable pieces. FUNCTIONs and SUBROUTINEs are similar in several ways. Both are independent program units, external to all other modules of the program. In addition, arguments are transmitted from a FUNCTION reference to a FUNCTION in the same way that arguments are transmitted to a SUBROUTINE. The major difference between FUNCTIONs and SUBROUTINEs is the way in which values are transmitted back to the calling program. A SUBROUTINE transmits values back to the calling program by way of output arguments, but a FUNCTION returns its value via the FUNCTION name. When the FUNCTION-value has been computed and control returns to the calling program, it is as if the FUNCTION reference were replaced by the value the FUNCTION computed. A RETURN statement in a FUNCTION causes the controller to return to the point where the FUNCTION was referenced. Let's look at the following FUNCTION to see how this comes about.

```
          REAL FUNCTION TAX(AMT)
          REAL AMT
          INTEGER CENTS, TBL(7), T
          DATA TBL(1),TBL(2),TBL(3),TBL(4),TBL(5),TBL(6),TBL(7)
        +     / 10  , 22  , 39  , 56  , 73  , 90  , 108 /

    C     CONVERT AMT TO CENTS (+0.5 FORCES PROPER ROUND OFF)
          CENTS = INT(100.00*AMT + 0.5)
          IF (CENTS .LE. 108)  GO TO 200
    C        COMPUTE 6 PER CENT SALES TAX
             TAX = AINT(6.0*AMT+0.5)/100.00
             RETURN
    C        USE TAX TABLE FOR AMOUNTS UNDER $1.08
    200      T=0
    210      IF (CENTS .LE. TBL(T+1))  GO TO 250
                T = T+1
                GO TO 210
    250      TAX = FLOAT(T)/100.00
             RETURN
          END
```

As you can see in the definition of the FUNCTION TAX, before returning, we assign the total tax to the name of the FUNCTION, as if the FUNCTION's name were a memory cell. This is how the FUNCTION gets its value. The value is then transmitted back to the statement that references the FUNCTION. Therefore, throughout the body of the FUNCTION, you may use the name of a FUNCTION as if it were a memory cell. The value of that "memory cell" when a RETURN is encountered becomes the value of the FUNCTION. Except for this, FUNCTIONs are written in the same way as SUBROUTINEs: header statement, parameter declarations, body, and END. The primary difference between them is the contexts in which they are used. A FUNCTION returns *one* value; a SUBROUTINE may return *any number* of values (through its arguments). A FUNCTION reference looks like prefix operator notation; a SUBROUTINE CALL looks more like a transfer of control. Choosing which to use is a matter of taste and convenience.

FUNCTION statement

forms

    type FUNCTION $f(p_1, p_2, \ldots, p_n)$
        FUNCTION $f(p_1, p_2, \ldots, p_n)$

    type is any data type

    f (the FUNCTION name) is an identifier

    $p_1, p_2, \ldots, p_n$ (the parameter names) are identifiers

    The body of the FUNCTION, that is, the statements between the FUNCTION statement and the corresponding END, must assign a value to the name f and must contain at least one RETURN statement. There must be at least one parameter in the parentheses.

    If *type* is omitted, implicit typing takes over.

meaning

    The value the FUNCTION computes when invoked is the value of its name when a RETURN statement is executed.

examples

```
REAL FUNCTION F(X)
INTEGER FUNCTION LOCSM(A,N)
FUNCTION G(X,Y,Z)
```

EXERCISES 7 4

1 What sequence of values will the REAL memory cell A be given by the following statements using built-in FUNCTIONs?

```
A = ABS(1.0 - 2.0)
A = ABS(A)*4.0
A = SQRT(ABS(2.0-A)*2.0)/2.0
```

2 What is wrong with the following FUNCTION definition?

```
REAL FUNCTION R
R = 2.0
RETURN
END
```

3 What value does FUNCTION TAX return if its argument is 3.49? How about 1.03?

4 What are the values of INT(5.0/3.0 + 0.5), INT(4.0/3.0 + 0.5), and AINT(5.0/2.0 + 0.5)? Do you see why we used similar expressions in the FUNCTION TAX?

5 Write a FUNCTION which duplicates the effect of the built-in FUNCTION ABS.

Section 7 5

Sorting—Using Variable Length Arrays

The managers of a marketing and sales research firm have asked us to help them out. Many customers come to their staff with lists of sales figures (usually either monthly or weekly) tabulated over several years. Normally the research firm begins by preparing a year-by-year listing of this data. For each year the sales figures are listed two ways. One is simply a month-by-month (or week-by-week) tabulation of the monthly (or weekly) sales amounts. The other lists the amounts in decreasing order, from the best sales period to the worst. In this way the research firm gets a picture of seasonal effects on the customer's sales.

The research firm's business has grown in recent years and the staff can no longer handle all of it. Consequently they have decided to turn the tabulations over to a computer. The sales figures will be punched on cards, with one group of cards for each year. The first card of each yearly group will have the year and the sales period type (MONTHLY or WEEKLY) punched on it. The remaining cards of the group will have the sales figures (in whole dollars) punched on them. The firm wants us to write a program to print the tabulations in order to save the staff this tedious job.

If you think about it, you will see that this is a relatively simple programming task except for the business of listing the sales figures in order of decreasing sales period. Up to that point it is simply a matter of READing values and printing them. No rearrangement is necessary because they come in chronological order. But in order to print the sales figures in order of decreasing sales periods, we need to rearrange the data. One way to do that is to put the sales figures into an array and, when necessary, to change the order in which they are stored. We will want the output from the program to look something like the sample below.

```
                     SALES TABULATION
              1976
      MONTHLY SALES FIGURES

            CHRONOLOGICAL                      BEST TO WORST
            MONTH        SALES                 MONTH        SALES
              1          6472                    12         10428
              2          4103                    10          9342
              3          2001                    11          8497
              4          2422                     1          6472
              5          3501                     6          5402
              6          5402                     7          5117
```

7	5117	8	4322
8	4322	2	4103
9	2173	5.	3501
10	9342	4	2422
11	8497	9	2173
12	10428	3	2001

SALES TABULATION

1976
WEEKLY SALES FIGURES

CHRONOLOGICAL		BEST TO WORST	
WEEK	SALES	WEEK	SALES
1	1647	49	2544
2	1500	52	2544
3	1399	45	2422
4	1822	41	2411
5	1021	50	2144
6	1059	43	2134
7	987	44	2111
8	855	51	2066
9	502	48	2032
10	408	46	2031
11	201	40	2011
12	422	42	1955
13	385	47	1902
14	638	4	1822
15	655	1	1647
16	588	25	1621
17	574	24	1534
18	788	2	1500
19	698	23	1422
20	755	39	1422
21	802	3	1399
22	621	29	1354
23	1422	26	1308
24	1534	28	1307
25	1621	30	1238
26	1308	27	1205
27	1205	31	1104
28	1307	6	1059
29	1354	5	1021
30	1238	32	987
31	1104	7	987
32	987	33	855
33	855	8	855
34	445	21	802
35	655	18	788
36	521	20	755
37	411	19	698
38	322	15	655
39	1422	35	655
40	2011	14	638
41	2411	22	621
42	1955	16	588
43	2134	17	574
44	2111	36	521
45	2422	9	502
46	2031	34	445
47	1902	12	422
48	2032	37	411
49	2544	10	408
50	2144	13	385
51	2066	38	322
52	2544	11	201

Because the line printer can't back up to print the columns under BEST TO WORST SALES MONTH, we'll have to store the sales information twice, once in chronological order and once in order of decreasing sales. When we arrange the sales figures in decreasing order, we must also arrange the corresponding month numbers to be printed beside the sales figures. Thus, in addition to the array

---

plan for sales report program

1 determine year of report
2 determine period of report (weekly or monthly)
3 process weekly or monthly data (sort and print)
4 repeat

---

storing the sales figures in chronological order, we need a pair of arrays to store the month numbers and sales figures in decreasing order. We'll use a SUBROU-TINE to arrange the data for the columns on the right. We'll call it SORT since it sorts data into a certain order. It will have three parameters: (1) the array containing the sales figures, (2) the array containing the corresponding month numbers, and (3) the number of elements in the arrays (12 or 52). The first two are both input and output parameters (when SORT is CALLed, the first two arguments will contain information in some order and SORT will rearrange the information) and the third is an input parameter.

Study the program below. We'll discuss the SORT subprogram once you understand its purpose.

```
COMMENT:  THIS PROGRAM MAKES SALES REPORT SUMMARIES
          INTEGER YEAR,PERIOD,MONTH
          DATA MONTH/1HM/
C         GET YEAR AND SALES PERIOD FROM FIRST CARD OF GROUP
   100    READ(5,1000) YEAR,PERIOD
   1000 FORMAT(I4,A1)
          IF ( YEAR .EQ. 0 )  STOP
          WRITE(6,1001)
   1001    FORMAT('1',21X, 'SALES TABULATION')
          WRITE(6,1002) YEAR
   1002    FORMAT(1X,I12)
C         CALL APPROPRIATE SUBROUTINE TO HANDLE
C         WEEKLY OR MONTHLY SALES PERIOD.
          IF ( PERIOD' .EQ. MONTH )  GO TO 200
            CALL WEEKLY
            GO TO 100
   200      CALL MNTHLY
            GO TO 100
COMMENT:  THE SUBROUTINES "WEEKLY" AND "MNTHLY" NEED NO
C         INFORMATION FROM THIS PROGRAM. THEREFORE, THEY'VE
C         NO ARGUMENTS.  THEY GET THEIR INFORMATION
C         FROM DATA CARDS AND PRINT THEIR RESULTS.
C         HENCE,  THEY DON'T NEED TO COMMUNICATE VALUES TO
C         OR FROM THE CALLING PROGRAM.
          END
```

```
      SUBROUTINE MNTHLY
      INTEGER SALES(12), MN(12), MNSALE(12), I
      WRITE(6,1000)
 1000 FORMAT(' MONTHLY SALES FIGURES'/
     +          '0',11X,'CHRONOLOGICAL',25X,'BEST TO WORST'/
     +          10X,'MONTH',9X,'SALES',18X,'MONTH',9X,'SALES')
      READ(5,1001) SALES
 1001 FORMAT(10I6)
C     SAVE SALES FIGURES AND MAKE A LIST OF MONTH NUMBERS
      I = 1
  100 MN(I) = I
      MNSALE(I) = SALES(I)
      I = I + 1
      IF ( I .LE. 12 )  GO TO 100
C     SORT INFORMATION ACCORDING TO DECREASING SALES.
      CALL SORT (MNSALE, MN, 12)
C     PRINT REPORT
      I = 1
  200 WRITE(6,2000) I,SALES(I),MN(I),MNSALE(I)
 2000 FORMAT(1X,I12,I16,18X,I3,I16)
      I = I + 1
      IF ( I .LE. 12 )  GO TO 200
      RETURN
      END


      SUBROUTINE WEEKLY
      INTEGER SALES(52), WK(52), WKSALE(52), I
      WRITE(6,1000)
 1000 FORMAT( ' WEEKLY SALES FIGURES'/
     +          '0',11X,'CHRONOLOGICAL',25X,'BEST TO WORST'/
     +          10X,'WEEK ',9X,'SALES',18X,'WEEK ',9X,'SALES')
      READ(5,1001) SALES
 1001 FORMAT(10I6)
C     SAVE SALES FIGURES AND MAKE A LIST OF  WEEK NUMBERS
      I = 1
  100 WK(I) = I
      WKSALE(I) = SALES(I)
      I = I + 1
      IF ( I .LE. 52 )  GO TO 100
C     SORT INFORMATION ACCORDING TO DECREASING SALES.
      CALL SORT (WKSALE, WK, 52)
C     PRINT REPORT
      I = 1
  200 WRITE(6,2000) I,SALES(I),WK(I),WKSALE(I)
 2000 FORMAT(1X,I12,I16,18X,I3,I16)
      I = I + 1
      IF ( I .LE. 52 )  GO TO 200
      RETURN
      END
```

Both of the above SUBROUTINEs use the SORT subprogram, but the arguments in the two CALLs are different. Different arrays of different lengths are in the arguments.

Now that the program is written, we must write the SUBROUTINE SORT. The problem of sorting numbers into decreasing order has been studied by many people and there are lots of solutions. Some are better than others. The method we describe here has at least two virtues: it is easy to understand, and it clearly demonstrates the uses of subprograms. We'll have more to say about other methods in Chapter 12.

Briefly, the idea is to locate the largest of the numbers and put it on top of the list and then to repeat the same process on the remaining unsorted numbers (from the second to the last). We keep repeating the process on shorter and shorter lists

until finally there are none left. The only tricky part of the process arises from the way in which the numbers are stored, which is in an array. When we find the largest number and want to put it on top of the unsorted portion of the list, we must find something to do with the number currently in the top position. It must go into the unsorted portion of the list, of course, and the natural place to put it is in the position vacated by the largest number. In other words, we interchange the largest number with the number on top of the unsorted portion of the list. Figure 7 5 1 illustrates the method.

The SUBROUTINE below uses a FUNCTION to locate the largest number in the unsorted part of the array and a SUBROUTINE to interchange the largest with the top number. You have already seen techniques for locating the largest number several times, so the FUNCTION should be easy to follow. You haven't seen a technique for switching the values in a pair of memory cells, however, and we'll get to that shortly.

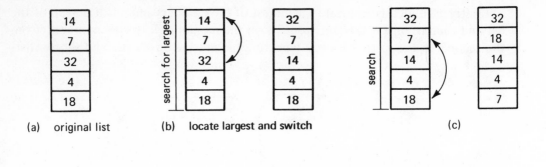

(a) original list   (b) locate largest and switch   (c)

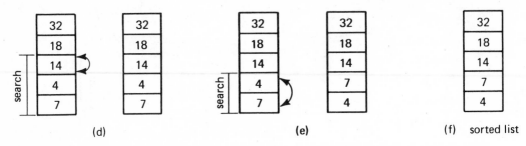

(d)   (e)   (f) sorted list

Figure 7 5 1   Sorting a List of Numbers

You will notice something unusual in the parameter declarations of the following subprograms. The array declarations have subprogram parameters for length declarators. This clearly illustrates the difference between parameter declarations and true declarations. Since parameter declarations describe already existing objects, the compiler is not required to reserve space for them. Consequently, the length of a subprogram parameter array may be specified by one of the variables in the parameter list. (If the array has more than one subscript, then the range of values for any one or all of the subscripts may be specified by variables in the

---

length declarator for parameter arrays

form

   $t\ p(list)$

   t is a Fortran data type
   p (a parameter array name) is an identifier
   list is a list of INTEGER parameter names and/or unsigned INTEGER constants

meaning

   The array p, which is a parameter in the subprogram being defined, will have the dimensions specified in *list* and the type t.

examples

```
SUBROUTINE VARLEN (A, B, N, C, D, M)
INTEGER N, M, A(N)
REAL B(4,N), C(M, N)
```

parameter list.) It is important to realize that this does not mean that any existing array actually has a varying length. All actual array declarations must have a constant length declarator; only parameter array declarations may have variables for length declarators. Furthermore, the value(s) of the parameter(s) declaring the dimension(s) of the array should not be changed by the subprogram because this would imply a change in the length of the actual array given in the argument list in the subprogram reference. No such change is possible.

VERBAL DESCRIPTION

Let TOP be 1.

Start loop:

locate largest element between TOP and end

interchange largest element with TOP element

increase TOP by 1

repeat unless TOP ⩾ length of array

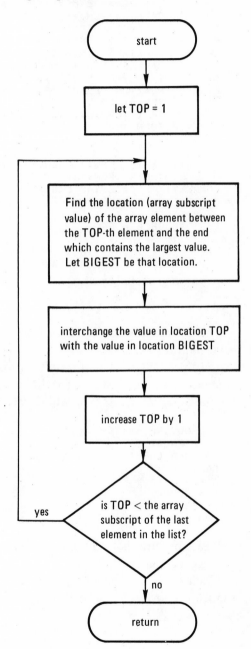

Figure 7 5 2   A Sorting Algorithm

```
            SUBROUTINE SORT (KEYS, OTHER, N)
            INTEGER N, KEYS(N), OTHER(N)
COMMENT:    ARRANGE THE VALUES IN "KEYS" AND "OTHER" INTO
C               DECREASING ORDER ACCORDING TO "KEYS"
            INTEGER TOP, BIGEST
            INTEGER LOCBIG
            TOP = 1
C       FIND LARGEST NUMBER IN "KEY"' BETWEEN "TOP" AND "N".
  100       BIGEST = LOCBIG(KEYS, TOP, N)
C           INTERCHANGE KEYS(TOP) WITH KEYS(BIGEST)
            CALL SWITCH (KEYS(TOP), KEYS(BIGEST))
C           TO AVOID MESSING UP THE CORRESPONDENCE BETWEEN
C           VALUES IN "KEYS" AND VALUES IN "OTHER", MAKE AN
C           IDENTICAL INTERCHANGE IN "OTHER".
            CALL SWITCH (OTHER(TOP), OTHER(BIGEST))
C           INCREMENT "TOP" TO REFLECT NEW TOP OF UNSORTED
C           PORTION OF ARRAYS.
            TOP = TOP + 1
            IF ( TOP .LT. N ) GO TO 100
            RETURN
            END

            INTEGER FUNCTION LOCBIG (A, FROM, TO)
            INTEGER FROM, TO, A(TO)
COMMENT:    LOCATE THE LARGEST NUMBER IN "A" BETWEEN A(FROM)
C               AND THE END OF THE ARRAY.
            INTEGER I
            LOCBIG = FROM
            I = FROM + 1
  100       IF ( I .GT. TO ) RETURN
            IF ( A(I) .GT. A(LOCBIG) ) LOCBIG = I
            I = I + 1
            GO TO 100
            END
```

The subprogram SWITCH, which interchanges the values in a pair of memory cells, requires explanation. It has three steps: (1) the value in the first cell is copied into a third cell so that it won't be lost in step 2, (2) the value of the second cell is copied into the first, and (3) the value in the third cell is copied into the second. If you think about it, you will realize that a two-step process simply won't work.

```
SUBROUTINE SWITCH (A,B)
INTEGER A, B
INTEGER COPYA
COPYA = A
A = B
B = COPYA
RETURN
END
```

Please be sure that you understand how this sorting method works by following through a small example. We'll want to use it again.

When our completed program was run using the data cards below, it produced the sales report you saw at the beginning of this chapter.

```
1976M
  6472  4103  2001  2422  3501  5402  5117  4322  2173  9342
  8497 10428
1976W
  1647  1500  1399  1822  1021  1059   987   855   502   408
   201   422   385   638   655   588   574   788   698   755
   802   621  1422  1534  1621  1308  1205  1307  1354  1238
  1104   987   855   445   655   521   411   322  1422  2011
  2411  1955  2134  2111  2422  2031  1902  2032  2544  2144
  2066  2544
0000
```

EXERCISES 7 5

1 Which of the following parameter declarations are legal and which aren't? If not, explain why not.

```
SUBROUTINE ONE(A, N,M)
INTEGER M,N, A(N,M)

SUBROUTINE TWO(A,N)
INTEGER N, A(10,N,4)

SUBROUTINE THREE(A,N)
INTEGER N, A(LENGTH)
```

2 What is wrong with the following SUBROUTINE?

```
SUBROUTINE WRONG(A,N)
INTEGER N, A(N)
N = N+1
A(N) = 0
RETURN
END
```

3 What would need to be changed in order to make our SUBROUTINE SORT arrange the numbers into increasing (rather than decreasing) order?

4 What would happen to INTEGER memory cells ONE and TWO if the statement CALL BADSWT (ONE, TWO) were executed?

```
SUBROUTINE BADSWT(A,B)
INTEGER A,B
A = B
B = A
RETURN
END
```

5 What is wrong with the statement CALL BADSWT (1, 2), given the above subprogram?

Section 7 6*

Random Numbers

There are many situations in computing in which we need to have access to random numbers. For this reason, most computer centers provide a subprogram which generates a random number each time it is called. Actually, the numbers it generates are usually called "pseudorandom" because they are produced by a deterministic program; every time you start the program over, you get the same sequence of pseudorandom numbers. However, the numbers pass a large number of statistical tests for randomness so that we can say that they act very much like true random numbers, whatever those are.

Can you know if an event is really random?

The pseudorandom numbers are usually uniformly distributed REAL numbers in the range from 0.0 to 1.0 (endpoints *not* included). In other words, the likelihood that a number will fall in a particular subinterval is the same as the likelihood that it will fall in any other subinterval of the same length. (A descriptive, albeit imprecise, way of saying this is: "All numbers between 0.0 and 1.0 are equally likely.") They are generated using the multiplicative congruential method—each new number is obtained from the last by multiplying it by a fixed multiplier and taking the last few digits of the product as the new random number.

It isn't our purpose to dwell on random numbers or random number generators here. We simply want to make sure that you have access to a random number generator since we will use random numbers in later chapters. If you don't have one easily available, you can copy SUBROUTINE RANDOM, which appears below. It has one parameter, an output parameter. When you CALL it, it will store a pseudorandom, uniformly distributed, REAL number in the memory cell you specify as its argument. This number will be greater than 0.0 and less than 1.0.

```
      SUBROUTINE RANDOM (X)
      REAL X
COMMENT:  THIS SUBROUTINE PRODUCES A SAMPLE "X" FROM A
C         UNIFORM DISTRIBUTION  ACROSS THE INTERVAL (0.0,1.0)
C  WARNING!  IF YOU INTEND TO GENERATE MORE THAN A THOUSAND
C            OR TWO RANDOM NUMBERS, USE SOME OTHER ROUTINE
C            TO GENERATE THEM.
C         FOR INFORMATION ON HOW WELL THIS TYPE OF RANDOM
C         NUMBER GENERATOR WORKS, SEE *THE ART OF COMPUTER
C         PROGRAMMING*, VOL. 2, D. KNUTH, ADDISON-WESLEY.
      INTEGER MOD
      REAL FLOAT
      INTEGER A, MULT, BASE
      DATA    A/19727/, MULT/25211/, BASE/32768/
      A = MOD(MULT*A, 32768)
      X = FLOAT(A) / FLOAT(BASE)
      RETURN
      END
```

Often it is very useful to have a FUNCTION which generates a random INTEGER between 1 and some given upper limit, each possible value having the same likelihood. The FUNCTION CHOOSE does this. It uses our SUBROUTINE RANDOM, but it could just as well use any random number generator with similar properties.

```
       INTEGER FUNCTION CHOOSE (N)
       INTEGER N
COMMENT:  THIS FUNCTION CHOOSES, AT RANDOM, ONE OF THE
C            INTEGERS 1, 2, 3, ...., N .
       REAL U
       CALL RANDOM(U)
       CHOOSE = INT(FLOAT(N)*U) +1
       RETURN
       END
```

PROBLEMS 7

1 Write a program which READs in 80 characters from a card, stores them in an array, prints them out, then reverses the array by making repeated CALLs to SUBROUTINE SWITCH (see Section 7 5), and finally prints out the reversed array.

2 Convert FUNCTION TAX (Section 7 4) so that it uses the sales tax rate from your state. Use it to print a table listing the tax on purchases of 1¢, 2¢, . . ., 200¢.

3 Write and test a SUBROUTINE that accepts an array of people's nicknames and that returns the name which comes first alphabetically and the one which comes last. Don't forget to set up a parameter to input the number of names.

4 Do a problem from Chapter 4 or 6, perhaps one you have already done, making use of FUNCTIONs and SUBROUTINEs and any other technique you can think of to make your program more clearly organized.

5 Write a LOGICAL FUNCTION called INHERE that has three parameters: (a) an array of people's names, (b) the number of names in the array, and (c) a variable which stores the name of a customer. INHERE should return the value .TRUE. if the customer's name appears in the array, and .FALSE. otherwise. Assume each name is short enough to fit in one memory cell.

6 Write a FUNCTION called LOG which has two parameters, BASE and X, and returns the largest INTEGER, LOG, such that BASE**LOG does not exceed X. For example, L = LOG(2,10) would result in L having the value 3, since $2^3 \leqslant 10$ but $2^4 > 10$.

7 Two cars are traveling down the highway at 55 mph, with the second car 70 feet behind the first. The first car suddenly slams on its brakes. Will the second car be able to stop in time to avoid ramming into the first? It will if its driver is able to slam on the brakes before the car has traveled 70 feet (right?). The time it takes the second driver to apply his brakes after seeing the brake lights on the car ahead is called his **reaction time**.

People's reaction times depend on a number of factors, such as how tired they are, how distracted they are, how drunk they are, etc., so it seems reasonable to model the reaction time as if it were a random variable.

Assume the driver's reaction time is a (uniform) random number between 0.5 and 1.0 second, i.e., is computed as

$$\text{react. time} = (1.0 + V)/2.0$$

where V comes from CALL RANDOM(V). Given the reaction time, you can compute the distance the second car travels and from that, tell whether or not there was a wreck.

Write a program that simulates 100 emergency braking situations and outputs the 100 different distances, the number of wrecks and the number of "close calls." If the second car stops less than one foot from the first but doesn't hit it, that's a close call.

8 Write and test a SUBROUTINE CONVERT whose input is an INTEGER and whose output is an array of INTEGERs that represent the input number in binary notation.

A number's binary representation can be computed by using the following algorithm, which builds up the binary representation *from right to left*.

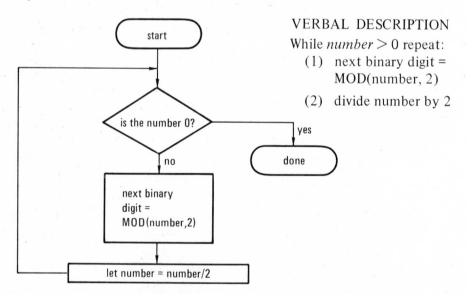

VERBAL DESCRIPTION
While *number* > 0 repeat:
  (1) next binary digit = MOD(number, 2)
  (2) divide number by 2

Computing the Binary Representation

9 Rewrite SUBROUTINE CONVERT so that it has an additional input parameter, a base to which to convert the input INTEGER's representation.

10 If the numbers produced by SUBROUTINE RANDOM (Section 7 6) were actually uniformly distributed between 0.0 and 1.0, and if we take a large sample, the average value should be 1/2 and the sample standard deviation should be $\sqrt{(1/12)}$. Test it to see how close it comes.

Write a FUNCTION MEAN that accepts two inputs, one an array of REAL values and one an INTEGER that specifies how many values are in the array. MEAN should return a REAL value that is the sample mean of the values in the input array.

$$\text{mean} = \frac{\sum\limits_{i=1}^{n} x_i}{n}$$

Write a FUNCTION STDDEV that returns the standard deviation of the values in the array it receives.

$$\text{sample std. dev.} = \sqrt{\frac{n \sum\limits_{i=1}^{n} x_i^2 - \left(\sum\limits_{i=1}^{n} x_i\right)^2}{n(n-1)}}$$

Use the two FUNCTIONs to test RANDOM. Generate 100 RANDOM numbers, and print out their mean and standard deviation. Then generate 200 RANDOM numbers and output their mean and standard deviation. Then 300, 400, . . ., 1000. How close are the means and standard deviations to $1/2$ and $\sqrt{(1/12)}$?

11 The 100 members of the Alpha Nu fraternity need a secret handshake by which they can identify each other. One night in a dream the spirit of Alpha Nu reveals a keen secret handshake to Joe College, ace football player, BMOC, and loyal Alpha Nudist. As Alpha Nudists go from class to class on campus, they meet each other at random. Whenever two randomly selected Alpha Nudists meet, if one knows the handshake, he teaches it to the other.

After each 10 random meetings, count how many Alpha Nudists know the secret handshake and print that count. Stop after 600 random meetings have occurred. Your output should resemble a histogram.

```
  10X
  20XXXX
  40XXXXXXXXXXXXXXXX
   •    •
   •    •
   •    •
 580XXXXXXXXXXXXXXXXXXXXXXXXXXXXXXXXXXXXXXXXXXXXXXXXXXXXXXXX
 590XXXXXXXXXXXXXXXXXXXXXXXXXXXXXXXXXXXXXXXXXXXXXXXXXXXXXXXX
 600XXXXXXXXXXXXXXXXXXXXXXXXXXXXXXXXXXXXXXXXXXXXXXXXXXXXXXXXXXXXX
```

Note: An implied do list of the same form as the one at the end of Section 6 6 is useful in printing the individual lines of this output. (We thank Gary Sager for this problem.)

12 If you are faimiliar with matrices and use them, here's a problem for you. Write three SUBROUTINEs that manipulate matrices.

a SUBROUTINE SCMLT(A,M,N,C)

A is an M X N matrix (two-dimensional array) of REAL values and C is a REAL. The SUBROUTINE multiplies matrix A by scalar C and returns the new value of A.

b SUBROUTINE ADD(A,B,C,M,N)

A and B are two M X N matrices which SUBROUTINE ADD adds together. Their sum is returned in the M X N matrix C.

c SUBROUTINE MULT (A,MA,NA,B,MB,NB,C,MC,NC)

multiplication of the MA X NA matrix A and the MB X NB matrix B, returning the product as the MC X NC matrix C. If A and B are not compatible (i.e., if NA ≠ MB) issue an error message.

Test your routines by verifying some equality like this

$$2 \times \begin{bmatrix} 1 & 0 & 0 \\ 0 & 1 & 0 \\ 0 & 0 & 1 \end{bmatrix} + 14 \times \begin{bmatrix} 1 & 0 & 0 \\ 0 & 1 & 0 \\ 0 & 0 & 1 \end{bmatrix} = \begin{bmatrix} 4 & 0 & 0 \\ 0 & 4 & 0 \\ 0 & 0 & 4 \end{bmatrix} \times \begin{bmatrix} 2 & 0 & 0 \\ 0 & 2 & 0 \\ 0 & 0 & 2 \end{bmatrix} \times \begin{bmatrix} 2 & 0 & 0 \\ 0 & 2 & 0 \\ 0 & 0 & 2 \end{bmatrix}$$

> NOTE: Problems 13 through 22 use the plotting ideas of Section 7 3.

13 Improve the output from the motorcyclist problem (problem 4 19 or 4 20) by plotting the cyclist's trajectory instead of just printing a numerical summary of his flight. If you feel ambitious, include in the picture a cross section of the canyon and a puff of dust where he lands. You could plot different symbols for the canyon boundary (perhaps +), trajectory (perhaps −), and dust (perhaps *).

14 Use the line printer to make a graph of the function $\sin(x)/x$ from $x = 0$ to $x = 10$, stepping in increments of 0.1. (Note: $\sin(x)/x = 1$ when $x = 0$, and all values of $\sin(x)/x$ are in the range −1 to 1.)

In plotting graphs like this, it is easier to orient the x-axis down the page rather than across. That way, the program can compute one value of the function, plot it on the current line across the page, and then step to the next value and plot it on the next line, etc.

The only tricky part might be translating values of the function (which lie between −1 and 1) to positions on the line to be printed (which typically run from column 1 to column 132). To figure out how far across the line to plot a particular value of $\sin(x)/x$, use the discretization formula

```
I = INT(100.0*(Y+1.0)/2.0) +1
```

where Y is a value of $\sin(x)/x$. Then I will be in the range 1 to 101 and you can plot Y with statements like

```
      INTEGER BLANK,STAR
      DATA BLANK/1H /, STAR/1H*/
         .
         .
         .
      WRITE(6,1000) (BLANK,K=1,I), STAR
 1000 FORMAT(1X,102A1)
```

which put an asterisk in the appropriate position across the page.

15 In problem 14 the discretization formula gives the value I if Y is in the range $-1.00 + (I - 1)*0.01$ to $-1.00 + I*0.01$. Use this fact to draw and label the axes of your plot.

16 Draw graphs of other functions using the techniques of problems 14 and 15. The discretization formula will continue to divide the range of values of the function into 100 equally spaced parts if you change the $(Y + 1.0)/2.0$ expression to $(Y - YMIN)/(YMAX - YMIN)$, where YMIN and YMAX are the smallest and largest values your function can take on.

   Note that you can shrink the plot of your function by making YMAX larger than the maximum value of the function and YMIN smaller than the minimum.

17 Use the techniques of problems 14, 15, and 16 above to plot the guitar signals described in problem 4 17. Since you no longer have to plot the curve by hand, you may want to increase the number of points that are plotted per cycle in order to get a more detailed picture of the wave forms.

18 Rewrite the SUBROUTINE PLOT so that instead of plotting only one point per CALL, its input contains all the points to be plotted in the picture in a pair of coordinate arrays. Plot the points line by line rather than all at once. In other words, let your plotting array be one-dimensional to represent one line. Start at the top of the image, and look through all the points to be plotted. Whenever you find one to be plotted, put a symbol at the corresponding horizontal position in your array. When you've cycled through all the coordinates to find those on the top line, print the line, and repeat the process for the next line down, and so on.

19 Design some SUBROUTINEs to use in conjunction with SUBROUTINEs PLOT, BLKOUT, and PRGRAPH, and use them to produce an interesting series of patterns. Here are some ideas:

   a SUBROUTINE NEGATE takes an array GRAPH as argument and turns every nonblank square into a blank and every blank into an asterisk.

   b SUBROUTINE INVERT takes a picture stored in GRAPH and turns it over (rotates 180°).

   c SUBROUTINE SKLTN takes a picture and turns every square which is completely surrounded by dark squares into a blank.

d SUBROUTINE MOVE takes a picture and two INTEGERs DX and DY and shifts everything in the picture along the *x*-axis DX squares (to the left for negative DX and to the right for positive DX); it also shifts the picture DY squares along the *y*-axis.

20 Spiral of primes

Compute all the prime numbers less than 59^2 (see problem 6 19 for an algorithm to use). Then plot the primes in the following way. Number a 59×59 grid of squares from the center out in a spiral. To figure the appropriate (I, J) subscript in the 59×59 array given a number *n*, use SUBROUTINE COORD below.

```
      SUBROUTINE COORD(N, I,J)
      INTEGER N, I,J
COMMENT:  THIS ROUTINE COMPUTES THE ARRAY SUBSCRIPT (I,J)
C            CORRESPONDING TO THE NUMBER N IN THE SPIRAL
C            NUMBERING OF THE LATTICE POINTS IN THE PLANE
      INTEGER SQRTN, R, CNR, RES, RESRES, QUAD, SR
      INTEGER RSGN(4), DSGN(4), ISIGN, OFFSET
      DATA RSGN(1),RSGN(2),RSGN(3),RSGN(4)/-1,+1,+1,-1/
      DATA DSGN(1),DSGN(2),DSGN(3),DSGN(4)/+1,+1,-1,-1/
C
C        ARRAY DIMENSIONS:  2*OFFSET-1  BY  2*OFFSET-1
      DATA OFFSET/30/
C
C        N=1 GOES IN CENTER
      IF ( N .GT. 1 )  GO TO 100
         I=OFFSET
         J=OFFSET
         RETURN
C        FIND THE NUMBER "R" SUCH THAT "N" IS IN THE R-TH
C            CONCENTRIC SQUARE ABOUT THE ORIGIN
  100 SQRTN = INT(SQRT(FLOAT(N))) +1
      IF ( (SQRTN-1)**2 .EQ. N )  SQRTN = SQRTN -1
      R = SQRTN/2
C        FIND THE SPIRAL NUMBER OF THE LOWER LEFT HAND CORNER
C            OF THE R-TH CONCENTRIC SQUARE
      CNR = (2*R-1)**2 +1
C        FIND THE NUMBER OF STEPS, COUNTING COUNTERCLOCKWISE
C            ALONG THE CONCENTRIC SQUARE FROM THE LOWER LEFT HAND
C            CORNER
      RES = N-CNR
C        DETERMINE EDGE NUMBER OF SQUARE (QUAD) AND
C            DIRECTION FROM ORIGIN (SIGNED RADIUS)
      QUAD = RES/(2*R)
      SR = ISIGN(R,RSGN(QUAD+1))
C        FIND SIGNED DISTANCE ALONG EDGE (RESRES)
      RESRES = DSGN(QUAD+1)*(MOD(RES,2*R) -R)
C        COMPUTE COORDINATE
      IF ( MOD(QUAD,2) .EQ. 0 )  GO TO 200
         I = SR +OFFSET
         J = RESRES +OFFSET
         RETURN
  200    I = RESRES +OFFSET
         J = SR +OFFSET
      RETURN
      END
```

22	21	20	19	18
23	8	7	6	17
24	9	1	5	16
25	2	3	4	15
10	11	12	13	14

etc.

21 Write a SUBROUTINE LINE(GRAPH,W,H,X1,Y1,X2,SYMBOL) that inserts a straight line made up of the character SYMBOL from (X1,Y1) to (X2,Y2) in the picture GRAPH (which as in the other plotting SUBROUTINEs is a $w \times h$ two-dimensional array). Assume the image region is a 1 × 1 square. If part of one of the lines goes off the edge of the GRAPH, insert an exclamation point at the boundary point nearest to the desired point. Use LINE to plot a tic-tac-toe board, using a minus sign for horizontal lines and an I or | for vertical lines.

22 Use SUBROUTINE LINE from problem 21 to plot a picture of the path taken by a person caught in the center of an unruly mob. Plot the person's new position each time he moves, assuming he moves five feet each time, but in a random direction. Use SUBROUTINE RANDOM from Section 7 6 to generate a random angle between 0.0 and 2π. Using the random angle, compute the next endpoint, and CALL LINE to fill in the path. Use different SYMBOLs for successive lines so you can follow the unfortunate person's path even though it may cross over itself from time to time.

23 Suppose you were running a pizza parlor and you wanted to figure out how many waitresses/waiters you should hire. If you have too few, then customers will have to wait a long time to be served and you'll lose business, but if you have too many, then you'll lose money paying them. You decide to simulate the process. You estimate that every minute the odds are 50/50 that a new customer will come in and that it takes three minutes of a waitress's time to serve each customer. Your program should simulate the arrival of 1000 customers and should print out the total amount of time customers spend waiting and the amount of time waitresses/waiters spend waiting. Try your program with one, two, and three waitresses/waiters to see how many it would be best to have.

Here are some hints about how you could write the program:

   a Have one main loop which corresponds to what happens each successive minute.

   b Have memory cells which keep track of the following things:

   □ How many customers are waiting: CWAIT

   □ How many waitresses/waiters are waiting: WWAIT

□ How many waitresses/waiters have just started waiting on a customer: WWAIT0
□ How many waiters/waitresses have been waiting on a customer for one minute: WWAIT1
□ How many waiters/waitresses have been waiting on a customer for two minutes: WWAIT2
□ How much (total) time customers have spent waiting: CTIME
□ How much (total) time waitresses/waiters have spent waiting: WTIME

VERBAL DESCRIPTION

Initialize.

Simulate one minute:
  Account for arriving customers.
  Update status of waitresses.
  Serve customers (as many as possible).
  Account for time people have spent waiting this minute.

Repeat (i.e., simulate next minute) unless it's closing time.

Print results.

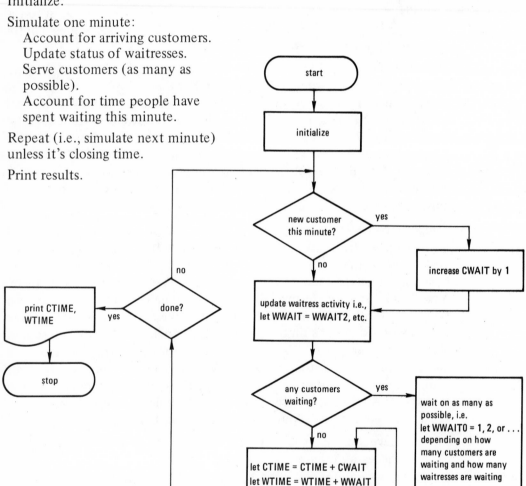

start

initialize

new customer this minute? — yes → increase CWAIT by 1

no

update waitress activity i.e., let WWAIT = WWAIT2, etc.

any customers waiting? — yes → wait on as many as possible, i.e. let WWAIT0 = 1, 2, or ... depending on how many customers are waiting and how many waitresses are waiting

no

let CTIME = CTIME + CWAIT
let WTIME = WTIME + WWAIT

done? — no (loop back) / yes → print CTIME, WTIME → stop

24 Boss Tweed Clothing does tons of direct mail advertising and has been getting a lot of complaints from people who have received more than one copy of its glossy four-color flyer. Boss Tweed has discovered that one of its big problems is that one of the companies it buys mailing lists from records the names like this:

Phillip K. Nerdly

and the others record them like this:

Nerdly, Phillip K.

Write a program which READs a name (up to 80 characters long) into an array, 1 character per element, and converts names written in the second form into the first form. Take care to think of the possibilities. Write and use a LOGICAL FUNCTION which returns .TRUE. if the rest of the name (all characters after the one specified by one of the arguments) are blank. (Why is it easier to go from form 2 to form 1 than vice versa?)

8 DO-LOOPS

Section 8 1

The DO Statement

By now you have read enough programs to have noticed that GO TO statements make a program difficult to read because you have to hunt all over the program for the statement labels. In addition, GO TO statements used without discretion can lead to programs with extremely contorted logic. It would make programs easier to read if there were some way to write loops without using GO TO statements. Fortran provides a little help in this direction with a GO TO-less, though highly restricted, loop construction known as the DO-loop. The DO-loop can be used whenever the looping is controlled by an INTEGER variable which increases by uniform increments on each pass through the loop, and the loop terminates when the variable exceeds some upper bound. Such a loop may be called a **counting loop** since the control variable is counting from some initial value to some final value.

A surprisingly large proportion of program loops are counting loops. This makes the DO-loop very useful. However, many Fortran programmers try to force their loops to fit this category even when they could be more clearly written in some other way. By this point, however, you should be familiar enough with looping in general that you will be able to choose the most appropriate construction.

HI FRIENDS!
FRIENDLY FRANK THE
STATEMENT SALESMAN HERE!
HAVE I GOT A DEAL FOR YOU!
TIRED OF USING COUNTERS AND
HAVING TO INITIALIZE THEM?
TIRED OF USING IF STATEMENTS
TO STOP LOOPS? TRY THE NEW,
IMPROVED, LEMON-FRESHENED
DO STATEMENT.

Here's an example of a DO-loop in use:

```
        INTEGER N,N1,N2, TOP
        TOP = 10
 COMMENT:  LIST THE SQUARES AND CUBES OF 1, 2, ..., TOP
        WRITE(6,1000)
  1000 FORMAT('   NUMBER    SQUARED    CUBED')
 COMMENT:  HERE'S THE DO-LOOP
        DO 10 N=1,TOP,1
           N2 = N**2
           N3 = N**3
   10      WRITE(6,2000) N,N2,N3
 2000      FORMAT(6X,I2,6X,I4,6X,I4)
        STOP
        END
```

output

NUMBER	SQUARED	CUBED
1	1	1
2	4	8
3	9	27
4	16	64
5	25	125
6	36	216
7	49	343
8	64	512
9	81	729
10	100	1000

Probably you can tell what's going on just by staring at the program and the output for a while. There are a number of formal rules, however.

Each DO-loop starts with a statement called a **DO statement**, which specifies five things:

    1   the control variable or **index**

    2   the **starting value** of the index

    3   the **upper bound** for the index

    4   the **increment** for the index

    5   the **range** of the DO-loop (that is, the statements which are part of the DO-loop)

The **index** must be an unsubscripted INTEGER variable. The **starting value**, **upper bound**, and **increment** must have positive INTEGER values. The **range** is specified by a statement label in the DO statement that indicates the last statement in the loop. Thus the loop includes all the executable statements *following* the DO statement up to and including the terminal statement. It is important to realize that the DO statement itself is *not* part of the loop; it merely sets up the loop. Nonexecutable statements, like FORMATs or DATA statements, may appear physically inside a DO-loop construct, but they are not part of the loop because they can't be executed.

The statements in the range of the DO-loop are repeated once for each value of the index, beginning with the starting value and increasing after each pass through the range by the specified increment until the upper bound is exceeded.

Let's dissect the DO-loop in the example above to see how it fits the rules. While we're at it, we'll write out a program that does exactly the same thing but which doesn't use a DO-loop. That way you can always refer to the non-DO-loop form if you have a question about some detail of how DO-loops work.

```
        DO-loop form                        non-DO-loop form

        DO 10 N=1,TOP,1              N = 1
          N2 = N**2             10   N2 = N**2
          N3 = N**3                  N3 = N**3
   10     WRITE(6,1000) N,N2,N3      WRITE(6,1000) N,N2,N3
                                     N = N+1
                                     IF(N.LE.TOP) GO TO 10
```

The DO statement comes first and specifies the number of times the loop will be repeated, and the values the index will take. The statement label specifies the range of the loop. In our example the range is all statements *after* the DO statement up to and including statement 10. The memory cell called N serves as the index, and its value is changed on each pass through the loop. The index N is initialized to the value 1 (the starting value) and is increased by 1 (the increment) on each pass. The statements of the loop are repeated as long as the index is less than or equal to the value of TOP (the upper bound). Compare the DO-loop to the equivalent form using the conditional GO TO again. You'll probably agree that the DO statement is easier to read, once you understand the notation.

Let's look at another example. Suppose you want to compute an approximation to the infinite sum $1 + 1/4 + 1/9 + 1/16 + \ldots + 1/n^2 + \ldots$. To see how the sum is progressing, you want to print it after every hundredth term has been added. This is a perfect situation for a DO-loop; while you are adding terms, you want to count to 100 over and over again and print out the sum each time you get to 100. The following program does this computation. It stops adding terms when they get very small.

```
COMMENT:  COMPUTE 1 + 1/4 + 1/9 + ... + 1/N**2 + ...
          REAL N, SUM
          INTEGER COUNT
COMMENT:  INITIALIZE SUM AND N
          SUM = 1.0
          N = 1.0
COMMENT:  ADD A HUNDRED TERMS
   10     DO 20 COUNT = 1,100,1
            N = N + 1.0
   20       SUM = SUM + 1.0/N**2
          WRITE(6,1000) SUM
 1000     FORMAT(' SUM SO FAR=', F10.7)
COMMENT:  ADD NEXT 100 TERMS UNLESS LAST TERM WAS VERY SMALL
          IF (1.0/N**2 .GT. 1.0E-6)  GO TO 10
          STOP
          END
```

output

```
SUM SO FAR= 1.6350819
SUM SO FAR= 1.6399713
SUM SO FAR= 1.6416173
SUM SO FAR= 1.6424434
SUM SO FAR= 1.6429400
SUM SO FAR= 1.6432716
SUM SO FAR= 1.6435086
SUM SO FAR= 1.6436864
SUM SO FAR= 1.6438248
SUM SO FAR= 1.6439356
```

Now that we've seen a couple of examples, let's look at a detailed description of the form and meaning of the DO statement.

There are lots of rules to remember about DO-loops.

1 The values of the DO-parameters (index, starting value, upper bound, and increment) may *not* be changed by any statement in the range.

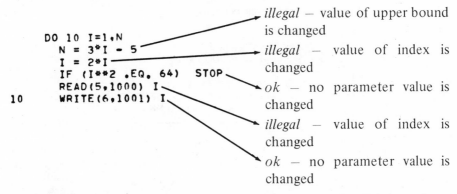

```
        DO 10 I=1,N
          N = 3*I - 5
          I = 2*I
          IF (I**2 .EQ. 64)   STOP
          READ(5,1000) I
  10      WRITE(6,1001) I
```

illegal — value of upper bound is changed

illegal — value of index is changed

ok — no parameter value is changed

illegal — value of index is changed

ok — no parameter value is changed

2 No statement may cause a transfer into the range of a DO-loop from outside the range.

```
        GO TO 10
        DO 10 IN=1,25
          IF ( (-N/2)*2 .EQ. NOW)   GO TO 20
  10      MODEM = IN*MODEM
  20    ZOMBIE = 2.0*3.14159
```

illegal — transfers into DO-loop range

ok — transfers outside range

3 The index of a DO-loop may be assumed to have a value only within the range of the DO-loop. Once the loop terminates the value is lost. The only exception is the case in which a transfer from inside the range to outside the range occurs before the loop has terminated normally.

```
        DO 100 IND=1,25
          IF ( (IND/3)*3 .EQ. NOW)   GO TO 200
  100     WRITE(6,1000) IND
        WRITE(6,1000) IND
        GO TO 300
  200   WRITE(6,1000) IND
```

ok — within loop, IND has a value

illegal — the DO-loop has terminated so IND has no value

ok — transfer to this point occurs before DO-loop termination

DO statement

forms

DO s $v = m_1, m_2$
DO s $v = m_1, m_2, m_3$

s is a statement label

v is an unsubscripted INTEGER variable

m_j is an unsigned INTEGER constant or an unsubscripted INTEGER variable (assumed to have a positive value)

meaning

The range of the DO-loop includes all executable statements after the DO statement up to and including the statement labeled s, the **terminal statement** or **object** of the DO-loop. The index v is initialized to m_1 and increased by m_3 after each pass through the statements in the range. (If m_3 is not present, it is assumed to be equal to 1.) The statements of the range are repeated as long as $v \leqslant m_2$.

examples

```
      DO 100 K=1,27
100      SUM = SUM + A(K)

      DO 200 LSMFT=LOW,N,3
         ALPHA = LSMFT + OFFSET
200      WRITE(6,1000) ALPHA
```

4 DO-loops may be nested. That is, the range of one DO-loop may be wholly inside the range of another. However, the ranges of two DO-loops may not overlap in any other way.

```
      DO 20 KATZ=1,142,2          DO 10 KATZ,1,142,2
         DO 10 LUMP=1,57             DO 20 LUMP=1,57
10          WRITE(6,2000)KATZ,LUMP  10  WRITE(6,2000) KATZ,LUMP
20       WRITE(6,4000)            20  WRITE(6,4000)
```

5 Nested DO-loops may have the same terminal statement, but if they do, then there cannot be a transfer of control to the terminal statement except from the innermost loop.

```
·DO 10 KATZ=1,142,2
    DO 10 LUMP=1,57
       IF(MIRE.GT.KATZ) GO TO 10
       WRITE(6,1000) KATZ,LUMP
10     WRITE(6,2000)
```

```
DO 10 KATZ=1,142,2
   IF(MIRE.GT.KATZ) GO TO 10
   DO 10 LUMP=1,57
10 WRITE(6,2000)
```

6 The terminal statement of a DO-loop must be executable and must not be a GO TO, STOP, DO, or RETURN, nor may it be an IF statement containing one of these. It may be a CALL statement though.

There are two fairly common techniques associated with DO-loops that programmers use to improve the readability of their programs. One is to indent the statements in the range of the DO-loops. The other is to place a CONTINUE statement at the end of the range of every DO-loop so that the DO statement and the CONTINUE act as visual "brackets" for the DO-loop. The CONTINUE statement has no effect other than to act as a place to attach a statement label.

> **CONTINUE** *is an executable statement. Its (rather unusual) meaning is to* do nothing. *It is often used as the terminal statement in the range of a* DO-*loop.*

EXERCISES 8 1

1 In the first DO-loop example program, what will be printed if TOP has the value −1?

2 In what way would the output of the second example program be changed if its DO statement was changed to

```
DO 20 COUNT = 1,100
```

3 How many lines will this bizarre and possibly senseless program print?

```
        INTEGER OUTER,INNER,MIDDLE
COMMENT:  THIS PROGRAM IS BIZARRE AND POSSIBLY SENSELESS.
C         READ IT AT YOUR OWN RISK.
        DO 100 OUTER=2,8,2
          DO 100 MIDDLE=OUTER,2,1
            DO 100 INNER=1,4,2
100           WRITE(6,1000)
1000          FORMAT(' LINE')
        STOP
        END
```

4 What's wrong with this?

```
        DO 110 I=1,10
100     N=N+I
110     WRITE(6,1100) I
1100    FORMAT(1X,I10)
        IF (N .LT. 100) GO TO 100
```

Section 8 2

DO-Loops and Arrays—A Great Team

Commonly the values stored in an array are related and must be dealt with in a very similar way, but one at a time, of course. Such situations are great opportunities to use DO-loops, resulting in a more efficient program which is easier to read, hence easier to debug. Here's part of a program which locates the smallest value in an array of numbers. We assume that an earlier section of the program has succeeded in READing N values into array positions ROSE(1), ROSE(2), . . . , ROSE(N).

```
        .
        .
        .
COMMENT:  FIND THE SMALLEST VALUE IN THE ARRAY "ROSE", THUS
C             FINDING THE FEWEST NUMBER OF PETALS ANY ROSE HAS.
C         FIRST ELEMENT IS SMALLEST SO FAR
          MINIM = ROSE(1)
C         SEARCH THE OTHER ELEMENTS FOR SMALLER ONES
          DO 300  HERE = 2,N
            IF (ROSE(HERE) .GE. MINIM)  GO TO 300
C           HERE IS A SMALLER VALUE.  UPDATE
            MINIM = ROSE(HERE)
  300     CONTINUE
C         DONE
          WRITE(6,3000) MINIM
 3000 FORMAT(' NO ROSE HAS LESS THAN', I5, ' PETALS')
          STOP
          END
```

You have seen the algorithm before. Notice the use made of the CONTINUE statement in statement 300. It provides a convenient place to go when, under certain conditions, you want to skip some part of the DO-loop range. In this case we wanted to skip the statement

```
    MINIM = ROSE(HERE)
```

unless we found a new minimum value.

A Chicago Peace has forty-five petals;   an *Austrian Copper* has five.

Nested DO-loops are convenient ways of dealing with two-dimensional arrays. To illustrate this, let's look again at the program that we saw in the first part of Section 6 4. That's where we first used two-dimensional arrays. We had an array which stored the results of a poll taken for our political candidate. We used the array

```
    REAL POLL(7,5)
```

and we wanted to know the average value in each column. Using DO-loops our program would look like the one below.

```
      REAL POLL(7,5), AVERGE, SUM
      INTEGER COLUMN, ROW
         .
         .
         .
      DO 200 COLUMN=1,5
        SUM = 0.0
        DO 100 ROW=1,7
          SUM = SUM + POLL(ROW,COLUMN)
100       CONTINUE
        AVERGE = SUM/7.0
        WRITE(6,1000) COLUMN, AVERGE
1000    FORMAT(' THE AVERAGE SUPPORT IN COLUMN', I3,
     +              ' IS', F7.3, ' PERCENT')
200     CONTINUE
      STOP
      END
```

Where they are appropriate, DO-loops help by providing a concise notation for a specific sort of loop. You already know how to write any sort of loop you want, so if the restrictions on DO-loops make them inappropriate to your problem, you know what to do.

EXERCISES 8 2

1 Look at the examples in Chapters 3 and 6 and see which of the loops could be appropriately written as DO-loops and which of them couldn't.

2 Alter the example which computes the smallest value in ROSE so that it finds the largest.

3 Alter the example which computes the smallest value in ROSE so that it also prints the number of memory cells in ROSE which have the smallest value.

Section 8 3*

Fads

> Skip this section
> if you feel like it.

Let's look at a situation in which the DO-loop is useful. As you know, many people believe that fads spread faster when they start on one of the coasts than when they start in the middle of the country. If this is true there must be some reason for it. We'll try to explain it by hypothesizing a fad spread mechanism and testing it on the computer to see if the results support the observation that fads spread faster from the coasts.

We will assume that fads spread by word of mouth and that a person's influence doesn't extend much beyond a small region around his home. (These assumptions can, of course, be criticized on many grounds, especially since we are long out of the nineteenth century, but let's forge ahead anyway.) Basically we are assuming that the percentage of people in a particular region who follow the fad on one day is changed (either up or down) by the percentages in neighboring regions. Let's divide the country up into regions by laying a 40 × 100 grid over the U.S. map. Each region is a small square with eight immediate neighbors: north, northeast, east, southeast, south, southwest, west, and northwest. The only exceptions are the border regions, which are, of course, missing one or more neighbors. Let's say that fads spread by an averaging mechanism: If the percentage of people in a particular region who follow the fad is $r\%$ today, and the percentages in the neighboring regions are $n\%$, $ne\%$, $e\%$, $se\%$, $s\%$, $sw\%$, $w\%$, and $nw\%$, then the percentage in the region tomorrow will be $(r\% + n\% + ne\% + e\% + se\% + s\% + sw\% + w\% + nw\%)/9$. If the region in question is on the border, then we'll leave the missing neighbors out of the average.

As a starting condition, we will assume that 100% of the people in a particular region, the home of the fad, decide to follow a fad on day 1 and that no one else knows about the fad until the next day, when it starts to spread according to our rules. We make a special case of the home of the fad: it stays at 100% at all times since the home town folks really love it. We'll let the simulation run for 60 days and then look at the results.

It will be easy to write the program. We can use a two-dimensional array to store the percentages. However, since the United States isn't rectangular, we will have to initialize some points of the array to special values which indicate that they are not part of the United States. We can use negative values for this purpose since they clearly are not possible percentages. We can read the coordinates of these outside regions from cards. Then we initialize the starting region (read from a card) to 100% and the remaining regions to 0%. The heart of the program is the part which computes the next day's percentages for each region. On each of 60 days we must look at each region, compute its new percentage, and record it in another rectangular array. This is the only complex part of the program, and it's made complex because we have to worry about what to do on the boundary points. Suppose we want to update the percentage at the position whose east-west coordinate is stored in EAST and whose north-south coordinate is stored in NORTH. We want to sum up the values in the nine memory cells around (NORTH, EAST).

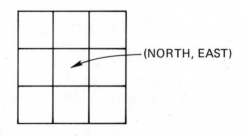

(NORTH, EAST)

This means we need two nested loops, one to go from NORTH − 1 up to NORTH + 1 and one to go from EAST − 1 up to EAST + 1. Then, at each of the nine places, we'll test to see if the stored value is negative (indicating a point outside the United States). If it is, we won't add its value in. Since this is such an important and basic part of the program, we've indented the statements that make it up.

The other important idea here is that when we compute the new percentage at a point, we can't just insert that new value back into the same array. If we did,

> *parallel process: a process which has subparts which function simultaneously*
>
> *serial process: a process whose subparts function one at a time (sequentially)*
>
> *In the fad problem we are using a serial process (our program running on a serial digital computer) to simulate a parallel process (the fad spread mechanism).*

then in trying to compute the new percentage for a neighboring point, one of the terms in the average would be wrong. That's why we need to use *two* arrays. The problem arises because this program is simulating a process that is going on simultaneously all over the country, i.e., it is a parallel process. Since the program can do computations for only one part of the country at a time, it has to retain the old percentages until it has all the new ones computed.

At the end of 60 days we print the results in the form of a rectangular display of symbols, one for each region. Rather arbitrarily we decide on the use of symbols shown in the Official Table of Symbols.

Official Table of Symbols

symbol	meaning
—	outside U.S.
blank	0 − 10%
1	10 − 20%
2	20 − 30%
.	
.	
.	
9	90 − 100%
*	home of fad

```
COMMENT:  PROGRAM TO TEST THE FAD THEORY.
C        TWO ARRAYS FOR PERCENTAGE OF SATURATION--ONE FOR
C        CURRENT DAY, THE OTHER FOR THE NEXT DAY
         REAL PCT(100,40), NXTPCT(100,40)
C        MEMORY CELLS FOR INPUT/OUTPUT
         INTEGER NTH(8), EST(8), LINE(100), SYMBOL(12), I
C        MEMORY CELLS FOR COMPUTATION OF NEIGHBORHOOD AVERAGES
         REAL AVE, NEAR
         INTEGER N, E, NLESS1, NPLUS1, ELESS1, EPLUS1
C        OTHER USEFUL VARIABLES
         INTEGER NORTH,EAST,DAY,HOMEE,HOMEN,I
         DATA SYMBOL(1)  /1H-/
         DATA SYMBOL(2)  /1H /
         DATA SYMBOL(3)  /1H1/
         DATA SYMBOL(4)  /1H2/
         DATA SYMBOL(5)  /1H3/
         DATA SYMBOL(6)  /1H4/
         DATA SYMBOL(7)  /1H5/
         DATA SYMBOL(8)  /1H6/
         DATA SYMBOL(9)  /1H7/
         DATA SYMBOL(10)/1H8/
         DATA SYMBOL(11)/1H9/
         DATA SYMBOL(12)/1H*/
C
C        INITIALIZE ALL REGIONS TO ZERO PER CENT
         DO 10 NORTH = 1,40
           DO 10 EAST = 1,100
  10         PCT(EAST,NORTH) = 0.0
C
C        GET BOUNDARY COORDINATES FROM DATA CARDS.
  20     READ(5,1000) EAST, NORTH
 1000    FORMAT(2I5)
           IF ( NORTH .EQ. 0 )  GO TO 30
           PCT(EAST,NORTH) = -11.0
           GO TO 20
C        READ THE LOCATION OF THE HOME OF THE FAD.
  30     READ(5,1000) HOMEE, HOMEN
C        FOR EACH OF 60 DAYS, UPDATE THE PERCENTAGES.
C
         DO 300 DAY = 1,60
C
C        COMPUTE NEW AVERAGE FOR EACH REGION (100*40=4000 AV'S)
         DO 100 NORTH = 1,40
           DO 100 EAST = 1,100
C            IF PCT(EAST,NORTH) IS LESS THAN 0.0, IT IS NOT IN
C            THE CONTINENTAL U.S. ITS PERCENTAGE WON'T CHANGE.
             IF ( PCT(EAST,NORTH) .GE. 0.0)  GO TO 40
               AVE = PCT(EAST,NORTH)
               GO TO 100
```

```
C                    COUNT THE NUMBER OF NON-BORDER REGIONS AROUND
C                    POSITION (EAST,NORTH) AND COMPUTE AVERAGE.
   40                NEAR = 0.0
                     AVE = 0.0
                     NLESS1 = MAX0(NORTH-1,1)
                     NPLUS1 = MIN0(NORTH+1,40)
                     ELESS1 = MAX0(EAST-1,1)
                     EPLUS1 = MIN0(EAST+1,100)
                     DO 60 N=NLESS1,NPLUS1
                        DO 50 E=ELESS1,EPLUS1
C                       TEST FOR BOUNDARY POINT
                        IF ( PCT(E,N) .LT. 0.0 )   GO TO 50
C                       ADD IN THIS NEIGHBOR.
                        AVE= AVE + PCT(E,N)
                        NEAR = NEAR + 1.0
   50                   CONTINUE
   60                CONTINUE
C                    FINISH BY TAKING NEW AVERAGE.
                     AVE = AVE/NEAR
C                    INSERT NEW VALUE.
  100                NXTPCT(EAST,NORTH) = AVE
C        NOW GET READY FOR THE NEXT DAY.
         DO 200 NORTH = 1,40
            DO 200 EAST = 1,100
  200          PCT(EAST,NORTH) = NXTPCT(EAST,NORTH)
C        REMEMBER--HOME PERCENTAGE STAYS AT 100.
         PCT(HOMEE,HOMEN) = 100.
  300    CONTINUE
C        PRINT THE RESULTS, ONE LINE AT A TIME.
         DO 500 NORTH=1,40
            DO 400 EAST = 1,100
C              FIGURE OUT WHAT SYMBOL GOES HERE AND INSERT IT.
               I = INT(PCT(EAST,NORTH)/10.0) + 2
  400          LINE(EAST) = SYMBOL(I)
C        PRINT PERCENTAGE SYMBOLS ON THIS LATITUDE.
  500    WRITE(6,5000) LINE
 5000    FORMAT(10X,100A1)
         STOP
         END
```

Figure 8 3 1 is the output of the program. As you can see, fads on the coast do *not* spread faster. Since the results of our model do not correspond to reality, we must not have understood the process. Perhaps the averaging mechanism we used to spread the fads is wrong. Perhaps people on the coasts are different from people in the middle of America. Perhaps both. Perhaps neither.

Central Fad

Coastal Fad

Figure 8 3 1 Output from the Fad Program

EXERCISES 8 3

1 Have a discussion with some friends about other ways to model the fad spread process. Might the mass media have an effect which makes our assumptions unrealistic?

PROBLEMS 8

1 Write a program which prints a tastefully formatted table of sines and cosines of the angles between 0.00 radian and 1.57 radians in steps of 0.01 radian.

2 Do a problem from an earlier chapter again. Choose one which is appropriately done using DO-loops. A number of the plotting problems in Chapter 7 are good ones to try.

3 The 324th Annual Pumpkin Growing Contest of the Future Farmers of Grand Fenwick has 16 entries this year. The weights of the pumpkins (in **tsernotecs**, the traditional measure of weight in Grand Fenwick) are shown below beside the names of the entrants.

Write a program which the judges could use to select the winner. Print a congratulatory message which lists the name of the lucky winner and tells how many tsernotecs the winning pumpkin weighs. (Thanks to the late Walter Orvedahl for this problem.)

weight (tsernotecs)	grower	weight (tsernotecs)	grower
60.4	Hans Von Smong	69.4	Katy Klunz
86.1	Karl Schultz	78.8	Hans Von Der Door
63.9	Hans Von Neumann	85.3	Hans Schultz
71.2	Kristina Hampker	50.4	Hans Hanson
105.3	Karl Schmidthorst	67.3	Katy Kleinholter
54.7	Hans Von Laughen	57.9	Hans Bratworst
91.6	Karl Von Hausdorf	94.7	Kris Von Steinholder

4 Supposedly, if you take more and more terms of the series $1 + (1/2) + (1/3) + (1/4) + \ldots + (1/n)$ you can get as large a total as you want. But if you just leave out a term here and there so that you have the series $1 + (1/4) + (1/9) + \ldots + (1/n^2)$ the sum never gets very large.

Write a program which prints an appropriately formatted table of the values of the two series for $n = 1, 2, 3, \ldots, 180$. Try to fit the entire table on one output page.

5 Revise the sorting algorithm in Section 7 5 so that it sorts arrays into increasing order and uses DO-loops.

6 Revise the politician problem as suggested in Section 8 2, adding a section which selects regions where the politician's support is more than 1.5 times the average. Print these locations with a message urging campaign workers to go there asking for money.

7 Using three nested DO-loops, print out all possible three-person games of "rock, paper, scissors." Associate an INTEGER value with each symbol—for instance, you could use a two-dimensional array organized like this:

NAMES	1	2	3	4	5	6	7	8
1	R	O	C	K				
2	P	A	P	E	R			
3	S	C	I	S	S	O	R	S

When the three DO-loop indices are 2, 2, and 3, that would correspond to player 1 holding out "paper," player 2 holding "paper," and player 3 holding "scissors."

Beside each game, print how many wins each player had in that particular game. Recall that "paper wraps rock," "rock breaks scissors," and "scissors cut paper." In the example above, player 3 would win against both player 1 and player 2.

Sample output:

	GAME			WINS	
PLAYER1	PLAYER2	PLAYER3	PLAYER1	PLAYER2	PLAYER3
ROCK	ROCK	ROCK	0	0	0
ROCK	ROCK	PAPER	0	0	2
SCISSORS	PAPER	ROCK	1	1	1

Count up how many wins each player has overall.

8 Use the idea for storing huge numbers (problem 6 18) to print out a table of powers of 2 from 2^0 to 2^{160}.

9 One of the methods used for analyzing a set of time series data for periodicity is to calculate an autocorrelation coefficient between values of the variate X_i and the same variate at a constant time lag X_{i+p}. The autocorrelation coefficient for a particular time lag p is given by

$$r_p = \frac{\Sigma(x_i x_{i+p}) - \dfrac{\Sigma x_i \Sigma x_{i+p}}{n-p}}{\sqrt{\left[\Sigma x_i^2 - \dfrac{(\Sigma x_i)^2}{n-p}\right]\left[\Sigma x_{i+p}^2 - \dfrac{(\Sigma x_{i+p})^2}{n-p}\right]}}$$

The summations extend over the range $i = 1$ to $i = n - p$. An examination of r calculated as a function of p indicates those lags or periods over which the data of the time series seem to be correlated. In other words, r will be large for time lags p that are periods of the variate x_i.

Consider the following data, representing the monthly rainfall on a certain watershed between 1901 and 1920. Obtain the autocorrelation coefficients for time lags of 1 to 25 months, printing each value as it is calculated.

RAINFALL IN INCHES

Year	Jan.	Feb.	Mar.	Apr.	May	June	July	Aug.	Sept.	Oct.	Nov.	Dec.
1901	0.14	1.04	1.61	1.63	1.45	1.41	0.01	0.13	0.01	0.05	0.19	0.45
1902	1.42	1.35	1.03	2.05	2.32	0.73	0.06	0.39	0.26	0.21	1.21	0.87
1903	1.31	1.14	1.76	1.85	1.76	1.32	0.11	0.24	0.09	0.37	0.29	1.59
1904	0.32	1.21	2.43	2.10	2.42	1.05	0.02	0.01	0.51	0.19	0.05	1.61
1905	1.07	0.47	1.82	1.92	3.17	1.04	0.03	0.13	0.27	0.26	1.07	0.92
1906	1.06	1.36	1.46	2.31	1.87	0.85	0.07	0.07	0.14	0.62	1.34	0.09
1907	2.04	1.13	2.64	0.95	2.17	1.93	0.09	0.32	0.36	0.32	0.42	1.42
1908	0.41	1.09	1.73	1.74	1.94	0.64	0.10	0.06	0.22	0.73	0.31	0.76
1909	1.71	0.87	1.93	1.42	3.03	1.52	0.00	0.23	0.08	0.93	0.59	1.21
1910	1.41	1.49	2.56	2.09	2.98	1.61	0.00	0.33	0.49	0.24	1.61	0.32
1911	1.33	1.20	0.42	1.67	2.55	1.06	0.13	0.15	0.36	0.15	0.16	1.05
1912	1.32	1.43	2.34	1.76	1.76	1.16	0.07	0.34	0.45	0.84	0.87	1.11
1913	0.95	1.18	1.34	2.04	3.21	1.24	0.10	0.23	0.13	1.01	0.54	0.69
1914	0.42	1.06	1.53	1.82	1.69	0.95	0.31	0.04	0.28	0.36	0.98	1.24
1915	2.61	0.64	1.75	1.94	2.63	1.13	0.05	0.33	0.22	0.09	0.04	0.92
1916	1.42	0.86	1.42	2.15	0.86	0.76	0.09	0.15	0.19	0.37	0.23	1.42
1917	1.17	1.24	2.03	0.61	2.42	0.84	0.13	0.33	0.42	0.19	0.75	0.76
1918	0.76	1.00	2.26	2.21	1.74	0.92	0.00	0.35	0.04	0.75	0.12	0.63
1919	1.61	0.34	1.72	2.20	1.74	1.70	0.21	0.25	0.34	0.27	0.39	1.32
1920	1.27	1.32	1.94	1.23	3.20	1.09	0.17	0.03	0.26	1.21	0.94	0.68

10 Suppose a zoologist comes to you with a collection of data. He had made a count of the number of prairie rattlesnakes (Crotalus viridis viridis) found on a square mile of land at various altitudes around Fort Collins, Colorado. The data he has gathered is summarized in the table below.

altitude	number of snakes
5000'	30
5300'	28
5800'	20
6000'	14
6500'	10
7000'	3

He suspects that the number of snakes s at altitude a can be expressed as a linear function

$$s(a) = Da + M$$

He asks you to try to determine from his data what would be reasonable values to take for the coefficients D and M.

Naturally, you want to choose values for D and M so that the observed data deviates as little as possible from the values predicted by your coefficients D and M. In other words you want

$$s(5000) \text{ to be close to } 30$$
$$s(5300) \text{ to be close to } 28$$
$$s(5800) \text{ to be close to } 20$$

One technique that is often used in cases like this is to choose values for D and M which minimize the sum of the squares of the deviations from the observed values. In other words, so that

$$(s(5000) - 30)^2 + (s(5300) - 28)^2 + (s(5800) - 20)^2 + (s(6000)$$
$$- 14)^2 + (s(6500) - 10)^2 + (s(7000) - 3)^2$$

(where $s(a) = Da + M$)

is as small as possible.

Your job is to write a program which READs an integer n from a card, then READs n measurements a_i, s_i from the following n cards, then calculates values for D and M by solving the following pair of linear equations (which solve the least squares problem posed above).

$$\left(\sum_{i=1}^{n} a_i^2 \right) D + \left(\sum_{i=1}^{n} a_i \right) M = \sum_{i=1}^{n} a_i s_i$$

$$\left(\sum_{i=1}^{n} a_i \right) D + nM = \sum_{i=1}^{n} s_i$$

The output from your program should include the values of D and M as well as the value of the square deviation (for the computed values D and M) divided by n, that is

$$\frac{1}{n} \sum_{i=1}^{n} (Da_i - M - s_i)^2$$

11 We got this problem from Professor Wm. M. McKeeman. Its basic structure is very similar to the fad program described in Section 8 3. We'll use a square two-dimensional array of INTEGER memory cells to represent a patch of skin. Each element in the array is either *healthy*, *sick*, or *immune*. In order to operate, the program needs three numbers. The first, an INTEGER which we'll call SICK, tells how many time steps a skin spot remains sick once it has been infected. The second, an INTEGER called IMMUNE, tells how many time steps a skin spot remains immune after it is through being sick. The third, a REAL named RATE, tells the odds (probability) that a sick spot will infect a neighboring healthy spot during the current time step.

To represent a healthy spot of skin, store a 0 in the corresponding array location. To start things off, make the whole patch of skin healthy except for the spot in the very center. Store a 1 in the location representing a skin spot when that spot becomes sick. For each time step, sweep through the entire array. At each position with a nonzero value, add 1 to reflect the passage of one unit of time. Then check to see if the spot has completed both its sick and its immune phase (i.e., if the value stored there is SICK + IMMUNE). If it is, restore that spot to the healthy state (0).

Next, still within the same time step, sweep through the array again. This time, stop at each spot that is sick and see if it infects any of its healthy neighbors.

If the fad program is clear to you, this program shouldn't be too hard. Just as in the fad program, you will need an auxiliary array so that the states of affairs at time step t and $t + 1$ don't get confused. Just as in the fad program you can convert INTEGERs into characters to make the output nice. We suggest a blank for healthy spots, an asterisk for sick spots, and a period for spots in the immune state.

By trying different values of the three numbers SICK, IMMUNE and RATE, you can observe a variety of "diseases": ringworm, blotches, measles, infestations that die out (cure themselves), and infestations that continue re-infecting recovered skin.

Note: The computation time increases rapidly with the size of the array of cells. Write the program so that you can easily change the size of the array in case you have time limit problems. Start with a 20 × 20 patch of skin.

9 DESIGNING RELIABLE PROGRAMS

Section 9 1

Introduction

Throughout this book we have used a systematic approach to the development of programs. Our design procedure is outlined in the box below.

---

steps in program design
1. *statement of the problem*
2. *description of the desired solution in terms of input, computation, and output*
3. *refinement of the solution through successive levels of detail*
4. *coding of the program in Fortran*

You know from experience that the process does not always proceed smoothly. Sometimes problems in coding (step 4 in box) will force you to revise your program design (step 3). Sometimes problems with the final program will force reconsideration of the statement of the problem (step 1) or the desired input/output behavior (step 2). (Review the Big Picture in Section 1 2.) Nevertheless, most programmers find that a systematic approach leads to correct programs more quickly than the helter-skelter technique (starting at step 4 instead of step 1).

Now that you've had some experience in writing programs and know most of the features of Fortran, you'll benefit from some review of the overall programming process. That's the purpose of this chapter. Here we'll study four case histories showing the development of programs of moderate complexity. In these case histories, we'll emphasize techniques often used by successful programmers: **top down design**, **structured programming**, **assertions**, and **verification**. These techniques are difficult to understand out of context, so we'll avoid abstract definitions at this point and introduce the terms as they arise in the program development process. The techniques aren't ends in themselves. They are methods which help in producing reliable programs, programs that process the input in the desired way to produce correct results. We don't claim that the use of these techniques will automatically produce error-free programs, but that the debugging process will be shortened. With badly designed programs, debugging often takes longer than writing the original program. Better design leads to reduced debugging time.

Section 9 2

Roman Numerals—An Example of Top Down Design

Our goal in this section is to write a program which converts INTEGERs into roman numerals. If the input to our program is the number 7, the output should be the roman numeral VII. The input 9 should be converted to IX. You probably remember from your grade school days that this conversion process is not entirely trivial. We'll have to analyze it carefully in order to write the program.

> **problem statement**: *Print numbers as roman numerals.*

To get a firm grasp on what we want our program to do, let's try to describe the output we want for a given class of inputs. You hardly ever see roman numerals these days except as dates on movies or buildings (used so it's hard to tell how old they are) and as page numbers in book prefaces. Therefore it's unlikely that we'd need roman numerals for numbers of more than four digits. We'll write our program with this in mind.

> **input/output description**
> *input:*   INTEGER *between 1 and 9999*
> *computation:* *convert to roman numeral*
> *output:*   THE ROMAN NUMERAL FOR _____ IS _____
> _input number_   _roman numeral_

To get a feeling for how the process works, let's look at a few conversions.

1	I
3	III
8	VIII
48	XLVIII
109	CIX
1066	MLXVI
1492	MCDXCII
1984	MCMLXXXIV

You can look at the conversion as a digit-by-digit process. To write the roman numeral for 1896 we first convert the first digit, the 1 in the thousands place, to the corresponding roman numeral M. The next digit, the 8 in the hundreds place, leads to the roman numeral DCCC. Now we have MDCCC, with two digits to go. The 9 in the tens place gives XC, the 6 in the units place, VI, and we end up with MDCCCXCVI. Of course, a 0 in any position adds nothing to the roman numeral: 105 becomes CV, the 0 in the tens place having no effect.

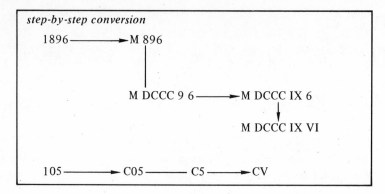

The conversion of 105 to CV brings up an interesting point. To make the process seem consistent with the digit-by-digit conversion of 1896, we actually went through an *extra step*: 105 to C05 is extra because the 05 part has a *leading zero*. We could have gone directly from 105 to C5, then on to CV, skipping the zero digit, but we have a feeling it will be easier to write the program if we treat leading zeros in the same way that we treat other digits. Since none of our numbers will have more than four digits, we can treat *all* inputs as if they had *exactly* four digits, viewing 105 as 0105 and 48 as 0048. Doing this we get a first stab at a conversion algorithm, as shown in Figure 9 2 1.

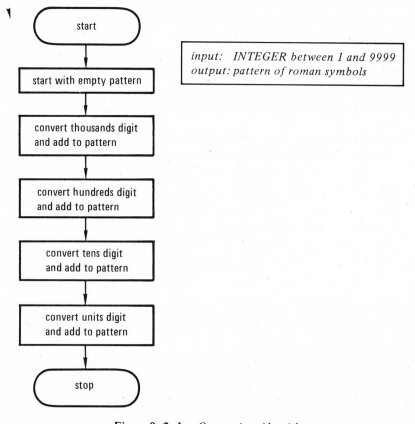

Figure 9 2 1   Conversion Algorithm

In converting a digit there are, of course, ten possibilities, one for each digit from 0 through 9. Each of these produces a pattern of roman symbols, and the roman symbols used depend on the position of the digit in the number (thousands, hundreds, tens, or units position). A zero digit is easy to handle. It produces no roman symbols, no matter what position it's in. The other patterns are more complicated. Study the accompanying table of digit conversions (Figure 9 2 2).

thousands place		hundreds place		tens place		units place	
0	(nothing)	0	(nothing)	0	(nothing)	0	(nothing)
1	M	1	C	1	X	1	I
2	MM	2	CC	2	XX	2	II
3	MMM	3	CCC	3	XXX	3	III
4	M$\overline{V}$	4	CD	4	XL	4	IV
5	$\overline{V}$	5	D	5	L	5	V
6	$\overline{V}$M	6	DC	6	LX	6	VI
7	$\overline{V}$MM	7	DCC	7	LXX	7	VII
8	$\overline{V}$MMM	8	DCCC	8	LXXX	8	VIII
9	M$\overline{X}$	9	CM	9	XC	9	IX

Figure 9 2 2   Table of Digit Conversions

Notice that there are three different symbols involved in the conversion list for each digit position. The units place uses the symbols I, V, and X; the tens place uses X, L, and C; the hundreds place, C, D, and M; and the thousands place, M, $\overline{V}$, and $\overline{X}$. Fortunately, the three symbols involved are used in a consistent way in each column. If we call the three symbols a, b, and c, then each column of the table is the same. We can condense the table (Figure 9 2 3).

thousands place	hundreds place	tens place	units place
$a = M$ $b = \overline{V}$ $c = \overline{X}$	$a = C$ $b = D$ $c = M$	$a = X$ $b = L$ $c = C$	$a = I$ $b = V$ $c = X$

0 (nothing)

1	a	4	ab	7	baa
2	aa	5	b	8	baaa
3	aaa	6	ba	9	ac

Figure 9 2 3   Condensed Table of Digit Conversions

Now we're getting somewhere! To convert a digit, no matter what position it's in, we need to know which digit it is (0 through 9) and the three necessary symbols. Digit conversion is then simply a matter of looking up an entry in the condensed table of digit conversions.

input: digit d (0, 1, 2, 3, 4, 5, 6, 7, 8, or 9)

symbols a, b, and c

output: pattern of symbols (possibly empty)

VERBAL DESCRIPTION

Select line d

  0: output (nothing)

  1: output a

  2: output aa

  3: output aaa

  4: output ab

  5: output b

  6: output ba

  7: output baa

  8: output baaa

  9: output ac

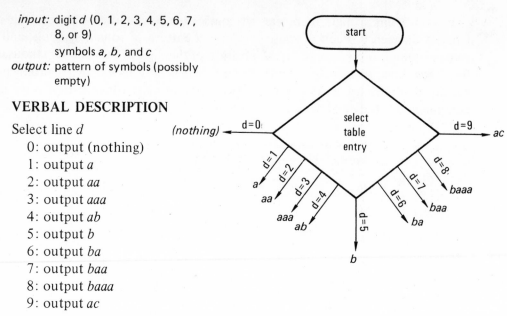

Figure 9 2 4   Digit Conversion Algorithm

Now let's consider what we've got. We have a way to produce a correct pattern of roman symbols given a digit and its position in the INTEGER being converted. We can put four of these digit conversions together and get a complete conversion. We still need a way to figure out which digit is in which position, given a Fortran INTEGER. It comes to us in one piece and we have to take it apart. Fortunately there is a built-in Fortran FUNCTION which will help us out: MOD. MOD gives us the remainder in the division of its two INTEGER arguments. If we give MOD the arguments 492 and 10, it returns the remainder 2 ($492 \div 10 = 49\ r2$). The remainder in a division by ten is the last digit in the dividend. That's how we get the units digit. To get other digits we simply shift them over to the units place via INTEGER division (remember, it's truncated) and pluck them off.

digit selection algorithm	
units digit:	MOD(I, 10)
tens digit:	MOD(I/10, 10)
hundreds digit:	MOD(I/100, 10)
thousands digit:	MOD(I/1000, 10)

Looking back over the pieces of our algorithm so far, we see that we have found techniques for converting each digit of the input number to the correct pattern of roman symbols, but we haven't yet decided how to add that pattern to the accumulating roman numeral. In fact, we haven't even decided how to accumulate the roman numeral. Suppose we decide to store the symbols of the roman numeral in an array, one symbol to each element. We can keep track of the number of symbols in a separate INTEGER memory cell N by updating the value of N each time we add some symbols to the roman numeral. Furthermore, the value of N will tell us where to put the symbols to be added each time we convert a digit of the input INTEGER.

Now that we've developed a plan, and understand each of the subproblems, we're finally ready to write some Fortran code. We'll use a SUBROUTINE named DIGIT to do the digit conversion so the main program will look very much like the conversion algorithm we originally described. The inputs to SUBROUTINE DIGIT will be the digit to be converted (an INTEGER), the three relevant roman symbols (Hollerith characters), the array in which the roman numeral is being accumulated (an array of Hollerith characters), and the current length of that array (an INTEGER memory cell). DIGIT will update the input array and its length in the appropriate way.

The program falls out of the development so naturally that it should be easy to understand the lightly annotated version which follows. We've used W for the symbol $\overline{V}$ and Y for $\overline{X}$. We've made the length of the array which stores the roman numeral 16. No roman numeral for a four-digit number can have more than 16 symbols. (The digit 8 has the longest roman equivalent, 4 symbols. Thus, 8888 would generate 16 symbols. Nothing could be longer.)

There is one final point we must bring up before you read the program. The digit conversion algorithm has to make a selection among ten different alternatives. We could implement this selection in Fortran by writing a series of IF statements, but there is a cleaner way to do it.

The situation is made to order for a special kind of statement that you don't know about yet: a multiple branch transfer of control called the **computed GO TO**. This GO TO statement, instead of specifying one place to go, specifies many possible destinations. One of them is selected based on the value of an INTEGER variable which is part of the statement.

---

computed GO TO statement

form
    GO TO $(s_1, s_2, \ldots, s_n), v$
    s_i is a statement label
    v is an unsubscripted INTEGER memory cell name

meaning
    Control is transferred to the vth statement in the list $s_1, s_2, \ldots, s_n$.
    If $v < 1$ or if $v > n$, results are unpredictable.

examples
```
INTEGER N, JMP, CASE
GO TO (85, 10, 100, 453), N
GO TO (465, 700, 25), JMP
GO TO (200, 100, 100, 200, 100, 400), CASE
```

If the value of the variable is 1, then the program jumps to the first statement in the list; if it is 2, to the second statement; and so on.

Here's our completed program for roman numerals:

```
COMMENT:  ROMAN NUMERAL PROGRAM
C              INPUT:  INTEGER, RIGHT JUSTIFIED, COL 1-4
C              OUTPUT:  INPUT INTEGER AND ITS ROMAN EQUIVALENT
C              VARIABLES:
C                 I--INPUT INTEGER
C                 R--ARRAY TO STORE ROMAN NUMERAL
C                 N--CURRENT NUMBER OF SYMBOLS IN R
       INTEGER I, R(16), N, J
       READ(5,1000) I
 1000 FORMAT(I4)
       IF (I .LE. 0)  GO TO 900
C      START WITH EMPTY ROMAN NUMERAL
       N=0
C      CONVERT 1000'S DIGIT, 100'S DIGIT, TENS, UNITS
       CALL DIGIT(MOD(I/1000,10), 1HM,1HW,1HY, R,N)
       CALL DIGIT(MOD(I/100 ,10), 1HC,1HD,1HM, R,N)
       CALL DIGIT(MOD(I/10  ,10), 1HX,1HL,1HC, R,N)
       CALL DIGIT(MOD(I     ,10), 1HI,1HV,1HX, R,N)
       WRITE(6,1001) I, (R(J),J=1,N)
 1001 FORMAT('0THE ROMAN NUMERAL FOR', I5,' IS ', 31A1)
       STOP
  900 WRITE(6,9000)  I
 9000 FORMAT('0****** NO ROMAN NUMERAL FOR',I5)
       STOP
       END

       SUBROUTINE DIGIT(D, A,B,C, R,N)
       INTEGER D, A,B,C, R(31),N
COMMENT:  INPUT:
C             D--NUMBER BETWEEN 0 AND 9
C             A,B,C--ROMAN SYMBOLS
C             R--ARRAY TO STORE ROMAN NUMERAL
C             N--CURRENT NUMBER OF SYMBOLS IN R
C          OUTPUT:
C             R,N--UPDATED BY CONVERTING D TO ROMAN SYMBOLS
       INTEGER CASE
       CASE=D+1
       GO TO (100,101,102,103,104,105,106,107,108,109), CASE
C         INPUT D=0, OUTPUT PATTERN=NOTHING
  100    RETURN
C         INPUT D=1, OUTPUT PATTERN=A
  101    R(N+1) = A
         N = N+1
         RETURN
C         INPUT D=2, OUTPUT PATTERN=AA
  102    R(N+1) = A
         R(N+2) = A
         N = N+2
         RETURN
C         INPUT D=3, OUTPUT PATTERN=AAA
  103    R(N+1) = A
         R(N+2) = A
         R(N+3) = A
         N=N+3
         RETURN
```

```
C           INPUT D=4, OUTPUT PATTERN=AB
  104       R(N+1) = A
            R(N+2) = B
            N=N+2
            RETURN
C           INPUT D=5, OUTPUT PATTERN=B
  105       R(N+1) = B
            N=N+1
            RETURN
C           INPUT D=6, OUTPUT PATTERN=BA
  106       R(N+1) = B
            R(N+2) = A
            N=N+2
            RETURN
C           INPUT D=7, OUTPUT PATTERN=BAA
  107       R(N+1) = B
            R(N+2) = A
            R(N+3) = A
            N=N+3
            RETURN
C           INPUT D=8, OUTPUT PATTERN=BAA
  108       R(N+1) = B
            R(N+2) = A
            R(N+3) = A
            R(N+4) = A
            N=N+4
            RETURN
C           INPUT D=9, OUTPUT PATTERN=AC
  109       R(N+1) = A
            R(N+2) = C
            N=N+2
            RETURN
            END
```

data

```
3649
```

output

```
THE ROMAN NUMERAL FOR 3649 IS MMMDCXLIX
```

The digit conversion SUBROUTINE seems long and bulky for such a simple idea, but it would be even worse if we had implemented it with IF statements. About the only way to shorten it is to leave out the comments, and that's dangerous. If you leave them out and later misplace the documentation you did on the program while developing it, you'll have a hard time maintaining the program in the future. You'll have to do most of the design work over again to figure out how the program works.

In case you were surprised to find the error message WRITE statement (statement 900) in the main program (we hadn't discussed it earlier), we're sure you realize that it's never a good idea to trust your input to be correct. It's always best to test the input for consistency with the assumptions your program makes about it. Sometimes this is very hard to do, but in our case, we only assume that the input is an INTEGER between 1 and 9999. If the program doesn't blow up on the READ statement, we know that the input is a four-digit INTEGER, and it's easy to check for one that's out of range (zero or negative).

EXERCISES 9 2

1   What are the four steps in program design?

2   Did we follow the four steps in sequence here? Which parts of this section correspond to which steps in top down design?

3   If the input INTEGER has fewer than four digits, the spacing on the output line will be bad. Describe a way to fix that problem.

4   Write computed GO TO statements that do the same as

a
```
IF (K .EQ. 1)  GO TO 10
IF (K .EQ. 2)  GO TO 20
IF (K .EQ. 3)  GO TO 30
```

Assume K is 1, 2, or 3.

b
```
      IF (I .GT. 2 .AND. I .LT. 5)  GO TO 100
      IF (I .LT. 6)  GO TO 200
300   ...
```

Assume I is positive and less than 7.

Section 9 3

Sorting Many Arrays—Assertions and Verification

Most computations in Fortran programs are made by successively changing the values of memory cells. Input values are brought into memory and manipulated under the direction of the program until the output values are found. All programs make certain assumptions about their input values, and it is good to be aware of those assumptions. Customarily (as in the roman numeral program of Section 9 2), we state these assumptions as comments in the program. We can think of these comments as **assertions** about the input values. When the values of memory cells are changed, they are changed for a purpose. The programmer can usually make assertions about relationships among the values stored in memory, assertions which will help a reader of the program determine the purpose of the changes. Even more important, they can help the programmer analyze the effects of the computations and verify that the results are correct. Let's look at an example.

Suppose you want to write a FUNCTION to find the subscript position in an array where the maximum value is stored. The inputs to the FUNCTION would be the array, call it A, and the number, N, of values stored in it. The output should be the subscript I such that the value stored in A(I) is larger (or at least as large as) any other value in the array. We wrote a similar subprogram in Section 7 5. We don't want to repeat the development process here, but we do want to rewrite the FUNCTION, adding relevant assertions about relationships among the variables.

```
      INTEGER FUNCTION LOCMAX(A,N)
      INTEGER N, A(N)
COMMENT:   LOCATE THE ELEMENT OF AN ARRAY CONTAINING THE
C          MAXIMUM VALUE
C            INPUT:
C               A--AN ARRAY OF INTEGER VALUES
C               N--THE NUMBER OF VALUES IN A
C            OUTPUT:
C               LOCMAX--AN INTEGER SUCH THAT A(LOCMAX) .GE. A(J)
C                                        FOR EACH J BETWEEN 1 AND N
      LOCMAX = 1
      DO 100 I=1,N
        IF (A(I) .GT. A(LOCMAX)) LOCMAX=I
C       ASSERTION:  AT THIS POINT A(LOCMAX) .GE. A(J)
C                                  FOR EACH J BETWEEN 1 AND I
 100    CONTINUE
      RETURN
      END
```

The assertion in the program can be verified by a simple mathematical proof. We don't want to go into mathematical proofs at this point, but if you're familiar with mathematical induction, you might want to look at the proof. In any case, a little thought will convince you of the correctness of the assertion. It is essentially a statement of the programmer's fundamental idea when he designed the program. Since I and N have the same value on the last pass through the loop, the assertion implies that when the RETURN is executed, $A(LOCMAX) \geqslant A(J)$ for each J between 1 and N. In other words, the value of the FUNCTION is correct.

---

inductive proof of assertion (skip this unless you're familiar with mathematical induction)

When $I = 1$, LOCMAX $= 1$ and $A(1) \geqslant A(1)$; hence the assertion is true when $I = 1$.

induction hypothesis: $A(LOCMAX) \geqslant A(J)$ for each J between 1 and I when $I = II$ $(II < N)$.

Suppose $I = II + 1$. Then either LOCMAX didn't change values on this pass through the loop or it did.

In the former case, we have $A(II + 1) \leqslant A(LOCMAX)$. This, together with the induction hypothesis, implies that $A(LOCMAX) \geqslant A(J)$, for each J between 1 and $II + 1$.

In the latter case, let p stand for the previous value of LOCMAX. The induction hypothesis says that $A(p) \geqslant A(J)$ for each J between 1 and II. The fact that LOCMAX has changed values implies that LOCMAX $= II + 1$ and that $A(II + 1) > A(p)$. Therefore, $A(LOCMAX) \geqslant A(J)$ for each J between 1 and $II + 1$.

This is a simple example, of course. But the same ideas apply in larger programs too. Let's look at one, a sorting problem.

What we want to do here is to print a list of personal statistics records (name, age, weight, and height for each of several persons) in order by weight, lightest to heaviest.

The input for the program will be a bunch of these personal statistics records, one to a card, followed by a terminal record containing the signal name END so that we'll know when we've reached the end of the records. We want the output to be the same list of records rearranged so that the weights are in order from lightest to heaviest.

> **input/output description**
>
> *input:* (a) one personal statistics record for each person, consisting of name, age, weight, and height;
> (b) terminal record with END in the name field
>
> *computation:* arrange the records by weights, lightest to heaviest
>
> *output:* list of all input personal statistics records in order of increasing weight

A first stab at designing our program is shown below. Since we've had a lot of experience with input and output loops of the kind we'll need here, there's not much point in spending time analyzing those processes here. The sorting process is the one we need to look at carefully.

> **personal statistics sorting algorithm**
>
> *1 bring records into memory*
> *2 compute arrangement by weight*
> *3 print records*

It is nearly always the case in a sorting problem that more than one array is involved. The example in this section involves four arrays, but the sorting subprogram we'll write will be useful for sorting, simultaneously, *any* number of corresponding arrays. The sorting process will be the same as in Section 7 5, but instead of rearranging the arrays themselves, we'll simply build an **index** which will tell us how they should be arranged. The first entry in the index will tell us where to find the array elements which come first in the ordering, the second entry will tell us

> **index:** *a list of numbers telling us how to arrange another list in alphabetical order; the first entry in index tells us which element in the list goes first, the second index entry tells us which goes second, and so on*

where to find the elements which should come second, and so on. Figure 9 3 1 pictures an index for some arrays containing the names, ages, weights, and heights of a group of children which we want to arrange in order from lightest to heaviest.

	names	ages	weights	heights	index	
1	BOB	5	45	46	3	(AMY lightest)
2	TED	6	39	45	4	(JOY 2nd)
3	AMY	3	27	32	5	(SUE 3rd)
4	JOY	4	31	36	2	(TED 4th)
5	SUE	5	33	38	1	(BOB heaviest)

Figure 9 3 1

The index will tell us what order the elements should come in. Our subprogram won't rearrange the arrays themselves so it won't need to know how many arrays are involved. All it will need to know is what values are in the array containing the **keys**, the values we want in increasing order. From that it can build the index, which will tell us what order to take the array elements in. We'll use a technique that can be used in conjunction with almost any sorting algorithm.

> **keys:** *a list of values which we want to know how to arrange in some particular order (e.g., increasing order)*

In the beginning, we set up the index as if the array were already in the correct order; that is, the index will have the entries 1, 2, 3, 4, and so on, to begin with. Then we rearrange the index until it correctly orders the keys. The trick is that we always refer to the keys *through the index*. Instead of referring to the *i*th key, we refer to the key designated by the *i*th entry in the index. If the keys array is called KEYS and the index array is called INDEX, then instead of referring to KEYS(I), we refer to KEYS(INDEX(I)). Whenever we want to interchange a pair of keys, we interchange the corresponding *index* entries (not the keys themselves). Since we are referring to the keys through the index anyway, it will be as if we had interchanged the pair of keys. Perhaps this is best explained pictorially, as in Figures 9 3 2 and 9 3 3.

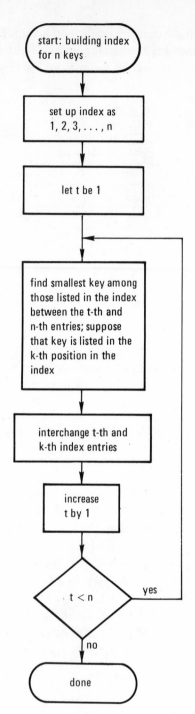

VERBAL DESCRIPTION

Set up index.

Find largest element in bottom section of array.

Interchange largest element with top element in bottom section.

Decrease size of bottom section.

Repeat unless bottom section contains only one element.

Figure 9 3 2   Sorting Algorithm

The subprogram below prepares an index for a list of keys in the way described by the flowchart of Figure 9 3 2. It has two input parameters: KEYS, an array of values we want to arrange in increasing order; and N, the number of values in the array KEYS. It has one output parameter, INDEX, an array which will tell us how to arrange the KEYS.

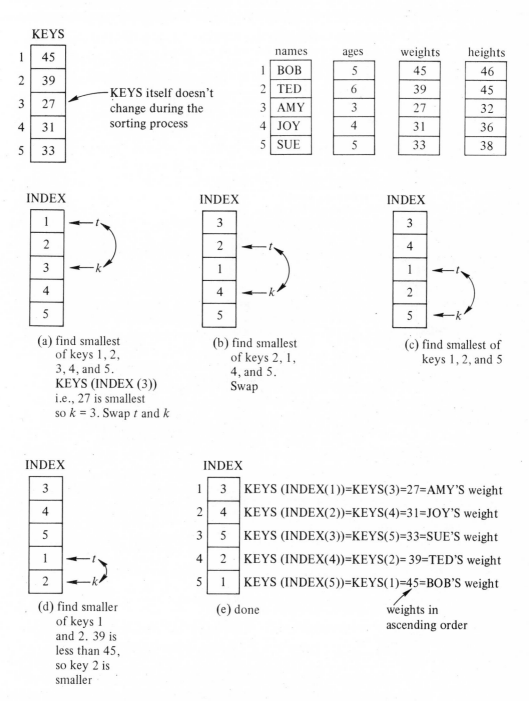

(a) find smallest
of keys 1, 2,
3, 4, and 5.
KEYS (INDEX (3))
i.e., 27 is smallest
so *k* = 3. Swap *t* and *k*

(b) find smallest
of keys 2, 1,
4, and 5.
Swap

(c) find smallest of
keys 1, 2, and 5

(d) find smaller
of keys 1
and 2. 39 is
less than 45,
so key 2 is
smaller

(e) done

weights in
ascending order

Figure 9 3 3 Arranging an Index

```
            SUBROUTINE INDSRT (KEYS, INDEX, N)
            INTEGER N, KEYS(N), INDEX(N)
   COMMENT:  THIS SUBROUTINE PERFORMS AN INDEX SORT.
   C            IT FILLS THE ARRAY "INDEX" WITH VALUES WHICH TELL
   C            US HOW TO ARRANGE THE ARRAY "KEYS" IN INCREASING
   C            ORDER.
   C          INPUT:
   C            KEYS--AN ARRAY OF INTEGERS
   C            N--THE NUMBER OF ENTRIES IN KEYS
   C          OUTPUT:
   C            INDEX--AN ARRAY CONTAINING ALL THE INTEGERS
   C                    BETWEEN 1 AND N ARRANGED SO THAT
   C                    KEYS(INDEX(1)).LE.KEYS(INDEX(2)).LE. ...
   C                    ETC.  UP TO KEYS(INDEX(N))
            INTEGER TOP, SM, LOCSM, NLESS1
   C        INITIALIZE INDEX
            DO 50 TOP=1,N
    50      INDEX(TOP)=TOP
   C        SORT
            NLESS1 = N-1
            DO 100 TOP=1,NLESS1
            SM = LOCSM(KEYS,INDEX, TOP, N)
            CALL SWITCH(INDEX(SM),INDEX(TOP))
   C        ASSERTION:  AT THIS POINT
   C        KEYS(INDEX(I)) .LE. KEYS(INDEX(I+1)), I=1 ... TOP
    100     CONTINUE
            RETURN
            END

            INTEGER FUNCTION LOCSM (KEYS,INDEX, FROM,TO)
            INTEGER FROM, TO, KEYS(TO), INDEX(TO)
   COMMENT: LOCATE THE SMALLEST VALUE
   C        INPUT:
   C          KEYS--AS IN SUBROUTINE INDSRT
   C          INDEX--AN ARRAY CONTAINING THE INTEGERS BETWEEN
   C                  1 AND "TO" (SCRAMBLED)
   C          FROM--AN INTEGER BETWEEN 1 AND "TO"
   C          TO--THE NUMBER OF ENTRIES IN KEYS AND INDEX
   C        OUTPUT:
   C          LOCSM--KEYS(INDEX(LOCSM)).LE.KEYS(INDEX(I))
   C                  FOR EACH I BETWEEN "FROM" AND "TO"
            INTEGER I
            LOCSM=FROM
            DO 100 I=FROM,TO
            IF (KEYS(INDEX(I)).LT.KEYS(INDEX(LOCSM))) LOCSM=I
   C        ASSERTION: AT THIS POINT
   C        KEYS(INDEX(LOCSM)).LE.KEYS(INDEX(J)) , J=FROM ... I
    100     CONTINUE
            RETURN
            END

            SUBROUTINE SWITCH (A,B)
            INTEGER A,B
            INTEGER COPYA
            COPYA = A
            A = B
            B = COPYA
            RETURN
            END
```

As in the LOCMAX program we studied before, the assertions stated in
INDSRT and LOCSM above can be verified by mathematical induction (or by

careful examination), and they make it clear that the SUBROUTINEs do what they were intended to do. Look at the assertion in the INDSRT routine. The assertion is true whenever the program passes through it. Therefore, it is true, in particular, the last time through the loop. On that last pass, TOP is equal to N, so that the assertion states that the computation the SUBROUTINE was written to perform has been completed. Since the output array is not changed beyond that point in time, the assertion (provided it's true, of course—you should verify this) proves that the SUBROUTINE is correct. You can go through a similar analysis of the assertion in the LOCSM routine.

We can use INDSRT to solve the problem of printing our list of children's names (along with their ages and weights) in order of their weights. All we need to do, once the information is stored in the arrays, is CALL our SUBROUTINE. We use the array that stores their weights as our argument, and provide an array to be used for an index. Then we will be able to print the arrays in the proper order by using the index. While we're at it, we may as well sort the arrays again so that we can also print the lists in order of increasing age. That will just involve another CALL to the SUBROUTINE.

```
COMMENT:   THIS PROGRAM READS A LIST OF CHILDREN'S NAMES,
C          AGES, WEIGHTS, AND HEIGHTS FROM CARDS, THEN PRINTS
C          THE LIST TWICE.  ONCE IN THE ORDER OF INCREASING
C          WEIGHT, THEN ONCE IN ORDER OF INCREASING AGE.
       INTEGER NAME(100), AGE(100), WGT(100), HGT(100)
       INTEGER N, I, X(100), FINIS
       DATA FINIS/3HEND/
C      STORE THE DATA
       N=0
 100   READ(5,1000) NAME(N+1),AGE(N+1),WGT(N+1),HGT(N+1)
 1000  FORMAT(A3, 3I3)
          IF (NAME(N+1) .EQ. FINIS)  GO TO 200
          N = N+1
          GO TO 100
COMMENT: FIRST SORT ON WEIGHTS.
 200   CALL INDSRT(WGT,X,N)
       WRITE(6,2000)
 2000  FORMAT('0CHILDREN BY INCREASING WEIGHT'/
      +        ' NAME      AGE     WEIGHT    HEIGHT')
       WRITE(6,3000) (NAME(X(I)),AGE(X(I)),WGT(X(I)),
      +                         HGT(X(I)), I=1,N)
 3000  FORMAT(' ',A3,3I10)
COMMENT: NOW SORT ON AGES.
       CALL INDSRT(AGE,X,N)
       WRITE(6,4000)
 4000  FORMAT('0CHILDREN BY INCREASING AGE'/
      +        ' NAME      AGE     WEIGHT    HEIGHT')
       WRITE(6,3000) (NAME(X(I)),AGE(X(I)),WGT(X(I)),
      +                         HGT(X(I)), I=1,N)
       STOP
       END
```

data

```
BOB   5  45  46
TED   6  39  45
AMY   3  27  32
JOY   4  31  36
SUE   5  33  38
END
```

output

```
CHILDREN BY INCREASING WEIGHT
NAME        AGE     WEIGHT      HEIGHT
AMY          3        27          32
JOY          4        31          36
SUE          5        33          38
TED          6        39          45
BOB          5        45          46

CHILDREN BY INCREASING AGE
NAME        AGE     WEIGHT      HEIGHT
AMY          3        27          32
JOY          4        31          36
BOB          5        45          46
SUE          5        33          38
TED          6        39          45
```

---

nonstandard subscripts

Many of the subscripts used in this program, like the $X(I)$ in NAME$(X(I))$, *are not ANSI standard subscripts. The standards require that expressions in subscripts be one of the following forms.*

$$k$$
$$v$$
$$v - k$$
$$v + k$$
$$c * v$$
$$c * v - k$$
$$c * v + k$$

c and k are unsigned INTEGER *constants*

v is an unsubscripted INTEGER *memory cell name*

To make our program fit the standards, we would need to declare an INTEGER *memory cell and assign it the value $X(I)$ whenever necessary. Thus the last WRITE statement in the program would be written:*

```
      DO 310 I=1,N
         J = X(I)
310      WRITE(6,3010) NAME(J),AGE(J),WGT(J),HGT(J)
```

EXERCISES 9 3

1   What statements would you add to the final program of this section so that it also prints the lists of children's names in alphabetical order?

2   What statements could you add to the program to make certain it didn't try to READ more cards than it had room for in its arrays?

3 The arrays are declared to be of length 100 in the program. But the array parameters in INDSRT are declared to be of length N, where N is one of the parameters. When INDSRT is CALLed, the parameter indicating the length of the arrays won't have a value equal to the actual declared array length. Do you think this should cause an error? Do you think it will cause an error? Why or why not?

Section 9 4

Simulating a Game of Craps

We are planning a trip to Las Vegas to gamble at the crap tables and wonder how much money we can expect to lose. If craps were a fair game, we would expect to come out about even. However, we know that it's not a fair game. There is a greater chance of losing than of winning, so we expect to come out a little behind. The question is, how far behind?

> **problem statement**: *Estimate expected losing rate at crap tables.*

A quick way of making an estimate of how far behind we expect to be after 1,000 games is to simulate the game on the computer (making use of the random number generator from Section 7 6). To simulate the game, we need to know the rules; they are depicted in Figure 9 4 1.

In plain English, the rules are: Roll the dice. If the sum of the spots is 7 or 11, you win immediately. If the sum of the spots is 2 ("snake eyes"), 3 ("craps"), or 12 ("box cars"), you lose immediately. Otherwise the number you rolled is called your **point**. You keep rolling until you get either your point, in which case you win, or a 7, in which case you have "crapped out," and you lose.

> *losing rate estimation algorithm*
> 1 *start out with no wins and no losses*
> 2 *simulate a game of craps*
> 3 *if the game was won, bump the number of wins; otherwise bump the number of losses*
> 4 *repeat from step 2 (simulation) unless number of games simulated is 1000*
> 5 *print number of wins and losses*

The rules of the game make it clear how to write the simulation part of the program. The only part of any difficulty is simulating the dice roll. To do this, we'll use a SUBROUTINE ROLL. When we call ROLL, it gives us the number (2, 3, 4, . . ., or 12) which came up on the dice. (ROLL will have one parameter, an output parameter.) To write this SUBROUTINE we can use the FUNCTION CHOOSE

VERBAL DESCRIPTION

Roll the dice. Select one of the following:

rolled 7 or 11: WIN.
rolled 2,3, or 12: LOSE.
rolled point = 4,5,6,8,9,or 10:
roll again:
if roll = 7 then LOSE.
if roll = point then WIN.
repeat from "roll again."

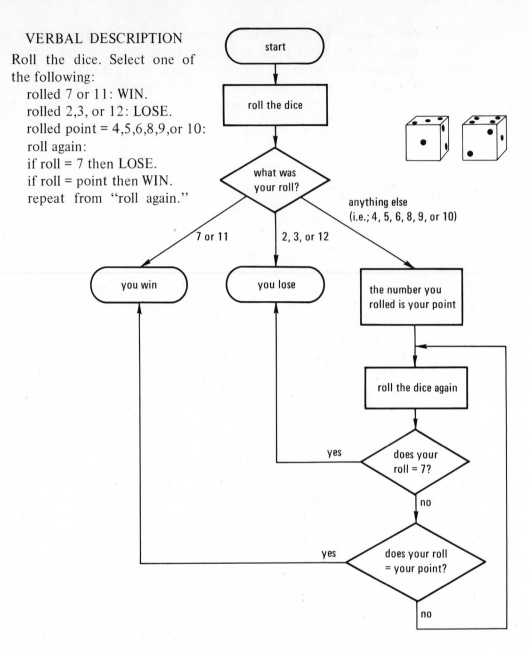

Figure 9 4 1   Rules of Craps

> *A philosophical question: The rules don't prohibit a game of craps from lasting forever. Should we worry about that in our program?*

236   Fortran for Humans

from Section 7 6. CHOOSE needs one argument, a positive INTEGER. The number it computes is an INTEGER between 1 and the value of its argument. Each possible value of CHOOSE has the same likelihood of being chosen. Therefore CHOOSE(6) gives us a number between 1 and 6, like rolling a die.

```
          SUBROUTINE ROLL (DICE)
          INTEGER DICE
          INTEGER CHOOSE
COMMENT:  "DICE" WILL BE SET TO A RANDOM VALUE 2, 3, ...., 12
C         LIKE ROLLING A PAIR OF DICE.
C             (FUNCTION CHOOSE IS FROM SECTION 7 6)
          DICE = CHOOSE(6) + CHOOSE(6)
          RETURN
          END
```

Note that it is crucial that we add together two random numbers uniformly chosen from 1 to 6 instead of just taking one number at random from 2 to 12. Look at the number of ways of getting the possible dice rolls. The table shows that the odds of getting a 7 are $6/36 = 1/6$. If we just used one random number uniformly chosen between 2 and 12, the odds would be $1/11$.

dice roll	number of ways of adding two numbers 1 to 6 to get the total	number of ways of getting one number 2 to 12
2	1	1
3	2	1
4	3	1
5	4 (i.e. 1+4, 2+3 3+2, 4+1)	1
6	5	1
7	6	1
8	5	1
9	4	1
10	3	1
11	2	1
12	1	1

In looking at the rules of the game, you probably noticed that after the initial dice roll, there is a fairly complicated series of tests which must be performed before deciding which of the three routes to take (win, lose, or roll again). We could make these tests using IF statements, but the program is clearer if we use the computed GO TO. It more accurately reflects the selection among several alternatives as expressed in the rules of the game.

> *the odds of winning at craps are about .493 (a little better than 49 out of 100).*

```
COMMENT:  PLAY 1000 GAMES OF CRAPS KEEPING A WIN-LOSS RECORD.
          INTEGER POINT, DICE, WINS, LOSSES
C         INITIALIZE WIN-LOSS COUNTERS
          WINS=0
          LOSSES=0
C         ROLL THE DICE
  1       CALL ROLL(DICE)
          GO TO (10,30,30,40,40,40,20,40,40,40,20,30,10), DICE
C         ERROR ...
 10          WRITE(6,1000) DICE
 1000     FORMAT(' ERROR--DICE ROLL=',I10)
          STOP
C         WIN ...
 20       WINS = WINS +1
          GO TO 50
C         LOSE ...
 30       LOSSES = LOSSES +1
          GO TO 50
C         ROLL BECOMES OUR POINT ... GO ON.
 40       POINT = DICE
 45       CALL ROLL (DICE)
C            TEST FOR UNLUCKY SEVEN (LOSE)
             IF (DICE .EQ. 7)   GO TO 30
C            TEST FOR POINT (WIN)
             IF (DICE .EQ. POINT)   GO TO 20
C            NO DECISION  ... ROLL AGAIN
             GO TO 45
C         GAME OVER...PLAY AGAIN UNLESS WE'VE PLAYED 1000 GAMES
 50       IF (WINS+LOSSES .LT. 1000)   GO TO 1
C         PRINT RESULTS
          WRITE(6,2000) WINS,LOSSES
 2000     FORMAT(' OUT OF 1000 GAMES, WE WON',I4,' AND LOST',I4)
          STOP
          END
```

output

```
OUT OF 1000 GAMES, WE WON 475 AND LOST 525
```

EXERCISES 9 4

1 How would you change the program to test the fairness of the game if the rule were that you lose if you get a 7 *or* an 11 while going for your point?

2 After rolling for a point, the rules require a three-branch selection. Devise a way to use the computed GO TO for this selection. (Note: This is a relatively hard exercise. If you don't get it in a few minutes, look at the answer.)

Section 9 5

Permutations

There is a big demand these days for short, modern-sounding corporate names. Coming up with a good name is a lengthy process, so it would be nice if we could develop a computer program to do part of the work, preferably the most tedious and uninteresting part. Many of the recent names (CITGO, EXXON, MILACRON, etc.) are based on acronyms. Since an acronym is just some arrangement of letters

> **acronym:** *a word formed from the initial letters or syllables of a compound term. For example, SOB is an acronym for Save Our Bay, a now defunct civic organization.*

or syllables each of which is the first part of a key word in the phrase you are trying to represent, it might be handy to have a little list of all the different ways in which these letters or syllables can be written. While reading through such a list, you might come across a particularly appealing arrangement. Then you could check to see if the corresponding arrangement of the key words would make sense. If so, you have come up with a nice acronym.

> **problem statement:** *Construct a program to print a list of all the possible arrangements of the key parts of an acronym.*

The idea of the program is simple—its input would be a list of letters and/or syllables from the key words, and its output should be all the possible orderings of the input list.

> **input/output description**
>
> input: *the key parts (letters or letter combinations) of an acronym*
>
> output: *a list of all possible arrangements of the key parts (one of these arrangements may be the good, catchy acronym we're looking for)*

Our general plan will be to start with the given arrangement of the acronym elements (the arrangement of the input list) and successively generate new arrangements, printing them as we go.

> **acronym arrangement algorithm**
> 1 *bring key parts into memory*
> 2 *start with the input arrangement*
> 3 *loop:*
>   a *print the current arrangement*
>   b *generate an arrangement not yet used*
>   c *repeat loop unless step 3 b was impossible*

Most of the steps in the acronym arrangement algorithm, as we now perceive it, are straightforward (things we've done before). The tricky part is step 3b, generating an arrangement we haven't yet seen. This will require careful analysis. Instead of trying to solve the rearrangement problem by working directly with the letters, let's look at the problem of generating arrangements of the numbers 1, 2, ..., n. Given an arrangement of numbers, we can generate an arrangement of the n key parts of an acronym simply by using each number to select a key part. For example, if the key parts are R, S, and I, then the number arrangement 3, 1, 2 leads to the acronym IRS.

It is natural to write down the various orderings or permutations of integers in lexical or dictionary sequence. In this sequence, the permutation 2 1 4 5 3 would come before the permutation 2 1 5 3 4 because, even though the first two digits of each are the same, the third digits differ, and the third digit of the first permutation is smaller than that of the second permutation. This is just like alphabetical order, but with numbers instead of letters. Our goal is to write a SUBROUTINE whose input is a list of INTEGERs in some order and whose output is that same list in a rearranged order. If we write the SUBROUTINE so that it always generates the *next* permutation in the lexical sequence, then no permutations will be repeated and none will be omitted. Once we have this SUBROUTINE, our acronym program will be easy to write.

The question is, given a certain permutation, how do you rearrange it so that it becomes the next permutation in the lexical sequence? This is not a trivial question, but if you think carefully, you will notice that what you want to change is the right-hand end or **suffix** of the permutation. Changes in the suffix make smaller jumps in the permutation's lexical position than changes in the left-hand end, and it's small changes in the lexical position that we're interested in. To make the smallest increase, we must rearrange the shortest suffix in which it is possible to make a lexical increase. It is not possible to make a lexical increase in a suffix in which the digits are already in decreasing order, because the only thing we can do to change a suffix is to interchange some of the integers that make it up, and any change would decrease that suffix's lexical position. Therefore, as a first step towards generating the next permutation, we want to pick the shortest suffix in which the digits are *not* in decreasing order.

For example, consider the permutation 4 1 3 5 2. The suffix 5 2 is already in decreasing order and therefore can't be increased. However, the suffix 3 5 2 isn't in decreasing order so we can increase it. How do we make the smallest possible increase (to get the next larger suffix)? To do this we interchange its first digit with the next larger digit in the suffix and arrange the remainder of the suffix in increasing order. Thus the suffix 3 5 2 would be changed to 5 2 3; the first digit (3) is exchanged with the next larger digit (5), and the remainder (3 2) is arranged in increasing order (2 3). Therefore 4 1 5 2 3 is the next permutation after 4 1 3 5 2.

Notice that if the sequence is entirely in decreasing order (5 4 3 2 1), we can't find a larger sequence in the lexical ordering. At this point, we'll be done.

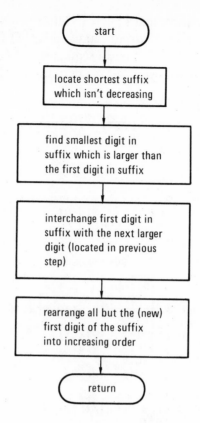

Figure 9 5 1 Algorithm for Finding the Next Permutation in Lexical Sequence

We have only one final observation to make before we write the SUBROUTINE: The suffix, exclusive of the first digit, remains in decreasing order after the interchange of the first digit with the next larger digit. Therefore, the rearrangement to get that part of the suffix into increasing order amounts to reversing it. To see this, consider a suffix $ab_1 \ldots b_k$, where a is the first number and b_1 through b_k are the remaining numbers, so that $b_1 > b_2 > \ldots > b_k$. Let b_i be the number in the suffix which is just larger than a. Then

$$b_1 > b_2 > \ldots > b_i > a > b_{i+1} > \ldots > b_k$$

because of the way b_i was selected. Therefore, after the interchange of a and b_i, the suffix becomes

$$b_i b_1 \ldots b_{i-1} a b_{i+1} \ldots b_k$$

which is in decreasing order except for the first digit.

Now we see how to write the SUBROUTINE. To locate the suffix, it must examine the input permutation from right to left until it finds a digit that is smaller than the one to its right. Then it interchanges that digit with the next larger one to its right and reverses the suffix (except for the first digit).

The following SUBROUTINE and associated subprograms accomplish this task. There are two input parameters: (1) an array containing the list of INTEGERs in the last used permutation and (2) an INTEGER indicating the number of entries in the list. There are two output parameters: (1) the list (input list) rearranged into the next permutation in lexical sequence and (2) a LOGICAL value, which is .FALSE. if the input list was the last permutation in the entire lexical sequence and .TRUE. otherwise.

```
      SUBROUTINE PERM (LIST, N, NEWPRM)
      INTEGER N, LIST(N)
      LOGICAL NEWPRM
C        INPUT:
C          LIST--A PERMUTATION OF 1 ... N
C        OUTPUT:
C          LIST--THE NEXT PERMUTATION IN LEXICAL SEQUENCE
C          NEWPRM--.FALSE. IF INPUT LIST WAS LAST (LEXICALLY)
      INTEGER SUFFIX, NXTLGR
      INTEGER K, L
      NEWPRM = .FALSE.
C        LOCATE SHORTEST INCREASABLE SUFFIX
      K = SUFFIX(LIST,N)
      IF (K .LE. 0)  RETURN
      NEWPRM = .TRUE.
C        INTERCHANGE FIRST DIGIT WITH NEXT LARGER ONE
      L = NXTLGR(K,LIST,N)
      CALL SWITCH(LIST(K),LIST(L))
C        REVERSE ALL BUT FIRST DIGIT
      CALL REVRSE(K+1,LIST,N)
      RETURN
      END


      INTEGER FUNCTION SUFFIX(LIST,N)
      INTEGER N, LIST(N)
COMMENT:  VALUE OF SUFFIX POINTS TO SHORTEST SUFFIX OF
C         "LIST" WHICH ISN'T DECREASING
      SUFFIX = N-1
 10   IF (SUFFIX .LE. 0)  RETURN
      IF (LIST(SUFFIX) .LT. LIST(SUFFIX+1))  RETURN
      SUFFIX = SUFFIX-1
C        ASSERTION:  AT THIS POINT
C          LIST(SUFFIX+1),LIST(SUFFIX+2),....,LIST(N) IS A
C          DECREASING SEQUENCE.
      GO TO 10
      END


      INTEGER FUNCTION NXTLGR(SX,LIST,N)
      INTEGER SX, N, LIST(N)
COMMENT:  THE VALUE OF "NXTLGR" POINTS TO THE SMALLEST VALUE
C         IN THE SUFFIX LIST(SX+1), LIST(SX+2), ...., LIST(N)
C         WHICH EXCEEDS LIST(SX)
C         ASSUMPTIONS:  LIST(SX+I),I=1...N-SX IS DECREASING
C                       SX < N
C                       LIST(SX) < LIST(SX+1)
      NXTLGR = N
 10   IF (LIST(NXTLGR) .GT. LIST(SX))  RETURN
      NXTLGR = NXTLGR-1
C        ASSERTION:  AT THIS POINT LIST(K) .LE. LIST(SX) FOR
C                    EACH K=NXTLGR+1 ... N
      GO TO 10
      END
```

```
        SUBROUTINE REVRSE(SX,LIST,N)
        INTEGER SX, N,LIST(N)
COMMENT:  REVERSES SUFFIX LIST(SX) ... LIST(N)
        INTEGER MIDDLE, K
        MIDDLE = (SX+N)/2
        DO 10 K=SX,MIDDLE
   10     CALL SWITCH(LIST(K),LIST(N-K+SX))
        RETURN
        END

        SUBROUTINE SWITCH(A,B)
        INTEGER A, B
        INTEGER COPYA
        COPYA = A
        A = B
        B = COPYA
        RETURN
        END
```

Now that we have the permutation generator, we can write our program to make a list of all possible acronyms from a given set of symbols. We'll use it to recount a bit of interesting history. It seems that, in the old days, compilers were called formula translators. Naturally, the development of the first formula translator was a long and arduous task, and when the program finally worked, the designers were very excited. One of them, it seems, went galloping down the halls shouting, "The formula translator ran!" Let's use that phrase to try to find an acronym for their compiler. We'll let FOR stand for "formula," T for "translator," and RAN stand for itself. You can see the results in the output section of the program listing below.

```
COMMENT:  PROGRAM TO GENERATE ACRONYMS.
C        VARIABLES:
C          LTRSYL --ARRAY STORING SYLLABLES AVAILABLE
C          P --ARRAY TO STORE PERMUTATIONS
        INTEGER LTRSYL(20), P(20), LEN, I, FINIS
        LOGICAL ANOTHR
        DATA FINIS/3H***/
C        GET SYLLABLES FROM DATA CARDS
        LEN = 0
   10   READ(5,1000) LTRSYL(LEN+1)
 1000   FORMAT(20A3)
          IF (LTRSYL(LEN+1) .EQ. FINIS)  GO TO 20
          LEN = LEN+1
          P(LEN) = LEN
          GO TO 10
C        GENERATE ACROMYMS, ONE PERMUTATION AFTER ANOTHER
   20   WRITE(6,2000) (LTRSYL(P(I)),I=1,LEN)
 2000   FORMAT(10X,20A3)
          CALL PERM(P,LEN,ANOTHR)
          IF (ANOTHR)  GO TO 20
        STOP
        END
```

```
data
    FOR
     T
    RAN
    ***
```

output

```
FOR T RAN
FORRAN T
  T FORRAN
  T RANFOR
RANFOR T
RAN T FOR
```

photo credit: Langsford, Raymond (197?), *A Pseudo-History of Computing*, Nonesuch Press, Inc., p. 37.

"The Formula Translator Ran!"

EXERCISES 9 5

1 List these permutations of the numbers from 1 to 5 in increasing lexical order.

1	2	3	4	5
2	3	5	4	1
5	4	2	3	1
5	4	3	1	2
3	2	5	4	1

2 By listing all the permutations of three numbers, verify that all possible acronyms based on FOR, T, and RAN are listed above.

244   Fortran for Humans

PROBLEMS 9

NOTICE: None of the problems in this chapter are particularly simple. If you take your time in the design phase and follow the organizational principles covered in this chapter, you will have a better time overall.

1 Construct a SUBROUTINE ARAB which accepts an array containing a number in roman notation and returns the equivalent INTEGER. (Note: This is an easier problem than going the other way.)

2 Write a program which performs addition, subtraction, multiplication, and division of roman numerals. Organize the program using SUBROU-TINEs which split up the work as shown below.

Problem statement: perform arithmetic on roman numerals.

First refinement:

```
                    ( start )
                        |
         +------------->|
         |              v
         |   +------------------------+
         |   | read roman numeral 1,  |
         |   | operator (+, -, *, /), |
         |   | and roman numeral 2    |
         |   +------------------------+
         |              |
         |              v
         |   +------------------------+
         |   | convert both roman     |
         |   | numerals to INTEGERs   |
         |   +------------------------+
         |              |
         |              v
         |   +------------------------+
         |   | perform desired        |
         |   | arithmetic on          |
         |   | the INTEGERs           |
         |   +------------------------+
         |              |
         |              v
         |   +------------------------+
         |   | convert result to      |
         |   | a roman numeral        |
         |   +------------------------+
         |              |
         |              v
         |   +------------------------+
         |   | print the equation as  |
         |   | roman numerals         |
         |   | (e.g., III + IV = VII) |
         |   +------------------------+
         |              |
         |              v
   yes   /----------------\
   +-----<     more?       >
         \----------------/
                 | no
                 v
             ( stop )
```

Notice that the module

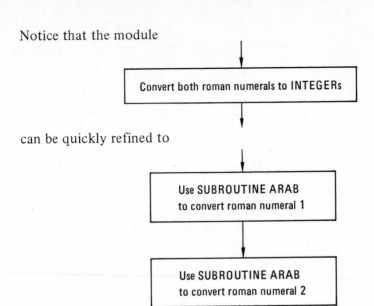

Convert both roman numerals to INTEGERs

can be quickly refined to

Use SUBROUTINE ARAB
to convert roman numeral 1

Use SUBROUTINE ARAB
to convert roman numeral 2

While the program you wind up with will be fairly large and does a rather complex task, by using the top down, successive refinement method, it is constructed quickly from small, manageable modules, many of which you already know how to write programs for.

Samples:

input			output
X	+	X	X + X = XX
X	/	L	X / L IS NOT REPRESENTABLE AS A ROMAN NUMERAL
IX	*	XI	IX * XI = XCIX
IV	–	XIII	IV – XIII IS NOT REPRESENTABLE AS A ROMAN NUMERAL

3 READ a value for *m* (the number of grades for each student). READ in *m* grades for each student, compute each student's average, and store the average grades in a one-dimensional array. Arrange the array of average grades in descending order and write out the ordered array. Finally, calculate and WRITE (with appropriate labeling) the number of average scores which fall in each of the percentile groups 1 to 10, 11 to 20, . . ., 91 to 100.

4 Compare the sorting method of Section 7 5 with the **bubble sort** (described below) by generating 1000 random numbers, sorting them each way, and counting how many times each routine compares pairs of numbers.

The bubble sort works like this: Go through the array element by element, comparing the current element with the next and reversing their order if the first is larger than the second. Keep doing this until you have gone completely through the array. Repeat until you complete one complete pass which requires no reversals. At that point you're finished—the array is in order.

WRITE the original numbers, the sorted numbers, and the number of comparisons made by the two different sorting methods. Each sorting method should be expressed as a SUBROUTINE.

5 Each of the following data cards has three pieces of information: the name of a football player, his number, and his weight. Write a program to read and print the arrays in four different orders. First in the original order, second in alphabetical order using the players' last names, third in order of their numbers, and fourth in order of their weights. (Hint: Use INDSRT from Section 9 3.)

Data:

SQUARE, JOHNNY	27	170
DUDA, PAUL	31	200
JULIANA, PAT	9	180
BLACKFORD, BOB	5	183
WILSON, MIKE	25	197
CASWELL, GERALD	95	240
DRISCOLL, MARK	8	175
BABICH, FRED	80	220
BATTLE, GREG	46	195
MONTGOMERY, CHARLES	63	255
ST. CLAIR, STEVE	87	195
STEWART, GUY	18	170
MOSS, JESSE	19	190
O'ROURKE, DAN	22	190

6 Bank Accounts

Write a program which creates and keeps track of bank accounts for up to 20 people. For each person, keep track of (a) the person's name, (b) the balance in his account, and (c) the number of withdrawals or deposits. A deposit will correspond to a data card such as

'MARY MOONY'   +303.02

and a withdrawal will correspond to a card like

'CAPT. BEEFHEART'   −2.00

Each time your program reads a card, check to see if there is an account for that person, and if not, create a new entry. If there already is an account, add or subtract the deposit or withdrawal and add 1 to the number of transactions. After there are no more data cards to read, your program should print the information it has compiled about each account.

Data:

FRANK FEEBLES	+ 100.00
RALPH WILLIAMS	+1901.74
RALPH WILLIAMS	+2794.25
BETTY FURNACE	+ 3.01
RALPH WILLIAMS	+ 470.00
HARRY IGNAZ	+ 25.00
FRANK FEEBLES	− 35.00
JESS UNRUH	+ 11.00
HAROLD STASSEN	+ 342.00
RALPH WILLIAMS	− 400.00
JESS UNRUH	−5243.00
MINNEY MOOS	+ 35.75
RALPH WILLIAMS	+7500.20
WAYNE ASPINALL	− .06
BETTY FURNACE	+ 3.01

HINT: Use several one-dimensional arrays to keep track of the accounts so that after the first three cards have been read, the arrays look like the following:

	NAME	BAL	TRANS
1	'FRANK FEEBLES'	100.00	1
2	'RALPH WILLIAMS'	4695.99	2
3			
4			

7 a Write a LOGICAL FUNCTION which takes the value .TRUE. if its INTEGER argument is a perfect square. (A number n is a perfect square if there is some other number k such that $n = k^2$).

   b Using nested loops (and the FUNCTION of part a), write a program which prints all the Pythagorean triples a, b, c, with a and b between 1 and 50. (A Pythagorean triple is three integers a, b, and c such that $a^2 + b^2 = c^2$.)

   c Write a program which prints out all of the (rare) Fermatean triples a, b, c, with a and b between 1 and 50. (A Fermatean triple is three integers a, b, and c such that $a^3 + b^3 = c^3$.)

8 A certain company rents time on five of its machines. Each time a customer uses a machine, he turns in a time card. At the first of each month the company sends out bills for the use of the machines for the past month.

   The rates on the machines are different for different customers and for different time periods during the day. Therefore, your first input will be ten price cards, each card specifying a price code (00–09) and the cost per hour for the price code.

Compute a bill for each customer which includes the following information:

  customer number

  machine number

  total hours and total costs for each machine used by the customer

  total cost for the customer

The time cards for the month are sorted by customer number but not by machine and contain the following information:

  customer number ($xxxxxxx$)

  price code (xx)

  machine number (1, 2, 3, 4, or 5)

  time in ($xx.xx$)

  time out ($xx.xx$)

Assume the time is given to the nearest hundredth of an hour on the 24-hour clock (e.g., 20.25 means 8:15 p.m.). (Thanks to Ed Noyce for this problem.)

9   Bicycle Registration

You are a programmer for a progressive college town that has a great deal of bicycle thievery. The town council decides to require everyone to register his or her bicycle so that there will be some chance of restoring captured stolen bikes to their original owners. Your job, should you decide to accept it, is to write a program which maintains and searches the data on bicycles. Your program must accept data cards of two different types:

new registrations

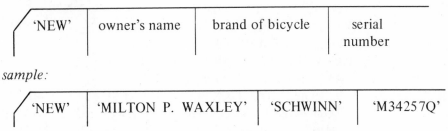

| 'NEW' | owner's name | brand of bicycle | serial number |

sample:

| 'NEW' | 'MILTON P. WAXLEY' | 'SCHWINN' | 'M34257Q' |

(If the serial number is scratched off, leave it blank.)

found bicycles

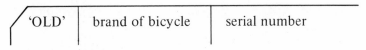

| 'OLD' | brand of bicycle | serial number |

Obviously, if a 'NEW' card comes in, you just add the information in. If an 'OLD' card comes in, there are two different situations. First, if the serial number of the recovered bike is known, you search the data and if such a bike has been registered, you print the owner's name (so he can be notified). Second, if the serial number has been scratched off, your program should print the names of everyone who owns that type of bike so they can be asked if the recovered bike is theirs. (Do not assume that the 'NEW' and 'OLD' cards have been separated.)

10 Typesetting

After months of searching, you find a job as a programmer for an ad agency. Your first assignment (given to you by your boss, who wears two-foot-wide ties, smokes mentholated cigars, and keeps calling you "baby") is to write a program which arranges ad copy. Your program READs the paragraph from cards and prints it out in the desired form. Desired forms are:

rectangle: fit as well as possible within margins n columns wide (run your program with $n = 50, 25,$ and 12)

triangle: fit as well as possible in a triangle shape with base at the bottom of the ad

Here is some ad copy to use, written in the triangle form.

YOUR
EYES, YOU
SAY? HOW COULD
YOU HAVE – EYE ODOR?
WELL, YOUR EYES ARE SO
CLOSE TO YOUR NOSE THAT YOU
GET USED TO THEIR SMELL. BUT DON'T
TAKE THE RISK OF OFFENDING OTHERS! USE
EYERON-F, THE GENTLE EYE FRESHENER AND
DEODORIZER. AVAILABLE IN THREE SIZES, GIANT,
JUMBO, AND FAMILY. (NOW LEMON-FRESHENED FOR
EVEN MORE PROTECTION.) GET SOME TODAY!

Your boss has changed his mind. He now wants the base of the triangle on the top. Write a new program. (Thanks to Raymond Langsford for this problem.)

11 Write a program which produces an array of shuffled cards, represented as the INTEGERs 1, 2, . . ., 52. If you establish an appropriate correspondence between INTEGERs and cards, you can compute the card's suit and denomination with expressions like (CARD – 1)/13 and MOD(CARD,13).

VERBAL DESCRIPTION

Start with 52 cards in your hand.

Choose a card from your hand at random and place it on the table (in a stack).

Repeat step 2 until you run out of cards in your hand.

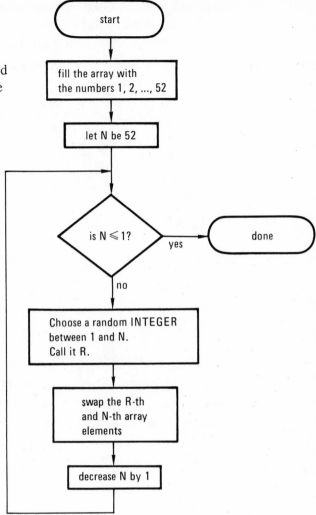

Shuffle Algorithm

Note: N is the number of cards left in your hand (array positions 1 to N). The stack on the table is array positions N + 1 to 52.

Write the shuffling algorithm as a SUBROU-TINE, and use it to shuffle a deck of cards. Print the shuffled deck one card at a time. If the jack of any suit comes up, use the FORMAT carriage control character + to "SLAP!" the jack.

KING OF CLUBS
TEN OF HEARTS
SEVEN OF HEARTS
FOUR OF SPADES
SLAP OF CLUBS
NINE OF SPADES
QUEEN OF SPADES

12 Design and write a program which deals a random bridge hand and displays it in the usual bridge notation.

NORTH
S: K J 3
H:
D: A Q 7 4
C: K Q 10 9 4 2

WEST
S: A 5 4
H: 8 7 4 3 2
D: K 9 6
C: A 7

EAST
S: Q 10 7 6
H: 10 5
D: J 10 5 3 2
C: 6 3

SOUTH
S: 9 8 2
H: A K Q J 9 6
D: 8
C: J 8 5

Use SUBROUTINE SHUFFLE from problem 11 to shuffle the deck.

13 Write an INTEGER FUNCTION GOREN which takes a bridge hand as an argument (i.e., an array of 13 INTEGERs that represent cards, as in problems 11 and 12 above) and returns the Goren point value of the hand.

10 ADDITIONAL STATEMENTS

Section 10 1

Introduction

The features described in this chapter are useful in special circumstances. Unless you have a solid grasp of the material in the first nine chapters, you may find some of these statements confusing. We suggest that you skim the chapter to get a feeling for what's available. Don't try to remember all the details on the first pass. When you come to an application that seems suited to one of the features covered here, read the details and try it out.

Section 10 2

Statement Functions

If there is an expression which appears repeatedly in your program, it may improve the clarity of your program to define a function which computes that expression. To do that, there is a simple notation you can use—the **statement function**.

Perhaps you are saying "but I thought we already . . . Isn't that what a FUNCTION is for?" Ah yes, but there's a difference here. The difference is not a conceptual one but a matter of implementation. There are differences in how FUNCTIONs and statement functions are declared; one consequence is that a statement function is available only within the program or subprogram where it is declared. Also, a statement function can compute just a single expression whereas a FUNCTION can compute any sort of algorithm you wish to write.

Statement functions are defined by writing the name of the function followed by its parameters in parentheses, an assignment operator, and finally the expression which the function is to compute. For example, if we wished to do a true rounding division of INTEGERs, we could define the statement function RNDDIV as

```
RNDDIV(I1,I2) = INT(FLOAT(I1)/FLOAT(I2)+0.5)
```

Since we want RNDDIV to return an INTEGER value, we would put the declaration

`INTEGER RNDDIV`

before the definition.

The definition of a statement function looks similar to an assignment statement, but the compiler can tell it's not since the function name is not declared as the name of an array (the only other possibility for a statement of this form is an array element assignment statement). In addition, statement function definitions must be placed *after* all declaration statements and *before* any executable statements.

The identifiers which appear as parameters in the definition of a statement function (I1 and I2 in our example above) are not memory cell names—they are there only to indicate what *types* of values (both INTEGER in the case of RNDDIV) the statement function will receive as arguments when it is referenced.

A statement function reference is identical to a FUNCTION reference—you write its name followed by the arguments you want it to use in its computation. For example, the following assignment statement contains a reference to the statement function RNDDIV.

`M = RNDDIV(2,3)`

As a result, M would be given the value 1.

---

statement function definition

form

$$f(a_1, a_2, \ldots, a_n) = e$$

f is an identifier (the function name)
each a_i is an identifier (the parameter names)
e is an expression.
There must be at least one parameter.

meaning

defines a statement function f which may be referenced anywhere in the program unit. A reference to the function is like placing the expression e (converted to the data type of f), with all occurrences of the parameters replaced by the corresponding arguments in the reference, in the place where the function reference occurs. Each actual argument in the reference must be of the type indicated by the corresponding parameter name in the definition.

examples

```
STDG(X) = EXP(-0.5*X**2)/SQRT(8.0*ATAN(1.0))
G(X,U,S) = STDG( (X-U)/S ) /S
```

It is legal (although it may make the meaning of the function reference obscure) to include memory cell names as well as the parameters in the expression that defines a statement function. To see what effect that will have, you may imagine that when a statement function is referenced, the values given for the parameters replace each appearance of them in the expression and then the resulting rewritten expression *replaces* the function reference. For instance, if we make these declarations:

```
REAL A, B, F, X, Z
```

and define this statement function:

```
F(X) = A*X + B
```

then, if later in the program we had

```
A = 1.0
B = 5.0
Z = F(2.0)
```

the result would be the same as

```
A = 1.0
B = 5.0
Z = A*2.0 + B
```

so Z would get the value 7.0.

The expression which defines a statement function may contain references to FUNCTIONs and to *previously defined* statement functions. This last rule prevents mind bogglers like

```
F(X) = G(X)
G(X) = F(X)
```

It is important to remember that statement function definitions are local to the program unit where they occur. They cannot be used in other program units without being redefined.

EXERCISES 10 2

1 Write a statement function called EX OR which returns the LOGICAL value .TRUE. if one (and only one) of its two arguments has the value .TRUE.

2 Write a statement function called SDIST which computes the distance between two points (x_1, y_1) and (x_2, y_2) using the square root of the sum of the squares distance measure.

3 Write a statement function called ADIST which computes the distance between (x_1, y_1) and (x_2, y_2) using the sum of the absolute values of the differences between x_1, x_2 and y_1, y_2 as the distance measure.

4 Write a statement function called TRNCD which takes two REAL parameters R1 and R2 and computes a REAL value equal to the truncated division of R1 by R2. For instance,

```
TRNCD(3.25,2.7999)
```

should yield the value 1.00.

5 Statement function RNDDIV works only when I1 and I2 have the same sign. Alter it so that it will work in all cases.

Section 10 3

Subprograms as Arguments to Subprograms

On occasion you may wish to define a FUNCTION or SUBROUTINE which accepts yet another subprogram as one of its arguments. One very common use of this is in subprograms which accept a FUNCTION from your program and then do something useful for you with it. Typical tasks are (1) plotting out its values over some range, (2) finding where your FUNCTION has maxima and minima, and (3) computing the area under your FUNCTION. Subprograms which do these things are no doubt available at your computer center.

Perhaps you recall from Chapter 7 that FUNCTIONs and SUBROUTINEs are said to be **external** subprograms because their definitions lie wholly without the program from which they are called and because they are compiled separately and independently from the main program and from each other. This means that when the compiler is dealing with one program unit, it doesn't look at other program units to decide if a particular identifier refers to a memory cell or to another program unit.

Let's examine the problem carefully. Suppose we have a SUBROUTINE called PLOT which accepts as arguments F (the FUNCTION whose values we want plotted), LIM1 and LIM2 (describing the range over which values are to be plotted), and DELTA (the stepsize).

```
      SUBROUTINE PLOT (F, LIM1,LIM2, DELTA)
      REAL F, LIM1,LIM2, DELTA
      REAL STEP, Y
      INTEGER POINT, I, BLANK, STAR
      DATA BLANK/1H /,   STAR/1H*/
      STEP = LIM1
100   Y = F(STEP)
      POINT = MAX0(1,MIN0(113,INT(10.0*Y)+49))
      WRITE(6,1000) (BLANK, I=1,POINT), STAR
1000  FORMAT(1X, 120A1)
      STEP = STEP+DELTA
      IF (STEP .LE. LIM2)   GO TO 100
      RETURN
      END
```

Look at statement 100. The form of the expression F(STEP) indicates that F is either an array or a FUNCTION. It can't be an array; if it were, there would be a declaration to that effect. Therefore, F must be a FUNCTION, and when SUBROUTINE PLOT is called, it will be informed of the FUNCTION's name. No problem here.

Now let's go to another program unit and look at a statement which CALLs SUBROUTINE PLOT. Suppose we want to plot out the values taken by the built-in FUNCTION ALOG10 (base 10 logarithm). We might write

```
CALL PLOT (ALOG10,1.0,10.0,1.0)
```

and hope that that would do the trick. However, "ALOG10" looks as if it could be a memory cell name. The only way for the compiler to tell that it is supposed to be a FUNCTION name is to look into SUBROUTINE PLOT and see how it uses its third argument. But the compiler doesn't look at SUBROUTINE PLOT while it is compiling the program containing the CALL. To solve the dilemma we must inform the compiler that ALOG10 stands for the FUNCTION called ALOG10, not a memory cell of that name. An EXTERNAL statement gives the compiler this information.

```
EXTERNAL ALOG10
```

If our main program makes several references to SUBROUTINE PLOT, say

```
EXTERNAL ALOG10, EXP, SIN
REAL      ALOG10, EXP, SIN
CALL PLOT (ALOG10,1.0,10.0,1.0)
CALL PLOT (SIN, -3.0, 3.0, 0.5)
CALL PLOT (EXP, -1.0, 0.0, 0.1)
STOP
END
```

output

then we must inform the compiler that ALOG10, EXP, and SIN are all names of external FUNCTIONs:

```
EXTERNAL ALOG10, EXP, SIN
```

We've seen an example where a FUNCTION name was an argument for a SUBROUTINE. Other combinations (e.g., a SUBROUTINE name as an argument for a FUNCTION) follow the same rules. Here's an example where a FUNCTION receives the name of another FUNCTION as an argument.

Suppose we have a number of FUNCTIONs we're trying out and we know (since we're going to divide by the result) that if any of our FUNCTIONs return the value 0, we're in trouble. For added safety we could define another FUNCTION called ZERCHK (ZERo CHecK) to protect us. Our main program is outlined below.

```
          .
          .
          .
      INTEGER FN1, FN2, FN3, X, Y, ZERCHK
      EXTERNAL FN1, FN2, FN3
          .
          .
          .
COMMENT:  TRY FN1, BUT BE CAREFUL
      Y1 = 100/ZERCHK(X,FN1)
COMMENT:  TRY FN2, BUT BE CAREFUL
      Y2 = 100/ZERCHK(X,FN2)
COMMENT:  TRY FN3, BUT BE CAREFUL
      Y3 = 100/ZERCHK(X,FN3)
          .
          .
          .
      END
```

We want ZERCHK to try out the FUNCTION and test the result to protect us from zero.

```
      INTEGER FUNCTION ZERCHK(ARG,FUNCT)
      INTEGER ARG, FUNCT
COMMENT:  COMPUTE THE VALUE OF "FUNCT"
      ZERCHK = FUNCT(ARG)
COMMENT:  TEST FOR ZERO
      IF (ZERCHK .NE. 0)  RETURN
COMMENT:  IT WAS ZERO, NOTIFY AND SAVE THE DAY
      WRITE(6,1000) ARG
 1000 FORMAT(' WITH ARGUMENT', I8,
     +          ' THE VALUE OF THE FUNCTION IS 0--BEWARE')
      ZERCHK = 1
      RETURN
      END
```

EXERCISES 10 3

1 Where must the EXTERNAL statement appear?

    a in the subprogram to warn it that one of its arguments is another subprogram

    b in your job control cards so that the compiler can figure out the necessary communication among subprograms

    c in your left ear

2 Would your program's performance be affected if you used EXTERNAL statements to declare every subprogram you reference?

Section 10 4

The DATA Statement

We have already seen the DATA statement, but in a restricted form. Here we cover the complete form and point out its manifold benefits.

There are three different ways to put values in memory cells: the assignment statement, the READ statement, and the DATA statement. The assignment statement computes a value and places the result in a memory cell. The READ statement takes values from data cards outside the program itself and places them into memory cells. Both of these statements are executable; that is, they cause the controller to take some action. The **DATA statement**, however, is *not* executable. It is an instruction to the compiler rather than to the controller. The DATA statement instructs the compiler to put initial values into specific memory cells, so that when the machine language version of your program begins to run, those memory cells will already have values.

DATA Statement

form

DATA $list_1 /c_1/$, $list_2 /c_2/$, . . . , $list_n/c_n/$

$list_k$ is a list of memory cell names or array elements. Subscripts in array elements must be constants.

c_k is a list of constants separated by commas. Any of these constants may be preceded by a replication factor $r*$, where r is an unsigned INTEGER constant. The replication factor $r*$ has the same effect that repeating the constant following it r times would have.

The number of constants in the list c_k must be same as the number of elements in $list_k$. A DATA statement may appear anywhere after the declarations (but before the END, of course).

meaning

instructs the compiler to place the constant values from the list c_k into the memory cells in the $list_k$, the first constant into the first memory cell, the second into the second, etc.

examples

```
INTEGER MONOID(3),FST,LST
REAL PI, WHALER(2)
DATA MONOID(1)/2/, MONOID(2)/4/
DATA FST,LST/4HALFA,4HMEGA/
DATA PI/3.1415926/, WHALER(1)/3.795/
DATA MONOID(1),MONOID(2),MONOID(3)/3*0/
```

Normally compile-time initialization is used only when the memory cells being initialized don't change values during execution. Using the DATA statement in this way lets you give names to constants, a practice which helps to make programs more readable and more easily modifiable. However, there are times when it is advantageous to use compile-time initialization for memory cells whose values will later be changed. One situation in which this is useful arises when a subprogram contains a computation which should be done only once during a computer run, even though the subprogram may be called several times.

For example, if we need a FUNCTION which computes the area of a circle given its radius, the FUNCTION will compute the product of π and the square of the radius. Therefore, the FUNCTION will need to know the value of π. Of course, we can simply write the value to the number of digits of accuracy appropriate to our machine, but then we'll have to go look up the value in a table. That's not so bad, even though it takes time we'd rather spend on something else, but

$\pi = 3.14159265$
35897932
$3846\ldots$

there is another disadvantage—if we give our FUNCTION to someone else whose computer carries a different accuracy in its REALs, he'll have to change the number in the program. Therefore, we decide to let the computer compute π for us to whatever accuracy it's capable of. To do this, we use the fact that $\pi/4 = \arctan (1)$. We compute PI using the assignment statement PI = ATAN(1.0) * 4.0. If we put the above assignment statement first in the FUNCTION it will compute a value for PI every time it is called. To avoid this unnecessary computation, we use a DATA statement to place the value .FALSE. in a LOGICAL memory cell. The first statement of the FUNCTION tests this memory cell. If it has the value .FALSE., its value is changed to .TRUE. and PI is assigned the value ATAN(1.0) * 4.0. If its value is .TRUE. (which it will be on every call to the FUNCTION except the first), then that assignment statement is skipped. Instead of having to compute π every time, the FUNCTION only has to perform a simple test and transfer.

```
      REAL FUNCTION AREA(RADIUS)
      REAL RADIUS
      REAL PI
      LOGICAL NOT1ST
      DATA NOT1ST/.FALSE./
      IF (NOT1ST) GO TO 10
         NOT1ST = .TRUE.
         PI = ATAN(1.0)*4.0
 10   AREA = PI*RADIUS**2
      RETURN
      END
```

EXERCISES 10 4

1 Which of the following are legal DATA statements? For those that are, say what values the memory cells would contain if the program were compiled. For those that aren't, say why. Assume the following declarations have been made and that the program contains only one of the DATA statements so that there is no problem with reinitialization.

```
INTEGER A,B,C(3)
REAL D,E, F(4)
DATA A,B/18,1/
DATA A,C,D/1, 3*7, 4.0/
DATA A/3/, E,F(1),F(2),F(3),F(4)/5*3.0/
DATA C(1),C(2),C(3)/1,2*5/, E/2/, D/1.0/
DATA C(?)/2/
DATA A,C(A)/2,3/
```

Section 10 5

The COMMON Statement

In Chapter 7, the chapter on subprograms, we said that statements in one program or subprogram could not affect the memory cells in another unless the memory cells in question were given to the subprogram as arguments. In other words, the only way two subprograms could have access to the same memory cells would be for one subprogram to call the other and use some of its memory cells as arguments. That wasn't the whole story.

There are times when it is handy for several subprograms to use some of the same memory cells without having to list them as parameters. Chapter 11 includes several programs in which a number of different subprograms access the same large block of storage using COMMON statements. This is probably the most frequent use of COMMON. In this chapter we'll show a number of different ways to use COMMON statements to do very simple tasks.

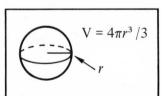

Suppose we want to write three FUNCTIONs, one to compute the volume of a sphere, given its radius, another to compute the volume of a cylinder, given its radius and height, and a third to compute the volume of a cone, given its radius and height. Each of these FUNCTIONs needs to use the value of PI. It would be nice to be able to put that value into some memory cell in the computer and use that memory cell in each of the FUNCTIONs. Of course, we could do this by adding an extra argument to each FUNCTION and supplying the value to the FUNCTION through that argument. The problem with this approach is that including the argument PI in every FUNCTION reference is a nuisance. What we need is an alternative way to allow subprograms to share memory cells.

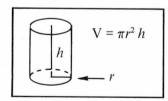

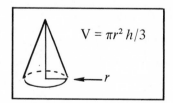

```
COMMENT: A CLUMSY WAY TO COMMUNICATE PI TO THE FUNCTIONS
        REAL VSHP, VCONE, VCYL
        REAL SPHERE, CONE, CYL
        REAL PI
        DATA PI/3.14159/
C
COMMENT:  COMPUTE THE VOLUME OF A SPHERE OF RADIUS 1.0
        VSPH = SPHERE(1.0,PI)
C
COMMENT:  COMPUTE VOLUME OF CONE, RADIUS 1.0, HEIGHT 2.0
        VCONE = CONE(1.0,2.0,PI)
C
COMMENT:  COMPUTE VOLUME OF CYLINDER, RADIUS 1.0, HEIGHT 2.0
        VCYL = CYL(1.0, 2.0, PI)
            .
            .
            .
```

The COMMON statement provides that alternative. Using a COMMON statement, we can set up a part of memory which can be used by any subprogram or program.

Before things get too involved, let's look at the example at hand. We want the three FUNCTIONs, SPHERE, CONE, and CYL, to be able to use a single memory cell whose value is π. To make this possible, we place a COMMON statement in each of the FUNCTIONs. A COMMON statement establishes a region of memory which may be accessed by any program unit. We name this region with a unique identifier which, as usual, is a string of six or fewer letters or digits beginning with a letter. We chose the name CONST in this example, as you see below. It is also possible to set up a COMMON region which is nameless; that is, its name may be blank.

```
REAL FUNCTION SPHERE(RADIUS)
REAL RADIUS
REAL PI
COMMON /CONST/ PI
SPHERE = (4.0/3.0)*PI*RADIUS**3
RETURN
END

REAL FUNCTION CONE(RADIUS,HEIGHT)
REAL RADIUS,HEIGHT
REAL PI
COMMON /CONST/ PI
CONE = HEIGHT*PI*RADIUS**2/3.0
RETURN
END

REAL FUNCTION CYL(RADIUS,HEIGHT)
REAL RADIUS,HEIGHT
REAL PI
COMMON /CONST/ PI
CYL = HEIGHT*PI*RADIUS**2
RETURN
END
```

COMMON statement

form

COMMON$/a_1$ /$list_1$ /a_2 /$list_2$ / . . . /a_n/$list_n$

a_k is an identifier or blank

$list_k$ is a list of unsubscripted memory cell names or array names separated by commas

If a_1 is blank, the first two slashes may be omitted. An array name in $list_k$ may be followed by a length declarator if its length is not declared elsewhere.

meaning

COMMON storage regions with labels a_k are set up, one area for each distinct label. Within the program unit in which this statement appears, the memory cells in region a_k are given the names in $list_k$ in the order specified by the list. If an array name appears in the list, all of its memory cells are included in the COMMON region. If two of the area names are identical, the effect is the same as if the elements in the second list were placed on the end of the first list.

example

```
REAL A(3), B(5), C
INTEGER X(3), Y(2), Z
COMMON /AREA1/ A,X,C  /AREA2/ Y,B,Z
```

sets up regions as follows

AREA 1		AREA 2	
	A(1)		Y(1)
	A(2)		Y(2)
	A(3)		B(1)
	X(1)		B(2)
	X(2)		B(3)
	X(3)		B(4)
	C		B(5)
			Z

As you can see, the COMMON statement labels a COMMON region in memory, the label being surrounded by slashes; then it names the memory cells to be included in the COMMON area. It is important to remember that the *label* is the only thing which can be communicated from one subprogram to another. The names of the individual memory cells within the COMMON area are local to the subprogram and *may* differ from one to another, although people usually choose to make them the same in all subprograms.

In our example of three FUNCTIONs using the COMMON area CONST, we did not include any statements giving PI a value. Of course, it would have to be given a value before any of the FUNCTIONs could be used. This could be accomplished in many ways. We will look at three ways. The first two are essentially different; the third is an embellishment of the second.

The first method is to assign PI a value in the main program before the FUNCTIONs are called.

```
      REAL VSHP, VCONE, VCYL
      REAL SPHERE, CONE, CYL
      REAL PI
      COMMON /CONST/ PI
      PI = 3.14159
C
COMMENT:  COMPUTE THE VOLUME OF A SPHERE OF RADIUS 1.0
      VSPH = SPHERE(1.0)
C
COMMENT:  COMPUTE VOLUME OF CONE, RADIUS 1.0, HEIGHT 2.0
      VCONE = CONE(1.0,2.0)
C
COMMENT:  COMPUTE VOLUME OF CYLINDER, RADIUS 1.0, HEIGHT 2.0
      VCYL = CYL(1.0, 2.0)
            .
            .
            .
```

The disadvantage of assigning PI a value in the main program is that the main program doesn't have any use for the value of PI, so it seems an inappropriate place to even have the memory cell PI around, let alone assign a value to it.

We can instruct the compiler to give values to memory cells located in COMMON areas by using a BLOCK DATA subprogram. Actually, "subprogram" is a misnomer here since a BLOCK DATA subprogram contains *no* executable statements and, therefore, isn't a program at all. A BLOCK DATA subprogram may contain only DATA statements and declarations of memory cells, arrays, and COMMON areas. No executable statements are allowed. (It can also contain EQUIVALENCE statements; see Section 10 6.) Its purpose is to instruct the compiler to put values into COMMON areas.

BLOCK DATA subprogram

form

    BLOCK DATA

    (declarations of memory cells, arrays, and COMMON areas;
    EQUIVALENCE statements)

    (DATA statements)

    END

meaning

    instructs the compiler to put values into COMMON areas (may
    not be used to initialize blank COMMON)

example

```
BLOCK DATA
REAL PI
COMMON /CONST/ PI
DATA PI /3.14159/
END
```

In the present example, the BLOCK DATA subprogram would look like the one in the box above. If we put this BLOCK DATA subprogram together with the three FUNCTIONs, SPHERE, CONE, and CYL, the main program no longer needs the COMMON statement because PI is given its value by the BLOCK DATA subprogram.

Another technique that we'll discuss computes a value for PI in the same way as the example in Section 10 4 on the DATA statement. If you have trouble understanding the scheme of the subprograms below, read that section again. Note that, no matter which of the three FUNCTIONs is called first, the value for PI is computed and assigned exactly once.

```
      REAL SPHERE, CONE, CYL,  VSHP, VCONE, VCYL
      VSPH = SPHERE(1.0)
      WRITE(6,1000) VSPH
 1000 FORMAT(' VOLUME OF SPHERE OF RADIUS 1 = ',F10.6)
      VCONE = CONE(1.0,2.0)
      WRITE(6,2000) VCONE
 2000 FORMAT(' VOLUME OF CONE OF RADIUS 1, HT 2 = ', F10.6)
      VCYL = CYL(1.0,2.0)
      WRITE(6,3000) VCYL
 3000 FORMAT(' VOLUME OF CYLINDER OF RADIUS 1, HT 2=',F10.6)
      STOP
      END

      REAL FUNCTION SPHERE(RADIUS)
      REAL RADIUS
      REAL PI
      LOGICAL NOT1ST
      COMMON /CONST/ PI, NOT1ST
      IF (NOT1ST) GO TO 10
        NOT1ST = .TRUE.
        PI = 4.0*ATAN(1.0)
 10   SPHERE = (4.0/3.0)*PI*RADIUS**3
      RETURN
      END
```

```
        REAL FUNCTION CONE(RADIUS,HEIGHT)
        REAL RADIUS,HEIGHT
        REAL PI
        LOGICAL NOT1ST
        COMMON /CONST/ PI, NOT1ST
        IF (NOT1ST) GO TO 10
          NOT1ST = .TRUE.
          PI = 4.0*ATAN(1.0)
   10   CONE = HEIGHT*PI*RADIUS**2/3.0
        RETURN
        END

        REAL FUNCTION CYL(RADIUS,HEIGHT)
        REAL RADIUS,HEIGHT
        REAL PI
        LOGICAL NOT1ST
        COMMON /CONST/ PI, NOT1ST
        IF (NOT1ST) GO TO 10
          NOT1ST = .TRUE.
          PI = 4.0*ATAN(1.0)
   10   CYL = HEIGHT*PI*RADIUS**2
        RETURN
        END

        BLOCK DATA
        REAL PI
        LOGICAL NOT1ST
        COMMON /CONST/ PI, NOT1ST
        DATA NOT1ST/.FALSE./
        END
```

output

```
    VOLUME OF SPHERE OF RADIUS 1 =    4.188790
    VOLUME OF CONE OF RADIUS 1, HT 2 =    2.094395
    VOLUME OF CYLINDER OF RADIUS 1, HT 2=  6.283185
```

There are a few other things you should know about COMMON areas. The first is that the total number of memory cells in a particular COMMON area must be the same in all subprograms in which is it declared. The names of the memory cells in the COMMON area don't have to be the same from one subprogram to the next, but the total length of a COMMON area must be the same from one program unit to another. The one exception is with blank COMMON. The length of the blank COMMON region need not be the same in every program unit. If it's not, the total length of the blank COMMON area is the maximum of its sizes in the various program units where it is declared.

Although COMMON areas are usually used to communicate values from one subprogram to another, they are occasionally used to save memory space. To use them for this purpose is tricky, however, and should be left to the accomplished programmer.

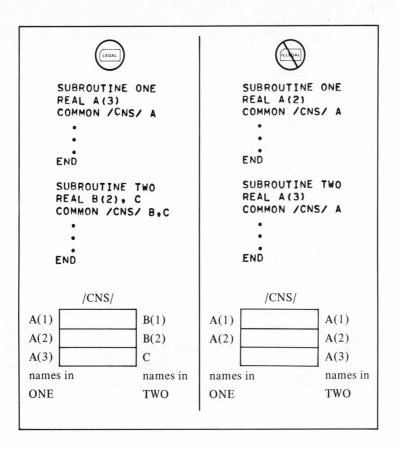

EXERCISES 10 5

1 Describe the correspondence between memory cells in the following SUB-
ROUTINEs.

```
SUBROUTINE ONE
REAL A(3), B, C(2)
COMMON /BLK1/A,B    /BLK2/C
A(2) = 1.0
C(1) = 1.0
RETURN
END

SUBROUTINE TWO
REAL B(3), C, D(2)
COMMON /BLK1/C,B    /BLK2/D
B(2) = 2.0
C = 2.0
RETURN
END
```

```
SUBROUTINE THREE
REAL Q(4), R, S
COMMON /BLK1/Q    /BLK2/R,S
Q(1) = 3.0
Q(2) = 3.0
Q(3) = 3.0
Q(4) = 3.0
R = 3.0
S = 3.0
RETURN
END
```

2   The following program calls the SUBROUTINEs of exercise 1. What does
it print?

```
      REAL A,B,C,D, E,F
      COMMON /BLK1/A,B,C,D    /BLK2/E,F
      CALL THREE
      CALL TWO
      CALL ONE
      WRITE(6,1000) A,B,C,D, E,F
 1000 FORMAT(1X,6F10.1)
      STOP
      END
```

Section 10 6

The EQUIVALENCE Statement

The effect of the EQUIVALENCE statement is to allow the programmer to
refer to a memory cell by more than one name. It can be used to conserve memory, allowing a region of memory to be used for different purposes in one program without sacrificing the practice of giving memory cells names indicative of
their use. The EQUIVALENCE statement must precede all executable statements,
but should follow all relevant declarations and precede all relevant compile-
time initializations.

> *Novice programmers who use the* EQUIVALENCE *statement are
> inviting trouble in the form of bugs which defy discovery.*

An EQUIVALENCE statement can increase the length of a COMMON area in
the forward direction. That is, it can add memory cells onto the end of the
COMMON area, but an EQUIVALENCE statement which implies a change in the
beginning of a COMMON area is illegal.

ok	*illegal*
EQUIVALENCE *extends* COMMON *region in* *forward direction*	EQUIVALENCE *implies* *new origin for* COMMON *region*

`REAL A(3), B(4), C(2)`
`COMMON /AREA/ A`
`EQUIVALENCE (A(2),B(2),C(1))`
	`REAL A(3), B(3)`
	`COMMON /AREA/ A`
	`EQUIVALENCE (A(1),B(2))`

/AREA/		/AREA/	
	A(1), B(1)		B(1)
	A(2), B(2), C(1)		B(2), A(1)
	A(3), B(3), C(2)		B(3), A(2)
	B(4)		A(3)

EXERCISES 10 6

1 Write all the names which can be used for memory cell A below in a list; similarly, write the alias groups for B, C(1), and C(2).

```
INTEGER A,B,C(2)
REAL X,Y(2)
EQUIVALENCE (A,Y(1),X), (C(1),Y(3)), (B,Y(2))
```

Section 10 7

Additional I/O Statements

The I/O devices we have been principally concerned with have been the card reader and the line printer. However, there are many other kinds of I/O equipment—card punches, paper tapes, magnetic tapes, disks, drums, plotters, and so on. Each kind of device has different advantages in terms of speed and convenience which we'll not dwell on here. Because of the great variety of I/O devices (some or all of which may be present at any particular computer center) it would be difficult for Fortran to provide different I/O statements for each device. In-

> *peripheral device:* any piece of hardware (other than the controller or memory) which is connected to a computer

stead, as you already know, devices are assigned numbers, and your READ and WRITE statements specify the peripheral device you wish to use by including a unit number. Since the correspondence between numbers and devices is not standardized, you will have to ask a local expert for the information. Often the number 5 identifies the card reader, 6 the line printer, and 7 the card punch. Beyond that, there is not even a hint of common usage.

The input and output statements we have been dealing with have always involved a *conversion*. As we have used them so far, input statements convert character strings (taken from our data cards) into INTEGERs, REALs, or whatever type is specified in the FORMAT. An output statement performs the reverse conversion from a representation of data in memory to a character string (normally printed on paper). The I/O device stores the information in a form very different from the way it would be stored in memory cells. This is quite natural, of course, because we have been using I/O devices primarily as a means of communication between human and computer.

However, I/O devices can be used as an extension of the computer's memory as well as a means of communication. When an I/O device is used for this purpose, the information on the I/O device might just as well be stored in essentially the same form as it would be stored in memory cells since that would avoid the conversion process. This is the reason for **unformatted I/O statements**. We use the word *unformatted* to mean that the form in which the data is stored in the I/O device is left up to the computing system being used, and hence is not specified by a FORMAT statement. Most computing systems choose a form essentially like the one used in representing data in memory cells, so that the I/O process involves very little computation.

Since unformatted I/O statements are used primarily to extend the computer's memory, the unit designated by an unformatted output statement should make records which can be read by some input device. The line printer, for example, would be an inappropriate unit for an unformatted I/O statement because the

---

unformatted I/O statement

forms
> READ (*u*) *list*
> WRITE (*u*) *list*
>
> *u* is a unit number
> *list* is an I/O list

meaning
> READs or WRITEs the values of the memory cells in *list* on unit *u* without changing their representation

examples
```
READ(10) X, (T(I), I=1,N)
WRITE(N) R,P,G
```

---

computer couldn't read the values back into its memory and the output would be wasted.

In order to use I/O devices as extended memory, you must be able to position the I/O device (e.g., at the beginning of the information or back one record). For this reason the REWIND and BACKSPACE statements are provided. The RE-WIND statement positions the I/O device at the beginning of the first record written on the device. An unformatted **record** is a set of values written by a single unformatted WRITE statement. The BACKSPACE statement positions the I/O device at the beginning of the record just previous to the one at which it is currently positioned. An I/O device, when stopped, is always positioned at the beginning of a record, and a READ statement must READ a whole record, even if some of the values in the record are not put into memory.

---

unit positioning statements

form
    REWIND u

meaning
    position unit u at beginning of first record

form
    BACKSPACE u

meaning
    position unit u at beginning of the immediately previous record.

form
    ENDFILE u

meaning
    place an end-of-file mark on unit u at the current position

examples
```
BACKSPACE 10
BACKSPACE N
REWIND 10
REWIND N
ENDFILE 10
ENDFILE N
```

Another I/O statement is used to mark the ends of files of information. The ENDFILE statement puts a special mark, called an end-of-file mark, on the I/O unit specificed. This mark terminates the series of records contained on the unit up to that point. Since many versions of Fortran provide a way to detect this special mark, it provides a way to insure that your program does not try to READ data which you haven't written on the I/O unit. (See, for example, the END-condition READ at the end of Section 3 3.) End-of-file marks are often used to separate logical blocks of information on I/O storage media (especially magnetic tape).

Most manufacturers provide additional (non-ANSI) direct access I/O statements, some allowing very useful and elegant manipulation of mass storage files. Since there is no standard notation, you'll have to dig the information out of the manuals provided by the manufacturers or ask local experts for advice on using these features.

EXERCISES 10 7

1 Find out about the different kinds of peripheral equipment available at your computer center. Perhaps some of it would be of great use to you.

Section 10 8

Variable FORMATs

Sometimes it is impossible to devise the FORMAT of a printed line or data card until the program has made some computations. For example, you may want to print from one to ten numbers on a line in fields of width five so that if there are fewer than ten numbers, they appear on the right-hand side of the line. Suppose there is a memory cell N whose value is the number of numbers you want to print on the line and that the numbers are stored in any array A. It would be nice if you could simply put variables in the FORMAT itself. Unfortunately, this is illegal, but with a little more effort we can get the desired effect.

```
            WRITE(6,1000) (A(I), I=1,N)
       1000 FORMAT(1X,  (11-N)  (5X)  ,  N I5)
```

This FORMAT *contains illegal uses of variables as repeat specifications.*

A **variable FORMAT** is an array containing a character string. That string must be a legal FORMAT specification. That is, it must be a string which could appear

variable FORMAT I/O statements

form
    READ (u,f) *list*
    WRITE (u,f) *list*
    WRITE (u,f)
    f is the name of an array containing a character string of FORMAT specifications surrounded by parentheses

meaning
    same as with constant FORMAT

after the word FORMAT in a FORMAT statement, including the parentheses. The I/O statement using the variable FORMAT is exactly the same as if it had used a normal FORMAT except that the name of the array containing the variable FORMAT now replaces the usual FORMAT label.

To get back to the problem at hand, recall that we wanted a FORMAT like this:

$$(1X, \boxed{} \qquad (5X, \boxed{} \qquad I5)$$

where the boxes represent character strings which will change from time to time. For example, if the first box contains the character 1, then the second should contain the characters 10. In order to be able to assign one of the necessary character strings to those parts of the FORMAT, we set up an array DIGIT containing them. For the FORMAT itself, we set up an array SKIP containing the parts of the FORMAT which are fixed and leave spaces in which to insert the variable portions. As you can see in the program fragment, before printing, we assign character strings to those variable parts of SKIP using the array DIGIT.

```
        INTEGER SKIPF(6), DIGIT(10)
        INTEGER N, I
COMMENT:   "SKIPF" IS THE VARIABLE FORMAT.
C          FILL IN THE PARTS THAT STAY PUT
C          (I.E., ALL BUT SKIPF(2) AND SKIPF(5))
        DATA SKIPF(1)/4H(1X,/, SKIPF(3)/4H(5X)/
        DATA SKIPF(4)/4H,   /, SKIPF(6)/4HI5) /
COMMENT:   INITIALIZE NUMERIC TO HOLLERITH CONVERSION ARRAY
        DATA DIGIT(1),DIGIT(2),DIGIT(3),DIGIT(4),DIGIT(5)
     +   /   1H1 ,   1H2 ,    1H3 ,    1H4 ,    1H5    /
        DATA DIGIT(6),DIGIT(7),DIGIT(8),DIGIT(9),DIGIT(10)
     +   /   1H6 ,   1H7 ,    1H8 ,    1H9 ,    2H10  /.
COMMENT: SUPPOSE THERE ARE 6 ITEMS TO APPEAR
        N=6
        SKIPF(2) = DIGIT(11-N)
        SKIPF(5) = DIGIT(N)
        WRITE(6,SKIPF) (I,I=1,N)
        STOP
        END
```

output

```
        1    2    3    4    5    6
```

EXERCISES 10 8

1 What FORMAT is used in our program when N has the value 3?

11 SOPHISTICATED USES OF ARRAYS

Section 11 1

Data Structures

Throughout this book we have been emphasizing the idea of breaking down the problem you are trying to program so that it will be easier to understand (more clearly organized) and hence easier to work with. In this chapter we will deal with an organizational idea which makes programming easier by making the details of your program directly analogous to the details of the problem you want to solve. The idea is to recognize some of the structure (relationships among subparts) of your problem, and after you feel you understand the structure of the problem, to assemble units of information in the computer memory into that structure. We call such assemblages of memory words **data structures**. Every program you have written has used memory cells in some way, so you have been using data structures all along. This is the first time that we will be very conscious of relationships among memory cells, however. Let's look at an example.

> *data structure: a group of memory cells organized in some manner*

Figure 11 1 1(a) contains the same information as Figure 11 1 1(b). Take a look at them. Which one is better? If your problem is "How many mothers are there?" then the organization in Figure 11 1 1(b) is probably best suited. However, if you are faced with the problem of determining more complex family relationships among people, then Figure 11 1 1(a) seems easier to use. Thus different organizations of the same data may be best suited to different problems.

What is it about Figure 11 1 1(a) that makes it easier to use to answer questions about relationships? One thing is that in the tree (Figure 11 1 1(a)), the closer two names are, the closer is the relationship between them, but there is no way to rearrange the list in Figure 11 1 1(b) so that this is true. In the tree, names along the same vertical line tend to be of the same generation, but this is obviously not true in the list. These and other reasons seem to make it easier to find your way around in the data when it is represented as a tree. More effort has gone into organizing the data in the tree than in the list, but this effort can pay off when the time comes to use the data.

This chapter deals with the organization of data as an important part of programming. Often, spending some time and thought organizing your data can result in a program which is not only easier to write and understand but also more efficient.

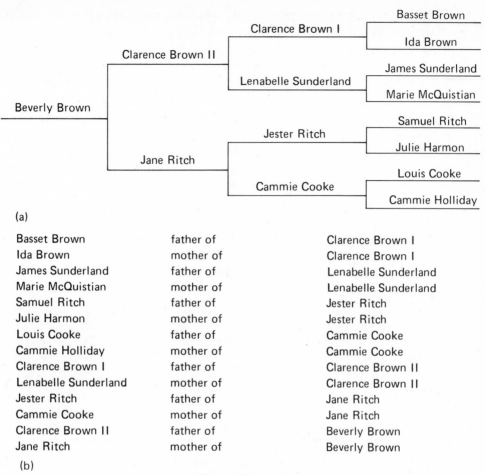

(a)

Basset Brown	father of	Clarence Brown I
Ida Brown	mother of	Clarence Brown I
James Sunderland	father of	Lenabelle Sunderland
Marie McQuistian	mother of	Lenabelle Sunderland
Samuel Ritch	father of	Jester Ritch
Julie Harmon	mother of	Jester Ritch
Louis Cooke	father of	Cammie Cooke
Cammie Holliday	mother of	Cammie Cooke
Clarence Brown I	father of	Clarence Brown II
Lenabelle Sunderland	mother of	Clarence Brown II
Jester Ritch	father of	Jane Ritch
Cammie Cooke	mother of	Jane Ritch
Clarence Brown II	father of	Beverly Brown
Jane Ritch	mother of	Beverly Brown

(b)

Figure 11 1 1

Of course, organizing the data in this way takes some careful thought. We hope that once you have studied these data structures you will be able not only to apply them to problems which you encounter, but also to make up new organizations of data suited to whatever problem is at hand.

Section 11 2

Multidimensional Arrays

We have used individual memory cells to store several different kinds of data. Fortran automatically maintains an internal organization for each memory cell. This internal organization is different for different types of data. For instance, REAL numbers are stored in a very different way from INTEGERs. Because of this internal organization, each memory cell alone could be considered a data structure, but people usually reserve the term **data structure** for organizations which involve a number of memory cells. We have used such organizations already. When we have had several related items of information, we have stored the items in an array, a data structure consisting of several memory cells grouped together and referred to under the same name. A subscript appended to the name distinguishes one item of the group from another—MEMBER(3) refers to the third memory cell in the array called MEMBER. Because Fortran includes a special notation for arrays (the subscript notation), they are very easy to use.

Memories in sequential digital computers are organized like one-dimensional arrays. Thus, all other more complex data structures are constructed from one-dimensional arrays. Fortran automatically does this additional organizing for us in the case of two- and three-dimensional arrays, but beyond that we're on our own.

Suppose, for a moment, that Fortran hadn't provided two-dimensional arrays. How could we organize the data in a one-dimensional array so that we could use it as if it were a two-dimensional array? There are many answers to this question, but the one we describe here is the most common—it's the one used by the Fortran compiler.

> *Why bother? There are two good reasons for going into the details of using one-dimensional arrays to represent two-dimensional arrays. First, it's a good introduction to the more complex techniques which follow. But more important, there are times when it is very helpful to know the details of the Fortran representation of two-dimensional arrays. For example, it determines the order of the elements when whole arrays are transmitted in I/O statements.*

If the array is to have m rows and n columns, then we need to use $m*n$ memory cells to represent it. Therefore, we declare a one-dimensional array (which we call TWODIM in our illustration) with $m*n$ memory cells. We organize this block of cells into n sections, each section having m cells in it. The first section of m cells represents the first column of the two-dimensional array we are creating, the second section represents the second column, and so on (see Figure 11 2 1). Remember, since there are m rows, each column has m elements in it.

If we want to find the place in the array TWODIM which represents the two-dimensional array element in the Ith row and Jth column, we skip down to the Jth section and pick the Ith element in that section. This means that TWODIM(M*(J − 1) + I) is the memory cell representing the two-dimensional array element normally designated by the pair of subscripts (I,J). Figure 11 2 1 shows the details for an array with two rows and three columns.

This method of organizing a two-dimensional array is often called the **column major form**; we say that we are storing the array "by columns."

Fortran stores two-dimensional arrays by columns. It can be helpful to know this when you are using them. For example, suppose you have declared an array REAL A(3,2) in the main program and you CALL a SUBROUTINE with that array and its dimensions as parameters: CALL SUBR A(3,2). If the SUB

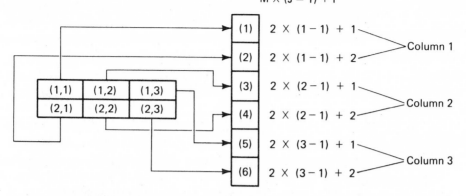

Two-dimensional array using two subscripts

Corresponding position in
one-dimensional array (Column Major Form)
$M \times (J - 1) + I$

Figure 11 2 1

> *We can make the array references appear very natural. We simply
> define an* INTEGER *valued function of two arguments (the row
> and column of the array element to be referenced) which com-
> putes the corresponding subscript in the one-dimensional array.
> For example, if the function is named S and we define it using an
> arithmetic statement function,*

```
        •
        •
        •
     INTEGER S,I,J,M,N
     S(I,J) = M*(J-1) + I
        •
        •
        •
```

> *then* TWODIM(S(I,J)) *refers to the (I,J)th element of the m-by-n
> array which we are representing.*

ROUTINE starts out like this, using N as the *first* length declarator,

```
SUBROUTINE SUBR(B, M,N)
REAL B(N,M)
   •
   •
   •
```

then you would have problems because the SUBROUTINE will place a different
organization on the array than does the main program. The diagram below shows
the memory cell names as they are in the main program on the left, and their
temporary names when the SUBROUTINE is CALLed on the right. You can see
that the subscripting is entirely different. It pays to know what you're doing when
you use two-dimensional arrays as arguments to subprograms.

```
A(1,1) ┌──────┐ B(1,1)
A(2,1) │      │ B(2,1)
A(3,1) │      │ B(1,2)
A(1,2) │      │ B(2,2)
A(2,2) │      │ B(1,3)
A(3,2) └──────┘ B(2,3)
```

EXERCISES 11 2

1 Draw a figure similar to Figure 11 2 1 showing the representation of a 3-by-4 array.

2 In setting up the column major representation of a two-dimensional array with m rows and n columns, what is the role of m? What is the role of n? Why is m more important than n? Could you set up the representation if you knew m precisely, but knew only that n was, say, smaller than 100? Will Barbara marry Jason? Will Jason leave Toni? Will Toni find happiness in the arms of Barbara? And what about the dog?

3 There is a similar representation of a two-dimensional array called the **row major form**. In this representation, an array with m rows and n columns is, again, represented by a one-dimensional array with $m*n$ memory cells. The array is divided into m sections, each section containing n memory cells and representing one row. Work out a formula which, given a subscript pair (I,J) designating the element in the Ith row and Jth column of the matrix, computes the place in the one-dimensional array which corresponds to the (I,J)th element of the matrix. In this row major representation is it more important to know the number of rows or the number of columns?

4 Where do the 1's go?

```
        INTEGER A(4,4)
        CALL ZAPDIA(A,2)
        STOP
        END

        SUBROUTINE ZAPDIA(B,M)
        INTEGER M, B(M,M)
        INTEGER I
COMMENT:  PUT ONES ON DIAGONAL
        DO 10 I=1,M
  10      B(I,I) = 1
        RETURN
        END
```

Section 11 3

Odd-shaped Arrays

It is easy to generalize from the two-dimensional case to see how to represent a three-dimensional array.

Suppose we want to represent an m-by-n-by-l three-dimensional array. The first subscript varies between 1 and m, the second between 1 and n, and the third be-

ANSI Fortran *allows* arrays of up to three dimensions.

tween 1 and l. Therefore, we need $m*n*l$ memory cells to represent the array, and we declare a one-dimensional array THREED with $m*n*l$ memory cells. We divide the array into l sections, each section having $m*n$ memory cells. In each of the sections we organize an m-by-n two-dimensional array in column major form. That is, we divide each of the l sections into n subsections, each subsection having m memory cells. To refer to the (I,J,K)th element of the three-dimensional array we go to the Ith memory cell of the Jth subsection of the Kth section. Then conceptual array element (I,J,K) corresponds to

$$THREED(M*N*(K-1) + N*(J-1) + I)$$

The $M*N*(K-1)$ term moves us to the Kth section of the array, the $N*(J-1)$ term moves us to the Jth subsection of that section, and the I term moves us to the Ith element of that subsection.

Perhaps you can begin to see a general scheme here for representing multidimensional arrays. Try to write down the formula for the four-dimensional case, given the range of each subscript.

The two-dimensional array we represented is rectangular in shape. That's just one of many possibilities. Think of the problem faced by a traveling pharmaceuticals salesman in West Texas. His district includes the towns of El Paso, Van Horn, Odessa, Big Spring, Midland, Abilene, Pecos, Lubbock, Amarillo, and Wichita Falls. He lives in Pecos and, since he must travel his route once every month, he wants to plan it carefully so that it will be as economical as possible. In other words, he wants to choose the shortest route, starting and ending in Pecos, which visits all ten of the towns in his district. Fortunately, the corner gas station has a table of intertown distances (Figure 11 3 1).

We want to write a program to find the shortest route. Obviously our program needs to know the intertown distances. How should we arrange the data from the table in the computer's memory cells? The table from the gas station looks like a normal two-dimensional array with a missing part. We will call it a **triangular array**. To present the triangular array, we can use an idea from our representation of rectangular two-dimensional arrays. One method of storing a rectangular two-dimensional array is the row major method (see exercise 11 2 2); that is, storage "by rows." We divide the array into sections, one section for each row. In the rectangular case, each row is the same length so it's easy to find the beginning of each section in the array. In this new triangular case, each row has a different length, and this complication makes it slightly more difficult to locate the beginning of each section.

	Abilene	Amarillo	Big Spring	El Paso	Lubbock	Midland	Odessa	Pecos	Van Horn
Amarillo	285								
Big Spring	110	225							
El Paso	466	581	356						
Lubbock	160	125	100	456					
Midland	150	265	40	316	140				
Odessa	200	315	90	266	190	50			
Pecos	262	377	152	204	252	112	62		
Van Horn	354	469	244	112	344	204	154	92	
Wichita Falls	150	235	260	616	215	355	405	467	559

Figure 11 3 1 Distance Table

Let's look at the details. The first row has one member, the second row has two members, the third, three, and so on up to the ninth row, which has nine members. Thus the first section of our one-dimensional array representing this triangular array should have one memory cell, the second section two memory cells, and so on. To find the fourth section, we have to skip over the first three. That means skipping over the first row (length one), the second row (length two), and the third row (length three). Altogether we skip over $1 + 2 + 3 = 6$ memory cells.

In general, to find the beginning of the kth section, you must skip over $1 + 2 + 3 + \ldots + (k - 1) = k * (k - 1)/2$ memory cells.

$$
\left.
\begin{array}{ccccc}
1 & + & 2 & + & 3 & + \ldots + & k \\
+ k & & + (k - 1) & + (k - 2) & + \ldots + & 1
\end{array}
\right\} = 2 \times (1 + 2 + 3 + \ldots + k)
$$

$$
(k + 1) + (k + 1) + (k + 1) + \ldots + (k + 1)
$$

$$
= k \times (k + 1) \qquad \frac{k(k + 1)}{2} = 1 + 2 + \ldots + k
$$

Thus the conceptual triangular array element (I,J) corresponds to

$$\text{TRIANG}(I * (I - 1)/2 + J)$$

where I, of course, may never be smaller than J. It is interesting that, unlike the case for rectangular arrays, here we don't need to know either the number of columns *or* the number of rows in order to refer to an element in the triangular array. Thus, the triangular array offers a surprising advantage over the rectangular structure.

To set up and use a triangular array, all you need to do is declare an array with as many memory cells as you need, that is, $n(n + 1)/2$ memory cells if the array is to have n rows. For our example, since there are ten towns, we need a nine-row triangular array, 45 memory cells in all.

Listing all ten towns both vertically and horizontally would result in the chart having ten unnecessary zeros in it.

The problem we are concerned with is to find the route of shortest length which visits all the towns and which starts and ends in Pecos. We will take a straightforward approach. (This, the **traveling salesman problem,** has been much-studied, and there are more efficient solutions, but we're looking for a simple solution rather than efficiency.) We simply compute the length of every possible route, and choose the shortest one. The difference between routes is the order in which the cities are visited. Therefore, we need a part of our program to step through all the possible orderings of the intermediate cities. This is what we called the "permutation problem" in Section 9 5, and there we wrote a SUBROUTINE which would produce a new ordering of a list each time it was CALLed. We designed the SUBROUTINE so that, if we CALLed it again and again, it would eventually produce all possible orderings of the original list and signal us, through one of its parameters, when it produced the final ordering. That SUBROUTINE can be put to good use here.

Figure 11 3 2 is an outline for our program. Try to follow the program using the flowchart as a guide. In the program the towns are referred to by their number in alphabetical order, 1 for Abilene, 2 for Amarillo, . . ., 9 for Van Horn, and 10 for Wichita Falls. We use a FUNCTION to compute the length of a route. The name PERM refers to the SUBROUTINE in Section 9 5.

You will notice that Pecos (town number 8) is left out of the compile-time initialization of the arrays which store routes the salesman might take. That's because we already know when he'll be in Pecos—he'll leave from there and he'll wind up there.

Our main program uses a FUNCTION LENGTH to discover how many miles it will take to travel a particular route. Since LENGTH must know the distance between towns, it is there that our triangular array appears. The values are entered into the array DIST through compile-time initialization, and the statement function BTWEEN is used to access values in it.

The order of the constants in the DATA statements which initialize the arrays TOWNS and DIST is determined by the organization of the arrays. TOWNS is a two-dimensional array organized by columns (according to the standard Fortran conventions—see Section 11 2). DIST is a triangular array which we organized by rows, as we explained in this section.

VERBAL DESCRIPTION

Initialize.

While there are still unexamined routes, repeat:

if next route is shorter than shortest route seen so far, store new route.

Print shortest route.

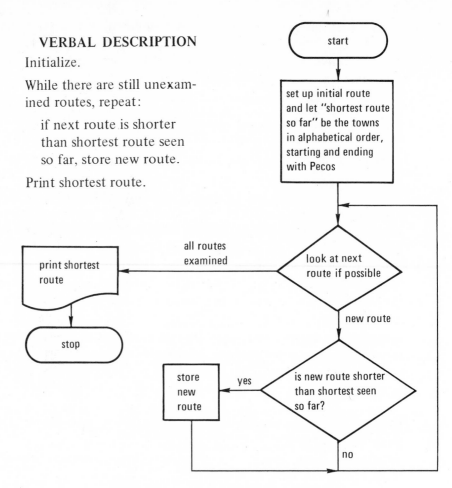

Figure 11 3 2   Finding the Shortest Circuit

```
COMMENT: FIND SHORTEST WEST TEXAS ROUTE
      INTEGER TOWNS(13,10),ROUTE(9),SHORTR(9),LENGTH,
     +       SLEN,L,N,T
      LOGICAL NEWPRM
C     THE FOLLOWING IS A NON-ANSI USE OF A DATA STATEMENT
C     SINCE IT NAMES ENTIRE ARRAYS AT ONCE.
      DATA ROUTE  /1,2,3,4,5,6,7,  9,10/,
     +     SHORTR /1,2,3,4,5,6,7,  9,10/
C     STORE TOWN NAMES.
      READ(5,1000) ((TOWNS(L,N), L=1,13), N=1,10)
 1000 FORMAT(13A1)
C     GET NEXT ROUTE
  100 CALL PERM(ROUTE,9,NEWPRM)
      IF (.NOT. NEWPRM) GO TO 200
C     IF NEW ROUTE IS SHORTER, SAVE IT.
      IF (LENGTH(ROUTE) .LE. LENGTH(SHORTR))
     +                        CALL STORE(ROUTE,SHORTR,9)
      GO TO 100
```

```
C      TRIED ALL ROUTES--PRINT SHORTEST
  200  SLEN=LENGTH(SHORTR)
       WRITE(6,2000) SLEN
 2000  FORMAT(' SHORTEST ROUTE (PRINTED BELOW) IS',I5,
      +            ' MILES LONG.')
       WRITE(6,2100)
 2100  FORMAT('0PECOS')
       DO 300 T=1,9
  300    WRITE(6,3000) (TOWNS(L,SHORTR(T)), L=1,13)
 3000    FORMAT(1X,13A1)
       WRITE(6,4000)
 4000  FORMAT(' PECOS')
       STOP
       END

       INTEGER FUNCTION LENGTH(R)
       INTEGER R(9)
       INTEGER BTWEEN, TOWN1, TOWN2, I, S, ROW,COL
       INTEGER DIST(45)
C      THE FOLLOWING IS A NON-ANSI USE OF A DATA STMT SINCE
C      IT NAMES THE ENTIRE ARRAY "DIST" AT ONCE.
       DATA DIST
      +          /285,
      +           110,225,
      +           446,581,356,
      +           160,125,100,456,
      +           150,265, 40,316,140,
      +           200,315, 90,266,190, 50,
      +           262,377,152,204,252,112, 62,
      +           354,469,244,112,344,204,154, 92,
      +           150,235,260,616,215,355,405,467,559/
C      STATEMENT FUNCTION TO COMPUTE SUBSCRIPT FOR TRIANGULAR
C      ARRAY.  THE ROW NUMBER IS ALWAYS 1 SMALLER THAN
C      THE TOWN NUMBER SINCE "ABILENE" IS NOT ONE OF THE ROWS
       S(ROW,COL) = ROW*(ROW-1)/2 + COL
       BTWEEN(TOWN1,TOWN2) = S(MAX0(TOWN1,TOWN2)-1,
      +                        MIN0(TOWN1,TOWN2)    )
C      START WITH DISTANCE FROM PECOS (TOWN 8) TO FIRST TOWN
C      IN ROUTE PLUS DISTANCE FROM LAST TOWN TO PECOS
       LENGTH = DIST(BTWEEN(8,R(1)))+DIST(BTWEEN(R(9),8))
C      ADD UP THE REST
       DO 100 I=1,8
  100    LENGTH = LENGTH + DIST(BTWEEN(R(I),R(I+1)))
       RETURN
       END

       SUBROUTINE STORE(A,B,LEN)
       INTEGER LEN, A(LEN), B(LEN)
       INTEGER I
       DO 100 I=1,LEN
  100    B(I) = A(I)
       RETURN
       END

data
       ABILENE
       AMARILLO
       BIG SPRING
       EL PASO
       LUBBOCK
       MIDLAND
       ODESSA
       PECOS
       VAN HORN
       WICHITA FALLS
```

```
SHORTEST ROUTE (PRINTED BELOW) IS 1482 MILES LONG.

PECOS
EL PASO
VAN HORN
ODESSA
MIDLAND
LUBBOCK
AMARILLO
WICHITA FALLS
ABILENE
BIG SPRING
PECOS
```

The traveling salesman problem would be a relatively hard one for a beginner to solve, yet the main program above is no harder to follow than the flowchart. Most of the work is done in subprograms, particularly PERM, the module we developed in Section 9 5.

EXERCISES 11 3

1 Why not store triangular arrays "by columns"?

2 How would you store an array shaped like this?

```
· · · · ·
  · · · ·     (upside-down
    · · ·      triangular array)
      · ·
        ·
```

3 The traveling salesman program in this section keeps recomputing the length of the shortest route so far. How can this be avoided? Is it worth it?

Section 11 4

Stacks and Queues

The data structures we've seen so far have been fixed in size. The data has been collected and manipulated, but the amount of data stored in the structures remains static once it has been collected. In this section we want to study some data structures that are useful when the amount of data varies dynamically during the computation. To implement these data structures in Fortran, we'll simply use auxiliary variables to keep track of what parts of a large fixed-length array are currently occupied. But before jumping into the details, let's look at a problem in which dynamic data structures are useful.

You may have noticed that railroad cars have small colored bars on their sides. These bars form an identification code for the cars, a code which can be read by machine and transmitted to a computer. The computer can be used to automate some parts of the railroad operation. Let's write a program which figures out how to do the switching operation that goes on in a classification yard (the switching area where trains are put together).

> **problem statement:** *Automate the procedure for putting trains together at Durham.*

Figure 11 4 1 shows the track layout of Durham, a small classification yard. Trains arriving at Durham leave their cars on track 1.

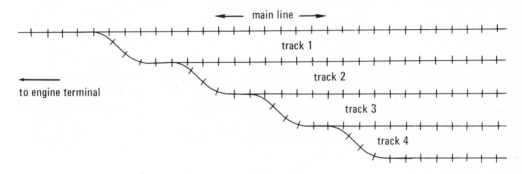

Figure 11 4 1 Durham Yard

There are three trains a day which leave Durham for three different destinations: Norfolk, Roanoke, and Portsmouth. Incoming trains include cars for all

> *classify: to put a car on the correct train*

three destinations, and must be broken up so that each car can be put into the proper train. Every morning the head office sends Durham a list of the cars which will be arriving and which trains (1, 2, or 3) they are to go out on. We'll write a program to print out detailed instructions which tell the crew working the switch engine how to classify all the cars in the yard. When the yard crew is finished with the classification, all three trains should be properly assembled: the Norfolk train on Track 1, the Roanoke train on track 2, and the Portsmouth train on track 3.

> **input/output description**
> *input:* a list of arriving car identification codes and the destination for each car
> *output:* a list of instructions for the yard crew

The classification technique used by the yard crew is well known to all railroad men. We have described it pictorially in Figure 11 4 2 and verbally in the classification algorithm box.

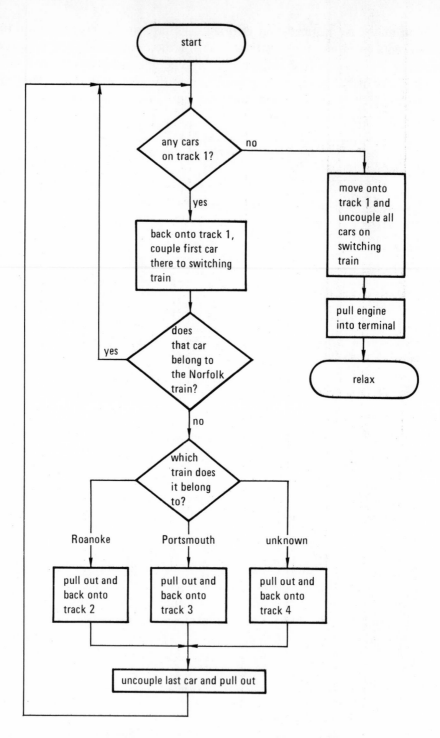

Figure 11 4 2 Classification Algorithm

```
classification algorithm

classification loop:
    While there are cars remaining on track 1, repeat the following
    operations:
        1  back onto track 1 and couple first car to switching train;
        2  if that car doesn't go to Norfolk, then (a) select destina-
           tion:
        Roanoke: pull out and back onto track 2;
        Portsmouth: pull out and back onto track 3;
        unknown: pull out and back onto track 4; and (b) un-
        couple last car and pull out.

finish up:
    Move the train of cars coupled to the switch engine to track 1
    and uncouple from engine.
    Pull engine into terminal and relax.
```

Looking at the flowchart (Figure 11 4 2), you will see that the rectangular boxes contain explicit instructions for the yard crew. (In a fully automated yard, they would be commands to the switch engine control system.) To prepare a sequential list of detailed instructions, our program can follow the classification algorithm, printing out an instruction each time it comes to a rectangular box. A typical list of instructions might be: Back onto track 1 and couple first car. Pull out of track 1 onto track 3. Uncouple last car and pull out. Back onto track 1 and couple first car . . .

```
classification program plan
1  store list of car-ID, train-membership pairs
2  record ID's of incoming cars (in order) as they
   go onto track 1
3  follow the classification algorithm, printing in-
   structions as they come up
```

We can think of track 1 as a dynamic data storage device. All the cars start out there and are removed and put back one at a time from the open end of the track. Because there is only one open end, the last car to go on will be the first car to come off the track. The last in, first out nature of track 1 puts it in a class of data storage devices known as **stacks** (also called **push-down stacks** and **LIFO** (last in, first out) **devices**).

Conceptually, a stack is a storage device in which elements may be added or removed only from the top. Traditionally, adding a new element to the top is called **pushing** the stack, and removing the top element is called **popping** the stack. We implement a stack by using an array (declared to be as large as our estimate of the greatest number of items that will ever be on the stack at one time) and a simple INTEGER memory cell (traditionally called the stack **pointer**) which stores the index (i.e., array subscript) of the current top element.

Durham Yard isn't really all that big. Only 200 cars will fit on track 1. That means that we can get by with 200 elements in the array we use to implement the stack representing track 1.

```
INTEGER TRACK1(200),FRONT1
```

When a train bringing cars to be classified backs onto track 1, the automatic scanner reads the car identification numbers and flashes them to the computer (we'll simulate that process by READing data cards). As each car passes the scanner, we want to push its identification number onto our stack.

```
         INTEGER TRACK1(200),FRONT1
         INTEGER IDNO
            .
            .
            .
100      READ(5,1000) IDNO
            .
            .
            .
         CALL PUSH(IDNO,TRACK1,FRONT1)
            .
            .
            .
```

Before going on with the program, let's resolve the problem of pushing a new value onto the stack. This amounts to putting the new value in the next available spot in the array and changing the pointer so that it indicates the new top element.

```
         SUBROUTINE PUSH(ELEMNT,STACK,TOP)
         INTEGER ELEMNT,STACK(200),TOP
COMMENT: STACK MANIPULATION ROUTINE: PUSH ON NEW
C        ELEMENT IF THERE'S ROOM.
         TOP=TOP+1
         IF (TOP .LE. 200) GO TO 100
C        OVERFLOW!
         WRITE(6,1000) ELEMNT
1000     FORMAT(' STACK OVERFLOW WHEN PUSHING',I10)
         STOP
C
100      STACK(TOP)=ELEMNT
         RETURN
         END
```

Looking at the classification algorithm, you can see that we'll also need a way to simulate the removal of cars from track 1. Cars are removed one at a time from the front. This corresponds to popping the stack, and we may as well use a SUBROUTINE named POP to do it. The input to POP will be the stack array and its stack pointer and the output will be the value of the top element and an updated stack and pointer to reflect the removal of the top element.

```
        SUBROUTINE POP(ELEMNT,STACK,TOP)
        INTEGER ELEMNT,STACK(200),TOP
COMMENT: STACK MANIPULATION ROUTINE: POP TOP
C          ELEMENT OFF STACK (UNLESS THE STACK IS EMPTY).
        IF (TOP .GT. 0) GO TO 100
C          IMPLOSION!
        WRITE(6,1000)
 1000   FORMAT(' STACK IMPLOSION')
        STOP
C
 100    ELEMNT=STACK(TOP)
        TOP=TOP-1
        RETURN
        END
```

Looking back over what we've put together, it appears that we've refined the steps of our program plan carefully enough to write the program. In reading the program below, refer often to the program plan and the classification algorithm to help you understand what's going on. Doing that, the program almost writes itself.

```
COMMENT: PROGRAM TO CLASSIFY TRAINS AT DURHAM YARD.
C          INPUT (DATA CARDS):
C               GROUP1: ONE CARD FOR EACH AVAILABLE
C                       TRAIN CAR.  CAR-ID: COL 1-3,INTEGER
C                       TRAIN MEMBERSHIP:COL 5-8,CHARACTER.
C               GROUP2: ONE CARD FOR EACH ARRIVING CAR
C                       CAR-ID:COL 1-3,INTEGER.
C               EACH GROUP FOLLOWED BY A BLANK CARD.
        INTEGER TRACK1(200),FRONT1
        INTEGER NXTCAR,CAR(200),TRAIN(200),N,BLNK
        DATA BLNK/4H    /
C
C       STORE CAR-ID. TRAIN-MEMBERSHIP PAIRS IN MEMORY.
        N=0
 100    READ(5,1000) CAR(N+1),TRAIN(N+1)
 1000   FORMAT(I3,1X,A4)
        IF (TRAIN(N+1) .EQ. BLNK) GO TO 200
        N=N+1
        IF (N .LT. 200) GO TO 100
C
        WRITE(6,1009) N
 1009   FORMAT(' THIS PROGRAM CANNOT HANDLE MORE THAN',I4,
     +              ' CARS.')
C
C       START WITH TRACK1 EMPTY.
 200    FRONT1=0
C
C       RECORD CAR-ID'S AS THE CARS ARRIVE AND ARE PUT
C       ON TRACK1.
 210    READ(5,1000) NXTCAR
        IF( NXTCAR .EQ. 0) GO TO 300
        CALL PUSH(NXTCAR,TRACK1,FRONT1)
        GO TO 210
C
C       CLASSIFY CARS
 300    CALL CLSSFY(CAR,TRAIN,N,TRACK1,FRONT1)
        STOP
        END
```

```
      SUBROUTINE CLSSFY(CARS,TRAINS,N,TRACK1,FRONT1)
      INTEGER CARS(200),TRAINS(200),N,TRACK1(200),FRONT1
      INTEGER NRFK,RNKF,PMTH,CAR,TRAIN,FNDTRN,PTR
      LOGICAL EMPTY
      EMPTY(PTR)=PTR .EQ. 0
      DATA NRFK,RNKE,PMTH /4HNRFK,4HRNKE,4HPMTH/
COMMENT: FOLLOW CLASSIFICATION ALGORITHM, PRINTING
C          INSTRUCTIONS FOR YARD CREW.
C       NAME USAGES--
C          EMPTY: STATEMENT FUNCTION TO TEST FOR EMPTY TRACK.
C          TRACK1,FRONT1: TRACK 1 SIMULATION STACK.
C          CARS,TRAINS: ARRAYS CONTAINING TRAIN ASSIGNMENT
C                       FOR EACH CAR.
C          N: N=NUMBER OF CARS IN THE YARD
C          CAR: CURRENT CAR BEING SWITCHED.
C          TRAIN: TRAIN ASSIGNMENT FOR CURRENT CAR.
C
C       PROCEED WITH CLASSIFICATION.
  100 IF (EMPTY(FRONT1)) GO TO 200
      CALL POP(CAR,TRACK1,FRONT1)
      TRAIN=FNDTRN(CAR,CARS,TRAINS,N)
      IF (TRAIN .EQ. NRFK) GO TO 100
      IF (TRAIN .EQ. RNKE) GO TO 110
      IF (TRAIN .EQ. PMTH) GO TO 120
C     UNKNOWN DESTINATION
      WRITE(6,1000)
 1000 FORMAT('0 PULL OUT, THEN BACK ONTO TRACK 4.')
      GO TO 130
C
C       CAR FOR TRAIN TO ROANOKE.
  110 WRITE(6,1010)
 1010 FORMAT('0PULL OUT.   THEN BACK ONTO TRACK 2.')
      GO TO 130
C
C       CAR FOR TRAIN TO PORTSMOUTH.
  120 WRITE(6,1020)
 1020 FORMAT('0PULL OUT.   THEN BACK ONTO TRACK 3.')
  130 WRITE(6,1030)
 1030 FORMAT('0UNCOUPLE ONE CAR , THEN RETURN TO TRACK 1.')
      GO TO 100
C
C     ALL CARS LEFT ATTATCHED TO ENGINE GO TO NORFOLK.
  200 WRITE(6,2000)
 2000 FORMAT('0BACK ONTO TRACK 1 AND UNCOUPLE ALL CARS.'/
     +        ' PULL OUT AND MOVE INTO ENGINE TERMINAL.'/
     +        ' DONE FOR THE DAY.  ')
      STOP
      END

      INTEGER FUNCTION FNDTRN(CAR,CARS,TRAINS,N)
      INTEGER CAR,CARS(200),TRAINS(200),N
COMMENT: FIND THE DESTINATION OF 'CAR'.
C       PARAMETERS--
C          CAR: ID OF CAR
C          CARS,TRAINS: ARRAYS GIVING CAR DESTINATION.
C          N: NUMBER OF CARS IN ENTIRE YARD.
      INTEGER I,UNKN
      DATA UNKN /4HUNKN/
      DO 100 I=1,N
        IF (CAR .NE. CARS(I)) GO TO 100
C        CAR-ID FOUND--RETURN DESTINATION.
        FNDTRN=TRAINS(I)
        RETURN
  100   CONTINUE
```

```
C         CAR NOT LOCATED--RETURN UNKNOWN AS DESTINATION.
          FNDTRN=UNKN
          RETURN
          END
```

data
```
    423 RNKE
    147 RNKE
    232 RNKE
    976 NRFK
    225 NRFK
    227 NRFK
    322 NRFK
    999 PMTH
    361 PMTH
    882 PMTH

    322
    232
    361
    147
    999
    423
    225
    882
    227
    976
```

output
```
    PULL OUT.  THEN BACK ONTO TRACK 3.

    UNCOUPLE ONE CAR , THEN RETURN TO TRACK 1.

    PULL OUT.  THEN BACK ONTO TRACK 2.

    UNCOUPLE ONE CAR , THEN RETURN TO TRACK 1.

    PULL OUT.  THEN BACK ONTO TRACK 3.

    UNCOUPLE ONE CAR , THEN RETURN TO TRACK 1.

    PULL OUT.  THEN BACK ONTO TRACK 2.

    UNCOUPLE ONE CAR , THEN RETURN TO TRACK 1.

    PULL OUT.  THEN BACK ONTO TRACK 3.

    UNCOUPLE ONE CAR , THEN RETURN TO TRACK 1.

    PULL OUT.  THEN BACK ONTO TRACK 2.

    UNCOUPLE ONE CAR , THEN RETURN TO TRACK 1.

    BACK ONTO TRACK 1 AND UNCOUPLE ALL CARS.
    PULL OUT AND MOVE INTO ENGINE TERMINAL.
    DONE FOR THE DAY.
```

The problems at the end of this chapter suggest other applications for stacks. Use the POP and PUSH routines we've developed here.

Stacks provide a way to store a variable number of items when items enter and leave from the same place (last in, first out). There are many situations in which items enter one place and leave another. For example, Figure 11 4 3 shows people standing politely in line. People enter the line at the BACK, and receive their tickets when they are at the FRONT. As time goes on, the line (or **queue**) shrinks and grows depending on the rates at which people enter and leave.

The most obvious way to represent a queue is a simple extension of the way we handled stacks. We'll just declare an array big enough, and now, instead of having just one variable keeping track of the top, we'll have *two*, one for the FRONT and one for the BACK.

Figure 11 4 3   A Queue

We start FRONT and BACK off with the value 0 to represent an empty queue. Now, to add an item VALUE (at the back), we can use the statements

```
BACK = BACK +1
QUEUE(BACK) = VALUE
```

and to remove an item (from the front), we use

```
FRONT = FRONT + 1
VALUE = QUEUE(FRONT)
```

Unfortunately, this scheme doesn't work all that well in practice. Suppose we put on one element, then take it off, then put it on, take it off, and so on. Even though at any point in time the queue is either empty or else has just one value in it, we will need an infinite number of memory locations. Not very practical.

A cure for this problem is to make the array circular. Study SUBROUTINE QADD to see what we mean. Statement 10 turns the array into a circle by making QUEUE(1) come after QUEUE(500).

```
      SUBROUTINE  QADD(QUEUE,FRONT,BACK,VALUE)
      INTEGER QUEUE(500), FRONT, BACK, VALUE
COMMENT:  MOVE BACK
      BACK = BACK + 1
COMMENT:  SEE IF WE NEED TO WRAP AROUND
  10  IF (BACK .GT. 500) BACK = 1
COMMENT:  NOW TEST FOR OVERFLOW
      IF (BACK .NE. FRONT)  GO TO 20
COMMENT:  OVERFLOW...
      WRITE(6,1000) VALUE
1000 FORMAT(' QUEUE OVERFLOW WHEN ADDING', I8)
      STOP
COMMENT:  INSERT VALUE
  20  QUEUE(BACK) = VALUE
      RETURN
      END
```

Often you will want to store more than one value in each queue element. For example, if you were writing a simulation of a supermarket and were using queues to represent shoppers waiting at the checkout stands, you might need to store three things for each shopper: the time the shopper entered the queue (so you can tell how long the shopper had to wait), the number of groceries (so you can tell how long it will take to get checked out), and whether or not the shopper has Tide-XK (so you can tell whether the shopper will be accosted by the people shooting TV commercials in the parking lot).

The solution is very simple—just declare an array for each queue you need and use the same FRONT and BACK values for all of the queues.

```
REAL TIME(500)
INTEGER THINGS(500), FRONT, BACK
LOGICAL TIDE(500)
```

To add in a shopper, just step BACK and insert the appropriate values into TIME(BACK), THINGS(BACK) and TIDE(BACK). The (enlarged) queue would look like this:

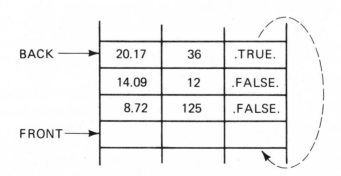

The dotted line is to remind you of our trick for more efficient use of memory space.

EXERCISES 11 4

1 If the elements you want to store in a stack are REAL numbers, what would you change?

2 Write a SUBROUTINE REMOVE(QUEUE, FRONT, BACK, VALUE) which removes the element at the front of QUEUE, puts its value in VALUE, and incorporates the "wraparound" usage of the array called QUEUE.

3 Add a test for an empty queue into your SUBROUTINE REMOVE. (If the queue is empty, there's nothing to be removed.)

Section 11 5

Strings

In the last section we saw data structures which required saving information about how many elements were currently being stored (TOP = the number of elements in a stack, for example). This information was kept separate from the elements being stored. In this section we will see a data structure in which length information is kept right with the elements being stored and in which other variables will be used to find where subparts of the information are kept.

Imagine that you are responsible for writing a program which processes bills. We'll suppose that, as the bills and checks come in, someone keypunches the amounts on a card and, if the bill has a comment (or complaint) written on it, that gets punched as well. Your program would update everyone's account on the basis of these cards. If there is a message, then it should be stored along with the person's account, and a list of people who had messages should be printed out so that someone could go over them later.

But now a problem arises—how much space should you leave for messages in the areas where accounts are stored? You know from experience that only a few people will write comments. If you leave the same amount of space for each person's message, then most of the space you set aside will be blank (and wasted). You decide that maybe you could store all the messages in one place and just use one word per account to tell where the message is (if there is one). This way you can set aside a much smaller amount of memory (see Figure 11 5 1).

Everything seems fine now, until it's time to decide how long a space to leave for each message. Some are long, like "I wish that next time your man comes he could stay longer because I had such a nice time telling him about my trip uptown and he said he was sorry but he had to rush off and he didn't get to taste my cherry cobbler," and some are short, like "@!!?#." The only way to get around leaving a huge space for each message is somehow to store them as variable length chunks. We will call each chunk a **string**.

Strings occur naturally in many nonnumeric computing tasks, such as linguistic analysis and text editing. String processing is so important that several languages have been developed (notably SNOBOL) especially for dealing with strings. We will describe a way to deal with them in Fortran.

First estimate the maximum space needed to store all the messages. Then declare an array of that size, e.g.,

`INTEGER STRING(1000)`

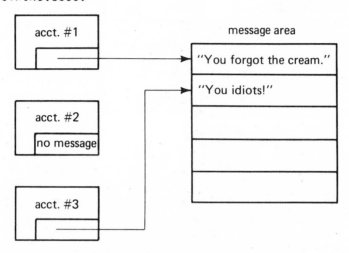

Figure 11 5 1   Storing Strings in Memory

Next, let's see how to store one message. Suppose it is "Two creams from now on." First, set aside memory cell STRING(1) and then just keep filling letters into successive memory cells in the array until the message is finished. Then put the number of memory cells used by the string into STRING(1).

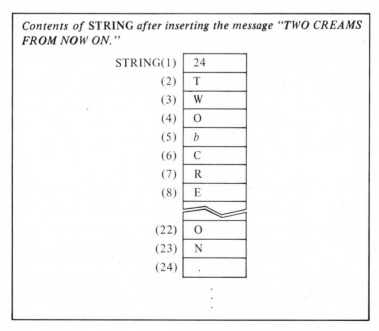

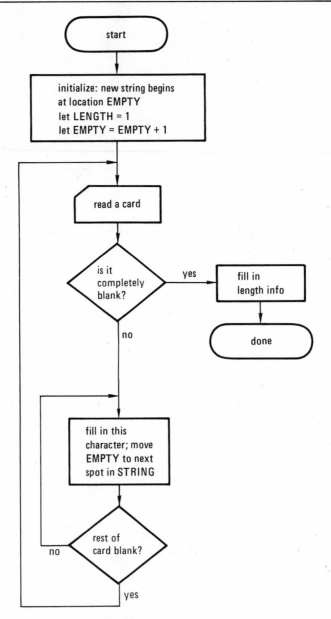

> *storing characters: Character information, unlike other data types, may be stored in memory cells of* any *type. We are using this quirk to store two types of information in the array* STRING: *(1) the* INTEGERs *indicating the length of the strings and (2) the characters which make up the messages.*

start

initialize: new string begins
at location EMPTY
let LENGTH = 1
let EMPTY = EMPTY + 1

read a card

is it completely blank? — yes → fill in length info → done

no

fill in this character; move EMPTY to next spot in STRING

rest of card blank? — no / yes

Figure 11 5 2   Message READing and Storing Algorithm

We can reference the string by providing a variable that records where in the array STRING the message starts. The first word of the string tells how long it is, so we know how far to go to find the whole message.

What if we want to add in another message? Well, we had better know where to store the message in the array STRING. We'll create a variable EMPTY that indicates where we can start filling. After the string "Two creams from now on" has been inserted, EMPTY would have the value 25.

Following this train of thought, and adding a few helpful features, we came up with the algorithm shown in Figure 11 5 2, and SUBROUTINE RDMESS. RDMESS READs a message from data cards, stores it as a string in STRING, keeps track of the next EMPTY spot in STRING, and returns a pointer to the new message. Since we need some way to tell when a message is over, we require that a blank card be placed at the end of each message. Since it is inconvenient for people to have to punch their message all the way to the end of each card, RDMESS simply throws away trailing blanks.

```
         SUBROUTINE RDMESS(NEWSTR)
         INTEGER NEWSTR
COMMENT: READ A MESSAGE FROM DATA CARDS, AND STORE IT IN
C           'STRING'.  RETURN 'NEWSTR', WHICH POINTS TO THE
C           NEW MESSAGE.  A MESSAGE CONSISTS OF AN ARBITRARY
C           NUMBER OF CARDS, FOLLOWED BY A CARD WHICH IS ALL
C           BLANKS.  IN ORDER TO ENSURE THAT EACH CARD HAS AT
C           LEAST ONE TRAILING BLANK (SO THE TEST CARRIED
C           OUT BY LOGICAL FUNCTION ALLBLE ('ALL BLANKS TO
C           END') IS GUARANTEED TO SUCCEED SOONER OR LATER),
C           WE MAKE ARRAY 'CARD' LENGTH 81 AND STICK A BLANK
C           AT THE END OURSELVES.
         INTEGER CARD(81),COLUMN,LENGTH,BLANK
         LOGICAL ALLBLE
         INTEGER STRING(1000),EMPTY
         COMMON EMPTY,STRING
         DATA CARD(81)/1H /,BLANK/1H /
C
C        INITIALIZE
         NEWSTR=EMPTY
         EMPTY=EMPTY+1
         LENGTH=1
C        READ A MESSAGE CARD.
  100    READ(5,1000) (CARD(COLUMN),COLUMN=1,80)
 1000    FORMAT(80A1)
         IF (.NOT. ALLBLE(CARD,1)) GO TO 200
C           RECEIVED BLANK CARD--END OF MESSAGE
            STRING(NEWSTR)=LENGTH
            RETURN
C
  200    COLUMN=1
C        FILL IT IN.
  300    STRING(EMPTY)=CARD(COLUMN)
            LENGTH=LENGTH+1
            EMPTY=EMPTY+1
            COLUMN=COLUMN+1
            IF (.NOT. ALLBLE(CARD,COLUMN)) GO TO 300
C        STICK IN ONE BLANK BEFORE GOING ON TO THE NEXT CARD
C        BECAUSE WE SKIPPED EVERY ONE OF THE TRAILING BLANKS.
         STRING(EMPTY)=BLANK
         LENGTH=LENGTH+1
         EMPTY=EMPTY+1
         GO TO 100
         END
```

```
         LOGICAL FUNCTION ALLBLE(CARD,COL)
         INTEGER CARD(81),COL
         INTEGER BLANK,LOOK
         DATA BLANK/1H /
C        IF ALL CHARACTERS IN 'CARD' FROM COLUMN NUMBER
C        'COL' UP TO COLUMN 81 ARE BLANK, RETURN '.TRUE.'.
         ALLBLE=.FALSE.
         LOOK=COL
  100    IF (CARD(LOOK) .NE. BLANK) RETURN
            LOOK=LOOK+1
            IF (LOOK .LE. 81) GO TO 100
C        YES, IT'S ALL BLANK.
         ALLBLE=.TRUE.
         RETURN
         END
```

So far, we have a way to READ and store variable length messages as strings. Since each string begins with a cell storing the string's length, printing out a message is easy (see exercise 4). But we can do *more*. Once we have a number of messages stored as strings it's fairly easy to manipulate them. We can hack them apart, add them together, or do a variety of text editing tasks.

Sometimes when you go back over something you've written, you want to cut the end of a sentence off because it runs on too long anyway, and sometimes you want to put two sentences together to make a longer message. Let's see how we could do those operations on strings. First, let's take chopping off the end of a string. We'll write a SUBROUTINE CHOP which will chop the last DROPNO characters from the string starting at location SENT in the array STRING.

```
         SUBROUTINE CHOP(SENT,DROPNO)
         INTEGER SENT, DROPNO
         INTEGER LENGTH
         INTEGER EMPTY, STRING(1000)
         COMMON EMPTY, STRING
COMMENT:  FIND HOW LONG STRING IS NOW
         LENGTH = STRING(SENT)
COMMENT:  COMPUTE LENGTH AFTER DROPPING "DROPNO" CHARACTERS
         LENGTH = LENGTH - DROPNO
COMMENT:  STICK IN NEW LENGTH
         STRING(SENT) = LENGTH
         RETURN
         END
```

Next, let's see how we might run two sentences together. This widely used string operation is usually called **concatenation**.

We face a problem here. Since we have packed the strings into our array as tightly as possible, we can't just copy the second string into the memory cells immediately following the first string. It usually won't fit without wiping out part of some other string. We'll have to abandon the two original strings and make a copy of the first, then the second, without its length information, then update the new string's length information, and finally, update the variable which pointed to the first string so that now it will point to the beginning of the concatenated result.

```
            SUBROUTINE CONCAT(STR1, STR2)
            INTEGER STR1, STR2
            INTEGER L1, L2, LOWLIM, UPLIM, S, FILL
            INTEGER EMPTY, STRING(1000)
            COMMON EMPTY, STRING
COMMENT:   FIND OUT HOW LONG THE FIRST STRING IS
            L1 = STRING(STR1)
COMMENT:   ALSO THE SECOND STRING
            L2 = STRING(STR2)
COMMENT:   COPY STRING "STR1" TO THE EMPTY REGION
            LOWLIM = EMPTY
            UPLIM = EMPTY + L1 - 1
            S = STR1
            DO 100 FILL = LOWLIM,UPLIM
               STRING(FILL) = STRING(S)
  100       S = S+1
COMMENT:   NOW COPY "STR2" (EXCEPT FOR ITS LENGTH INFO)
            LOWLIM = UPLIM + 1
            UPLIM = LOWLIM + L2 - 2
            S = STR2 + 1
            DO 200 FILL = LOWLIM,UPLIM
               STRING(FILL) = STRING(S)
  200       S = S+1
COMMENT:   SET POINTER TO NEW STRING AND UPDATE LENGTH INFO
            STR1 = EMPTY
            STRING(STR1) = L1 + L2 - 1
COMMENT:   UPDATE "EMPTY" POINTER
            EMPTY = EMPTY + STRING(STR1)
            RETURN
            END
```

You may wonder what happens to all the old strings we abandoned in the CONCAT routine. You might think they're now just wasted space. That's right. A solution to this problem of wasted space is the concept of **garbage collection**. We will not go into this in detail, but the main idea is that if your program tries to create a new string and finds that there's not enough room between EMPTY and the end of the array STRING, it calls a subprogram which rearranges the strings so that all the abandoned ones now become empty space.

You'll get a chance to learn more uses for strings in the problems at the end of the chapter.

EXERCISES 11 5

1 Look at SUBROUTINE RDMESS. Where should a test be placed to prevent storing a message which is too long for the available space in memory?

2 If the string starting at S1 looks like:

| 16 | C | O | M | E | | O | N | | P | E | O | P | L | E | |

and S2 looks like:

| 22 | S | M | I | L | E | | O | N | | Y | O | U | R | | B | R | O | T | H | E | R |

what does the string starting at S1 look like after executing CALL CONCAT(S1,S2)?

3 If the string starting at S1 looks like:

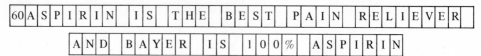

`60 A S P I R I N _ I S _ T H E _ B E S T _ P A I N _ R E L I E V E R _`

`A N D _ B A Y E R _ I S _ 1 0 0 % _ A S P I R I N`

and the one starting at S2 looks like:

`17 T H E _ B E S T _ A S P I R I N`

what does the string starting at S1 look like after:

```
CALL CHOP(S1,48)
CALL CONCAT(S1, S2)
```

4 Write a SUBROUTINE called PRINTS which takes one argument that points to a string and which prints that string.

Section 11 6

Lists

In the string data structures of Section 11 5, the strings vary in length, giving us a flexible data structure (collection of strings) made up of a number of sub-structures (individual strings). We've seen a progression of increasingly general data structures, from fixed-size, fixed-shape structures (arrays), through variable-size, fixed-shape structures (stacks and queues), and on to variable-size, variable-shape structures (collections of strings). Each string in a collection of strings is a variable-sized, fixed-shape data structure, but the whole collection can be thought of as having variable shape since its subparts are varying independently of one another.

In this section we want to study a data structure with even greater flexibility. In this new data structure, even the units of information can vary in both size and shape. Each unit is called a **list** (or **linked list**) and is made up of data items each of which contains information about how to find neighboring data items. Thus it is possible to change not only the number of data items, but also the relationships between contiguous data items. Before, these relationships remained constant. (In a string each letter has the preceding and following letters for its neighbors, a fixed relationship.) We use lists in applications where it is important to vary both the number of data items and their interrelationships.

There have been a great number of predictions made about the use of computers in the home. Whether they come true or not will depend to a large extent on whether people can come up with really useful things for home computers to do and write programs to carry them out. Let's do some preliminary work on a system which keeps track of grocery supplies and generates shopping lists.

Each item of information will consist of the name of a grocery product and a number. As an example, BEANS, REFRIED 2 would stand for two cans of refried beans. The number will stand for the number on hand, the number purchased, or the number used, depending on the context in which we find the data item.

> **problem statement:** *Develop an automated grocery inventory manager for the home.*

What we have in mind here is a computer program which will automatically keep track of the groceries on hand, itemized by grocery product, and print out shopping lists of items needed. To keep track of supplies, the program will need to be informed, via data entry (READ), when items are used or purchased. The program will be inconvenient to use because the user will have to punch a data card for every purchase and for every time a product is used, but by the time home computer systems become commonplace, scanners like those used in automated checkout stands at supermarkets may be cheap enough to be used in the home. These scanners read the machine coded labels (**universal product code**) on grocery products. With the availability of scanners, the program will be easy to use. Instead of punched card data entry, containers can be passed over a scanner built into the kitchen counter before putting them on the shelf (or throwing them out, in the case of empties), and the computer can get its information on supplies from the scanner. This kind of a home computer, product scanner system will probably become practical in the near future, so it isn't too soon to start designing the programs to control it. In fact, looking a little further into the future, it may become practical to connect your home computer to computers in supermarkets via telephone lines and have your computer automatically shop around for the best prices and place orders for delivery to your door.

We want our program to READ data cards containing information like that shown below.

```
USED        WHEATIES,10 OZ.      1
BOUGHT      BEER,CAN             6
USED        MILK,HALF GAL.       1
SUPPLIES
SHOP
```

Treating each data card as a command, the program should respond by deleting or adding items to the list of supplies or the shopping list or respond by printing the current list of supplies or the shopping list. The input/output description, Figure 11 6 1, makes these ideas more explicit.

The most complicated parts of the program will be the parts that manipulate the various lists. (The rest of the program is made up of familiar components.) From a conceptual point of view, there's little difference betweeen the lists we'll be using and one-dimensional arrays. Lists are made up of elements, one after another in sequence, like arrays. The primary differences are

1 We have direct access to only the first element in a list (in an array we have direct access, via the subscript, to any element).

2 The number of elements in a list can change (the number of elements in an array is fixed, once declared).

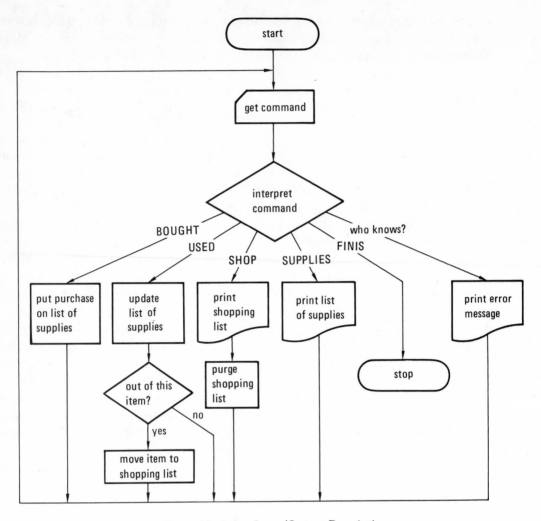

Figure 11 6 1   Input/Output Description

3 Elements can be added to or deleted from any part of the list without rearranging the rest of the list (in arrays this can only be done at the tail end).

The first property above is a disadvantage. To get to the fourteenth element in a list, we have to start at the top and move from element to element until we get to the fourteenth one. We'll put up with this undesirable feature in order to have the second property. We need the second property in our grocery inventory program because we have two lists, the list of supplies and the shopping list, which are constantly changing in size. Of course, we could use two arrays to store the lists, but we'd have to declare their (fixed) lengths in the beginning, and many elements would end up unused most of the time. Worse yet, there would be no dynamic flexibility. Unused elements in the shopping list array couldn't be used for the list of supplies, even if the shopping array was almost empty at the same time the list of supplies was full. (Note that this is a frequently occurring situation. When the shelves are stocked, the shopping list is small.)

Each element in a list has two parts, a **data part** and a **pointer part**. The data part contains the information the element stores. The pointer part tells how to find the next element in the list. Figure 11 6 2 is a diagram of a typical shopping list and a list of supplies (kitchen list). The pointer part is represented by an arrow. The first element in the shopping list contains the entry EGGS, the second, BUTTER, and so on. There is also a pointer to the first element. It is called the **list pointer** and is the only route of access to the list. This is why we can get at only the first element directly.

shopping list

EGGS ⟶ BUTTER ⟶ WHEATIES ⟶ PEACHES

kitchen list

OLIVES,1 ⟶ PEAS,3 ⟶ JELLO,6 ⟶ COKE,10 ⟶ FLOUR,5

Figure 11 6 2   Some Lists

It's all very well to draw pictures of data values connected by arrows—but how can we implement this organization in Fortran? The key to a solution is to see what is constant in a given list structure. The answer is the shape of each list element. In our problem each list element consists of a word, or a word and a number, and an arrow which points to another element. Although the number of elements on a particular list may vary, so that individual lists shrink and grow, the total amount of memory available to your Fortran program is fixed. That means that the total collection of elements is a fixed-sized collection of fixed-shape objects—an array of some sort.

We want to store an item description, a number, and a pointer in each list element. We'll allow six memory cells per element: four for the description, one for the number, and one for the pointer. Therefore, we'll need six arrays, one for each of the six memory cells per element.

```
INTEGER N1(1000),N2(1000),N3(1000),N4(1000),
  +         QUANT(1000),NEXT(1000)
```

A subscript value between 1 and 1000 identifies one spot in each of the six arrays, altogether making a single list element. A pointer, then, is just a subscript. Given a particular element, the value in the array NEXT at that position gives the subscript value of the succeeding element. A pointer value of 0 (not a legitimate subscript value) will mean "end of list." The only other thing we need is a memory cell which stores a pointer to the beginning of the list. Follow through Figure 11 6 3 to see how the two lists as drawn on the left half of the figure are stored in the arrays on the right.

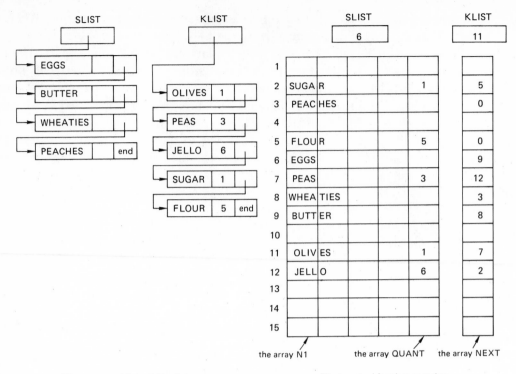

The way we think of the lists

Their actual implementation

Figure 11 6 3

Now that we have the basic idea of how lists are implemented, let's follow through our grocery list program piece by piece, pausing to inspect specific examples of list manipulation—creation of lists, searching, adding elements, and so forth.

Here's our main program:

```
COMMENT: ORGANIZE AND MAINTAIN AN INVENTORY OF GROCERIES.
C        GENERATE A SHOPPING LIST.
C        INPUT:THERE ARE 5 DIFFERENT FORMS OF INPUT CARD
C            1 'BOUGHT' CARDS SPECIFY NEWLY
C                PURCHASED ITEMS
C            2 'USED' CARDS SPECIFY SUPPLIES THAT HAVE
C                BEEN USED
C            3 'SHOP' CARDS REQUEST A SHOPPING LIST
C                TO BE PRINTED OUT
C            4 'SUPPLIES' CARDS REQUEST A PRINT OUT OF
C                THE STOCK ON HAND
C            5 'FINIS' CARDS TERMINATE PROCESSING
C        OUTPUT: THE PROGRAM ISSUES SHOPPING LISTS AND/OR
C                INVENTORY LISTS ON COMMAND
```

```
C
C             DATA STRUCTURES: THE LISTS ARE IMPLEMENTED AS
C                              LINKED LISTS, MADE UP OF ELEMENTS
C                              WHICH HAVE 6 SUBFIELDS. 4 FOR A
C                              DESCRIPTION OF THE ITEM, 1 FOR
C                              QUANTITY, 1 TO INDICATE THE NEXT
C                              ELEMENT ON THE LIST.  ALL LIST
C                              ELEMENTS RESIDE IN COMMON.
        INTEGER N1(1000),N2(1000),N3(1000),N4(1000),
     +          QUANT(1000),NEXT(1000),END
        COMMON N1,N2,N3,N4,QUANT,NEXT,END
        INTEGER KLIST,SLIST,FREE,COMAND,CASE,C1,C2,
     +          L1,L2,L3,L4,Q
        WRITE(6,2000)
 2000 FORMAT('1',10X,'KITCHEN SYSTEMS,INC.'///)
        END=0
C       SET UP FREE LIST
        FREE=0
  100   IF (FREE .GT. 999) GO TO 200
            NEXT(FREE+1)=FREE
            FREE=FREE+1
            GO TO 100
C       TO BEGIN WITH BOTH 'KLIST' AND 'SLIST' ARE EMPTY
  200   KLIST=END
        SLIST=END
COMMENT: PROCESS INPUT COMMANDS.
  300   READ(5,3000) C1,C2,L1,L2,L3,L4,Q
 3000 FORMAT(2A4,1X,4A4,1X,I4)
        CASE=COMAND(C1,C2)
        GO TO (310,320,330,340,350,360),CASE
C
C       'BOUGHT' A NEW ITEM.
  310   CALL RESTCK(L1,L2,L3,L4,Q,FREE,KLIST)
        WRITE(6,3100) Q,L1,L2,L3,L4
 3100 FORMAT(' BOUGHT ',I3,2X,4A4)
        GO TO 300
C
C       'USED' SOME STUFF
  320   CALL USED(L1,L2,L3,L4,Q,KLIST,SLIST)
        WRITE(6,3200) Q,L1,L2,L3,L4
 3200 FORMAT(' USED ',I3,2X,4A4)
        GO TO 300
C
C       'SHOP'-PING LIST WANTED
  330   WRITE(6,3300)
 3300 FORMAT('0HERE IS YOUR SHOPPING LIST')
        CALL PRNLST(SLIST)
        WRITE(6,3350)
 3350 FORMAT('0')
C       FLUSH SHOPPING LIST.
  335   IF (NEXT(SLIST) .EQ. END) GO TO 338
            CALL MOVE(SLIST,NEXT(SLIST),FREE)
            GO TO 335
C       SPECIAL CASE FOR FIRST ELEMENT ON SLIST.
  338   NEXT(SLIST)=FREE
        FREE=SLIST
        SLIST=END
        GO TO 300
```

```
C
C        'SUPPLIES' LISTING WANTED
  340    WRITE(6,3400)
  3400   FORMAT('0SUPPLIES ON HAND:')
         CALL PRNLST(KLIST)
         WRITE(6,3350)
         GO TO 300
C
C        'FINIS'--BAIL OUT
  350    STOP
C
C        WHO KNOWS WHAT COMMAND WE GOT?
  360    WRITE(6,3600) C1,C2
  3600   FORMAT('0',2A4,' IS NOT A COMMAND, WHAT',
       +         ' DID YOU HAVE IN MIND?')
         GO TO 300
         END
         INTEGER FUNCTION COMAND(C1,C2)
         INTEGER C1,C2
COMMENT: CONVERT COMMAND WORDS INTO NUMBERS:
C            'BOUGHT'=1
C            'USED'=2
C            'SHOP'=3
C            'SUPPLIES'=4
C            'FINIS'=5
         INTEGER WORDS(5,2)
         DATA WORDS(1,1),WORDS(1,2)/4HBOUG,4HHT  /,
       +      WORDS(2,1),WORDS(2,2)/4HUSED,4H    /,
       +      WORDS(3,1),WORDS(3,2)/4HSHOP,4H    /,
       +      WORDS(4,1),WORDS(4,2)/4HSUPP,4HLIES/,
       +      WORDS(5,1),WORDS(5,2)/4HFINI,4HS   /
         COMAND=1
  100    IF ((C1 .EQ. WORDS(COMAND,1)
       +         .AND. C2 .EQ. WORDS(COMAND,2))
       +            .OR. COMAND .GT. 5) RETURN
         COMAND=COMAND+1
         GO TO 100
         END
```

As you can see from its comments, the main program is a direct implementation of the input/output description in Figure 11 6 1. The only addition is the initialization section which sets up the free list (explained shortly) and the other two lists. We'll discuss this section first.

The statements up to statement 300 set up the lists. There will be three lists altogether. You already know about the kitchen list and the shopping list, but the other list, the **free list**, is new. The purpose of the free list is to keep track of currently unused list elements. Most of the time there will be some elements on the kitchen list and some on the shopping list, but the total number of elements on those two lists together will not exhaust the list space (hopefully). It is these leftover elements that we keep on the free list. When we need to add an element to one of the other lists, we simply take an element off the free list, put appropriate values in it, and add it to the other list. When we delete an element from the kitchen list or shopping list, we put it on the free list for later use.

In the beginning, all of the list elements are unused, so they all go on the free list. To put all the elements on the free list, we link them all together and set the head pointer FREE so that it points to the first element. The kitchen list and the shopping list, on the other hand, are empty in the beginning, so we set their head pointers KLIST qand SLIST to "end of list" (END = 0).

Once a list has been constructed (either the kitchen list or the shopping list), printing it out is just a matter of repeatedly checking to see if we're at the end of the list and, if not, printing the description and quantity fields, then moving on to the next element.

> *finding the next list element: If* NEXT *is the array containing the pointers to the next list elements, and we are currently looking at the element in array position N, then* NEXT(N) *is the subscript of (pointer to) the next element in the list.*

```
      SUBROUTINE PRNLST(LIST)
      INTEGER LIST
COMMENT: PRINT OUT ALL ITEMS ON 'LIST'.
      INTEGER N1(1000),N2(1000),N3(1000),N4(1000),
     +        QUANT(1000),NEXT(1000),END
      COMMON N1,N2,N3,N4,QUANT,NEXT,END
      INTEGER CUREL
      CUREL=LIST
  100 IF (CUREL .EQ. END)   RETURN
        WRITE(6,1010) N1(CUREL),N2(CUREL),N3(CUREL),
     +                N4(CUREL),QUANT(CUREL)
 1010   FORMAT(6X,4A4,I6)
        CUREL=NEXT(CUREL)
        GO TO 100
      END
```

SUBROUTINE ADD puts new elements on lists. First it fills in the item description and quantity parts of the list element at the front of the free list, and then it rearranges pointers to cut the element off the free list and install it at the front of the new list (whose head pointer is denoted by LIST in the SUBROUTINE). Figure 11 6 4 shows the necessary pointer changes pictorially. If you study it in conjunction with SUBROUTINE ADD, you should be able to figure out what's going on.

```
      SUBROUTINE ADD(M1,M2,M3,M4,Q,FREE,LIST)
      INTEGER M1,M2,M3,M4,Q,FREE,LIST
COMMENT: CREATE A NEW ELEMENT BY REMOVING THE FIRST
C        ELEMENT OF THE 'FREE' LIST, FILLING IT UP WITH 'M1'
C        THRU 'M4','Q', AND INSERTING IT INTO 'LIST'.
      INTEGER N1(1000),N2(1000),N3(1000),N4(1000),
     +        QUANT(1000),NEXT(1000),END
      COMMON N1,N2,N3,N4,QUANT,NEXT,END
      INTEGER SAVE
      N1(FREE)=M1
      N2(FREE)=M2
      N3(FREE)=M3
      N4(FREE)=M4
      QUANT(FREE)=Q
      SAVE=FREE
      IF (FREE .NE. END)  GO TO 100
        WRITE(6,1000)
 1000   FORMAT(' OUT OF ROOM ON FREE LIST.  SORRY')
        STOP
  100 FREE = NEXT(FREE)
      NEXT(SAVE)=LIST
      LIST=SAVE
      RETURN
      END
```

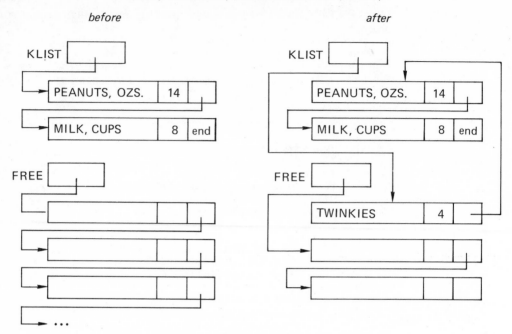

What SUBROUTINE ADD does to add the
entry TWINKIES, 4 to the kitchen list (KLIST)

before   *after*

Figure 11 6 4   ADDing a New Element to KLIST

When a grocery item is used up, we want to remove its list element from the kitchen list and put it on the shopping list. After the shopping list has been printed, we move the elements on it to the free list for later use. Both movements involve the same pointer manipulations. In both there are two cases, determined by whether the element to be moved is the first element of its list or not. If the element is the first element, we must alter the head pointer of the list. If it's not the first element, we must alter the pointer field (NEXT) of the previous element. Look back at the main program. Statements 335 up to (but not including) 340 use SUBROUTINE MOVE to handle elements which are *not* at the front of the shopping list (SLIST), and the three statements starting with 338 MOVE elements which *are* at the front. If it's not clear to you what's going on, try drawing pictures like those in Figure 11 6 4.

```
      SUBROUTINE MOVE(PRED,ELEMNT,LIST)
      INTEGER PRED,ELEMNT,LIST
COMMENT: *NEXT(PRED)* CURRENTLY POINTS TO *ELEMNT*.
C        PULL *ELEMNT* OUT AND STICK IT ON THE FRONT
C        OF *LIST*.
      INTEGER N1(1000),N2(1000),N3(1000),N4(1000),
     +        QUANT(1000),NEXT(1000),END
      COMMON N1,N2,N3,N4,QUANT,NEXT,END
      NEXT(PRED)=NEXT(ELEMNT)
      NEXT(ELEMNT)=LIST
      LIST=ELEMNT
      RETURN
      END
```

```
      SUBROUTINE RESTCK(M1,M2,M3,M4,Q,FREE,LIST)
      INTEGER M1,M2,M3,M4,Q,FREE,LIST
COMMENT: IF ITEM IS ALREADY IN STOCK, JUST ADD TO QUANT.
C        OTHERWISE, CREATE A NEW ITEM AND STICK IT ON 'LIST'
      INTEGER N1(1000),N2(1000),N3(1000),N4(1000),
     *        QUANT(1000),NEXT(1000),END
      COMMON N1,N2,N3,N4,QUANT,NEXT,END
      INTEGER LOOK
      LOGICAL EQUAL
      LOOK=LIST
  100 IF (LOOK .NE. END) GO TO 200
C        MAKE A NEW ENTRY.
      CALL ADD(M1,M2,M3,M4,Q,FREE,LIST)
      RETURN
C        FIND IT YET?
  200 IF (EQUAL(M1,M2,M3,M4,LOOK)) GO TO 300
      LOOK=NEXT(LOOK)
      GO TO 100
C
C        FOUND IT
  300 QUANT(LOOK)=QUANT(LOOK)+Q
      RETURN
      END
```

RESTCK uses the LOGICAL FUNCTION EQUAL to tell if it has found the item it's looking for. This is simply a matter of comparing descriptions (one Fortran IF for each of the four memory cells containing the description).

```
      LOGICAL FUNCTION EQUAL(M1,M2,M3,M4,PLACE)
      INTEGER M1,M2,M3,M4,PLACE
C     EQUAL RETURNS .TRUE. IF THE DESCRIPTION IN THE LIST
C     ELEMENT POINTED TO BY 'PLACE' IS THE SAME AS M1,M2,ETC
      INTEGER N1(1000),N2(1000),N3(1000),N4(1000),
     *        QUANT(1000),NEXT(1000),END
      COMMON N1,N2,N3,N4,QUANT,NEXT,END
      EQUAL=.FALSE.
      IF (M1 .NE. N1(PLACE)) RETURN
      IF (M2 .NE. N2(PLACE)) RETURN
      IF (M3 .NE. N3(PLACE)) RETURN
      IF (M4 .NE. N4(PLACE)) RETURN
      EQUAL= .TRUE.
      RETURN
      END
```

The bookkeeping we must perform when an item has been used up is very similar to the process of restocking. We search for the item, find it, and subtract the quantity used from the quantity listed. If the subtraction exhausts the supply, we move the item to the shopping list.

After the purchase has been made, we want to add it to our inventory. Figure 11 6 5 shows the algorithm we'll follow for restocking the list of kitchen supplies after a purchase has been made. First we search for the item. If we find it on the kitchen list, we add the quantity purchased to the currently listed quantity. If we don't find it, we put the product description and quantity into a new list element and add it to the list.

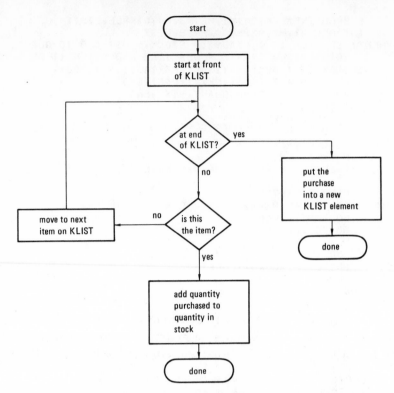

Figure 11 6 5 Restocking Algorithm

```
      SUBROUTINE USED(M1,M2,M3,M4,Q,KLIST,SLIST)
      INTEGER M1,M2,M3,M4,Q,KLIST,SLIST
COMMENT: SEARCH 'KLIST' FOR AN ITEM DESCRIBED AS 'M1', ....,
C          'M4'.  IF FOUND, SUBTRACT Q UNITS FROM THE
C          QUANTITY IN STOCK.  IF QUANTITY IS NOW ZERO, MOVE
C          ELEMENT TO SHOPPING LIST ('SLIST').
      INTEGER N1(1000),N2(1000),N3(1000),N4(1000),
     +          QUANT(1000),NEXT(1000),END
      COMMON N1,N2,N3,N4,QUANT,NEXT,END
      LOGICAL EQUAL
      INTEGER LOOK,PRVIUS,SAVE
C      FIRST SEE IF THE SOUGHT FOR ITEM IS AS THE VERY FRONT
C      OF THE LIST.
      IF (.NOT. EQUAL(M1,M2,M3,M4,KLIST)) GO TO 90
C        YES IT IS.
        QUANT(KLIST)=QUANT(KLIST)-Q
        IF (QUANT(KLIST) .GT. 0) RETURN
C          WE'RE OUT OF THIS ITEM.  TACK IT ONTO SLIST.
          SAVE=KLIST
          KLIST=NEXT(KLIST)
          NEXT(SAVE)=SLIST
          SLIST=SAVE
          RETURN
C      IF THE ITEM WASN'T THE FIRST ELEMENT, LOOK DEEPER.
 90     PRVIUS=KLIST
        LOOK=NEXT(KLIST)
 100    IF (LOOK .NE. END) GO TO 200
          WRITE(6,1000) M1,M2,M3,M4
 1000     FORMAT(' THERE MUST BE SOME MISTAKE HERE.'/
     +           ' HOW COULD WE HAVE USED SOME ',4A4/
     +           ' WHEN THERE WAS NONE IN STOCK?')
          RETURN
```

```
C        IS THIS THE ITEM?
200      IF (EQUAL(M1,M2,M3,M4,LOOK)) GO TO 300
C   HAVEN'T FOUND IT YET, MOVE TO NEXT ITEM IN 'KLIST'.
         PRVIUS=LOOK
         LOOK=NEXT(LOOK)
         GO TO 100
C
C        FOUND IT, UPDATE RECORDS.
300      QUANT(LOOK)=QUANT(LOOK)-Q
C        IF WE'RE OUT OF IT (HEH HEH), ADD TO SHOPPING LIST.
         IF (QUANT(LOOK) .LE. 0) CALL MOVE(PRVIUS,LOOK,SLIST)
         RETURN
         END
```

At this point you've seen routines for doing all the list manipulation we need for the grocery inventory problem. Below, you can see what happened when we ran the program.

```
data
        BOUGHT    SPAN OLIVES,JAR        3
        BOUGHT    RIPE OLIVES,CAN        5
        BOUGHT    TORTILLAS,FLOUR       24
        BOUGHT    CHEESE,JACK,OZS       30
        BOUGHT    HOT CHILIES,CAN        1
        BOUGHT    REFRIED BEANS,CAN      3
        SUPPLIES
        USED      CHEESE,JACK,OZS        6
        BOUGHT    TOMATO SAUCE,CAN       2
        BOUGHT    BEER,CAN              12
        BOUGHT    ALKA SELZER            1
        BOUGHT    PINTO BEANS OZS       16
        BOUGHT    TWINKIES               4
        BOUGHT    LETTUCE,OZS            5
        BOUGHT    HOT CHILIES,CAN        1
        BOUGHT    MILK,CUPS              8
        BOUGHT    SPAGHETTI,OZS         12
        BOUGHT    PEANUTS,OZS           14
        USED      BEER,CAN               1
        USED      TORTILLAS,FLOUR        6
        USED      SPAN OLIVES,JAR        2
        USED      HOT CHILIES,CAN        1
        USED      RIPE OLIVES,CAN        1
        USED      REFRIED BEANS,CAN      1
        USED      CHEESE,JACK,OZS       12
        USED      LETTUCE,OZS            2
        USED      BEER,CAN               1
        USED      PEANUTS,OZS            1
        USED      BEER,CAN               1
        USED      PEANUTS,OZS            4
        USED      BEER,CAN               2
        USED      PEANUTS,OZS            6
        USED      BEER,CAN               4
        USED      PEANUTS,OZS            3
        USED      BEER,CAN               3
        USED      SPAN OLIVES,JAR        1
        USED      ALKA SELZER            1
        USED      TWINKIES               1
        BOUGHT    HOT CHILIES,CAN        2
        BOUGHT    BREAD,WHL WHT          1
        SHOP
        SHOP
        SUPPLIES
        FINIS
```

output

KITCHEN SYSTEMS,INC.

```
BOUGHT    3   SPAN OLIVES,JAR
BOUGHT    5   RIPE OLIVES,CAN
BOUGHT   24   TORTILLAS,FLOUR
BOUGHT   30   CHEESE,JACK,OZS
BOUGHT    1   HOT CHILIES,CAN
BOUGHT    3   REFRIED BEANS,CA

SUPPLIES ON HAND:
        REFRIED BEANS,CA      3
        HOT CHILIES,CAN       1
        CHEESE,JACK,OZS      30
        TORTILLAS,FLOUR      24
        RIPE OLIVES,CAN       5
        SPAN OLIVES,JAR       3


USED     6   CHEESE,JACK,OZS
BOUGHT    2   TOMATO SAUCE,CAN
BOUGHT   12   BEER,CAN
BOUGHT    1   ALKA SELZER
BOUGHT   16   PINTO BEANS OZS
BOUGHT    4   TWINKIES
BOUGHT    5   LETTUCE,OZS
BOUGHT    1   HOT CHILIES,CAN
BOUGHT    8   MILK,CUPS
BOUGHT   12   SPAGHETTI,OZS
BOUGHT   14   PEANUTS,OZS
USED     1   BEER,CAN
USED     6   TORTILLAS,FLOUR
USED     2   SPAN OLIVES,JAR
USED     1   HOT CHILIES,CAN
USED     1   RIPE OLIVES,CAN
USED     1   REFRIED BEANS,CA
USED    12   CHEESE,JACK,OZS
USED     2   LETTUCE,OZS
USED     1   BEER,CAN
USED     1   PEANUTS,OZS
USED     1   BEER,CAN
USED     4   PEANUTS,OZS
USED     2   BEER,CAN
USED     6   PEANUTS,OZS
USED     4   BEER,CAN
USED     3   PEANUTS,OZS
USED     3   BEER,CAN
USED     1   SPAN OLIVES,JAR
USED     1   ALKA SELZER
USED     1   TWINKIES
BOUGHT    2   HOT CHILIES,CAN
BOUGHT    1   BREAD,WHL WHT

HERE IS YOUR SHOPPING LIST
        ALKA SELZER           0
        SPAN OLIVES,JAR       0
        BEER,CAN              0
        PEANUTS,OZS           0
```

```
HERE IS YOUR SHOPPING LIST        ┌ notice that the
                              ←────┘ previous command
                                     flushed this
SUPPLIES ON HAND:                    shopping list.
    BREAD,WHL WHT          1
    SPAGHETTI,OZS         12
    MILK,CUPS             8
    LETTUCE,OZS           3
    TWINKIES             3
    PINTO BEANS OZS      16
    TOMATO SAUCE,CAN      2
    REFRIED BEANS,CA      2
    HOT CHILIES,CAN       3
    CHEESE,JACK,OZS      12
    TORTILLAS,FLOUR      18
    RIPE OLIVES,CAN       4
```

EXERCISES 11 6

1 We declared each of the arrays used for list elements to be 1000 cells long. What restriction does this place on the total number of grocery items our program can deal with?

2 Redraw Figure 11 6 3 showing all unused list elements tied together on a list pointed to by memory cell FREE.

3 What (few) changes would need to be made so that there is also a command ADD that lets you add new items to the shopping list without using up items from the shelves?

PROBLEMS 11

1 Verify that Fortran stores two-dimensional arrays using column major form. Declare a one-dimensional array

    INTEGER TEST(16)

in your main program. In each memory cell TEST(i), store i. Now send TEST as an argument to a SUBROUTINE VERIFY which lists a two-dimensional array

    INTEGER A(4, 4)

as a parameter. Within VERIFY, print the values in A, column by column. They should come out 1, 2, 3, 4, 5, 6, 7, . . ., 16.

2 Redo problem 1, only this time include a number N as one of SUBROUTINE VERIFY's parameters. Use N as a variable dimension, i.e.,

    INTEGER A(N, N).

Then CALL the SUBROUTINE several times, giving N different values. Within VERIFY, print out the values in the array and study how it is arranged in each case.

3 Use our traveling salesman program (Section 11 3 and Section 9 5) on a problem of interest (or practical value) to you. For example, go to a company that makes deliveries of some sort and find out the route their truck takes. Then get a map and find the distances between all stops they must make. See if the route they use really is the shortest. Tell them if it's not.

4 One of the most unpleasant features of the kitchen system in Section 11 6 is that if you don't type the product description exactly the same way each time, the system doesn't know it's dealing with the same item and will proliferate list entries. Character-by-character equality is too strict a criterion for telling whether two item descriptions match.

Devise and test several more lenient matching schemes. Here are a few ideas:

a ignore all punctuation marks
b ignore position on the line (i.e., " cheese" and "cheese " are surely the same item)
c ignore vowels (is this too extreme?)

5 Change the grocery inventory program of Section 11 6 to make it easier to check the shopping list from time to time before making the decision to actually go grocery shopping. As it is, the program deletes all the items from the shopping list after printing, assuming the person requesting the list will now go shopping. In practice, the list may be short and shopping unnecessary. In cases like this the shopping list should be retained. One way to alleviate this problem would be to have the program ask the user whether he intends to go shopping before dropping the list. In other words, after printing the shopping list, the program should print the question: GOING SHOPPING? If the answer is yes, the shopping list should be dropped as before. If no, then it should be retained.

6 A great many board games use a hexagonal grid (early American settlers played Agon on a hex grid, and the majority of the hundreds of battle simulation board games use hex grids). The reason is simple—unlike on a square grid, the distance from a given cell to each of its neighbors is the same. Some people like hexagonal grids just because they look prettier than square grids.

Write a collection of subprograms which implement a hexagonal array, including

a LOGICAL FUNCTION ISNBR(H1,K1,H2,K2), which returns .TRUE. if hex cells (H1,K1) and (H2,K2) are neighbors
b SUBROUTINE NBR(H1,K1,NUMB,H2,K2), which, given hex cell (H1,K1), returns in (H2,K2) the NUMBth neighbor of (H1,K1).

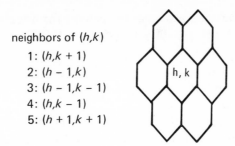

neighbors of (h,k)

1: $(h,k + 1)$
2: $(h - 1,k)$
3: $(h - 1,k - 1)$
4: $(h,k - 1)$
5: $(h + 1,k + 1)$

Use your hex manipulation routines to solve the following problem, which is useful in considering certain strategies in battle games. Given a hexagonal array, with armies placed on certain cells, are all pieces of the army connected? That is, does every army have at least one neighboring cell that also has an army on it?

7 Another odd-shaped array that is sometimes useful is the **polar array**. By computing the subscript properly, a one-dimensional array may be organized into the form shown below.

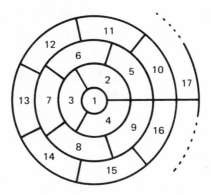

We've chosen this form so that the area that corresponds to each memory cell is about the same. The area of the ring between radius $R - 1$ and radius R is proportional to

$$R^2 - (R - 1)^2 = 2R - 1$$

Thus, we've placed $2R - 1$ locations in each ring of radius R (1 for $R = 1$, 3 for $R = 2$, 5 for $R = 3$, etc.)

We will refer to memory cells in the polar array by giving one value for the radius R and one for the angle THETA. When THETA is 0, to find our way to the memory cell corresponding to the radius R, we must skip over the first $R - 1$ rings; thus we must skip over $1 + 3 + 5 + \ldots + (2R - 3)$ locations. The next location will then correspond to the memory cell at radius R and angle 0. Hence, the formula for computing the appropriate array subscript for this cell is

$$(R - 1)^2 + 1$$

> *Amazing, but true: the sum of the first n odd numbers is n^2*

Now all we need is a term to account for nonzero THETAs. Since the ring at radius R has $2R - 1$ values for the THETA term, the THETA term is

$$((2*R - 1)*THETA))/360$$

We have carefully parenthesized the expression so that INTEGER division helps us out.

Thus, given a value R (1 or greater) and a value THETA (0 to 359), we use the memory cell whose subscript is

$$(R - 1)**2 + 1 + ((2*R - 1)*THETA)/360$$

Figure out how many memory cells must be in the array when we want to have a polar array whose maximum radius is RMAX. Write a statement function to convert (R, THETA) values into the appropriate array subscripts. Write a program which implements a polar array and test it by first storing values at various (R, THETA) positions and then printing out the array to verify that the values you stored went into the correct positions.

If you feel like it, write a FUNCTION CONVRT that will accept values for THETA in any range and return a value in the proper range (0 to 359). For example,

CONVRT (710) returns 350

and   CONVRT (–90) returns 270

8 Devise a scheme for going from (R, THETA) values to array subscripts which organizes a one-dimensional array into a polar array of the form

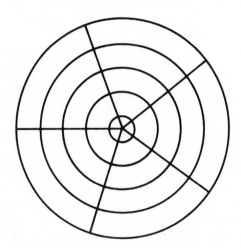

9 Do problem 8 11 (ringworms) using polar arrays.

10 Suppose you are running a supermarket and you have four checkout counters. You would like to run one of them as an "express lane," but you're not sure where to set the limit which determines who may use the express lane. You decide to write a computer simulation and compare the

effects of different limits on how quickly 200 shoppers (who buy a random amount of groceries and come to be checked out at random times) get checked out.

Here's the strategy of the program: Let the current time be T. For each shopper, generate two random numbers. The first, TENTER, gives the time the shopper arrives at the checkout area and the second, TOUT, gives the length of time it will take for the checker to check the shopper out (once the process starts). For each checkout counter, keep track of the shoppers waiting by using a queue. If there is some shopper already at the head of one of the lines who will be checked out before TNEXT = T + TENTER, check him out (so that T is now T + TOUT). Keep testing until there are no more to be checked out up to time TNEXT. Then enter the shopper who has arrived (thus making T = TNEXT), using the following strategy:

If the TOUT value associated with this shopper is below the LIMIT, he may enter the express lane if he chooses. Otherwise he should be put in the lane with the fewest people waiting.

Optional: Decide which line the next shopper goes to on a more elaborate basis—perhaps on how many people in a line *and* the TOUT associated with the last person in that line (as if the shopper is also estimating how many groceries the people already in line have).

Print the results of your simulation in a form that makes it easy to compare the results. Run the program for several different values of LIMIT.

11 Write a program which creates and maintains a list of people's names and their telephone numbers. Your program should maintain the links in the list so that the names are in alphabetical order. A list element should have the general structure shown below.

name	phone number	link
JOHNSON, JAMES E.	415-321-2300	⟶

The input for your program should be punched cards in one of two types:

    a new entry card: name   phone number

    b ALPHABETIC LISTING

If your program sees a card of type **a** it should add the name and phone number to the list in the appropriate place. If it sees a card of type **b** it should print out all the names and phone numbers in its list in alphabetical order.

12 Alter the program of problem 11 so that it maintains a doubly linked list. The first link will be unchanged and the second link will order the list according to increasing phone number.

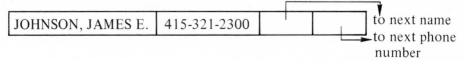

JOHNSON, JAMES E. | 415-321-2300 | | | to next name
to next phone number

Now your program should accept one more kind of input card:

   c NUMERIC LISTING

If your program sees a card of type **c** it should print a listing of names and phone numbers in order of increasing phone number (thus creating a cross-reference phone book).

13 A **graph**, for the purposes of this problem, is a number of nodes together with a set of line segments connecting some of those nodes.

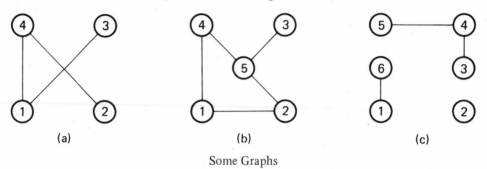

(a)   (b)   (c)

Some Graphs

A **path** in a graph is a set of its line segments connecting one node to another. A graph is called **connected** if there is a path between each pair of nodes. In the drawing above, (a) and (b) are connected graphs but (c) is not connected. The object of this problem is to write a LOGICAL FUNCTION which decides whether the graph described by its parameters is connected or not.

An easy way to describe a graph is by using a triangular array containing LOGICAL values. The value .TRUE. indicates that a line segment is present between the two nodes determined by the row and column number of that entry in the array; .FALSE. indicates the absence of a connecting segment. Graphs (a), (b), and (c) correspond to triangular arrays (a), (b), and (c). Your LOGICAL FUNCTION should have two parameters: (1) a triangular array describing a graph and (2) an INTEGER indicating the number of nodes of the graph. The FUNCTION should return the value .TRUE. when the graph is connected and .FALSE. otherwise.

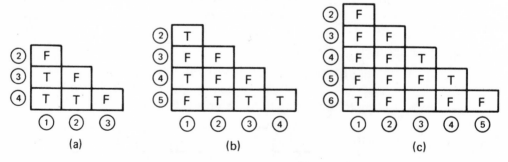

(a)   (b)   (c)

The Same Graphs as Triangular Arrays

318   Fortran for Humans

Use the following algorithm to determine connectedness.

INITIALIZE: initialize a stack of nodes by placing node 1 on it

HOOK: add to the stack all nodes which are connected to the top element on the stack by a path consisting of a single line segment

DECIDE: (a) if the stack contains all nodes, return the value .TRUE.

(b) if no nodes were added in the HOOK step, return the value .FALSE.

(c) otherwise, repeat from HOOK

14 Devise a data structure with internal links to describe your graphs. Rewrite the algorithm of problem 13 so that it uses your new data structure rather than the triangular array representation of a graph.

15 Make up a data structure of your own, basing it on some complex real world problem you are interested in. Write down a precise description of how your data structure works. See if you can explain it to someone else in the class. If you can, write the Fortran statements necessary to implement it. If you can't, your description must not be detailed enough, so try again.

16 Write a program which carries out the logic for the following traffic light system.

The s's in the drawing represent sensors, and the lights should follow the following rules. If no sensors are on, cycle the lights the same as if all sensors were on. If only one sensor is on, let that car go (give it a green light). Traffic on College has priority, so if sensors on College and on Prospect stay on, let more time pass with green for College than green for Prospect. Cars going straight have priority over cars turning.

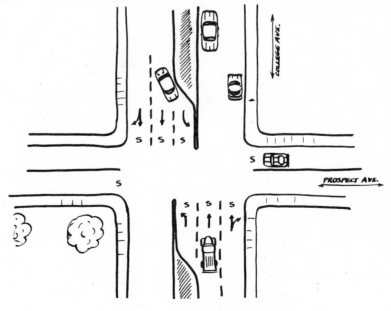

Make up a number of data cards each of which represents a car, and have on the card some representation of which way the car wants to go and what time he arrives at the light. You may ignore yellow lights. Each time the light changes, print out the current situation: e.g., if at time 10.0 the lights on Prospect are green and there are three cars waiting to proceed north on College and one waiting in the left turn lane to turn west onto Prospect, then print out:

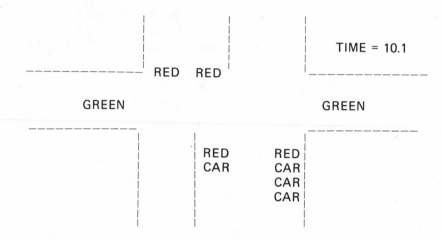

Select some appropriate data structure to store cars that are in the intersection. Queues or lists would do.

17 Write a program to print random sentences. Begin by writing a number of rules for generating sentences, using a period at the beginning to distinguish between words that are part of the rules from words which may appear in sentences.

Example:

Rule 1	.sentence	=	.nounph	.verb	
Rule 2	.sentence	=	.nounph	.verb	.nounph
Rule 3	.nounph	=	.article	.noun	
Rule 4	.nounph	=	.noun		
Rule 5	.verb	=	BIT		
Rule 6	.verb	=	JUMPED		
Rule 7	.verb	=	SWALLOWED		
Rule 8	.article	=	THE		
Rule 9	.noun	=	HORSE		
Rule 10	.noun	=	COW		
Rule 11	.noun	=	PILL		

Algorithm for forming sentences:

   a Start a stack with *.sentence.*

   b Find the first rule in the stack (i.e., the first word in the list which starts with a period) and replace it by the definition of that rule (e.g., the definition of the rule .article above is THE). If there is more than one definition for the rule, then choose at random *one* of these definitions.

   c If there are no more words in the stack which start with a period, print out the sentence. Otherwise, repeat step 2.

You may want to use two stacks, DONE and WORKIN, to store the partially completed sentences, as shown in the example below:

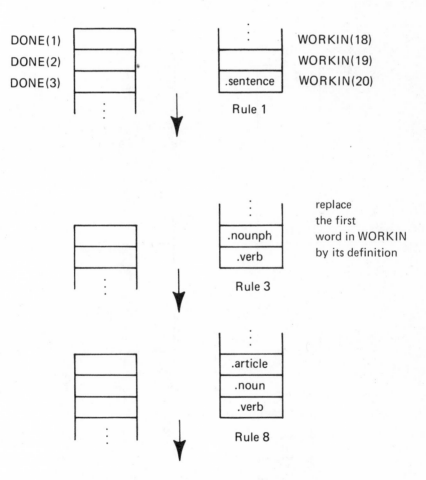

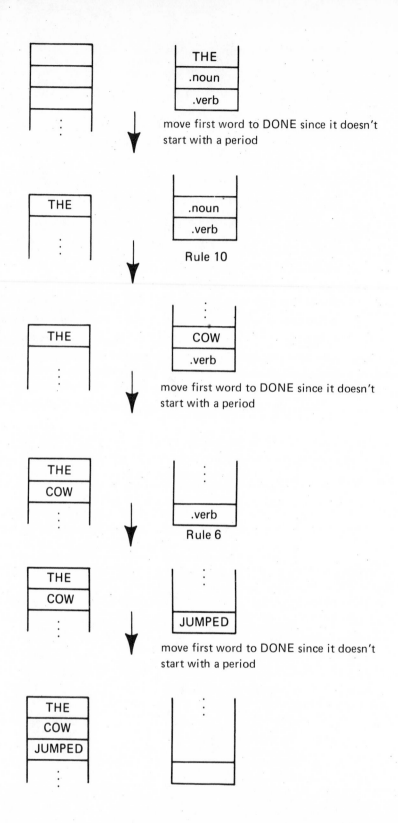

move first word to DONE since it doesn't start with a period

Rule 10

move first word to DONE since it doesn't start with a period

Rule 6

move first word to DONE since it doesn't start with a period

18 In Morse code each letter is coded into a group of dots and dashes. To represent a Morse code message on data cards, we can use periods (.) for dots and minus signs (−) for dashes. The letters in the coded message can be separated by one space and the words by two spaces. The end of the message can be signified by a slash (/). For example, the following is a message containing two words:

$$...b---b...bb...b.b-/$$

The cards may be considered contiguous. That is, words or letter codes may be continued from one card to the next.

Write a program which READs a coded message from cards and prints it out in letters. (The message should be written in International Morse Code—see any encyclopedia or Boy Scout manual for a description of it.) Try to write the program in such a way that it makes *no* assumptions about the length of the message. To do this you will probably find the following subprograms helpful. One of them delivers the next character in the coded message, no matter what card or where on the card the character comes from. The other "prints" the message, one character at a time. Actually it saves its input characters until it has a whole line and prints them all at once. For this reason, it has two arguments. The second argument should be .FALSE. until the last CALL. Then it should be .TRUE. to tell the routine to print the characters it's been saving even if the whole line isn't full. This is necessary to avoid losing the contents of a partially filled last line.

---

*buffering: The technique of saving parts of an output record in memory until a whole record is accumulated is known as **buffering** the output. The array used to save the partial records is called a **buffer**. Input can be handled similarly when partial records are needed in sequence. The SUBROUTINEs GETCH and PRNCH are input and output buffering routines.*

```
        SUBROUTINE GETCH(CH)
        INTEGER CH
COMMENT: "CH" IS ASSIGNED THE VALUE OF THE NEXT CHARACTER
C          IN THE INPUT STREAM.
        INTEGER CARD(80),CURSOR,MOD
        DATA CURSOR/0/
C
C       GET NEXT RECORD IF BUFFER IS EMPTY.
        IF (CURSOR .NE. 0) GO TO 200
           READ(5,1000) CARD
  1000     FORMAT(80A1)
           CURSOR=1
C       PUT NEXT CHARACTER IN "CH" AND INCREMENT "CURSOR".
  200   CH=CARD(CURSOR)
        CURSOR=MOD(CURSOR+1,80)
        RETURN
        END

        SUBROUTINE PRNCH(CH,DUMP)
        INTEGER CH
        LOGICAL DUMP
```

```
COMMENT: "CH" IS PLACED IN THE LINE TO TO BE EVENTUALLY
C          PRINTED.  THE LINE IS PRINTED IF IT IS FULL AND
C          WE APE AT A WORD BOUNDARY (SPACE).
C          IF "DUMP" IS .TRUE., LINE IS PRINTED REGARDLESS.
      INTEGER LINE(100),CURSOR,I,HYPHEN,BLANK
      DATA CURSOR/0/,HYPHEN/1H-/,BLANK/1H /
C     PUT "CH" IN "LINE".
      CURSOR=CURSOR+1
      LINE(CURSOR)=CH
      IF (.NOT. ((CURSOR .GE. 60   .AND.
     +                          LINE(CURSOR) .EQ. BLANK   .OR.
     +                              DUMP) GO TO 200
      WRITE(6,1000) (LINE(I), I=1,CURSOR)
      CURSOR=0
      RETURN
C     PRINT LINE WITH HYPHEN IF WE JUST CAN'T HOLD ANY MORE.
  200 IF (CURSOR .LT. 100) RETURN
      WRITE(6,1000) LINE,HYPHEN
      CURSOR=0
      RETURN
 1000 FORMAT(' ',101A1)
      END
```

19 Add a feature to the grocery inventory program of Section 11 6 that allows the user to maintain his stocks of individual items at any desired level. Some people may want to keep an extra sack of flour in the house at all times to avoid running out. Or two extra boxes of Wheaties and a carton of milk. It all depends on the person. What you need to do is add another list which the user can set up in the beginning to specify the products and quantities that he wants to keep an extra supply of. In order to decide whether to put a product on the shopping list, the program will have to check for an entry on this new stock maintenance list and compare the amount on hand to the quantity entered there. Some products won't be on the stock maintenance list. Those products should be handled as before (put them on the shopping list only when the present supplies are exhausted).

20 Suppose you are working in the credit department of a lumber yard. There are a good many contractors with active accounts at the yard. The yard must send bills every month to those contractors who have made purchases. Your job is to automate the process. Design a program to print the monthly statements based on charge tickets accumulated over the month.

Each charge ticket will correspond to one purchase and will contain the contractor's name, account number, a description of his purchase, and the cost. (Your program will READ one card with this information on it for each purchase.)

To print an itemized list for each customer, you'll have to keep a list of charges for each customer making purchases this month. Since the number of customers can vary from month to month, you should keep the head pointers for these lists in yet another list (making a list of lists).

21 In problem 20 above, there is no provision made for returning goods. Expand the program to accept return tickets and deduct the cost (less a 10 percent restocking charge) from the bill. Itemize the returns as well as the purchases.

12 SEARCHING AND SORTING

Section 12 1

Introduction

Some problems occur so often that people have spent a great deal of time inventing and comparing alternative algorithms which solve them. In this chapter we'll look at two such problems in detail to give you some ideas about how to compare different algorithms. Both problems are seemingly simple, but in fact people are still learning a lot from trying to find ever-better solutions. The first problem is that of **searching** or looking in an array for a particular stored value. The second is **sorting**, or given an array of values, manipulating it so that the values wind up in order. You've seen solutions to both of these problems in the first part of the book; here you will see some solutions which are better.

Section 12 2

Searching

Our problem here is how to store numbers in an array if you are going to have to look up specific ones later.

One place the problem arises is in assembling, maintaining, and using files of information about people (data banks). In Section 9 3 we saw a way of using several arrays, one for each type of information. There we let the subscripts link the various pieces of information together—for example, letting the ith memory cell in each array correspond to the information stored about the ith person. For example, suppose we want a file of information to help prepare paychecks. For each person, we'd need to record (1) a social security number, (2) an hourly wage, (3) the number of income tax deductions claimed, and (4) whether or not they've elected to have company health insurance. If there are not more than 2000 employees, we'd declare the arrays

```
INTEGER SOCSEC(2000), HRWAGE(2000), DEDUCS(2000)
LOGICAL INSURE(2000)
```

and the first part of our "data bank" might look like Figure 12 2 1.

	SOCSEC		HRWAGE		DEDUCS		INSURE
1	275307041	1	375	1	2	1	.FALSE.
2	444226810	2	425	2	1	2	.TRUE.
3	721337726	3	326	3	5	3	.TRUE.
	⋮		⋮	4	⋮		⋮

Figure 12 2 1

The information stored about the second person is that her social security number is 444226810, her hourly wage is $4.25, she has claimed one deduction, and it is .TRUE. that she has the company health insurance. (Note that we've stored wages as INTEGERs instead of REALs so that we don't have to worry about round-off errors.)

Now when the records showing how many hours each person worked this week come in, we must find the information stored about that person to be able to compute his pay for the week. Suppose one such record is

soc-sec-no = 721337726   hrs worked = 36.5

As we have things set up, we would have to search in the SOCSEC array until we found an entry with the value 721337726. We would find it in SOCSEC(3), so we would know that the information about this person is stored in HRWAGE(3), DEDUCS(3), and INSURE(3). In this case, that wouldn't take much effort, but on the average we would have to look through about half of the employees before we found the one we wanted. There is a much faster way. Suppose that we stored things so that the person's social security number *was the array subscript value of the memory cells where his records were stored.* Then if memory cell ID contained a particular person's social security number, the cells

HRWAGE(ID), DEDUCS(ID) and INSURE(ID)

would contain the information we want. This way, no matter whom we're looking for, once we know his social security number, we can immediately find the desired information.

No doubt you can see the trouble with our scheme. It requires that the arrays be as long as the largest possible social security number! If we had only 2000 employees, we'd still need 999,999,999 memory cells in each array, even though 999,997,999 of them wouldn't be used for anything. Inserting new records and retrieving old ones is very fast and easy, but the memory requirements are simply unacceptable.

"Aha!" you may say. "Why not just give each employee a number between 1 and 2000?" Then we could use the same technique but would need only 2000 spaces in each array.

That solution is also unacceptable because it would mean that each employee would have to learn his employee number (and a number for his bank, his savings and loan, and every organization that wanted to use this efficient and convenient—for the computer—way of storing information). That's just the sort of thing that makes people say that computers are dehumanizing.

The only acceptable way of utilizing a data bank such as we're describing is a combination of the techniques we've described—give each person a small number, but never let him know it. Instead, store an array which makes the correspondence between his social security number (or, even better, his name) and the number you want to use internally. To find a person's records, first locate his social security number, then use the corresponding element in the internal number array to retrieve his records. If you turn back a few pages, you'll see that this is equivalent to the way we started! Thus, no matter how much information you want to store about each person, the only acceptable ways of accessing that information involve looking up a number (or name) in an array.

Now that we've resigned ourselves to the fact that we must look in an array to locate the information we want, let's concentrate on that problem. The most obvious way is the simple one we already mentioned. Look at the contents of the first memory cell and see if that's the one we want. If so, then we're done. If not, we'll look at the second, and so on. We'll call this a **sequential search**. Figure 12 2 2 describes the process, assuming the array we're searching is named PEOPLE and the value we're looking for is PERSON.

This algorithm will work fine as long as PERSON really is in the array PEOPLE somewhere. If there's been a typing error, or PERSON represents a new employee, then the algorithm gets into trouble because it doesn't check to make sure it doesn't keep going past the end of the array. As long as we're going to fix *that*, let's change it so that if PERSON doesn't appear in the array, we'll make a new entry. Let the memory cell NENTRY store the number of entries (people's names or numbers) stored in the array.

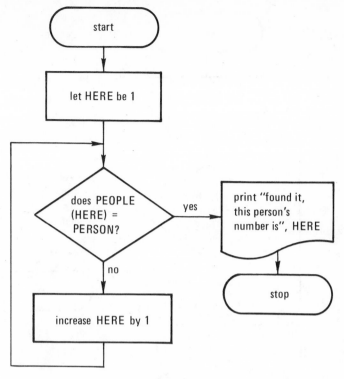

Figure 12 2 2

Making a new entry is very easy. We just add 1 to NENTRY since there's now one more person stored and then stick in PERSON (see Figure 12 2 3). If there are NENTRY people, then finding a PERSON takes NENTRY/2 steps on the average. If the PERSON isn't in the array, it takes NENTRY steps to discover that fact. Sequential search is very easy, but it can take a long time even on a very fast computer. For instance, if there are 10,000 people on a company's payroll, it would take

$$\underbrace{10{,}000}_{\substack{\text{number of} \\ \text{searches}}} \quad * \quad \underbrace{10{,}000/2}_{\substack{\text{average steps} \\ \text{per search}}} = 50{,}000{,}000 \text{ steps}$$

to find the information needed to compute all the paychecks.

There is a situation that we're all familiar with that is very similar to the one we're facing. Suppose you are given someone's name and a phone book and are asked to find that person's phone number. If the phone book listings were in no particular order, you'd have to carry out the sequential search algorithm to find the name you're looking for! Except in a very small town, that would be a horrendous task. Fortunately, the phone company has had the good sense to put the listings in alphabetical order so that you have some hope of finding the name

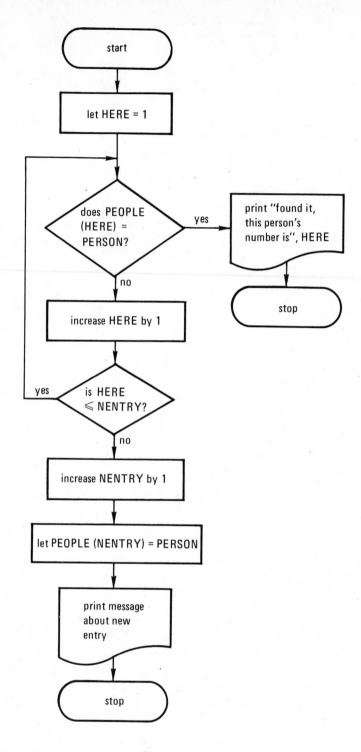

Figure 12 2 3

you want (or discovering that it's not listed) before your eyes fall out. Obviously, it would be faster to find an entry in an array if the array were arranged in a nice order. If the array is in increasing order, we can use the following algorithm, which is related to the way you look up a number in a phone book.

We'll use two variables, one called LOW, which stores an array index value that we know is lower than the place we want, and a memory cell HIGH, which is higher than the place we want. Before we look anywhere, we know that 0 is lower than the place we want, and the NENTRY + 1 must be higher than the place we want. Then we'll start looking. Since we don't yet know anything except that the place we want is somewhere in between LOW and HIGH, we might as well look in the *middle*, guessing that the place we want is just as likely to be in the first half of the array as the last half. The middle value is, of course, PEOPLE((LOW + HIGH)/2). Maybe that's the value we wanted. If so, we've finished. If *not*, then we can tell if the value we wanted is before the middle or after the middle just by comparing the value PERSON to the value PEOPLE((LOW + HIGH)/2). If PERSON is not equal to PEOPLE((LOW + HIGH)/2) then we know that if PERSON appears at all, it (1) lies *above* the middle or (2) lies *below* the middle. In either case we continue the process, changing the value of LOW in the first case or HIGH

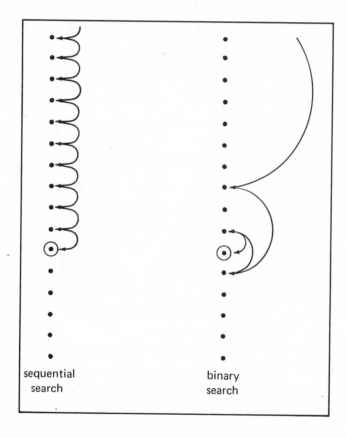

sequential
search

binary
search

in case (2). If LOW and HIGH ever get so close together that there are no entries between them, we know that PERSON wasn't in the array at all! We call this kind of search **binary search** because at each step we eliminate about one half of the alternatives. The flowchart in Figure 12 2 4 describes the search more precisely.

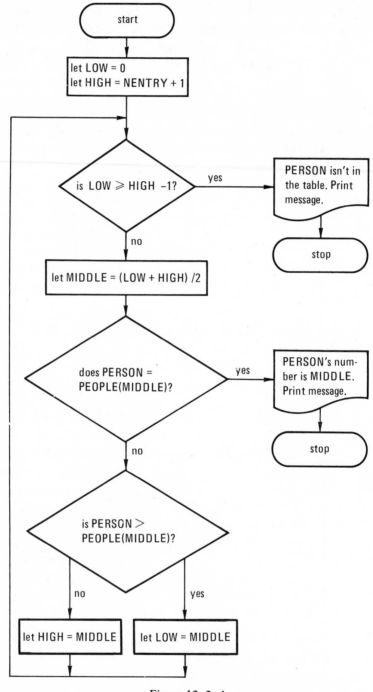

Figure 12 2 4

Since we eliminate about half of the alternatives each time around the loop, after one time there are NENTRY/2 alternatives left, after two times there are NENTRY/(2*2) left, after three times there are NENTRY/(2*2*2) left, and after n times there are NENTRY/2^n left. We stop if there can't be more than one alternative left, that is when NENTRY/$2^n \leqslant 1$. Solving for n, we find that the most steps it could ever take is $n = \log_2$ (NENTRY). Now to look up the information to compute the payroll for our company of 10,000, it takes no more than

$$\underset{\substack{\text{number of} \\ \text{searches}}}{10{,}000} \quad * \quad \underset{\substack{\text{maximum time} \\ \text{per search}}}{\log_2 (10{,}000)} \quad = \quad 133{,}000 \text{ steps}$$

which is many, many fewer than the number required by the sequential method.

While the binary search method is much better for looking things *up* than the sequential method, it's a little worse when we have to put a new person into the array. In the sequential scheme, to put in a new person, we just stick the number (or name) in at the bottom. In the binary scheme we must insert the new person in the right place so that the array stays in order.

If you look at the binary search flowchart (Figure 12 2 3), you'll see that when we discover that PERSON doesn't appear in the array, we at least know where it should be—it should be at position LOW + 1. All we need to do then is to slide all entries after LOW down one position and then stick in PERSON. On the average, that will take NENTRY/2 steps. Here's a complete binary search routine. It takes an array called PEOPLE as an argument along with a PERSON to look for, and it returns the position of PERSON in the array if it found it, or the position of PERSON after PERSON was inserted.

There are yet more algorithms for searching an array. One very common technique involves **hash coding**. Here the idea is a compromise between speed and the amount of memory you are willing to allow your program to use. It is a takeoff on a storage method we briefly passed over earlier in this chapter. Recall that we noted that it would be very convenient to do insertions and retrievals if we just let the person's social security number be the array subscript associated with his records, but that it required an absurd amount of memory. We can get some of the same effect by just taking (say) the last three digits of the social security number and using that as an array subscript. Now we need only 999 memory cells instead of 999,999,999. However, it is likely that two people's social security numbers will have the same last three digits. This means that the numbers we get are not unique and there must be some way of telling which specific person we are looking for. There have been many, many algorithms proposed and used to do this. Since bad luck (what if the last three digits of the social security numbers of all your employees are the same!) can make hash coding degenerate into sequential search, and good luck (what if they are all different?) can make hash coding extremely fast, statistical studies are needed to recommend one technique over another.

Yet another technique for searching arrays is of value when items must often be deleted (during depressions, for example). This technique (using **AVL trees**) requires an even more elaborate structuring of the array than does binary search.

```
          SUBROUTINE BINARY(PERSON,PEOPLE,NENTRY,HERE)
          INTEGER PERSON, NENTRY, PEOPLE(100), HERE
COMMENT:  BINARY SEARCH ALGORITHM TO FIND "PERSON" IN THE
C         ARRAY "PEOPLE" .
C             IF "PERSON" IS NOT FOUND, IT IS INSERTED.
          INTEGER LOW, HIGH, MIDDLE, SHIFT
C         IF "PERSON" IS IN THE ARRAY, IT MUST BE BETWEEN
C         THE FIRST AND LAST POSITION IN THE ARRAY.
          LOW = 0
          HIGH = NENTRY + 1
C         ARE "LOW" AND "HIGH" TOO CLOSE TOGETHER?
   10     IF ( LOW .GE. HIGH-1 )  GO TO 200
C            LOOK IN THE MIDDLE
             MIDDLE = (LOW+HIGH)/2
C            EXIT IF FOUND
             IF ( PERSON .EQ. PEOPLE(MIDDLE) )  GO TO 100
C            PROCEED IN TOP OR BOTTOM HALF OF ARRAY
             IF ( PERSON .GT. PEOPLE(MIDDLE) )  GO TO 20
             HIGH = MIDDLE
             GO TO 10
   20        LOW = MIDDLE
             GO TO 10
C
C         FOUND IT...RETURN ITS POSITION
  100     HERE = MIDDLE
          RETURN
C
C         NOT PRESENT.. INSERT IT
  200     SHIFT = NENTRY
  210     PEOPLE(SHIFT+1) = PEOPLE(SHIFT)
          SHIFT = SHIFT - 1
          IF ( SHIFT .GE. LOW+1 )  GO TO 210
          NENTRY = NENTRY + 1
          PEOPLE(LOW+1) = PERSON
          HERE = LOW +1
          RETURN
          END
```

If you are interested in hash coding or AVL trees, problem 12 1 lists some references for further study.

There is no doubt some absolute limit to how good an algorithm can be for searching and inserting values in arrays on current digital computers. As parallel computers become more common, probably a new crop of commonly occuring problems will become the focal point of the race to find the fastest, most efficient algorithms.

EXERCISES 12 2

1   Try the following game to convince yourself of the speed of the binary search strategy. Pick a number between 1 and 1000. See how many guesses a friend makes before he gets the number if after each guess, you tell him whether his guess was "high" or "low." The binary search algorithm guarantees that at most ten guesses are needed.

Section 12 3

Sorting

The binary search algorithm made use of an array that we maintained in a particular order. In this section we'll see a sorting algorithm which uses another way of ordering an array to cut down on the amount of work that must be done. The sorting technique we used in Section 7 5 and Section 9 3 is slow; it takes an amount of time proportional to the square of the number of items to be sorted. In this section we'll see a sorting method which sorts a list in an amount of time proportional to the number of entries times the logarithm of the number of entries. This seemingly small difference, multiplying the number of entries by itself as opposed to multiplying by its logarithm, can be amazingly large.

n	n^2	$n\log_{10} n$
10	100	10
100	10,000	200
1,000	1,000,000	3,000
10,000	100,000,000	40,000
.	.	.
.	.	.
.	.	.

The main idea is to organize the array of numbers to be sorted into a **tree** structure. Up to now we have tended to think of an array as providing a sequential, linear structure: array position i comes *before* position $i + 1$ and *after* $i - 1$. Here we'll organize things so that an element in the array is associated with one position that comes before it, called its **predecessor**; and two that come after it, called its **successors**, specifically, its **left successor** and its **right successor**. Since each array element has *two* successors, our trees are **binary trees**. One particularly easy way of effecting this structure is to let array position 1 be the **root** of our tree (a root is a position which has no predecessor—it's the *first* position) and to let positions 2 and 3 be its successors. In general, if we are at position i, then the left successor will be the array element at position $2*i$, the right successor will be at position $2*i + 1$, and the predecessor will be at position $i/2$ (recall that division of INTEGERs loses any fractional part so that the predecessor of positions 2 and and 3 is the same, namely the array element at position 1). Figure 12 3 1 shows the organization implied by our scheme.

Notice that (depending on how many memory cells we have in the array) some positions have no successors, and one position might have just one successor (as does position 5 here). If there are NKEYS (for Number of KEYS) elements

> *key: an item to be sorted*

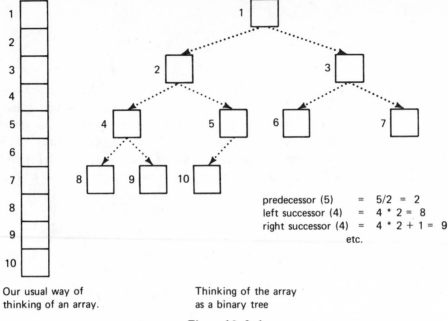

predecessor (5)   =   5/2 = 2
left successor (4)   =   4 * 2 = 8
right successor (4)   =   4 * 2 + 1 = 9
                                etc.

Our usual way of
thinking of an array.

Thinking of the array
as a binary tree

Figure 12 3 1

in the array, then we can tell if position *i* has any successors by testing whether or not 2 * *i* is less than or equal to NKEYS.

It is this conceptual structure which will let us create the efficient algorithm we've promised. This algorithm (due to Floyd* although our version is based mainly on Stone's** presentation) is divided into two phases.

In Phase I we will take the unsorted array and rearrange it until we have a binary tree with certain special properties. In Phase II we will produce the sorted array by repeatedly removing the largest value from the binary tree and then patching the tree up.

The binary tree we'll produce in Phase I consists of a partially sorted version of the original array. The tree will have the property that the value stored at each position is larger than the value stored at any successor position. We've said that this tree is *partially* sorted because if you follow any path in the tree from the root down through the successors, the values stored at those positions will be in decreasing order. Such a tree automatically has the property (which we'll use in Phase II) that the largest value of all is stored at the root node. Figure 12 3 2 illustrates the states the array to be sorted will go through. Notice that all the properties we said the binary tree would have do in fact hold in the tree we've drawn.

It probably seems odd to you that a tree structure like this could be of any

---

*R. W. Floyd, "Algorithm 245," *Comm. ACM*, vol. 7, no. 12 (1964), p. 701.

**H. S. Stone, *Introduction to Computer Organization and Data Structures*, (McGraw-Hill, 1972), pp. 257–263.

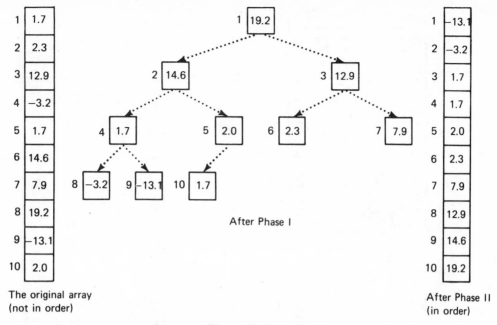

After Phase I

The original array
(not in order)

After Phase II
(in order)

Figure 12 3 2

help in sorting an array. If so, think of it this way: Suppose you have in your possession a bunch of bags of gold which you want to number according to increasing weight. You also have a very accurate, but difficult to operate, scale which will compare the weights of two bags of gold. That is, at each weighing you can determine which of two bags is heavier. Since it takes so long to make a weighing, you want to retain as much information as possible from each weighing in the hope of doing as few weighings as possible.

Let's take an example with four bags and see how you might proceed. You don't have any choice in the beginning but to weigh some pair of bags, so let's say you start with bag A and bag B, and suppose A turns out to be heavier. You don't want to forget anything, so you write down an *A* above a *B* (with a line between them) indicating that bag A is heavier than bag B. Now let's say you weigh bag A and bag C and that bag A is again heavier. Now you know that bag A is the heaviest of the three bags A, B, and C (but you don't know which of B and C is heavier), so you draw a diagram containing an *A* on the top level and a *B* and a *C* on a lower level with lines extending down from *A* to *B* and *C* to indicate that bag A is heavier than bags B and C. Now you want to see where bag D fits into the scheme, so you weigh bag D and bag B. Let's say bag D is heavier. Now you don't know quite how to draw the diagram. You know *D* should go above *B*, but you don't know if it should also be above *A*. Therefore, you weigh bag A and bag D. Let's say D is again heavier. Then *D* should go on the top level with *A* on the second level (a line from *D* to *A* indicates that bag D is heavier than bag A). *B* and *C* should go on the bottom level (connected to *A* by lines indicating that bag A is heavier than bags B and C).

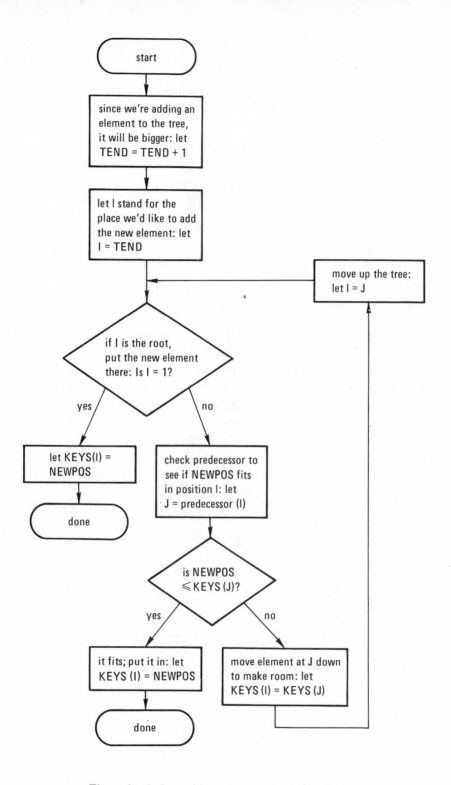

Figure 12 3 3 Adding a New Value to the Tree

Now you know bag D is the heaviest and bag A is the next heaviest. The only question left is the relation between bag B and bag C. (The diagram clearly shows this since *B* and *C* are on the same level. Therefore, you weigh bag B and bag C, finding that, say, C is heavier, and put the bags into increasing order by weight.

This is, of course, a special case; we have only four bags. Nevertheless, you can see that our diagrams, which looked like the trees we talked about earlier, helped us decide what weighings to make. Sorting values in Fortran is a similar problem. You can compare only two values at a time and you don't want to make any extra comparisons if you can help it. Perhaps it is not surprising, then, that the idea of thinking of the array to be sorted as a tree helps. In the case of four objects our previous method (Sections 7 5 and 9 3) would need six comparisons, whereas we needed only five using the tree notation. Try a similar approach with five bags of gold and see how well you can do. Our old technique would need ten comparisons.

The flowchart in Figure 12 3 3 describes an algorithm for adding the next element to a partially completed binary tree in Phase I. In the flowchart we are to add the value NEWPOS into the tree made up of positions 1 through TEND (Tree END) of the array KEYS. The algorithm starts by trying to add NEWPOS at the very bottom of the tree. If it doesn't belong there, then the value from the predecessor of the bottom spot is moved to the bottom and the process repeats. NEWVAL moves up the tree until it finds a place where it fits properly.

To create the original binary tree, we'll use our algorithm to insert one value at a time until they're all in the tree. After the tree is formed, we're through with Phase I. We are then assured that the largest value of all is in the root position.

In Phase II we collapse the tree one value at a time and build the sorted list of numbers from the bottom of the array up. Each time we take the value from the root node, we'll put it in the proper place at the bottom (since it is the largest remaining value). At the end of Phase II, the entire array will be in increasing order.

Each time we remove the largest remaining value in the tree (the value at the root), we'll have to manipulate the rest of the tree so that it again has the properties we desire. Let's follow this at the point when the tree looks like this:

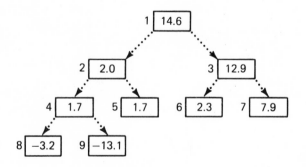

We remove the root value (14.6), and we must alter the remaining tree so that each element exceeds its successors. Thus we want to alter it by repeatedly moving up the larger value from the emptied spot's successors.

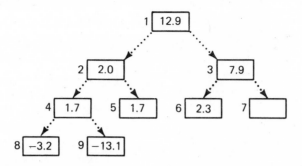

We see that everything is fine and that we no longer need position 7 since the value there was moved up in the process of patching up the tree. The only hitch is that we are supposed to put the largest element on the *bottom*; that is, position 9 rather than position 7. Fortunately this isn't any harder than the process we just described. After having removed the root, we know that we must fix up the remaining tree by inserting the value from position 9 somewhere. We'll just start at the top. Either the value from position 9 should go there, or else one of the values from the two successors of the top position goes there. We can tell which by choosing the largest of the three. If it was one of the successors, we move it up, leaving an empty position there. Then we repeat the process on the part of the tree below the empty position. Eventually we will find a legitimate place to put the value from position 9. Once it is in place, we put the largest value (14.6 in this case) into position 9 and go on to the next step of Phase II. In the next step, the tree will be smaller (in this case TEND would decrease to 8). The step we just described corresponds to the changes shown in Figure 12 3 4.

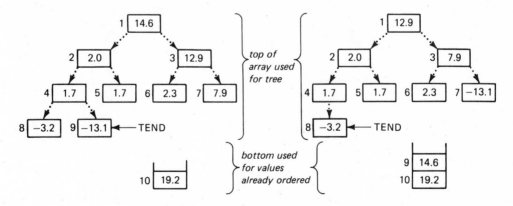

Figure 12 3 4

Figure 12 3 5 is an outline for a step of Phase II. In it, BOTPOS is the value we want to remove from the bottom of the array to make room for the largest value.

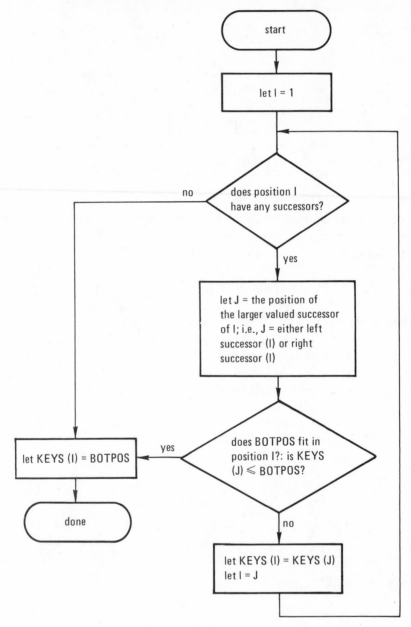

Figure 12 3 5   Repositioning the Largest Remaining Value after
Having Removed the Root

A program for the sorting algorithm we've been discussing follows. Each step of Phase I (the flowchart of Figure 12 3 3) is performed by SUBROUTINE CREATE; each step of Phase II (the flowchart of Figure 12 3 5) is performed by

SUBROUTINE FIXUP. The sorting program, SUBROUTINE TSORT (for Tree SORT), can be used to sort an array of REALs.

```
      SUBROUTINE  T SORT (KEYS, NKEYS)
      INTEGER NKEYS
      REAL KEYS(NKEYS)
COMMENT:  THIS SUBROUTINE CARRIES OUT AN EFFICIENT SORTING
C         ALGORITHM BASED ON THE 'TREESORT' TECHNIQUE OF
C         R. FLOYD.  IT CONSISTS OF TWO PHASES.  PHASE I
C         CONSTRUCTS A PARTICULAR BINARY TREE.  PHASE II
C         TEARS THAT TREE APART, ONE VALUE AT A TIME, TO
C         PRODUCE A REARRANGEMENT OF "KEYS" INTO INCREAS-
C         ORDER.
      INTEGER I, T END
      REAL BOT POS, NEW POS
C
COMMENT:  FIRST PUT THE VALUES INTO THE DESIRED BINARY TREE
C         CONFIGURATION.   KEYS(1) BY ITSELF IS ALREADY A
C         TREE OF THE CORRECT FORM SO START BY ADDING
C         KEYS(2)  TO THE TREE
      T END = 1
      DO 100 I = 2,NKEYS
        NEW POS =  KEYS(I)
 100     CALL CREATE (KEYS, NKEYS, T END, NEW POS)
C
COMMENT:  NOW THAT THE TREE HAS BEEN SET UP, PULL THE TOP
C         POSITION OUT, STORE IT IN THE BOTTOM AND FIX UP
C         THE TREE
      T END = N KEYS
 200  BOT POS =  KEYS(T END)
      KEYS (T END) =  KEYS(1)
C     THE TREE IS NOW ONE SPOT SMALLER
      T END = T END  -1
      CALL FIX UP  (KEYS, NKEYS, T END, BOT POS)
      IF ( T END .GE. 2)  GO TO 200
C
COMMENT:  DONE
      RETURN
      END

      SUBROUTINE CREATE  (KEYS, NKEYS, T END, NEW POS)
      INTEGER T END, NKEYS
      REAL KEYS(NKEYS), NEW POS
COMMENT:  THIS SUBROUTINE INSERTS THE KEY "NEW POS"
C         INTO THE PARTIALLY FORMED BINARY TREE STORED IN
C         "KEYS"
      INTEGER I, J, PRED
COMMENT:  STATEMENT FUNCTION FOR PREDECESSOR
      PRED(I) = I/2
C
COMMENT:  THE TREE WILL BE LARGER BY ONE POSITION
      T END = T END + 1
COMMENT:  AT FIRST TRY TO PUT THE NEW KEY ON THE BOTTOM
      I = T END
COMMENT:  HAVE WE LOOKED ALL THE WAY BACK TO THE ROOT?
 100  IF (I .LE. 1)  GO TO 200
COMMENT:  NO, DOES "NEW POS" FIT IN POSITION I
      J = PRED(I)
      IF ( NEW POS .LE. KEYS(J) )  GO TO 200
COMMENT:  NO, 'NEW POS' MUST FIT FURTHER UP THE TREE
      KEYS(I) = KEYS(J)
      I = J
      GO TO 100
```

```
       COMMENT:  FOUND THE PROPER PLACE FOR "NEW POS".  INSERT IT.
       200   KEYS (I) = NEW POS
             RETURN
             END

             SUBROUTINE  FIX UP (KEYS, NKEYS, T END, BOT POS)
             INTEGER T END, NKEYS
             REAL KEYS(NKEYS) , BOT POS
       COMMENT:  THIS SUBROUTINE ACCEPTS A BINARY TREE WITH A
       C         MISSING ROOT AND FIXES IT UP, FINALLY INSERTING
       C         "BOT POS" IN THE BLANK SPOT LEFT BY THE FIX UP.
             INTEGER I, J, L SUCC, R SUCC
       COMMENT:  STATEMENT FUNCTIONS FOR LEFT SUCCESSOR AND
       C         RIGHT SUCCESSOR
             L SUCC(I) = I*2
             R SUCC(I) = I*2 +1
       COMMENT:  START AT THE ROOT
             I = 1
       COMMENT:  IF I HAS NO SUCCESSORS, WE'RE DONE
       100   IF (L SUCC(I) .GT. T END)  GO TO 300
             J = L SUCC(I)
       COMMENT:  IF I HAS JUST ONE SUCCESSOR, GO ON
             IF ( R SUCC(I) .GT. T END )  GO TO 200
       COMMENT:  COMPARE VALUES AT THE TWO SUCCESSOR POSITIONS
             IF ( KEYS(J) .LT. KEYS(R SUCC(I)) )  J = R SUCC(I)
       COMMENT:  DOES "BOT POS" BELONG HERE?
       200   IF ( KEYS(J) .LE.  BOT POS )  GO TO 300
       COMMENT:  SLIDE UP POSITION OF LARGEST SUCCESSOR
             KEYS (I) = KEYS (J)
             I = J
             GO TO 100
       COMMENT:  INSERT 'BOT POS'
       300   KEYS (I) = BOT POS
             RETURN
             END
```

This might seem to be a lot of mental effort to produce a sorting algorithm, but in a practical situation it can save an amazing amount of computer time.

To give you a rough idea about how much better this sorting technique is than the one in Section 7 5, let's refresh your memory about the sorting routine there. The way it works is by going through the entire array and finding the largest element. It moves that element to the top and then looks in the rest of the array for the largest remaining element, moves that to the second position and continues. If there are NKEYS values in the array, then we'll make NKEYS searches for the largest element; the first search is through all NKEYS spots in the array, the last is through just one. On the average we look through about NKEYS/2 places. Thus, to sort the array, we go through about NKEYS * (NKEYS/2) steps.

In the sorting scheme we've shown you here, each step we make proceeds not through the entire array but merely along a *path in the binary tree structure*. By looking at some binary trees, you should be able to convince yourself that no path in a binary tree can be longer than $\log_2$ (NKEYS). (An easy way to see this is to observe that the nth horizontal level of a binary tree contains 2^n entries, hence 2^n cannot exceed NKEYS.)

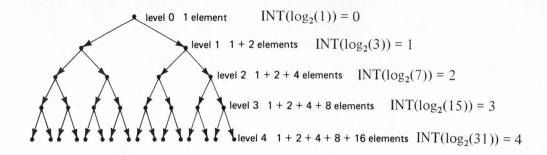

level 0 1 element $INT(\log_2(1)) = 0$

level 1 1 + 2 elements $INT(\log_2(3)) = 1$

level 2 1 + 2 + 4 elements $INT(\log_2(7)) = 2$

level 3 1 + 2 + 4 + 8 elements $INT(\log_2(15)) = 3$

level 4 1 + 2 + 4 + 8 + 16 elements $INT(\log_2(31)) = 4$

Since we have to search through two paths for each value in the original array (one path to build the tree and another to pull out the largest value and fix up the tree), the total numbers of steps can't be more than

$$2*NKEYS*\log_2(NKEYS)$$

Our old scheme takes a number of steps that is proportional to $(NKEYS)**2$ while our new scheme requires a number of steps that is proportional to $NKEYS *\log_2(NKEYS)$. No matter what the constants of proportionality are, if NKEYS is big enough, our new scheme will take fewer steps than our old scheme. Use the new scheme!

PROBLEMS 12

1 Write programs for two or more hash coding storage schemes and compare their behavior. A discussion of such schemes may be found in

> Harold S. Stone, *Introduction to Computer Organization and Data Structure,* McGraw-Hill, 1972, Chapter 11.

Some specific hash coding schemes are in

> J. R. Bell, "The quadratic quotient method: a hash code eliminating secondary clustering," *Comm ACM.* vol. 13, no. 2, 1940, pp. 107–109.

> J. R. Bell and C. H. Kaman, "The linear quotient hash code," *Comm ACM*, vol. 13, no. 11, 1970, pp. 675–677.

> W. D. Maurer, "An improved hash code for scatter storage," *Comm ACM*, vol. 11, no. 1, 1968, pp. 35–38.

> R. Morris, "Scatter storage techniques," *Comm ACM.* vol. 11, no. 1, 1968, pp. 38–44.

2 If you are interested in the searching problem, do some reading on AVL trees. The following articles will give you a start.

> G. M. Adel'son-Velskii and E. M. Landis, "An algorithm for the organization of information," *Dokl. Akad. Nank CCCP, Mathemat.,* vol. 146, no. 2, 1962, pp. 263–266.

> Caxton C. Foster, "Information storage and retrieval using AVL trees," *Proc. ACM Nat'l Conf.,* 1965, pp. 192–205.

3 If you are interested in sorting, do some reading on the subject. The following references will give you a start.

C. A. R. Hoare, "Quicksort," *Comm ACM*, vol. 4, no. 7, 1961, p. 321.

R. W. Flyod, "Tree sort," *Comm ACM*, vol. 7, no. 12, 1964, p. 701.

R. Sedgewick, "Quicksort," Computer Science Dept. Technical Report STAN–CS–75–492, Stanford Univ.

D. Knuth, *The Art of Computer Programming*, vol. 3, Addison-Wesley, 1973.

J. W. J. Williams, "Heapsort," *Comm ACM*, vol. 7, no. 6, 1964, pp. 347–348.

4 Write a program that makes a plot of "number of elements in the array" vs. "average time needed for search" for (a) the sequential search algorithm and (b) the binary search algorithm. Such plots are called **timing diagrams**. Compute the average by timing a separate search for each value in the array and averaging the times.

5 Write a program which makes a timing diagram for (a) the sorting technique of Section 7 5 and (b) the sorting technique of Section 12 3. (To get an average, generate several random-valued arrays.)

6 Find someone who does a lot of sorting and ask what technique he's using. If it's not a tree sort, ask him if he'd be willing to try your tree sort program. Observe the results. (For some very special situations, other sorting techniques may be faster.)

13 GENERALIZATIONS ABOUT PROGRAMMING

Section 13 1

Other Languages

There have been literally thousands of higher-level computer languages defined. There have been hundreds of higher-level languages developed far enough that someone has actually used them. The most we can do here is to give brief discussions about a few widely used languages. Our goal is to help you see Fortran in a wider context.

BASIC, a language developed in 1965 at Dartmouth University, is widely used on time-sharing computer systems. In BASIC, each line is given a number, and the commands in a BASIC program are carried out in order of their line numbers. This allows BASIC programs to be altered easily. Memory cells are named with either a single letter or a letter followed by a digit. The assignment statement is of the form

statement number LET *memory cell name = expression*

for example: 20 LET X = 2 * Y + 1/3

The IF statement has the form

statement number IF *relation* THEN *statement number*

for example: 30 IF X = 0 THEN 500

and means, if the *relation* is true, then transfer control to the listed *statement number.*

BASIC allows the definition of functions like Fortran statement functions, and has a very primitive form of SUBROUTINE. BASIC is often used as a beginning language in time-sharing situations where a number of users can be simultaneously writing, checking and running their programs. It is one of the few high-level languages available on home microcomputers.

Here's a sample BASIC program which asks the user for a value for memory cell N and then sums the first N numbers. We let it count from N down to 1 (unlike Fortran DO-loops, BASIC's built-in loop structure allows negative values for its parameters). Statements which begin with REM are comments (REMarks).

```
10 REM:   SUM FIRST N NUMBERS
20 PRINT "N=";
30 INPUT N
40 REM:   NOW COMPUTE THE SUM
50 LET S = 0
60 FOR T = N TO 1 STEP -1
70    LET S = S + T
80    NEXT T
90 REM:   END OF LOOP.  PRINT RESULT
100 PRINT "THE SUM OF THE FIRST "; N; " NUMBERS IS"; S
110 GO TO 20
120 END
```

COBOL is a business data processing oriented language which was designed starting in 1959 by a committee. One of the goals was to create a language that was more like English than Fortran. This was done by using English words to make up commands, but the language is still very much a computer language—a person unfamiliar with COBOL couldn't just sit down and produce a valid program.

COBOL makes file manipulation and the handling of various kinds of data more convenient than in Fortran. It also makes it easy to create and manipulate quite complex and useful data structures. In addition, it virtually forces the programmer to produce well-documented (orderly, well-commented) programs. For these reasons it is widely used in business applications. For many of the same reasons, however, COBOL programs take more time to write (they are more wordy) than Fortran programs, and on many systems they require more computer resources (time and memory). We'll show one sample statement. Variable names are made up of letters, digits, and hyphens and may be up to 30 characters long.

```
IF TIME-SPENT EXCEEDS OVER-TIME OR EQUALS LIMIT
         THEN MOVE PAY TO STORE.
```

This is equivalent to the Fortran statement

```
IF (TIMES.GT.OVERT .OR. TIMES.EQ.LIMIT) STORE=PAY
```

Algol is a lanuguage designed for computing numerical algorithms. It was defined initially by an international committee which started meeting in 1958. That committee, its successors, and other workers have produced Algol 58, Algol 60, Algol W, and Algol 68. One of the nice features of Algol is that legal programs are defined by means of a formal grammar. This at once makes Algol less restrictive in its syntactic form and makes Algol programs more orderly in overall organization (compared to Fortran).

In Algol, any sequence of statements may be made into a syntactic unit by bracketing the statements with the reserved words *begin* and *end*. In Fortran, if

> *"Algol is Fortran done right."*
> —*Bruce Knobe, 1973*
>
> *"PASCAL is Fortran done right."*
> —*Raymond Langsford, 1976*

we wish to perform several statements only when an IF test is .TRUE., we must use GO TO statements to jump to those statements. In Algol, we can simply make the statements into a *begin-end* block, keeping the statements close to the test, which makes the program easier to read. In Algol, the assignment operator is := and a semicolon is used to mark the end of a statement (in Fortran, the end of a card marks this). The Algol statement

>*if* pointer > upperlimit *then*
>>*begin*
>>>overflow:=*true;*
>>>save:=node
>>*end*
>*else*
>>*begin*
>>>slacknodes[pointer] :=node;
>>>pointer:=pointer+1
>>*end;*

is equivalent to these Fortran statements:

```
         IF (POINTR .GE. UPLIMIT)   GO TO 200
         SLKND(POINTR) = NODE
         POINTR = POINTR+1
         GO TO 300
200      OVERFL = .TRUE.
         SAVE = NODE
300      .
         .
         .
```

Algol is a pleasant language to use and has attracted considerable attention within the computer science academic community, but has not obtained the widespread use that Fortran and COBOL have.

PL/I is a language defined and developed by IBM. It arose out of a series of meetings and reports issued from 1963 through 1966. At first the purpose was to define a successor to Fortran IV, but this was abandoned for the more ambitious goal of creating a language which combines and generalizes all the features of Fortran, COBOL, Algol and JOVIAL (a language not discussed here).

This effort produced a language that has an enormous number of statements and forms, and which is useful for an extremely wide range of tasks. It is a rare PL/I programmer who knows and uses all of the features.

PL/I compilers are very complex and elaborate and tend to require a large amount of space and time. This may explain why PL/I has not yet become more dominant.

The following statement (it is, in fact, syntactically just one statement although it does have other statements as subparts) may convey a feeling for the possibilities.

```
     IF TIME>LIMIT THEN PUT FILE(TWO)LIST(N,3,X+1,0);
     ELSE DO N=1 TO TOTAL BY NUMB1
          TIME = TEST(TIME,N);
     END;
```

APL is a language designed in the early sixties by K. E. Iverson. One of its biggest attractions is its convenient notations for vector and matrix manipulation. For example, the average of the numbers stored in a vector **X** can be stored in A by the statement

$$A \leftarrow (+/X) \div \rho\ X$$

APL is widely available on interactive computer systems which can be reached by phone and connected to special typewriter terminals located in the home or office. It is also available on some stand-alone portable computers.

Many APL programmers amuse themselves by trying to see how much of a program they can condense into one line. (This practice was inadvertently encouraged by early APL time-sharing systems which always completed the operations specified on one line before moving to the next customer. Thus, the more the programmer could put on a line, the faster his program would run.) A famous folk-theorem states that any APL program can be written in one statement. However, these "one-liners" are usually obscure and unnecessarily hard to understand.

SNOBOL is a series of languages developed at Bell Laboratories. The main advantage of these languages is in the creation and manipulation of the string data structure (see Section 11 5). It is easy to create strings and search them for occurrences of specific substrings, so SNOBOL has found frequent use by people doing linguistic analyses. The following statements are written in SNOBOL4.

```
SAMPLETEXT           = "JUST WHAT THE WORLD NEEDS"
GLOBEPATTERN         = "WORLD" | "EARTH" | "GLOBE"
SAMPLETEXT    GLOBEPATTERN      :S(FOUND)
```

The first line lets the variable SAMPLETEXT stand for the string "JUST WHAT THE WORLD NEEDS". The second line lets the variable GLOBEPATTERN stand for a *pattern* which will match either the string "WORLD" or the string "EARTH" or the string "GLOBE". The last line is a **pattern match statement**. If the pattern GLOBEPATTERN matches SAMPLETEXT, that is, if any of the strings "WORLD", "EARTH", or "GLOBE" appear as substrings of the string that is the value of SAMPLETEXT, then the pattern match succeeds (as it does in this example). Since the match succeeds, the statement with the label FOUND is carried out next.

In 1959, a group at MIT led by John McCarthy began work on the language **LISP**. Although it is based on a scheme for representing partial recursive functions, it has seen use in a wide number of symbol manipulation tasks. Many "artificial intelligence" programs have been written in LISP and it has inspired a number of newer languages (PLANNER, CONNIVER, LISP70, etc.). LISP (as well as SNOBOL) was designed to deal with symbolic rather than numeric information; manipulating *numbers* is somewhat inconvenient in LISP. The basic structure of LISP is the **list structure**. Both data and programs have the same structure. Thus, it is easy to write LISP programs which write and alter other LISP programs.

Here is a LISP function which returns the value T (true) if its two arguments (given the names STRUCTURE1 and STRUCTURE2) are identical list structures.

It uses these primitive functions:

        ATOM   which is True if its argument is an atom (the
                          atom is the basic element of LISP much
                          as a **number** is the basic element of For-
                          tran) rather than a list structure

        EQ   which is True if its two arguments are the
                          same atom

        CAR   which returns the first element of a list

        CDR   which returns the rest of a list (after the first
                          element)

```
(EQUAL                                          (LAMBDA
     (STRUCTURE1 STRUCTURE2)            (COND
        ((ATOM STRUCTURE1)    (EQ STRUCTURE1 STRUCTURE2))
        ((ATOM STRUCTURE2)    NIL)
        ((EQUAL (CAR STRUCTURE1) (CAR STRUCTURE2))
            (EQUAL (CDR STRUCTURE1) (CDR STURCTURE2)))
        (T    NIL)                                      )))
```

In slightly less obscure terms, the above program says:

If STRUCTURE1 is an atom then

        if STRUCTURE1 and STRUCTURE2 are the same
                then T
                 else False (NIL)

otherwise,

if STRUCTURE2 is an atom, the answer is False (NIL)

        since STRUCTURE1 isn't an atom

otherwise,

if the first element of STRUCTURE1 is EQUAL to the first element
        of STRUCTURE2 then the answer depends on
        whether or not the rest of STRUCTURE1 is
        EQUAL to the rest of STRUCTURE2

otherwise,

the answer is False (NIL).

If you fought through all that you will have noticed that the very definition of EQUAL involved references to itself. Thus LISP allows (in fact encourages) **recursive** programs. Algol, PL/I and SNOBOL also allow recursive programs.

There are many, many more computer languages available. There are whole *classes* of languages we haven't mentioned. For instance, there are languages designed to help write simulation programs, such as GPSS, SIMSCRIPT, and SIMULA.

Since every higher-level language that has received any kind of wide use is general (that is, theoretically you can write a program in that language that will compute anything that is computable), the choice of language is based on convenience. Different languages make solving different types of problems easier (or harder).

Section 13 2

Some Opinionated Opinions

This is the computer age, so they say. Man couldn't have gotten to the moon if it hadn't been for computers. Computers are giant brains, capable of making flawless, logical decisions in incomprehensively small fractions of a second. Computers are controlling us, dehumanizing us. "Computer designed" means "better." Computers never make mistakes and they never go on strike. You put data into a computer and it gives you answers. Computers draw pictures and write music; computers play chess; computers control airplanes and missiles; they keep tabs on your every credit transaction, phone call, and suspicious move. Movie computers respond to spoken requests with smooth tongued, seemingly pragmatic but actually borderline psychotic, logic. Computers are good; computers are evil.

Perhaps these "media" notions about computers seem hopelessly at odds with the view of computers you have seen in this book. At least *we* think that they are different. Perhaps a few words about the way we think of computers will help you come to your own conclusions about what computers are or should be or can be . . .

We think that computers are (1) useful tools and (2) fun. The second point is, of course, very subjective, and we certainly don't mean to imply that learning the intricacies of Fortran FORMAT statements or reading floods of obscure error messages is particularly enjoyable. We just mean that wracking our brains to describe some process, programming our description, and seeing the consequences of our program is enjoyable. It's fun to play around with programs, seeing large changes in the program's behavior with seemingly tiny changes in its exact form.

We see computers as tools just as people see mathematics as a tool, that is, as something which can be used to help you do something you want to do. Computer programs can be used as models of processes that go on in the real world. For example, an architect could write a computer program to study the effects of wind loads on a building he is designing; a linguist could use a computer program to describe a way he thinks people might analyze sentences; a neurophysiologist could write a computer program to describe the way he thinks a certain part of a nervous system operates. The program doesn't replace the reality of the process under study any more than writing a mathematical equation to describe how electrical current behaves in a resistor replaces a real resistor. A computer program is easier to change and experiment with than a real building or an electrical circuit but it can't really replace them—it *can* be used to help understand them.

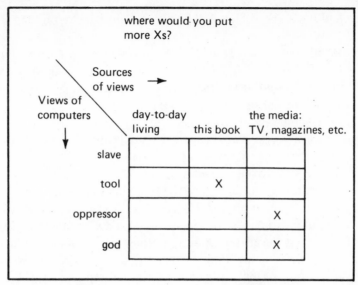

where would you put more Xs?

	day-to-day living	this book	the media: TV, magazines, etc.
slave			
tool		X	
oppressor			X
god			X

Views of computers ↓   Sources of views →

An important side issue here is that if we view computers as tools, then we have no more reason to trust the results we get than we do with any other tool. No theory or analysis becomes more (or less) true because it was done on a computer (or adding machine, slide rule, or abacus).

Yet another side issue is that viewing computers as tools says nothing about their limitations. If you want to ask, "Is it possible for a computer to be the world chess champion?" we would have to say that we don't see why not. No master-level chess playing programs exist today but there's no known reason why one could not be written. Such questions are really questions about *algorithms*, not computers, because any general purpose computer can, theoretically, carry out anything that is computable.

> *Computer programs exist today which play:*
> *an unbeatable game of Kalah*
> *a strong game of checkers*
> *a moderately good game of chess*
> *a rancid game of Go*

OK. If what we say is true, then why are there troubles? Why are we increasingly discovering that, say, a mistake in our credit card bill can go on unfixed for months, piling up spurious interest charges? Why do we get answers like "I'm really sorry you're having trouble, but your account is on the computer."

No doubt someone you know has had some sort of "computer trouble." We have a friend who signed up for meal plan A in his dorm, but was billed for meal plan B. He finally went to the person in charge of the billing, and she pulled out a huge book of computer printout, leafed through until she found his name and then announced, "You're on Plan B." He said, "But I have a copy of the form I

> *The thing to fear is not that computers are gods; the thing to fear is people who think that computers are gods.*

sent you and it's marked Plan A." She said, "No, you're on Plan B, *it says so right here*."

Yes, you might say, it's true that the problem shows up when someone in an organization puts too much faith in something just because it came out of a computer, but *if the computer weren't there, it couldn't have happened to begin with.* Hah! *Not so*, we would say.

We know (second hand) of a nice old person who was working designing airplanes just before World War II (not for the winning side incidentally). Part of the design necessitated solving some sets of differential equations that were so difficult that they could not be solved directly. Today, we'd just get a stored program from the computer center and have the machine grind out approximate solutions. This person had no computers. Instead there was a large room full of women (called "computer girls"), each one sitting at a desk with an adding machine. The method for solving the differential equations was to write out a series of instructions for each woman, including instructions saying which other woman to get partial results from. After a week or so, the "computer girls" would produce the desired answers.

The point here is *not* just the well-known fact that what the computer does is determined by its program, which was written by a human. Ultimately it is a human who is responsible for what happens. The people who are responsible are the ones who set up an organization, determine where their data comes from, how it is to be manipulated, and what is to be done with the results. It doesn't matter that it was a computer that printed out an erroneous credit balance or the wrong meal plan. The same wrong results could have been produced by humans; the problem is in the structure of the organization. Perhaps computers have made things worse because they are a new, modern gadget that can be blamed for the errors of a faulty organization. Perhaps computers make it easier to get by with bad manners. But we believe these abuses will gradually diminish.

There are numbers of lessons to be learned about good programming from all the bad programming we come into contact with daily. For instance, it should be clear to you that a few simple IF statements could immediately halt such absurdities as sending someone an erroneous utility bill for one million dollars. The only reasonable way to program is to admit that there are going to be errors, and to put in tests for them. In the case of billing programs, any bill that is much different from the average should be detected and set aside for someone to examine.

Another bad practice that arises is using abbreviations where the full word is needed for clarity. Programmers tend to fall into this sort of thing, perhaps because early programming languages (like Fortran) require such short memory cell names. This problem can be circumvented if programmers would keep in mind the principle that their programs should be understandable not only to themselves and their computer, but also *to other humans.*

> *"I'm going down to SFOF to get an RFP for the EVA PEX," he said clearly.*

Enough of this.

So far, computers have been extensively employed by the military, widely employed by technologically sophisticated industries, and used for accounting and record keeping by most other large organizations. Certainly these sorts of uses of large-scale computing will continue to grow, hopefully to yield such things as automated libraries, energy saving communication devices (since there will be less need for business trips), and better scheduled mass transit systems, but we suspect that the most noticeable new uses of computers will be more personal. In the future, we expect that computers will make steady intrusions into our everyday lives. To us, the pocket calculators, the barroom "pong" games, and hobbyists' microcomputers are portents of a dramatic domestication of computers. Now that computers are getting into the hands of the kid on the corner, the crackpot inventor, the lemonade stand tycoon, watch out! It will be fun. The technology for producing small, inexpensive computers already exists. What is currently lacking is just the sort of thing this book is about—programs to do interesting tasks. It is clear that computer hardware will continue to undergo revolutionary decreases in size and cost. What will continue to be necessary are new programs and people with good ideas about what to program. With the understanding of programming concepts you've received from this book, you should be in good shape to cope with and help control computers in the future.

PROBLEMS 13

1 Next time you come up against "the computer" in some way (phone company, your school, the IRS, a computer dating agency), try to learn something about how computers really fit into their operation. What image of how they use computers do they try to project?

2 Think up some useful, fun or zany products that could be made using tiny, inexpensive computers. Write a Fortran program that emulates your product. Some suggestions are:

    a a fish hook that analyzes the fish around it and scares away types you don't want to catch

    b a pen that measures the surface it's writing on and makes appropriate changes in the ink flow rate

    c a typewriter that checks your spelling

    d a pipe that regulates the flow of air so as to produce a smoke of just the right temperature

    e a program that writes Fortran textbooks

    f . . .

*

APPENDICES

A STRUCTURED PROGRAMMING STRUCTURES

In Section 1 2, Section 5 1, and Section 9 1 we outlined a systematic approach to programming in four steps. The third step, gradual refinement from a notation suited especially to the problem into operations easily described in Fortran, can be viewed as a language design process. You start with a language very close to the problem you're trying to solve and gradually refine the level of detail in the statements, keeping a "target language" (something close to a computer language) in mind. Many programmers have found that using Fortran as a direct target language often leads to rather jumbled programs. One of the major problems seems to be the temptation to jump around in the program with the unrestricted use of GO TO statements. The number of possible routes through the program increases dramatically when jumping statements are used carelessly. As the number of possible routes increases, the programmer's intended flow of control becomes more obscure. Restricting the control structure of the program can lead to a more transparent program. The easiest programs to understand are those that start at the beginning and proceed in a straight line until the end—no branching. But most problems don't allow such simple solutions, and some branching is needed.

There are basically two kinds of branching structures that are needed when the target language is Fortran (or any other iterative languages such as Algol, PL/I, PASCAL, BASIC, etc.) These structures are **looping** and **selection**. Loops are normally restricted to the one-entry, one-exit types described in Section 3 3 (pre-test or post-test). Selection is generally one of two forms, two-way selection (**if-then-else**) and multiple branch selection (**select case *x* from**: *list of cases*). If you'll try to use these control statements in preference to the branch-with-abandon philosophy, it is likely that your programs will be easier to develop and debug. This is not to say that using these control statements alone will guarantee good programs. Thoughtless use of any programming technique will produce rotten programs. You must use judgment and art to come up with good results.

structured flow
of control

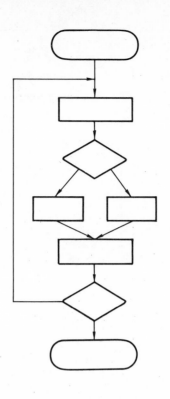

spaghetti-like
flow of control

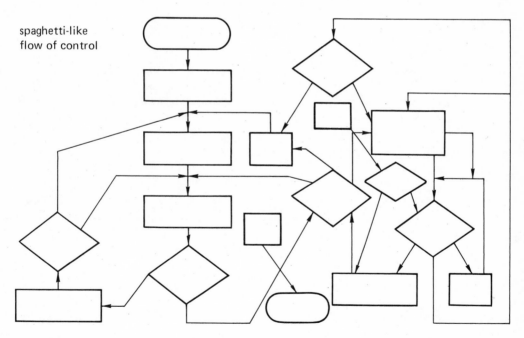

looping control statements

pre-test

form

> **while** *condition*
> **do** *sequence of statements*
> **end of loop**

meaning

> Check *condition*. If *true*, do the *sequence of statements* and repeat. If *false*, proceed from the statement after **end of loop**.

example

> while $x > 0$
> > do let $y = y * x$;
> > > let $x = x - 1$
> >
> > end of loop

post-test

form

> **loop**
> > *sequence of statements*
> > **repeat unless** *condition*

meaning

> Perform the *sequence of statements*. Check *condition*. If *false*, repeat. If *true*, proceed from next statement.

example

> loop
> > let $p = p * a$;
> > let $i = i + 1$
> > repeat unless $i > n$

selection control statements

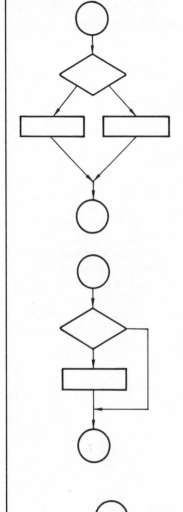

two-branch

form
> if *condition*
> > **then** *sequence of statements 1*
> > **else** *sequence of statements 2*
> > **end if**

meaning
> Check *condition*. If *true*, perform the first *sequence of statements*, and proceed from the statement after the **end if**. Otherwise, perform the second *sequence of statements* and proceed after the **end if**.

example
> if $x > y$
> > **then** let $m = x$;
> > > let $i = 1$
> > **else** let $m = y$;
> > > let $i = 2$
> > **end if**.

The **else** *sequence of statements* can be omitted, leaving an **if-then** statement.

example
> if $x > 0$ then let $y = 1/x$

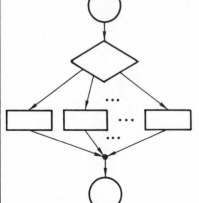

multiple-branch

form
> select case x from
> > *a: sequence of statements;*
> > *b: sequence of statements;*
> >
> > .
> > .
> > .
> >
> > *etc.*
> >
> > .
> > .
> >
> > end of cases

meaning

Compare x to the case headings a, b, etc. until finding a matching case ($x = a$ or $x = b$ or . . .). Then perform the associated *sequence of statements* and proceed from the statement after the **end of cases**.

examples

select case n **from**
>   1: error;
>   2: snake eyes; lose;
>   3: craps; lose;
>   7 or 11: win;
>   12: box cars; lose;
>   other: **let** *point* = n;
> **end of cases.**

select case *keyword* **from**
>   BOUGHT: update list of supplies;
>   USED: update list of supplies;
>   **if** item is exhausted
>   **then** add to shopping list;
>   PRINT: print out shopping list;
>   SUPPLIES: print out list of supplies;
> **end of cases.**

Note that this simple loop

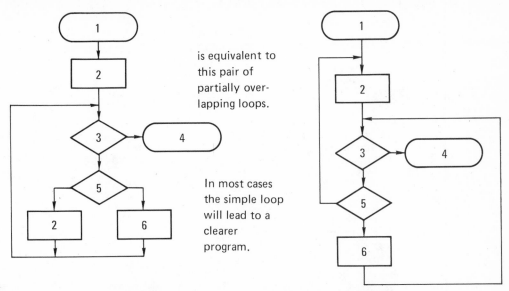

is equivalent to this pair of partially overlapping loops.

In most cases the simple loop will lead to a clearer program.

Of course, if any of the boxes contain more than a few statements, you'll want to make them subprograms; especially 2, since it must be repeated to avoid the overlapping loops.

There has been much discussion of ways to implement the above control structures in Fortran. Suggestions range from purely mechanical translation to careful tailoring to individual situations. You'll have to think about it and adopt your own philosophy and style. There is no magic technique which makes programming easy. It takes a lot of thought, like any other intellectual activity— writing, painting, potting, or whatever. If you practice programming thoughtfully, you will eventually learn to use the techniques wisely.

implementing *if-then-else* in Fortran

$$\text{if } x > y$$
$$\text{then let } m = x$$
$$\text{else let } m = y$$
$$\text{end if;}$$
$$\text{let } x = x/m;$$
$$\text{let } y = y/m;$$

```
        IF (X .LT. Y) GO TO 110              IF (X .GE. Y) GO TO 110
           GO TO 120                            M=Y
C       THEN                                    GO TO 120
  110      M=X                           110     M=X
           GO TO 130                     120    X=X/M
C       ELSE                                    Y=Y/M
  120      M=Y
           GO TO 130
  130    CONTINUE
         X=X/M
         Y=Y/M
```

Mechanical   Adapted
Implementation   Implementation

implementing *while* loops in Fortran

$$\text{while } x > 0$$
$$\text{do let } y = y * x;$$
$$\text{let } x = x - 1$$
$$\text{end of loop;}$$
$$\text{let } f = y$$

```
C       WHILE X>0                     100    IF (X .LE. 0) GO TO 110
  100   IF (.NOT. X .GT. 0) GO TO 110        Y=Y*X
C       DO                                   X=X-1
          Y=Y*X                              GO TO 100
          X=X-1                       110    F=Y
          GO TO 100
  110   CONTINUE
C       END OF LOOP
        F=Y
```

Mechanical   Adapted
Implementation   Implementation

implementing *repeat* loops in Fortran

> loop
> > let $p = p * a$;
> > let $i = i + 1$
> > repeat unless $i > n$

```
C     LOOP                              100   P=P*A
  100 CONTINUE                                I=I+1
      P=P*A                                   IF (I .LE. N) GO TO 100
      I=I+1
C     REPEAT UNLESS I>N
      IF (.NOT. I .GT. N) GO TO 100
```

Mechanical   Adapted
Implementation   Implementation

B HOW TO READ A FORTRAN MANUAL

Computer manuals have a reputation for obscurity. However, it is important that you know how to read one. It is even more important that you know *when* to read one. Manuals are written in a very compact style; few words are wasted. They are very precise; every detail is specified. Because manuals state all the details in as few words as possible without any particular emphasis on the more important details, they are very hard to read. In fact, they are nearly impossible to read unless you know what you're looking for. If you are trying to learn how to write a *program* in Fortran, the manual will be of no use to you. If you are trying to learn how to write a Fortran *statement*, the manual will help. In other words, manuals are not written to teach generalities; they are written to specify details. Once you understand this fact, you will be a lot more comfortable with, and less critical of your manual.

The Fortran manual must specify two things about each statement: its form (syntax) and its meaning (semantics). Most manuals describe the form of a statement in a notation which uses standard Fortran characters (the capital letters, the digits 0 through 9, and the special characters) in the precise way that they *always* occur in the statement. The parts of the statement which may vary are specified by small letters. We have used a similar convention in the descriptions of Fortran statements in this text and in the MiniManual.

> special
> characters:
>
> +
> –
> *
> /
> =
> ;
> .
> (
>)

For example, the form of the assignment statement might be described in a Fortran manual as follows:

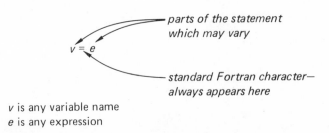

parts of the statement which may vary

standard Fortran character— always appears here

$v = e$

v is any variable name
e is any expression

The forms that v and e may take are described elsewhere in the manual. The meaning of the assignment statement might be described as follows:

The expression e is computed. If v has the same type as e, then the value computed is stored in v. If not, then both v and e must be of an arithmetic type (INTEGER, REAL, or DOUBLE PRECISION). The value computed is then converted to the type of v and stored in v. A table of legal conversions follows.

Table of Conversions

e type / v type	INTEGER	REAL	DOUBLE PRECISION	COMPLEX
INTEGER	none required	truncate fractional part	truncate fractional part	not permitted
REAL	change to floating point equivalent	none required	drop low order fractional part	not permitted
DOUBLE PRECISION	change to double precision equivalent	change to double precision equivalent	none required	not permitted
COMPLEX	not permitted	not permitted	not permitted	none required

Note that the above description doesn't give any hints about what to do with assignment statements; it assumes you already know. The description of the assignment statement may seem fairly clear to you, but let's look at a description of the CALL statement, as it might appear in a manual.

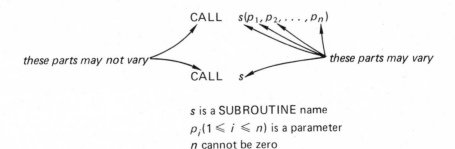

CALL $s(p_1, p_2, \ldots, p_n)$

these parts may not vary

these parts may vary

CALL s

s is a SUBROUTINE name
$p_i (1 \leqslant i \leqslant n)$ is a parameter
n cannot be zero

A parameter may be a constant, variable name, or expression. Variables are called by name; constants and expressions are called by value.

Control is transferred to the subroutine *s*. The CALL statement is completed when a RETURN in *s* returns control to the statement following the CALL statement.

In the case of the CALL statement, you need to know a lot of jargon to understand the description ("call by value," for example). This jargon may or may not be explained in the manual (or anywhere else).

You will be able to get the main idea about all the standard Fortran statements from this book. Details of ANSI standard statements appear in the ANSI Fortran MiniManual. Nonstandard statements specific to the system you are using are described in your local manual. As you progress as a programmer you will need your local manual more and more, especially to use the available mass storage devices (tapes, disks, etc.).

Remember, as you use our ANSI MiniManual or your own local manual, that the purpose of a manual is to describe the form and effect of all Fortran statements, not to tell how to compose the statements into a useful program.

C ANSI Fortran MiniManual

If you're down in the computer center late at night trying desperately to get a program to run and you can't remember all the options and restrictions associated with DO-loops, look here.

Contents

Definitions

address

a label (symbolic or numeric) identifying a memory cell;

an array **subscript**;

the value of a **pointer**

algorithm

directions for doing something;

more formally: a collection of rules which, when carried out, solve a specified problem in a finite number of steps;

less formally: what all God's chilluns got

alias

an alternate name or label;

when a memory cell has several names (through EQUIVALENCE statements) the memory cell is said to have aliases

alphanumeric

alphameric (see **character**)

ANSI Fortran

a computer language defined in standards maintained by the American National Standards Institute, Inc.

array

a collection of memory cells, individual members of which may be referenced by a single identifier followed by a numeric value (the **index** or **subscript**);

the memory cells which comprise a **subscripted variable**

argument

a value which serves as an input to a **subprogram**

binary I/O

see **unformatted I/O**

bit

a binary digit (0 or 1)

bug

an error;

a statement or pattern of statements which causes an error

byte

a directly addressable eight-bit storage element in IBM 360/370 core memory;

a small, fixed-size chunk of information (usually eight bits) on an I/O medium or in memory

chad

the material removed to make holes in punched cards or tape

> *WARNING: Use of chad as confetti is* dangerous. *Sharp edges can cause eye injuries. This is* no joke. *Use* **chard** *instead.*

chard

a vegetable with large leaves and succulent stalks

character

numeric character: a decimal digit, one of

$$0\ 1\ 2\ 3\ 4\ 5\ 6\ 7\ 8\ 9$$

alphabetic character: a capitalized letter, one of

$$A\ B\ C\ D\ E\ F\ G\ H\ I\ J\ K\ L\ M\ N\ O\ P\ Q\ R\ S\ T\ U\ V\ W\ X\ Y\ Z$$

alphameric: a numeric or alphabetic character (in some literature, this term is synonymous with **character**)

special character: one of

$$.\ ,\ \$\ +\ -\ *\ /\ )\ (\ =\ b$$

(where b represents the blank character)

other character: anything not mentioned above that you can find: % ? ! a b c, etc. Only the alphamerics and special characters are included in the ANSI standards.

compiler

a program which translates Fortran statements into the lower-level language appropriate for your computer

computer

a machine which can perform arithmetic operations, make logical decisions, and perform many other symbol manipulation tasks by automatically following the instructions in a computer program

controller

the part of the conceptual computer which carries out commands;

the part of the conceptual computer other than memory or input/output

debug

to locate and remove **bugs**

default

a value or condition which is assumed unless explicitly overridden

defined

having a value;

having been specified;

for instance, a memory cell's value is **defined** once it has been given a value by an assignment, input statement, or compile-time initialization

disk

a **random access I/O device** containing a stack of spinning magnetic storage plates

documentation

information prepared for humans describing a program or collection of related programs

drum

random access I/O device containing a spinning magnetic recording cylinder

element

one of a collection of things;

an **array element** is a memory cell in an array

executable statement

a statement which is a command to the **controller** rather than an instruction to the **compiler**;

assignment statements of any kind, transfer of control of any kind (including STOP and CONTINUE), input/output of any kind

Fortran

a computer language which either conforms to or closely resembles ANSI Fortran

head

see **read/write head**

identifier

a name (of a simple memory cell, array, subprogram, etc.)

I/O device

equipment which reads or writes data on an input or output medium

I/O medium

material used for storing data (e.g., computer paper, 80-column cards, magnetic tape)

index

a label which identifies one of a group of items;

an **array subscript**;

to point out each member of a collection (usually a collection of **array elements**)

initialize

to prepare for a process to begin;

to give starting (initial) values to memory cells

JCL

job control language;

statements in this language tell the operating system which system programs you are using (e.g., Fortran compiler); look on the walls of your computer center for the JCL for Fortran programs

key

in sorting, the values which determine the sorted arrangement are called the **keys**

key word

a sequence of characters making up a distinguishing part of a statement;

for example: STOP

                DO

                FORMAT

memory cell

the basic unit of memory in Fortran;

note: memory cells of differing data types may occupy a different number of physical storage units

mode

type

module

a **program unit** or collection of program units which make a logical subunit of an overall program

multipunch

a pattern of holes created by striking more than one key in the same column of a card;

to create such a pattern by striking several keys while holding down the MLT PCH key

nonexecutable statement

a statement which is not a command to the **controller**: END, EQUIVALENCE, COMMON, FORMAT, etc.

object

a Fortran item, element or unit;

i.e., a memory cell, an array, a subprogram, a statement, a constant, etc.

object of a DO-loop

the last statement in the range of a DO statement

operating system

a program which supervises the running of all programs on the computer system (see also **JCL**)

operator

+ − * / ** are arithmetic operators;

.NOT. .AND. .OR. are LOGICAL operators

parameter

an **identifier** used to specify the form and type which an **argument** to a **subprogram** will have;

the control variable, initial value, upper bound, or increment of a DO statement

pointer

a memory cell which stores an **address** or **subscript**

precision

the degree to which a value discriminates between measured quantities;

a value correct to two digits is more *precise* than one correct to only one digit since the first discriminates among a hundred possibilities, the second among only ten

program

a self-contained collection of program units including exactly one main program

program fragment

part of a program, used to illustrate some particular point

program unit

the main program, a FUNCTION, a SUBROUTINE, or a BLOCK DATA subprogram

a sequence of Fortran statements followed by an END statement

random access I/O device

an I/O device whose read/write head can move in a nonsequential way, thus making the data retrieval time almost independent of the location of the data on the I/O device (e.g., **disk, drum**)

record

a set of data items treated as a unit; for instance, the sequence of 80 characters on a punched card

recursive

self-referential;

a **recursive** subprogram is one which includes a reference to itself (possibly through some sequence of references to other program units);

using repeated obscenities

simple variable

a memory cell which is not subscripted

specification statement

a nonexecutable statement;

an instruction to the compiler which provides information about memory cells other than their data type (DATA, EQUIVALENCE, etc.)

statement

a single Fortran command

storage unit

the basic physical unit of memory used for Fortran variables. INTEGERs, REALs, LOGICALs occupy one storage unit. COMPLEX and DOUBLE PRECISION variables occupy two storage units.

four bytes on IBM 360/370; 60 bits on CDC 6000/7000 and CYBER; 48 bits on Burroughs 5000; 36 bits on DEC 10; 32 bits on most minicomputers

structured programming

an approach to programming which leads to understandable, correct computer programs

subprogram

a program unit other than the main program;

a FUNCTION or SUBROUTINE

subscript

a value designating a particular element of an array

subscripted variable

an **array**;

an array **element**

temporary

the result of an expression or subexpression which is not assigned directly to a memory cell in the program

type

the interpretation placed on a stored bit pattern, e.g., LOGICAL, INTEGER, REAL;

mode

typical rule

"This form may be used only if not before the last preceding comma, or in an ASSIGNed GO TO but not before *any* executable statement except STOP or PAUSE when these do not have the optional trailing octal constant."

unformatted I/O

a type of I/O designed for machine–machine communication as opposed to human–machine communication

unsigned INTEGER constant

a nonzero INTEGER constant not preceded by a plus or minus sign

 comma alert

used to draw attention to obscure places in specific statements where a comma must or may not appear (the triangle points to the place in question)

 forbidden usage

used to identify illegal, invalid usages

 legitimate usage

used to identify valid examples

The Price of Freedom from Syntax Errors is Eternal Vigilance

Syntax + Semantics/3

The syntax of a language is its correct grammatical form. Virtually all of the syntax of ANSI Fortran is described herein.

The semantics of a language is the meaning of its grammatical constructs. Some of the semantics of Fortran is explained herein. The rest is explained in the first thirteen chapters.

Entries have the following general organization.

Major topic category

Specific topic name

| precise definition of allowed forms |

comments, special things to notice

  examples of legal usage

  examples of illegal usage, with brief explanations of the errors

Material covered by gray shading is either an extension of or in disagreement with standard Fortran as described in ANSI X3.9–1966.

The examples assume that all identifiers which begin with

C	are COMPLEX
D	are DOUBLE PRECISION
I–N	are INTEGER
P–Q	are LOGICAL
R–Z	are REAL

Program Form

statement entry

The conventions for preparing programs for the Fortran compiler are based on the 80-column punched card. Even if your input medium is not punched cards, you will have to observe these conventions when you type (or punch) your Fortran programs.

There are four fields in a Fortran line.

columns 1–5	label field
column 6	continuation field
columns 7–72	statement field
columns 73–80	identification field

These fields are described in detail below.

label field

Statements may be labeled for reference from other statements by placing a label anywhere within columns 1 to 5 inclusive.

continuation field

The statement field may be continued over up to 19 lines by placing any mark other than 0 (zero) in column 6 of the continuation line(s). Comment lines may not be continued in this way, but may be extended over several lines by placing a C in column 1 of each of the lines.

statement field

Fortran statements must be written entirely within the statement field, columns 7 to 72 inclusive.

identification field

Columns 73 to 80 are ignored by the Fortran compiler and may be used for any desired purpose. They are often used to mark each line of a program with a code for program identification and line sequencing. (Sometimes lines get scrambled by mistake.)

comment lines

A C in column 1 of any line directs the compiler to ignore the line. This provides a way for programmers to document the workings of their programs within the program itself. This internal form of documentation is valuable because, unlike external documentation, it stays with the program and doesn't get lost.

A multiple-line comment must have a C in column 1 of each line.

blanks

Blank characters are ignored in the statement field and label field except in character (Hollerith) constants.

data

The fields on a data card (line) are determined by the FORMAT indicated by the READ statement. All 80 columns may be used.

statement labels

An unsigned, nonzero INTEGER with up to five digits placed anywhere in columns 1 through 5.

> *Statement labels identify Fortran statements for purposes of referencing them from other statements.*

Statement labels must be on the first line of a multiple-line statement and on no other line of the statement.

LEGAL	ILLEGAL	
100	0	zero not allowed
34100	−1.2	non-INTEGER
5	+19	no + allowed
37	123456	too many digits
999	LOOP:	ridiculous

Fortran Program

A Fortran program consists of one or several program units which, together, describe a self-contained computation to be performed. The program must contain exactly one main program.

main program

A main program is a program unit which is *not* headed by a FUNCTION, SUBROUTINE, or BLOCK DATA statement.

subprogram

A subprogram is a program unit headed by a FUNCTION, SUBROUTINE, or BLOCK DATA statement.

program unit

A program unit is an executable program unit or a BLOCK DATA subprogram.

---

executable program unit

header:	a FUNCTION or SUBROUTINE statement (omit header in main program)
specifications:	a sequence of specification statements (not including any DATA statements) and/or FORMAT statements
local functions:	a sequence of statement function definitions (no forward references to other statement functions allowed), FORMAT statements, and/or DATA statements
program part:	a sequence of executable statements, FORMAT statements, and/or DATA statements (including at least one executable statement)
terminator:	an END statement

The sequence of parts of an executable program unit must be as shown in the definition box.

When the header part is omitted, the program unit is a main program.

Specifications and local functions may be omitted. (Omissions usually affect the meaning of the program unit, of course.)

END statement

The END statement is not executable.

END instructs the compiler to stop compiling the current program unit and prepare to compile another program unit.

            END

            100 END
                 ENDS HERE

Basic Constituents

Constants

A constant is a fixed value involving no computation.

INTEGER constant

May include a leading + or −, otherwise all numeric characters.

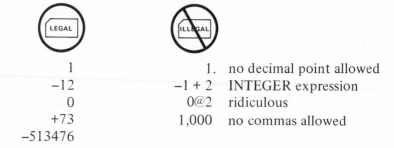

LEGAL	ILLEGAL	
1	1.	no decimal point allowed
−12	−1 + 2	INTEGER expression
0	0@2	ridiculous
+73	1,000	no commas allowed
−513476		

REAL constant

May include a leading + or −; must have a decimal point or a decimal point shift factor (may have both). A decimal point shift factor is an E followed by an INTEGER constant.

LEGAL	ILLEGAL	
−.01	−01	needs decimal point
1.002	1. + 2.	REAL expression
6.02E+23	4.*10.**10	ditto
.5E−12	Z11100	no Z allowed

COMPLEX constant

Two REAL constants, enclosed by parentheses, separated by a comma. First REAL is the real part, second REAL the imaginary part.

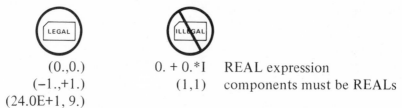

LEGAL	ILLEGAL	
(0.,0.)	0. + 0.*I	REAL expression
(−1.,+1.)	(1,1)	components must be REALs
(24.0E+1, 9.)		

DOUBLE PRECISION constant

Like a REAL constant, but carries greater accuracy. Shift factor is written with a D instead of E.

3.1415926D0	4	INTEGER
+1.0D+6	1,000.0	no commas allowed
−7.7777D−20	3.2E19	REAL

LOGICAL constant

Corresponds to two-valued logic. The periods at each end distinguish LOGICAL constants from identifiers.

.TRUE.	TRUE	needs periods
.FALSE.	NO	not even close

Character (Hollerith) constant

Character constants may be used in FORMAT, CALL, and DATA statements.

'TRA LA LA'	"TRA LA LA"	should be single, not double quotes
'Y NOT?'	'S DOG	needs closing quote
'APPLE''S BAY'	'APPLE'S BAY'	quotes don't match
9HTRA LA LA	9GHAA HA HA	should be 9H, not 9G
1H	GEEWHIZ	needs quotes
13HGUZORNENPLATZ	0H	constant must not be zero

Hollerith notation

$nHc_1c_2 \ldots c_n$
n is an unsigned INTEGER constant
c_i is a character

four equivalent FORMATs:

```
1000   FORMAT('1','CHECKING ACCOUNT SUMMARY')
2000   FORMAT(1H1,24HCHECKING ACCOUNT SUMMARY)
3000   FORMAT('1CHECKING ACCOUNT SUMMARY')
4000   FORMAT(25H1CHECKING ACCOUNT SUMMARY)
```

identifier

A string of one to six letters and/or numerals beginning with a letter

A1	1A	starts with number
BAT MAN	BRUCE WAYNE	too long
HNGRY	%GREED	illegal character
RST	R, S-T	illegal characters
X12345	X1234567	too long
SLOPE		

simple variable name

an identifier; an unsubscripted memory cell name

subscripted variable

an identifier followed by from one to three subscript expressions separated by commas

A(1,2,3)	A<1,2,3>	angle brackets not allowed
COST(M,N+2)	COSTLINESS(M,N)	name too long
TYPE(23)	(23) TYPE	name must go first

FUNCTION reference

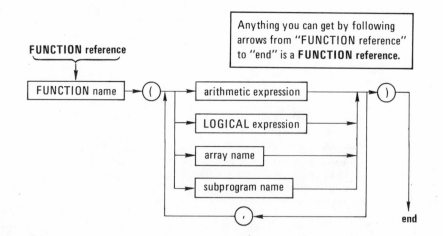

Anything you can get by following arrows from "FUNCTION reference" to "end" is a **FUNCTION reference.**

The number of arguments in a FUNCTION reference must be consistent with the FUNCTION definition.

The data types of the arguments in a FUNCTION reference must be the same as the data types of the corresponding parameters in the FUNCTION definition.

When you forget to declare an array, the compiler often mistakes references to the array for FUNCTION references.

```
X=SIN(Y**2 + 1.3)
M=3**MIN0(MAX0(I,2*K), -10)
IF (COS(X) .LT. 0.0)  GO TO 100
```

```
SIN(0.0)=0.0            sin(0.0) is not a memory cell, it's a value
READ(5,1000) ALOG(1.7)  ALOG(1.7) is not a memory cell, it's a value
```

Specification Statements

Specification statements give the compiler information about memory cells.

> **type statement (declaration)**
> *type* $a_1(s_1), a_2(s_2), \ldots, a_n(s_n)$
> *type* is a data type
> a_i is an identifier
> s_i is a list of up to three length declarators for the array
> $\quad$ a_i (must be unsigned INTEGER constants unless a_i is
> $\quad$ a parameter name in the current subprogram)
> $\quad$ (s_i) is omitted unless a_i is an array

A type statement declares the data type associated with a list of memory cells.

In subprograms, variables may be used as length declarators for array parameters. The variable length declarators must be parameters themselves.

Arrays may be declared only once in a program unit. An array declared in a type statement may not be subsequently declared in a DIMENSION or COMMON statement.

Arrays declared in type statements may be included in COMMON regions by listing their names without length declarators.

Memory can be allocated in single chunks (unsubscripted memory cells) or larger blocks (arrays). The compiler needs to know the data type of the values to be stored in the memory cells at the time of allocation because different types need memory cells of different lengths. The type can be declared explicity in a declaration statement or assumed according to the implicit typing rules.

Declaration of array parameters in subprograms doesn't involve memory allocation but takes the same form as memory allocating declarations.

```
INTEGER M,N,LOT(25)
REAL XYLO
LOGICAL PLATO(2,4,8)
COMPLEX C1,C2
DOUBLE PRECISION DRIFT(14),D12,DWARF2
```

```
INTERGER M,N,LOT(25)    misspelling
REAL 3.14159            must be an identifier, not a constant
LOGICAL (2,4,8)PLATO    array length info comes after identifier
DEVIOUS C1,C2           not a type
REAL YNOT(0)            array length may not be zero
INTEGER K(+2)           array length must be unsigned
```

> ## EXTERNAL statement
>
> EXTERNAL *list*
>
> *list* is a list of FUNCTION and/or SUBROUTINE names separated by commas

Whenever a program name (i.e., FUNCTION or SUBROUTINE name) is used as an argument in a CALL statement or FUNCTION reference, that subprogram name must be declared to be EXTERNAL. Otherwise it may be interpreted as a local memory cell under the implicit typing rules.

An EXTERNAL statement may be used to override built-in intrinsic FUNCTION names so that the names may be used for user defined FUNCTIONs.

```
EXTERNAL SIN,COS,USERFN
EXTERNAL SIGN,ABS,MOD
```

```
REAL X(10)
EXTERNAL X        only subprograms can be external
```

Data Type Chart

type	storage units per variable
INTEGER	1
REAL	1
LOGICAL	1
DOUBLE PRECISION	2
COMPLEX	2

You can use the number of storage units per variable to figure out which variables are sharing storage in complicated EQUIVALENCE schemes.

---

implicit type declarations

If an identifier does not appear in a type statement of any kind, then

if it begins with A through H } it is assumed to be
or O through Z } REAL

if it begins with I through N } it is assumed to be
} INTEGER

DIMENSION statement

DIMENSION *list*

list is a list of array declarators like those which may be used in type statements.

Array length information may be given only once in a program unit.

Array sizes may be specified in a DIMENSION statement. The data types of the arrays concerned should be previously established, unless implicit types are being used.

```
DIMENSION A(10)
DIMENSION X(10,15),Y(103)
```

```
DIMENSION X          lacks array length info
DIM Y(10)            no abbreviations allowed
DIMENSION A,B(10,12)
```

DATA statement

DATA $list_1/c_1/$, $list_2/c_2/$, . . . , $list_n/c_n/$

$list_k$ is a list of (possibly subscripted) memory cell names, separated by commas. Subscripts must be unsigned INTEGER constants.

c_k is a list of constants separated by commas. Any of these constants may be preceded by a replication factor $r*$, where r is an unsigned INTEGER constant. The replication factor $r*$ has the same effect that repeating the constant following it r times would have. The list c_k must have the same number of elements as $list_k$.

DATA statements give values to memory cells at compile time only. If those values are changed during execution, they remain changed, no matter how many times the program passes through the point at which the DATA statement is located.

Data types of initialization constants must match the types of the corresponding memory cells.

DATA statements may appear anywhere in a program unit after the specification section and prior to the END statement.

```
DATA X/1.72/, Y/3.17/
DATA A,P/.?., .TRUE./, C/(0.0,1.0)/
INTEGER MT(10)
DATA MT(3),MT(1),MT(10)/1,0,0/
```

```
DATA X/Y/              no variables allowed in constant list
DATA X/1.2, 3.7/       more constants than memory cells
DATA X,Y/1.0/          more memory cells than constants
DATA X/1/              data types don't match
```

The examples assume that all identifiers which begin with

C	are COMPLEX
D	are DOUBLE PRECISION
I–N	are INTEGER
P–Q	are LOGICAL
R–Z	are REAL

COMMON statement

COMMON/a_1/$list_1$/a_2/$list_2$/ ... /a_n/$list_n$

a_k is an identifier or blank
$list_k$ is a list of unsubscripted memory cell names or array names separated by commas

If a_1 is a blank, the first two slashes may be omitted. An array name in $list_k$ may be followed by a length declarator if its length is not declared elsewhere.

COMMON statements establish regions of memory which are **global** in the sense that they are accessible to any program unit. Each of these regions has a name. One legal name is the blank name; this region is known as the **blank common** region. Regions with nonblank names are known as **labeled COMMON** regions. A program unit gains access to a COMMON region via a COMMON statement naming that region and the memory cells therein.

COMMON names: Each subprogram (or main program) which uses a COMMON region must declare the region with a COMMON statement. A COMMON region is a collection of contiguous storage units. The names referring to these storage units may differ in different subprograms. It is the order of the memory cell and array names in the COMMON statement which determines which names will be associated with which storage units.

> *COMMON safety:* To be safe, for each COMMON region, punch a "COMMON *deck*" *of memory cell and array declarations and a single* COMMON *statement. Duplicate the deck for each program unit that uses the* COMMON *region.*

If a program unit contains COMMON statements referring to the same COMMON region more than once, the memory cells involved are sequentially included in the region in the order in which they occur in the COMMON statements.

Array sizes may be declared in COMMON statements, but array size information may be given only *once* in a program unit.

 sequence of COMMON statements

```
COMMON A(3),M,X,R(10)
COMMON /BLK1/Y,B//T(100)
```

 sequence

```
COMMON A,M,X      } a variable may appear in
COMMON /BLK/X,Y   } only one COMMON block
```

> **EQUIVALENCE statement**
>
> **EQUIVALENCE** $(list_1), (list_2), \ldots, (list_n)$
>
> $list_k$ is a list of memory cell names (possibly subscripted with a constant subscript). Not more than one of the elements in $list_k$ can be in a COMMON statement.

EQUIVALENCE statements may extend COMMON regions by adding more memory cells to the end of the regions. EQUIVALENCE statements implying new starting points for COMMON regions are in error.

An EQUIVALENCE statement may imply an extension on the end of a COMMON region but may not imply any other rearrangement in a COMMON region.

> *If it is 3 A.M. and you're still here because you used an* EQUIVALENCE *statement, it serves you right.*

Different COMMON regions may not overlap in the computer memory. Therefore, two different COMMON regions may not both contain the same memory cell.

To figure out the correspondence between storage units involved in complicated EQUIVALENCE schemes, use the Data Type Chart on page 386.

```
EQUIVALENCE (A,B)
EQUIVALENCE (X,Y,R),(D(10),C(387,2))
```

```
EQUIVALENCE (X)
EQUIVALENCE (A,B)(T,Z)
```

Expressions

arithmetic expressions

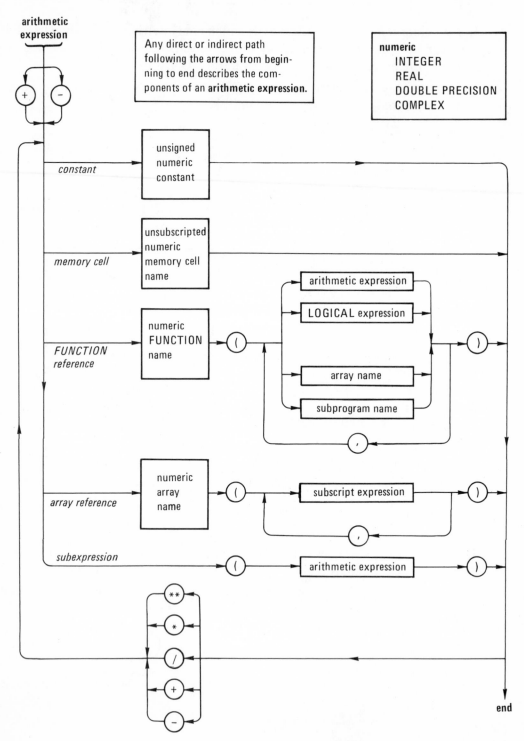

The number and data type of arguments in a FUNCTION reference must correspond to the function definition.

The number of and values of subscripts in an array reference must correspond to the array length declarators.

Other facts concerning the form and meaning of arithmetic expressions follow.

```
20.
3*INT(SQRT(X+Y))+1
ZN(14)+Z1(I*J,3)/X
-(X**Y)*(3.14/(Y+X))
+RATS
```

```
M*-4              adjacent operators not allowed
X+'4'             character value cannot be added
X*(Y/(1.4/T)      parentheses not balanced
```

precedence

An arithmetic expression is evaluated in the following order:

1   evaluate expressions in parentheses

2   ** exponentiations

3   * / multiplication or division

4   + – addition or subtraction (both binary and unary)

5   When faced with two operators at the same level, if they are exponentiations, proceed right to left, otherwise proceed left to right

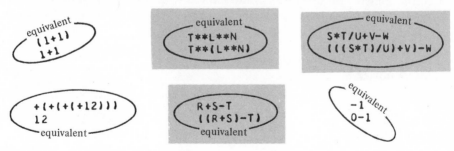

A unary + or – is equivalent to a binary + or – with 0 as the first operand.

data types of arithmetic expressions

A+B, A−B, A*B, or A/B

type of A \ type of B	type of result			
	INTEGER	REAL	DOUBLE PRECISION	COMPLEX
INTEGER	INTEGER	⊘	⊘	⊘
REAL	⊘	REAL	DOUBLE	COMPLEX
DOUBLE PRECISION	⊘	DOUBLE	DOUBLE	⊘
COMPLEX	⊘	COMPLEX	⊘	COMPLEX

A**B (exponentiation)

type of A \ type of B	type of result			
	INTEGER	REAL	DOUBLE PRECISION	COMPLEX
INTEGER	INTEGER	⊘	⊘	⊘
REAL	REAL	REAL	DOUBLE	⊘
DOUBLE PRECISION	DOUBLE	DOUBLE	DOUBLE	⊘
COMPLEX	COMPLEX	⊘	⊘	⊘

If an arithmetic expression contains constants, memory cell names, array names, and function references all of the same type t, the expression is of type t.

If the above case does *not* hold, the expression is of **mixed mode** (mixed type). The type of the expression then is the type of the longest, most complicated operand.

It is illegal to attempt to raise a negative value to a REAL or DOUBLE PRECISION power.

Mixed mode operations produce a result according to the following principles:

1 Conversions are made locally, that is, the two numbers involved in the operation being performed determine the type of the result.

2 Conversion is made in the direction of the longest, most intricate type.

troublesome cases

−1**N	evaluates to −1	exponentiation first
1./3.+0.D0	≠ 1.D0/3.	due to conversion rules

ANSI subscript expressions

$$k$$
$$i$$
$$i - k$$
$$i + k$$
$$c * i - k$$
$$c * i + k$$

c and k are INTEGER constants and i is an unsubscripted INTEGER memory cell name.

LOGICAL expressions

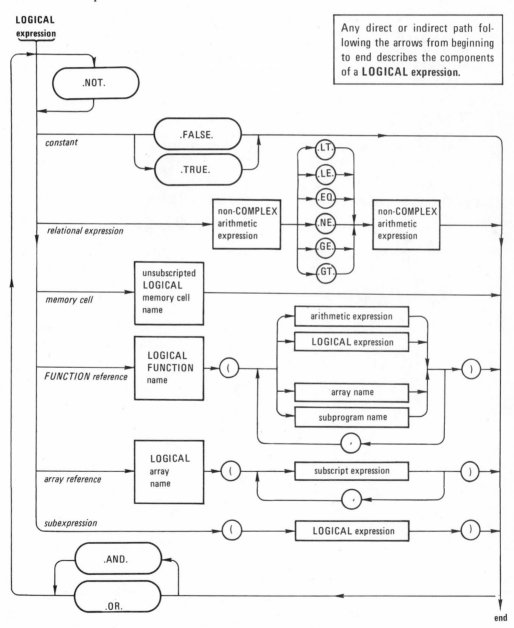

> Any direct or indirect path following the arrows from beginning to end describes the components of a **LOGICAL expression.**

If one side of a relational expression is of type INTEGER, then the other side must also be of type INTEGER.

Relational operators (.EQ., .NE., LT., etc.) cannot have COMPLEX or LOGICAL operands.

See comments about array and FUNCTION references in **arithmetic expressions** above.

LOGICAL operators (.NOT., .AND., and .OR.) can have LOGICAL operands *only*.

```
.TRUE.
PLATO(2*I)
QUIZIT  .OR.  X .LT. 10.7
POOBEE .AND.  .NOT. POOBEE
X*Y .GT. 3.1  .AND.  I .NE. 0
```

```
X    .AND.  Y .LT. 3.14   X isn't of type LOGICAL
QUIZIT .EQ. .TRUE.        QUIZIT AND .TRUE. are not numeric
```

precedence

A LOGICAL expression is evaluated in the following order:

1   evaluate terms in parentheses and relational expressions
2   .NOT.
3   .AND.
4   .OR.
5   go left to right

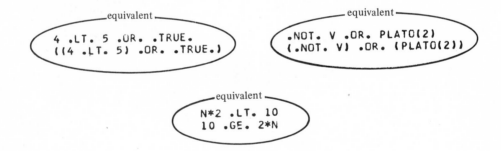

equivalent
```
4 .LT. 5 .OR. .TRUE.
((4 .LT. 5) .OR. .TRUE.)
```

equivalent
```
.NOT. V .OR. PLATO(2)
(.NOT. V) .OR. (PLATO(2))
```

equivalent
```
N*2 .LT. 10
10 .GE. 2*N
```

Assignment

---

assignment statement

$v = expr$

v is a memory cell name, possibly subscripted, and *expr* is an expression whose data type is assignment compatible with v.

If v and *expr* are not of the same data type but are assignment compatible, then *expr* is evaluated and the result is converted to the type of v. See the Conversion Chart below.

```
ISLE=1
T12=19.27
C2=(0.0,-1.0)
RACK(2)=RACK(2)+1.0
```

```
3=AT
A**2+B**2=C**2
P=3          P is logical
```

The examples assume that all identifiers which begin with

C	are COMPLEX
D	are DOUBLE PRECISION
I–N	are INTEGER
P–Q	are LOGICAL
R–Z	are REAL

To deduce the result of a conversion from type *a* to type *b,* start from the type *a* oval and follow the arrows along the most direct route to the type *b* oval, noting conversions as you go.

If you can't get to *b* from *a,* then *a* and *b* aren't assignment compatible.

"none" means no conversion necessary

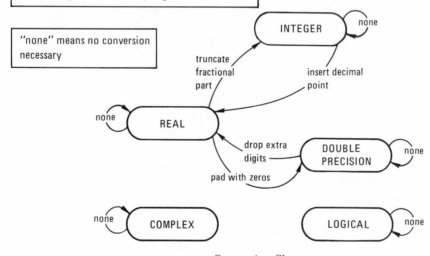

Conversion Chart

Transfer of Control

The default flow of control is sequential, from statement to statement. This flow may be altered by control statements.

GO TO

> ## GO TO s
>
> s is the statement label of an executable statement within the same program unit

```
GO TO 1000
GO TO 7543
```

```
GO TO *-1
GO TO F007     not legal statement labels
GO TO N
```

> ## computed GO TO statement
>
> GO TO $(s_1, s_2, \ldots, s_n)$, v
>
> s_i is a statement label
> v is an unsubscripted INTEGER memory cell name

Control is transferred to the vth statement label in the list.

Each s_i must be the label of an executable statement in the current program unit.

If the value of v is not between 1 and n, the results are unpredictable.

```
GO TO (10,20,20),JAX
GO TO (10,10,20,47,92,10),LOIN
```

```
GO TO (10,10,20,47,92,10),2*LOIN    2*LOIN isn't a simple memory cell name
GO TO (10,20,20) JAX                needs a comma
```

> ## ASSIGN statement
>
> ASSIGN s TO v
>
> s is a statement label
> v is an unsubscripted INTEGER memory cell name

The label s must be the label of an executable statement in the current program unit.

The memory cell v must also be used in an ASSIGNed GO TO statement.

ASSIGNed GO TO statement

GO TO $v, (s_1, s_2, \ldots, s_n)$

v is an unsubscripted INTEGER memory cell name

s_i is a statement label

Each s_i must be the label of an executable statement in the current program unit.

The memory cell v must have been given one of the values s_i by an ASSIGN statement.

```
ASSIGN 20 TO IBIS
ASSIGN 40 TO JAX
GO TO JAX,(10,40,92)
GO TO IBIS,(20,40)
```

```
ASSIGN IBIS=20
ASSIGN 42*3 TO JAX        42*3 isn't a statement label
GO TO JAX(10,40,92)       needs a comma
GO TO IBO(2),(10,10,30)   control variable may not be subscripted
```

---

logical IF statement

If (*logexpr*) *stmt*

logexpr is any LOGICAL valued expression

stmt is any executable statement except a DO or logical IF

The statement *stmt* is performed only when *logexpr* is .TRUE..

Unless *stmt* is performed and alters the flow of control, the next statement performed is the one following the logical IF.

The following construction serves no purpose which couldn't be served by omitting the IF statement.

```
     IF (N .EQ. 10) GO TO 100
100  X=EXP(Y)
```

If you have used such a construction, (i.e., a conditional transfer to the next statement in sequence), change your program to say what you meant.

```
IF  (P) STOP
IF  (NUML .EQ. 10) WRITE(6,1000) A,B,C
IF  (3.14159 .GE. X) GO TO 10
IF  (XRAY .LT. 0.0) XRAY=-XRAY
```

```
IF  P STOP                              needs parentheses
IF  (P) IF (3 .EQ. 4) GO TO 10          IF may not have another as right part
IF  (JJ .LT. 3 .OR. .GT. 1) X=2.        not a legitimate logical expression
IF  (P),STOP                            unwanted comma
```

> The examples assume that all identifiers which begin with
> | C | are COMPLEX |
> | D | are DOUBLE PRECISION |
> | I–N | are INTEGER |
> | P–Q | are LOGICAL |
> | R–Z | are REAL |

---

arithmetic IF statement

IF (*arithexpr*) s_{neg}, s_{zero}, s_{pos}

arithexpr is an arithmetic expression

s_{neg}, s_{zero}, and s_{pos} are statement labels

Control is transferred to one of the statement labels: s_{neg} if *arithexpr* has a negative value, s_{zero} if *arithexpr* has a zero value, and s_{pos} if *arithexpr* has a positive value.

Each of the statement labels must designate an executable statement in the current program unit.

The value of *arithexpr* cannot be COMPLEX.

```
IF  (IBIS-10) 10,10,20
IF  (X*100.-25.*Y) 9,10,11
IF  (2.+XRAY) 1,20,20
```

```
IF  (IBIS .GT. 10) 10,10,20     cross between LOGICAL and arith. IF
IF  X*100.-25.*Y 9,10,11        needs parentheses
IF  (2.+XRAY),1,20,20           extra comma
```

> ## DO statement
>
> DO *s* *v* = *start, bound, increment*
> DO *s* *v* = *start, bound*
>
> *s* is a statement label
> *v*, the DO **index**, is an unsigned INTEGER memory cell name
> *start, bound,* and *increment*, the **DO parameters**, are unsigned
> INTEGER constants or unsubscripted INTEGER memory cell
> names

The **range** of a DO-loop is the statements after the DO statement up to and including statement *s*, the **object** of the DO-loop.

The statements in the range are repeated once for each value of the index *v* in sequence beginning at *v* = *start* and increasing in steps of *increment* as long as *v* doesn't exceed *bound*. Thus the DO statement

```
DO 100 I=3,9,4
```

would cause the statements in its range to be performed twice, first for I = 3, then for I = 7.

If *bound* is smaller than *start*, the statements in the range will be performed once with *v* = *start*. (This degenerate case is not legal in ANSI Fortran.)

It is illegal to transfer from outside the range of a DO-loop to arrive inside the range without passing through the DO statement itself, thus setting the index to the value *start*. This implies that no GO TO or arithmetic IF outside the range of a particular DO-loop may list a destination inside the range. (The one exception to this rule, the extended range construction, is so awkward that we'll not discuss it.) It also implies that DO-loops cannot be partially overlapped as shown below.

```
        DO 100 I=1,10
        DO 200 J=1,10
100        CONTINUE
200        CONTINUE
```

DO-loops may be nested.

If a DO-loop terminates normally (i.e., by performing the object statement with *v* equal to the last value indicated by the DO parameters), then the index *v* no longer has a value.

On the other hand, if a DO-loop terminates by exiting via a GO TO or arithmetic IF before normal termination, then the index *v* still has the last value it took while the DO-loop was being performed.

All of the DO parameters, *start, bound, increment*, must be strictly positive.

Any attempt in the range of a DO-loop to change the value of *v, start, bound,* or *increment* is an error.

If nested DO-loops have the same object statement, any transfer to the object statement is considered to refer to the end of the *innermost* loop, thus such transfers from anywhere except within the range of the innermost loop are illegal.

```
DO 10 KAZ=ICE9,MONOID,3
DO 2700 IK=52,97
DO 999 LAMB=1,100,1
```

```
DO 10 X=ICE9,MONAD(2),3      bound may not be subscripted
DO 2700 I7=52,95+2           95+2 not legal
DO 999 LAMB=100,1,-1         increment may not be negative (or zero)
DO 999,LAMB=1,100,1
```

CONTINUE statement

A CONTINUE statement instructs the controller to proceed in the usual control sequence. It is in the class of executable statements.

> CONTINUE is the purest statement.

CONTINUE statements are often used as objects of DO-loops.

```
        CONTINUE            PROCEED
100     CONTINUE           CONTINUE 100
```

STOP and PAUSE statements

STOP
STOP *n*
PAUSE
PAUSE *n*

n is a string of up to five octal digits (digits between 0 and 7)

STOP terminates execution of your program.

> STOP is the most powerful statement

STOP *n*, on most systems, is equivalent to STOP. On some systems, it causes the indicated value to appear on the operator's console or the printed output.

PAUSE, on most systems, is equivalent to CONTINUE. On some systems, it causes temporary termination of your program, sends the constant (if given) to the operator's console, and resumes execution at the statement after the PAUSE on a signal from the operator.

```
STOP
STOP 10
PAUSE
PAUSE 20
```

```
STOP AT ONCE
STOP 'HAVE A BEER'
STOP 10*2
REFRESH
STOP 1984
```

subprogram control statements

CALL and RETURN are covered under the heading **subprograms**.

END is under the heading **Fortran program**.

I/O Statements

I/O statements are used to bring values into the computer memory (input) or to transmit values from the computer memory. The values brought into the memory by input statements are often read from punched cards, but may be read from other storage devices. Similarly, values transmitted from memory are often written on paper, but may be written on other storage media.

I/O list

· a list of memory cell names and/or implied do lists separated by commas

---

Output statements use I/O lists to designate memory cells whose values are to be written onto an output medium.

Input statements use I/O lists to designate the memory cells in which to store the values obtained from the input device.

Memory cells in an input list are given values in the order in which they occur in the list.

An I/O list may contain *memory cell names* (possibly subscripted), *array names* (implying all the elements in the array are elements in list, ordered from the lowest subscript to the highest), or implied do lists.

```
Z
A,B,K(2,3)
I,((K(L,M),L=1,3),M=1,20,2)
```

```
Z+2           not a memory cell or array name
'INPUT',A     character constant illegal
```

---

implied do list

$(list, i = k_1, k_2)$
$(list, i = k_1, k_2, k_3)$

list is an I/O list
i is an unsubscripted INTEGER memory cell name
k_1, k_2, and k_3 are nonzero unsigned INTEGER constants of
unsubscripted INTEGER memory cell names

Implied do lists may be nested.

The INTEGER memory cell *i* is called the **index** or **control** variable. It takes the **initial value** k_1, then increases to the **upper bound** k_2 by **increments** of k_3 or by increments of 1 if k_3 is omitted. Thus the implied do list has the effect of repeating its *list* part several times ($1 + (k_2 - k_1)/k_3$ times, to be exact) with all occurrences of the control variable *i* replaced by the appropriate value in each repetition of the *list*.

```
(K(J),J=1,3)
(A,2,ICE9=1,13,4)
(A,ICE9,RAMP(ICE9),ICE9=32,N,M)
((LAMBDA(I,J),I=1,10),J=10,100,10)
```

```
((LAMB(ICH),ICH,ICH=1,10),(SHEEP(ICK),ICK,ICK=1,10),L=1,2)
```

```
(K(X),X=1,20)              X is not an INTEGER
(A,2,ICE9=1,10+N,4)        10+N illegal
((LAMBDA(I,J),I=1,10)J=10,100,10)   needs a comma
```

The examples assume that all identifiers which begin with

C	are COMPLEX
D	are DOUBLE PRECISION
I–N	are INTEGER
P–Q	are LOGICAL
R–Z	are REAL

PRINT/WRITE statement

PRINT *f, list*

PRINT *f*

WRITE(*unit, f*) *list*

WRITE(*unit, f*)

list is an output list

f is a FORMAT statement label or an array containing the (*spec*) part of a FORMAT statement represented by character values

unit is an unsigned INTEGER constant or unsubscripted IN-TEGER memory cell

Transmits values to paper output or other output medium (designated by *unit*) such as punched cards, magnetic tape, etc.

PRINT transmits values to the line printer.

unit = 6 normally designates the line printer
unit = 7 normally designates the card punch (check with local experts)

The line printer always uses the first transmitted character on a line as the carriage control. The carriage control character is not printed.

carriage controls

blank	single space
0 (zero)	double space
1	eject (print at top of next page)
+	overprint previous line

The *list* is the driving force. All values in *list* are sent to the output device.

If *list* is omitted, the characters sent to the output device are the literal descriptors and spacing descriptors in *f* which precede the first data descriptor in *f*.

```
PRINT 1000
PRINT 3000, (Y(I),(Z(I,J), J=1,N), I=1,M)
PRINT AFMT, B,Z(4,3)

WRITE(6,1000) A
WRITE(7,ASKFMT) (M(I),I=1,N)
WRITE(6,4621)
WRITE(M,2030) X
```

```
PRINT,1000, A          extra comma
WRITE(6,2000) (3-X)*2  I/O list may not include expression
WRITE(X,1000) Y(3)     X must be INTEGER
```

ANSI Fortran MiniManual   403

Transfers values from data cards or other input medium (*unit*) to memory.

The card reader is the implied input device for the READ *f, list* and READ *f* forms.

unit = 5 is normally the card reader (check with local experts).

The FORMAT *f* describes the layout of the input records.

If *list* is omitted, one data card (record) is skipped (on the input *unit*).

Character values may be stored in a memory cell of any data type.

The *list* is the driving force; all memory cells in *list* will be given values. The system issues an error message if the input *unit* runs out of records before the *list* is completed.

```
READ 1000, A
READ 2000, (Y(K), K=1,N)
READ AFMT, A,M,X
READ(5,1000) A
READ(5,AFMT) A,M,X
READ(NT,2010) B, (Y(K),K=L,LU,3)
```

```
READ(5,9999) X+Y          X + Y is not a memory cell
READ(5,9898),A,B,C        extra comma
READ(X,1000) A,B,C        X is not an INTEGER
READ,1000, A              too many commas
READ 1000 A               not enough commas
READ(9) N, (A(I), I=1,N)
READ(ILP) BIGARA
READ(17)
```

The examples assume that all identifiers which begin with

C   are COMPLEX
D   are DOUBLE PRECISION
I–N   are INTEGER
P–Q   are LOGICAL
R–Z   are REAL

---

unformatted READ statement

READ(*u*) *list*

u, the unit number, is an INTEGER constant or unsigned INTEGER memory cell name

list is an input list which may be omitted

If *list* is omitted, one record is skipped.

If *list* doesn't exhaust a full record, the rest of the record is skipped.

```
READ(9) N,(A(I),I=1,N)
READ (ILP)BIGARA
READ(17)
```

```
READ(4*I)A      unit can't be an expression
READ (X) A      unit must be of type INTEGER
```

---

unformatted WRITE

WRITE(*u*)*list*

u and *list* are as in the unformatted READ

An **unformatted record** is what is written by a single unformatted WRITE statement.

```
WRITE(11) N,(P(I),I=1,N)
WRITE(ILP) X,GIGARA
```

```
WRITE(6) N,(A(I),I=1,N)      the line printer can deal with
                             character output only
```

I/O device positioning

> REWIND *unit*
> BACKSPACE *unit*
> ENDFILE *unit*
>
> *unit* is an unsigned INTEGER constant or unsubscripted INTEGER memory cell

REWIND positions the I/O head of *unit* at the point where data begins or may begin.

BACKSPACE positions the I/O head at the beginning of the record immediately preceding the present record, or at the beginning of the data if the current record is the first record.

ENDFILE places an end-of-file mark on *unit* at the current position of the I/O head.

```
REWIND 9
REWIND NT
BACKSPACE JP
ENDFILE 17
```

```
REWIND(9)
BACKSPACE,3
```
no parentheses allowed
no comma allowed

FORMATs

See Section 4 10 for further details.

A FORMAT describes an I/O record or records.

> ### FORMAT statement
>
> FORMAT (*spec*)
>
> *spec* is a list of FORMAT descriptors (i.e., data descriptors, literal descriptors, spacing descriptors, slashes, or groups of these) separated by commas. Slashes serve as delimiters, so commas should be omitted around slashes. Every FORMAT must have a statement label.

A FORMAT statement must always be labeled.

The (*spec*) part of a FORMAT may be stored in an array as a series of Hollerith values. This array may then be used as a **variable FORMAT** in an I/O statement.

```
10    FORMAT('1')
1505  FORMAT(I3,A5,2G11.2/A10)
2307  FORMAT(' ',2('NO.',I3,' IS NOT',L2/))
```

```
      FORMAT('1')              needs statement label
1505  FORMAT(3*I2)             *not legal
2307  FORMAT(' ',2(2I123PF7.0))  ambiguous, needs comma
```

data descriptors

> **G**$w.d$ REAL field of width w; d significant digits for REAL output

G11.4
G20.7
G28.16

G3.7 d must be smaller than w
GW.D w and d can't be variables

> **I**w INTEGER field of width w

I10
I3
I22

IK w must be a constant
I+2   no sign allowed
I3.2 no decimal point allowed

> **F**$w.d$ REAL field of width w; d decimal places on output

F10.0
F8.1
F30.16

F3.7 d must be smaller than w
FN.K w and d must be constants

E*w.d* REAL field of width *w*; scientific notation with *d* fractional digits on output

E15.7
E12.3

E10.7   *w – d* must be at least 7

D*w.d* DOUBLE PRECISION field of width *w*; scientific notation with *d* fractional digits on output

D15.7
D23.16

D20.16   *w – d* must be at least 7

For COMPLEX *values, use two* REAL *data descriptors.*

L*w* LOGICAL field of width *w*

L9
L1
L22

L9.1
L3**2   *w* can't involve computation

A*w* character field of width *w*

A10
A1
A22

AN   *w* must be constant
A12.0

sP scale factor; shifts decimal point in subsequent REAL or DOUBLE PRECISION fields; *s* may be negative

```
1000 FORMAT(3PE12.2,F10.4,D24.16,-2PF9.1,I2,D9.0)
```

affected by 3P   affected by –2P

Literal descriptors are simply character (Hollerith) constants used in FORMATs.
(See MiniManual **Constants** section.)

On output, the *n* characters in the literal descriptor are transmitted directly to the
output record. On input, the *n* characters in the corresponding field in the input
record replace the characters in the literal descriptor.

What!?!
Yes! The FORMAT *itself is altered when the* READ *transmits*
characters to the literal descriptor.

LEGAL

`◆ARCHETYPAL SYSTEMS INC.◆`
`23HARCHETYPAL SYSTEMS INC.`

`1H◆`

ILLEGAL

`22HARCHETYPAL SYSTEMS INC.`
`            SYSTEM`

carriage control characters

' ' or 1H (blank)	move down the page one line before printing	single space
'0' or 1H0 (zero)	move down the page two lines before printing	double space
'1' or 1H1 (one)	move to the top of the next page before printing	eject page
'+' or 1H+ (plus)	don't move paper	overprint

spacing descriptor

*n*X   skip the next *n* characters in the I/O record

LEGAL

ILLEGAL

3X	−10X	no sign allowed
10X	3.1X	can't skip a fractional number of characters
29X	X10	number goes before X

repeat specifications, groups, and record separators

A **repeat specification** is an unsigned INTEGER constant n which is placed immediately to the left of a data descriptor or a group of FORMAT descriptors. Its effect is the same as that of writing the data descriptor or group n times (separated by the appropriate commas, of course).

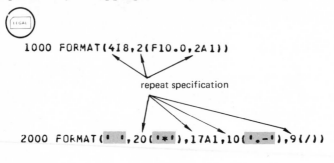

```
1000 FORMAT(4I8,2(F10.0,2A1))
```

repeat specification

```
2000 FORMAT(' ',20('*'),17A1,10('.-'),9(/))
```

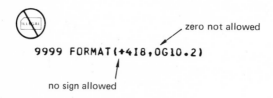

zero not allowed

```
9999 FORMAT(+4I8,0G10.2)
```

no sign allowed

A format descriptor **group** is a parenthesized list of FORMAT descriptors. Groups may be nested to a depth of two in the *spec* list in a FORMAT statement.

When there are more I/O list elements than data descriptors in the FORMAT, the FORMAT scan is repeated, starting from its **rightmost group**, including the group's repeat specification if it has one. In other words, the repeat scan starts at the repeat specification preceding the left parenthesis which matches the next to last right parenthesis in the FORMAT. If there are no groups in the FORMAT, the repeat scan starts at the beginning of the FORMAT.

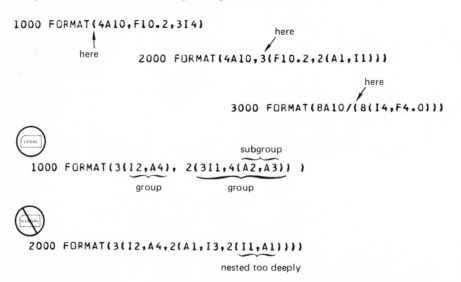

```
1000 FORMAT(4A10,F10.2,3I4)
```
here

```
2000 FORMAT(4A10,3(F10.2,2(A1,I1)))
```
here

```
3000 FORMAT(8A10/(8(I4,F4.0)))
```
here

subgroup

```
1000 FORMAT(3(I2,A4), 2(3I1,4(A2,A3)) )
```
group   group

```
2000 FORMAT(3(I2,A4,2(A1,I3,2(I1,A1))))
```
nested too deeply

A **slash** (/) is used in a FORMAT to separate one record description from another. It must be used whenever a FORMAT describes more than one I/O record (e.g., more than one output line or more than one data card).

```
1000 FORMAT(8A10/3I4)   This FORMAT describes two data cards
```

```
2000 FORMAT('1',A50/'0',10G11.4/)
```
This FORMAT describes three output lines. Each one contains a carriage control character. The last line is totally blank.

Subprograms

See definitions under the heading **Fortran program**.

SUBROUTINEs

SUBROUTINE statement

SUBROUTINE *name* $(p_1, p_2, \ldots, p_n)$
SUBROUTINE *name*

name, the name of the SUBROUTINE, is an identifier
p_k, a parameter, is an identifier

The body of a SUBROUTINE (the statements between the SUBROUTINE statement and the END statement) must contain at least one RETURN.

A SUBROUTINE, unlike a FUNCTION, has no *type*.

```
SUBROUTINE DIV(I,J)
SUBROUTINE PRN
```

```
SUBROUTINE S(A(3))      illegal parameter
SUBROUTINE RT(X(K))     illegal parameter
SUBROUTINE (X,Y,Z)      no name
SUBROUTINE X(1.3,T)     illegal parameter
```

```
CALL DIV(3,N)
CALL PRN
CALL ST(Y**2,3HCAT)
CALL SRT(A,N)
```

```
CALL DIV(3 N)      needs comma to separate arguments
CALL PRN( )        if PRN takes no arguments, leave off parentheses
CULL SRT(A,N)      misspelling
```

CALLing Sequence

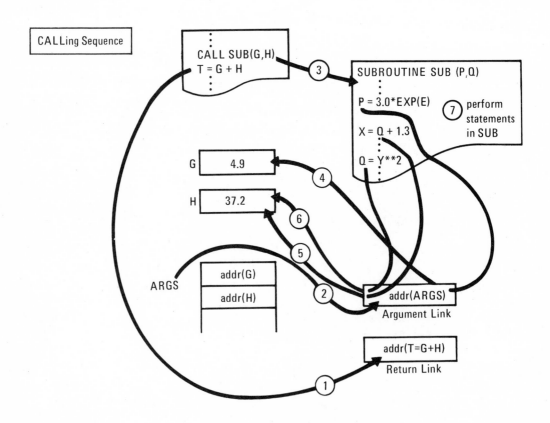

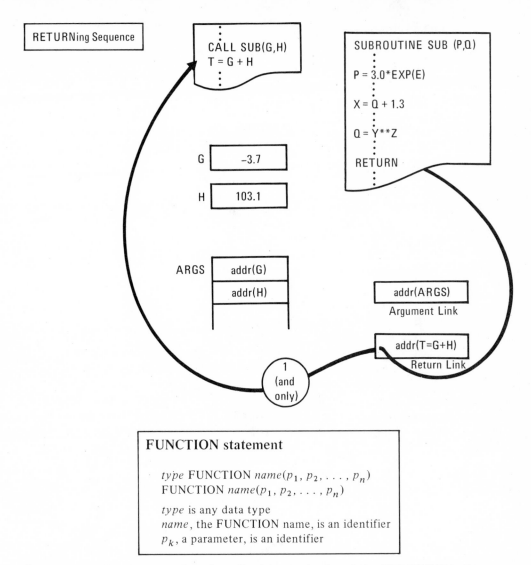

```
CALL SUB(G,H)
T = G + H
```

```
SUBROUTINE SUB (P,Q)

P = 3.0*EXP(E)

X = Q + 1.3

Q = Y**Z

RETURN
```

| G | –3.7 |
| H | 103.1 |

| ARGS | addr(G) |
| | addr(H) |

| addr(ARGS) |
| Argument Link |

| addr(T=G+H) |
| Return Link |

1 (and only)

FUNCTION statement

type FUNCTION *name*$(p_1, p_2, \ldots, p_n)$
FUNCTION *name*$(p_1, p_2, \ldots, p_n)$

type is any data type
name, the FUNCTION name, is an identifier
p_k, a parameter, is an identifier

Throughout the computation described in the body of the FUNCTION, the *name* of the FUNCTION is used like a memory cell name, the value of the FUNCTION is the value of its *name* when a RETURN statement in the body of the FUNC-TION is performed. There must be at least one RETURN in a FUNCTION.

```
INTEGER FUNCTION NXT(X,Y)
LOGICAL FUNCTION PER(AS,BE,CEE)
REAL FUNCTION XTM(Z,I)
COMPLEX FUNCTION CDV(C1,C2)
FUNCTION D(X,Y,Z)
```

```
REAL FUNCTION RND      a FUNCTION must have at least one parameter
REAL FUNCTION RND()    a FUNCTION must have at least one parameter
FUNCTION Z(3)          illegal parameter
```

FUNCTION reference

See listing under the heading **Fortran program**.

RETURN statement

RETURN

A RETURN statement returns control to the place where the subprogram was called.

A SUBROUTINE or FUNCTION may have several RETURN statements and *must* have at least one.

---

statement function definition

$f(p_1, p_2, \ldots, p_n) = expr$

f, the function name, is an identifier
p_i, a parameter name, is an identifier
expr, the function's value, is an expression whose data type may be converted to the type of the identifier f

---

The type of f must be established prior to the statement function definition and must be assignment compatible with *expr*. All statement function definitions must appear before any executable statement in the program unit.

Statement functions are local to the program unit where they are defined, hence they cannot be referenced in other program units and cannot be listed in EXTERNAL statements.

When you forget to declare an array, the compiler sometimes mistakes assignments to array elements for statement function definitions since they have the same form.

The *expr* part of a statement function definition may refer to *previously defined* statement functions only (see FUNCTION references under the heading **Fortran program**).

References to statement functions are made in the same way as references to external FUNCTIONs.

Parameters in statement functions may not be placeholders for subprograms or array names. Thus, F(X,G) = G(X) is not a legal statement function definition.

```
POS(X) = X .GT. 0.0
P(Q1,Q2) = (Q1 .AND. Q2) .OR. .NOT. P1
TRUNC(X) = FLOAT(INT(X))
IN(X,Y,Z) = AMAX1(X,Y,-Z,U,1.0)
HI(ISCUS) = 2**ISCUS
CROTAT(C) = C*(0.0,1.0)
STDG(X)=EXP(-0.5*X**2)/SQRT(ATAN(1.0)*4.0)
G(X,U,S)=STDG((X-U)/S)/S
```

```
P(4,7) = .TRUE.        illegal parameter
P(Q1,Q2) = 3.9         illegal type conversion
```

BLOCK DATA subprogram

    BLOCK DATA

    ↑ *declarations of memory cells, arrays, and* COMMON *areas;*
    ↑ EQUIVALENCE *statements*
    ↑ DATA statements
    END

BLOCK DATA subprograms are used for compile-time initialization of memory cells in COMMON regions.

All compile-time initializations of memory cells in COMMON regions must be done in BLOCK DATA subprograms.

Blank COMMON may not be initialized at compile time.

```
BLOCK DATA                          BLOCK DATA
REAL YES                            REAL YES
LOGICAL PRAPS                       LOGICAL PRAPS
COMMON /SETUP/ YES, PRAPS          COMMON /SETUP/ YES, PRAPS
DATA PRAPS/.TRUE./                  PRAPS=.TRUE.           no executable
END                                 END                    statements
                                                           allowed
```

Built-in FUNCTIONs

Built-in FUNCTIONs are FUNCTIONs that the ANSI standards require that every version of Fortran provide. To use them in your program you need merely write their name followed by appropriate arguments. Your local version of Fortran may well provide additional ones. Check your local manual to find out.

In the following table, the first column is a formal FUNCTION reference using the letters *i, r, d,* and *c* in place of the arguments to stand for the type of value that the actual argument should be. The letters *i, r, d,* and *c* stand for the data types INTEGER, REAL, DOUBLE PRECISION, and COMPLEX respectively. The second column describes the computation that the FUNCTION performs. The third column states the data type of the resulting FUNCTION-value. The fourth column says whether the FUNCTION is intrinsic or external (this is explained on page 418).

A few of the built-in FUNCTIONs allow *two or more* arguments. That is, one reference to the FUNCTION may have two arguments, and another five arguments. In those cases, we write the formal FUNCTION reference with dots in the argument list; e.g., MAX0 $(i_1, i_2, \ldots, i_n)$ to indicate that a variable number of arguments is allowed.

FUNCTION reference	value computed	type of value	external (E) or intrinsic (I)
ABS(r)	absolute value of r	REAL	I
IABS(i)	absolute value of i	INTEGER	I
DABS(d)	absolute value of d	DOUBLE	I
CABS(c)	modulus of c	REAL	E
CMPLX(r_1,r_2)	$r_1 + r_2\sqrt{-1}$	COMPLEX	I
REAL(c)	real part of c	REAL	I
AIMAG(c)	imaginary part of c	REAL	I
CONJG(c)	CMPLX(REAL(c), –AIMAG(c))	COMPLEX	I
DBLE(r)	DOUBLE PRECISION version of r	DOUBLE	I
SNGL(d)	REAL version of d	REAL	I
EXP(r)	e^r ⎧ e is the base	REAL	E
DEXP(d)	e^d ⎨ of natural	DOUBLE	E
CEXP(c)	e^c ⎩ logarithms	COMPLEX	E

FUNCTION reference	value computed	type of value	external (E) or intrinsic (I)
FLOAT(i)	REAL version of i	REAL	I
INT(r)	$\{$ INTEGER version of r with $\}$	INTEGER	I
IFIX(r)	$\{$ fractional part truncated $\}$	INTEGER	I
AINT(r)	FLOAT (INT(r))	REAL	I
IDINT(d)	INTEGER version of d	INTEGER	I
ALOG(r)	natural logarithm of r	REAL	E
DLOG(d)	natural logarithm of d	DOUBLE	E
CLOG(c)	principle value of log(c)	COMPLEX	E
ALOG10(r)	base 10 logarithm of r	REAL	E
DLOG10(d)	base 10 logarithm of d	DOUBLE	E
MAX0($i_1, \ldots, i_n$)	largest of the arguments	INTEGER	I
AMAX1($r_1, \ldots, r_n$)	largest of the arguments	REAL	I
DMAX1($d_1, \ldots, d_n$)	largest of the arguments	DOUBLE	I
MAX1($r_1, \ldots, r_n$)	INT(AMAX1($r_1, \ldots, r_n$))	INTEGER	I
AMAX0($i_1, \ldots, i_n$)	FLOAT(MAX0($i_1, \ldots, i_n$))	REAL	I
MIN0($i_1, \ldots, i_n$)	smallest of the arguments	INTEGER	I
AMIN1($r_1, \ldots, r_n$)	smallest of the arguments	REAL	I
DMIN1($d_1, \ldots, d_n$)	smallest of the arguments	DOUBLE	I
MIN1($r_1, \ldots, r_n$)	INT (AMIN1($r_1, \ldots, r_n$))	INTEGER	I
AMIN0($i_1, \ldots, i_n$)	FLOAT (MIN0 ($i_1, \ldots, i_n$))	REAL	I
DIM(r_1, r_2)	$r_1 -$ AMIN1(r_1, r_2)	REAL	I
IDIM(i_1, i_2)	$i_1 -$ MIN0 (i_1, i_2)	INTEGER	I
MOD(i_1, i_2)	$i_1 - (i_1/i_2)*i_2$ (remainder)	INTEGER	I
AMOD(r_1, r_2)	$r_1 -$ AINT(r_1/r_2)$*r_2$	REAL	I
DMOD(d_1, d_2)	$d_1 -$ FLOAT(IDINT(d_1/d_2))$*d_2$	DOUBLE	E
SIGN(r_1, r_2)	sign of r_2 times ABS(r_1)	REAL	I
ISIGN(i_1, i_2)	sign of i_2 times IABS(i_1)	INTEGER	I
DSIGN(d_1, d_2)	sign of d_2 times DABS(d_1)	DOUBLE	I
SIN(r)	trigonometric sine of r radians	REAL	E
DSIN(d)	trigonometric sine of d radians	DOUBLE	E
CSIN(c)	sine of c	COMPLEX	E

FUNCTION reference	value computed	type of value	external (E) or intrinsic (I)
COS(r)	trigonometric cosine of r radians	REAL	E
DCOS(d)	trigonometric cosine of d radians	DOUBLE	E
CCOS(c)	cosine of c	COMPLEX	E
TANH(r)	hyperbolic tangent of r	REAL	E
ATAN(r)	angle $(-\pi/2$ to $\pi/2)$ whose tangent is r	REAL	E
DATAN(d)	angle $(-\pi/2$ to $\pi/2)$ whose tangent is d	DOUBLE	E
ATAN2(r_1, r_2)	arctan(r_1/r_2) in the quadrant of the vector(r_1, r_2)	REAL	E
DATAN2(d_1, d_2)	arctan(d_1/d_2) in quadrant of (d_1, d_2)	DOUBLE	E
SQRT(r)	square root of r	REAL	E
DSQRT(d)	square root of d	DOUBLE	E
CSQRT(c)	square root of c	COMPLEX	E

Built-in FUNCTIONs are divided into two classes, external and intrinsic. Normally, you don't need to worry about the difference since a FUNCTION reference looks the same for an external FUNCTION as it does for an intrinsic FUNCTION. However, you can run into problems if you want to give FUNCTIONs you define names identical to intrinsic FUNCTION names. In this case you will have to declare the FUNCTIONs to be EXTERNAL in the program units which reference them.

some other helpful FUNCTIONs

If you see one you need, copy it whole since these are *not* part of the ANSI
standard library.

```
      INTEGER FUNCTION ROOF(ARG)
      REAL ARG
COMMENT: "ROOF" RETURNS THE SMALLEST INTEGER WHICH IS NOT
C     LESS THAN ARG (ROUND UP).
      ROOF=INT(ARG)
      IF (ARG .LE. 0.0) RETURN
      IF (ARG .EQ. FLOAT(INT(ARG))) RETURN
      ROOF=ROOF+1
      RETURN
      END

      INTEGER FUNCTION FLOOR(ARG)
      REAL ARG
COMMENT: "FLOOR" RETURNS THE LARGEST INTEGER WHICH IS NOT
C     GREATER THAN ARG (ROUND DOWN)
      FLOOR=INT(ARG)
      IF (ARG .GE. 0.0) RETURN
      IF (ARG .EQ. FLOAT(INT(ARG))) RETURN
      FLOOR=FLOOR-1
      RETURN
      END

      INTEGER FUNCTION ROUND(ARG)
      REAL ARG
      REAL SIGN
COMMENT: CLASSICAL ROUNDING
      ROUND=INT(ARG+SIGN(.5,ARG))
      RETURN
      END

      REAL FUNCTION POS(ARG)
      REAL ARG
      REAL DIM
COMMENT: IF ARG .GE. 0 THEN ARG, ELSE 0.
      POS=DIM(ARG,0.0)
      RETURN
      END

      REAL FUNCTION SGN(ARG)
      REAL ARG
COMMENT: +1,0, OR -1 ACCORDING TO WHETHER "ARG" IS
C     .GT., .EQ., OR .LT. ZERO.
      SGN=+1.
      IF (ARG .GT. 0.) RETURN
      SGN=-1.
      IF (ARG .LT. 0.) RETURN
      SGN=0.
      RETURN
      END
```

D Answers to Exercises

ANSWERS TO EXERCISES 1 3

1 Making "Pineapple Sliders"—Verbal Description

Sift together
   1 cup all purpose flour
   1 tsp. baking powder
   1/4 tsp. salt

In a separate bowl mix together (with wire whip)
   2 eggs
   1/2 cup granulated sugar
   1/2 cup brown sugar

Add
   1 tsp. vanilla
   1/2 cup chopped walnuts
   1 8 oz. can, crushed, unsweetened pineapple (drained)

Slowly add the flour mixture and blend thoroughly.
Bake in a slightly greased 8" square aluminum pan for 30 minutes at 350°.
Cool on rack for 5 minutes and cut into bars.
Roll in confectioner's sugar while warm.

"Pineapple Sliders" courtesy of C. M. Drotos.

Thanks to everybody who wrote in telling us how much they liked pineapple sliders.

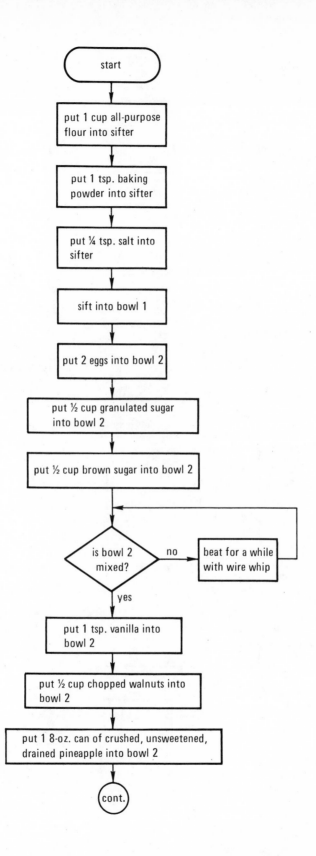

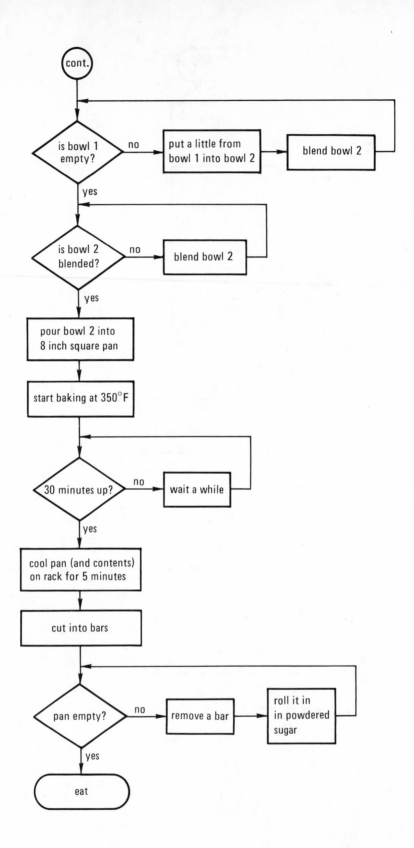

ANSWERS TO EXERCISES 1 4

3 controller: executes statements of program

memory: cells in which instructions and data are stored

I/O: provides for communication between human and computer

4 The memory cell is a device which stores information; its name allows us to locate it for purposes of examining or changing its contents; its value is what's in it at a given point in time.

ANSWERS TO EXERCISES 1 5

1 Add the following statement between STATEMENT 1 and STATEMENT 2

STATEMENT 1.5 Look at the value in memory cell B. If it is less than zero, stop.

2 We will need several memory cells: SUM to store the running total of the numbers, N to keep track of the number of numbers, NUM to store the numbers, one at a time, and ST1, ST2, . . . , ST9 in which to store the statements.

card number	memory cell which stores this statement	statement
1	ST1	Store 0 in SUM
2	ST2	Store 0 in N
3	ST3	Remove top card from the card reader stack; copy the number on it into NUM. Discard the card. (If there were no cards, get next instruction from ST7.)
4	ST4	Look at the values in NUM and SUM, add them together, and store the result in SUM.
5	ST5	Look at the value in N, add 1 and store the result in N.
6	ST6	Get your next instruction from ST3.
7	ST7	Look at the values in SUM and N, divide the former by the latter, and store the result in SUM.
8	ST8	Send the string "AVERAGE IS", followed by the number in SUM to the printer.
9	ST9	Stop.
10	none	Comment: End of program. Now comes the data.
11	none	14
12	none	17
13	none	3
14	none	-4
15	none	8

3 We will need several memory cells: LONGEST to store the longest name seen, NAME to store the names on the cards, one at a time, and ST1, ST2, ..., ST6 to store the statements of the program.

card number	memory cell which stores the statement	statement
1	ST1	Remove the top card from the card reader stack and copy the character string on it into LONGEST. Discard the card.
2	ST2	Remove the top card from the card reader stack and copy the value on it into NAME. Discard the card. (If there were no cards on the card reader stack, get your next instruction from ST5.)
3	ST3	Look at the strings in LONGEST and NAME and copy the longer one into LONGEST.
4	ST4	Get your next instruction from ST2.
5	ST5	Send the string "THE LONGEST NAME IS", followed by the value of LONGEST, to the printer.
6	ST6	Stop
7	none	Comment: End of program. Now comes the data.
8	none	J E Birk
9	none	D E Farmer
10	none	P Das
11	none	P G McCrea
12	none	C C Cheung
13	none	D L Milgram

ANSWERS TO EXERCISES 2 1

1 23SKIDOO is illegal because it starts with a digit.
SKIDOO23, FLIMFLAM, TONY THE TIGER and FORTRAN are illegal because they have more than six characters.
SALE3, TORQUE and JUICE are legal memory cell names.

2 INTEGER VERYLONG is illegal because the memory cell name is too long.
INTERGER Q is illegal because INTEGER is misspelled.
REAL A, 149.2 is illegal because 149.2 is not a memory cell name.

3 `INTEGER AJAX,FOAM`

4 The REALs are 41.7, 692.0, and −896.721.

ANSWERS TO EXERCISES 2 2

1 A and B are 10 and 2, respectively.

2 Memory cell B takes on the values 24, 3, and −38 at successive points in time (B contains only one of the values at a time, of course).

3 −AT = 2 and CAT + DOG = FIGHT are illegal because their left hand sides are expressions rather than memory cell names. CAT + DOG − 3, of course, is hopelessly illegal since it doesn't even have an assignment operator.

4 SOUP contains, at successive points in time, the values 15, 61, 1, 2, and 0.

5
```
INTEGER FIRST
FIRST = 2
FIRST = FIRST*4
FIRST = FIRST + 1
```

ANSWERS TO EXERCISES 2 3

1 The second is illegal because it contains expressions and constants instead of just memory cell names. The third one is illegal because it has no unit number or FORMAT number. The last one is illegal because it has a comma immediately after the parenthesis.

2 70.40*bb*12

ANSWERS TO EXERCISES 2 4

1 *data*

$$1.25$$
$$4.27$$
$$27.92$$
$$132.00$$
$$9.42$$
$$-237.26$$
$$0.0$$

output

NEW BALANCE IS*b*$*bb*64.90

2 READ(5,3000) A+B,2 is illegal because A+B and 2 are values, not memory cell names.

WRITE(6,4000),A is illegal because the comma before the A is improper.

```
3          INTEGER A,B,C,D,S
           READ(5,1000) A,B,C,D
   1000 FORMAT(I3,I3,I3,I3)
           S=A+B+C+D
           WRITE(6,2000) S
    200 FORMAT(' ',I4)
           STOP
           END
```

data
```
    10 15   7 10
```

output
```
    42
```

ANSWERS TO EXERCISES 3·2

1   It corresponds to a statement label.

2   The first two statements are OK.

The third statement contains the illegal relation .EG.

The fourth statement contains the illegal relation .SGT.

The last statement lacks parentheses and has an illegal comma. It should look like this

```
    IF (Y .EQ. 0) GO TO 20
```

```
3          REAL BALNCE, TRANS
           READ(5,1000)BALNCE
   1000 FORMAT(F7.0)
     20 READ(5,1000) TRANS
           IF (TRANS .EQ. 0) GO TO 30
           BALNCE=BALNCE-TRANS
           GO TO 20
     30 WRITE(6,2000) BALNCE
   2000 FORMAT(' ',F7.2)
           STOP
           END
```

data
```
    456.03
    78.36
    -25.39
    45.22
    -75.42
    0.0
```

output
```
    433.26
```

ANSWERS TO EXERCISES 3 3

1 IF (PRICE .GT. 999.0) GO TO 20

Note: It is not wise to test for exact equality of REALs because they are represented to limited precision.

2
```
      INTEGER FIVES
      FIVES=0
10    FIVES=FIVES+5
      WRITE(6,1000) FIVES
1000    FORMAT(I15)
      IF (FIVES .LT. 100) GO TO 10
      STOP
      END
```

output
```
        5
       10
       15
       20
       25
       30
       35
       40
       45
       50
       55
       60
       65
       70
       75
       80
       85
       90
       95
      100
```

3 Change the loop as shown below.

```
      .
      .
      .
      N=0.0
      SUM=0.00
      READ(5,1000) PRICE,WGT
10    SUM = SUM + PRICE/WGT
      N = N + 1.0
      READ(5,1000) PRICE,WGT
      IF (PRICE .GT. 0.00) GO TO 10
      .
      .
      .
```

ANSWERS TO EXERCISES 3 4

1 The inner loop in the knitting algorithm is "1st row: K2, P2, repeat from
* across"; the inner loop in the bank balance program is the one which
READs the old balance and transactions. The outer loop in the knitting
algorithm is the repetition of the first row until 60 inches; the outer loop
in the bank balance program is the one which begins by READing the
social security number and ends by printing the new balance.

2
```
      INTEGER SOCSEC
      REAL BALNCE,TRANS
100   READ(5,1000) SOCSEC
1000  FORMAT(I9)
      IF (SOCSEC .LT. 0) STOP
      WRITE(6,1010) SOCSEC
1010  FORMAT('0SOCIAL SECURITY NUMBER: ',I10)
      READ(5,1020) BALNCE
1020  FORMAT(F20.0)
      WRITE(6,1030) BALNCE
1030  FORMAT('    $',F7.2,' PREVIOUS BALANCE')
      WRITE(6,1040)
1040  FORMAT(' TRANSACTIONS')
200   READ(5,1020) TRANS
      IF (TRANS .EQ. 0.0)  GO TO 300
      BALNCE = BALNCE - TRANS
      IF (TRANS .GT. 0.0)  GO TO 210
       TRANS = -TRANS
       WRITE(6,2001) TRANS
2001     FORMAT('    $', F7.2, ' DEPOSIT')
       GO TO 200
210      WRITE(6,2010) TRANS
2010     FORMAT('    $', F7.2, ' CHECK')
       GO TO 200
300   WRITE(6,3000) BALNCE
3000  FORMAT(10X,'NEW BALANCE:    $', F7.2)
      GO TO 100
      END
```

data
```
276407566
456.32
 22.98
 33.54
-291.55
 54.39
 0.0
175504244
332.53
 22.03
-329.41
 22.11
  0.0
      -1
```

```
output
    SOCIAL SECURITY NUMBER:   276407566
      $ 456.32 PREVIOUS BALANCE
    TRANSACTIONS
      $   22.98 CHECK
      $   33.54 CHECK
      $ 291.55 DEPOSIT
      $   54.39 CHECK
              NEW BALANCE:     $ 636.96

    SOCIAL SECURITY NUMBER:   175504244
      $ 332.53 PREVIOUS BALANCE
    TRANSACTIONS
      $   22.03 CHECK
      $ 329.41 DEPOSIT
      $   22.11 CHECK
              NEW BALANCE:     $ 617.80
```

ANSWERS TO EXERCISES 4 2

1 $12 + 2$ and $4 * 2$ are INTEGER expressions; the term constant is restricted to values involving no computations and no memory cells.

12.75, 1.0, −127.5, are REAL constants. The others are INTEGER constants.

2 2 and +2 are INTEGER constants

−2.01E3.2 and 300E30. contain illegal decimal point shift factors

The others are legitimate REAL constants.

ANSWERS TO EXERCISES 4 3

1 The expression is evaluated like $0 - 1**4$. Exponentiations are performed before subtractions; hence, the result is −1.

2
```
MOUSE + (CAT*(DOG**2))
((SEX+DRUGS)-(SKIN*FLICK))+(BUSTER**(BROWN**SHOES))
(ROCK/ER)/FELLOW
```

3 Negative values can't be raised to REAL powers

4 2.0, 2.0, 0.0, 4.0, 4.0

5 AB is a single identifier in Fortran.

ANSWERS TO EXERCISES 4 4

1 2.0
   −2
   3
   1.0
   3.0
   1.0001

2 No, since

$$\text{tangent}\,(\alpha) = \frac{\text{sine}\,(\alpha)}{\text{cosine}\,(\alpha)}$$

and both SIN and COS are provided.

ANSWERS TO EXERCISES 4 5

1 ```
INTEGER NICKS,CENTS
NICKS=CENTS/5
```

2      4.175    goes into    BAR4
         3.2      goes into    BAR3
       0.96     goes into    BAR0
    −2.98    goes into    no BAR, but terminates loop
    496.1     goes into    no BAR, but evokes an error message

    What bar do you go into?

## ANSWERS TO EXERCISES 4 7

1   a   (2.8, −7.4)

   b   (−1.0, 0.0)

   c   the COMPLEX number whose real part is the value contained in A and whose imaginary part is the value of B

   d   the complex conjugate of ZETA

2   No

3   a   true

   b   false

   c   false

   d   false (roundoff errors sometimes could cause a small difference.)

4   a   true

   b   heaven's no!

   c   true

   d   false

## ANSWERS TO EXERCISES 4 8

1  ```
.TRUE.
.TRUE.
.FALSE.
.TRUE.
.FALSE.
.TRUE.
```

2 ```
      IF (X.GT. 0 .AND. X .LT. 10) STOP
   30 ...
```

3  ```
      IF (X .GT. 10 .OR. X .LT. 0) STOP
   30 ...
```

4   (A .AND. .NOT. B) .OR. (B .AND. .NOT. A)

5   Statements 10, 11, 12, and 13 should read

```
10    EXPOFF=.TRUE.
11    EXPDEF=.FALSE.
12    YNGOFF=.TRUE.
13    YNGDEF=.TRUE.
```

ANSWERS TO EXERCISES 4 9

1   We would have to alter the DATA statement so that NAMES1 is initialized to 4HJONE and so that NAMES2 is initialized to 1HS. Also, it would be only fair to change FORMAT 2000 so it says JONES instead of SMITH.

2
```
      INTEGER COL1,COL2,COL3,COL4,COL5,DOLLAR
      DATA DOLLAR/1HS/
      READ(5,1000) COL1,COL2,COL3,COL4,COL5
1000  FORMAT(5A1)
      IF (COL1 .EQ. DOLLAR) GO TO 100
      IF (COL2 .EQ. DOLLAR) GO TO 100
      IF (COL3 .EQ. DOLLAR) GO TO 100
      IF (COL4 .EQ. DOLLAR) GO TO 100
      IF (COL5 .EQ. DOLLAR) GO TO 100
      WRITE(6,2000)
2000  FORMAT(' NOPE')
      STOP
100   WRITE(6,3000)
3000  FORMAT(' YES, THERE WAS A $ SIGN')
      STOP
      END
```

data
```
48.23
```

output
```
NOPE
```

3   Yes. (It's true that there is *no* Exercise 3 in Section 4 9, but we thought that since there are a few exercises we don't give answers for, it's only fair we give a few answers we don't have exercises for.)

ANSWERS TO EXERCISES 4 10

1   a   REAL, F5.3 or INTEGER, I3
    b   INTEGER, I1
    c   INTEGER, *rAw*
        where *r* and *w* depend on the length of the names and your computer system
    d   REAL, F15.2

2   FORMAT 1000 is equivalent to ('*b*', 3I3, F12.2) which has a different effect from FORMAT 1001. The other pairs leave identical effects.

3   You can put it anywhere you want as long as it contains a decimal point.

4 It describes a data card with 120 columns (most have only 80).

5 Two numbers per card in the two fields, columns 1–10, and columns 11–20.

6 One solution is: `6000 FORMAT(A20,3(F10.0,10X))`

7 A +6.02E+23

   B +60.2E+230   too large on most systems (overflow)

8 A = bb123400.0bA = b.123E+06bA = bbb.1E+06
   A = b1234000.0bA = 1.234E+05bA = bb1.2E+05
   A = bbb12340.0bA = b.012E+07bA = bbb.0E+07

9   `WRITE(6,7000)`
    `7000 FORMAT('1'/100('  FORMAT IS A TRICKY LANGUAGE'/))`

   Note: This will start on the second line of a page.

10 `IN FIRST PLACE WAS BO`
    `THERE WERE 2 TIED FOR IT`

    `IN SECOND PLACE WAS MO`
    `THERE WERE`

   (*Note*: Here's a place where gobbling up the FORMAT to the next data descriptor has an undesirable result.)

ANSWERS TO EXERCISES 6 1

1 If the values in memory cells I and J are the same and that value is a legal subscript for B, then B(I) and B(J) denote the same cell.

2

0	1	1	2	3
5	8	13	21	34

3 `B(3) = B(I)` legal; but since I has the value 3, nothing is changed

   `B(I) = B(I-1)` legal; changes value of B(3) to value contained in B(2)

   `B(J) = B(2*I)` legal; changes value of B(7) to value contained in B(6)

   `B(4) = B(J-1) + B(I*J-21)` illegal; B(I*J–21) refers to B(0), which doesn't exist

   `B(2*I) = B(J+4)` illegal; B(J + 4) refers to B(11), which doesn't exist

   `B(1.7) = 0` illegal; REAL subscripts aren't allowed

4 No arrays would be needed, as shown in the program below.

```
      COMMENT--PROGRAM TO LIST THE WESTERN STATES, THEIR
      C        SALES TAX RATES, AND THE AVERAGE RATE OVER THE
      C        WESTERN STATES.
            REAL T,SUM,AVE
            INTEGER S,N
      C
            SUM=0.0
            N=0
       100  READ(5,1000) S,T
      1000  FORMAT(A2,F7.0)
              WRITE(6,1010) S,T
      1010    FORMAT(' ',A2,F7.3)
              SUM=SUM+T
              N=N+1
              IF (N .LT. 11) GO TO 100
      C
            AVE=SUM/11.0
      C
            WRITE(6,2000) AVE
      2000  FORMAT('0AVERAGE WESTERN STATES SALES TAX IS',
          +                                      F7.3)
            STOP
            END
```

```
      data
       WA 0.045
       ID 0.03
       MT 0.00
       OR 0.04
       WY 0.03
       CA 0.06
       NV 0.03
       UT 0.04
       CO 0.03
       AZ 0.04
       NM 0.04
```

```
      output
      (input values copied here . . .)
        AVERAGE WESTERN STATES SALES TAX IS    .035
```

5 `REAL A(10)`	legal
`INTEGER A(13-2)`	illegal; no computation allowed in length declarator
`INTEGER A(I)`	illegal; no variable allowed in length declarator
`REAL A(150), BOK(3472)`	legal
`REAL X(15.0)`	illegal; length declarator must be INTEGER
`LOGICAL QS(23), PS(47)`	legal

ANSWERS TO EXERCISES 6 2

1   We need 12 cells in the arrays because the information on the "**" card will have to be stored somewhere. Since there will be up to 11 response cards, we need a twelfth cell to include the information from the "**" card.

2   Change the STORE DATA and COMPUTE AVERAGE sections of the program as shown below.

```
C       STORE DATA
        SUM=0.0
        N=0
100     READ(5,1000) S(N+1),T(N+1)
1000    FORMAT(A2,F7.0)
            IF (S(N+1) .EQ. FIN)  GO TO 200
            SUM=SUM+S(N+1)
            GO TO 100
200     AVE=SUM/N
```

3   Since N will be zero when the computer reaches the COMPUTE AVER-AGE section of the program the computer will attempt to divide by zero, resulting in an error. To avoid this, change the statements between statements 200 and 210 in the program to the ones below.

```
200     IF (N .NE. 0) GO TO 205
            WRITE(6,2000)
2000        FORMAT(' NO DATA FOR TAX PROGRAM')
            STOP
205     SUM=0.0
        K=1
```

4   Increase the length of the arrays S and T to 51. That's all!

5   The program will try to use nonexistent array elements. Change the statement GO TO 100 in the STORE DATA section of the program to the following sequence of statements.

```
        IF (N .LE. 11) GO TO 100
            N=N-1
            WRITE(6,2009) N
2009        FORMAT(' ONLY',I3,' RESPONSE CARDS ALLOWED FOR.'/)
```

```
6       COMMENT--PROGRAM TO LIST THE WESTERN STATES WITH
C               BELOW AVERAGE SALES TAX RATES.
        INTEGER S1,S2,S3,S4,S5,S6,S7,S8,S9,S10,S11
        REAL T1,T2,T3,T4,T5,T6,T7,T8,T9,T10,T11,SUM,AVE
        INTEGER FIN
        DATA FIN/2H**/
C
C       SET ALL TAX RATES TO ZERO INITIALLY SO THAT UNUSED
C       CELLS WILL NOT CONTRIBUTE TO SUM IN STATEMENT 200.
        DATA T1,T2,T3,T4,T5,T6,T7,T8,T9,T10,T11/11*0.0/
```

```
C
C      STORE DATA AND ACCUMULATE SUM
       SUM=0.0
       N=0
       READ(5,1000) S1,T1
 1000  FORMAT(A2,F7.0)
       IF (S1 .EQ. FIN) GO TO 200
       N=N+1
       READ(5,1000) S2,T2
       IF (S2 .EQ. FIN) GO TO 200
       N=N+1
       READ(5,1000) S3,T3
       IF (S3 .EQ. FIN) GO TO 200
       N=N+1
       READ(5,1000) S4,T4
       IF (S4 .EQ. FIN) GO TO 200
       N=N+1
       READ(5,1000) S5,T5
       IF (S5 .EQ. FIN) GO TO 200
       N=N+1
       READ(5,1000) S6,T6
       IF (S6 .EQ. FIN) GO TO 200
       N=N+1
       READ(5,1000) S7,T7
       IF (S7 .EQ. FIN) GO TO 200
       N=N+1
       READ(5,1000) S8,T8
       IF (S8 .EQ. FIN) GO TO 200
       N=N+1
       READ(5,1000) S9,T9
       IF (S9 .EQ. FIN) GO TO 200
       N=N+1
       READ(5,1000) S10,T10
       IF (S10 .EQ. FIN) GO TO 200
       N=N+1
       READ(5,1000) S11,T1
       IF (S11 .EQ. FIN) GO TO 200
       N=N+1
C
 200   AVE=(T1+T2+T3+T4+T5+T6+T7+T8+T9+T10+T11)/N
C
       WRITE(6,2000)
 2000  FORMAT(' STATES WITH BELOW AVERAGE SALES TAX'/)
       IF (T1  .LE. AVE  .AND. N .GE. 1 ) WRITE(6,2010) S1
       IF (T2  .LE. AVE  .AND. N .GE. 2 ) WRITE(6,2010) S2
       IF (T3  .LE. AVE  .AND. N .GE. 3 ) WRITE(6,2010) S3
       IF (T4  .LE. AVE  .AND. N .GE. 4 ) WRITE(6,2010) S4
       IF (T5  .LE. AVE  .AND. N .GE. 5 ) WRITE(6,2010) S5
       IF (T6  .LE. AVE  .AND. N .GE. 6 ) WRITE(6,2010) S6
       IF (T7  .LE. AVE  .AND. N .GE. 7 ) WRITE(6,2010) S7
       IF (T8  .LE. AVE  .AND. N .GE. 8 ) WRITE(6,2010) S8
       IF (T9  .LE. AVE  .AND. N .GE. 9 ) WRITE(6,2010) S9
       IF (T10 .LE. AVE  .AND. N .GE. 10) WRITE(6,2010) S10
       IF (T11 .LE. AVE  .AND. N .GE. 11) WRITE(6,2010) S11
 2010  FORMAT(' ',A2)
       STOP
       END
```

data
```
WA 0.045
ID 0.03
MT 0.00
OR 0.04
WY 0.03
CA 0.06
NV 0.03
UT 0.04
CO 0.03
AZ 0.04
NM 0.04
**
```

output
```
STATES WITH BELOW AVERAGE SALES TAX

ID
MT
WY
NV
CO
NM
```

Imagine changing this program to handle all 50 states!

```
7    COMMENT:  MAKE A BAR GRAPH FROM DISTANCE DATA.
          INTEGER BAR(6), NUMB
          REAL DIST
     C        INITIALIZE BAR HEIGHTHS
          NUMB = 1
      5   BAR(NUMB) = 0
            NUMB = NUMB+1
            IF (NUMB .LE. 6)  GO TO 5
     C        READ DISTANCES AND ACCUMULATE BAR SUMS
     10   READ(5,1000) DIST
   1000 FORMAT(F10.0)
            IF (DIST .LT. 0.0)  GO TO 200
     C        DROP FRACTIONAL PART TO DETERMINE BAR SUM AFFECTED
          NUMB = DIST
     C        INCREMENT APPROPRIATE BAR COUNTER
          IF (NUMB .LE. 5)  GO TO 30
            WRITE(6,2009) DIST
   2009     FORMAT(' DISTANCE', F7.1, ' IS OUT OF RANGE.')
            GO TO 10
     30     BAR(NUMB+1) = BAR(NUMB+1) + 1
            GO TO 10
     C    PRINT RESULTS
    200   WRITE(6,2000)
   2000 FORMAT('1BAR    HEIGHT')
          NUMB = 0
    210   WRITE(6,2100) NUMB, BAR(NUMB+1)
   2100 FORMAT(' ', I2, I7)
            NUMB = NUMB+1
            IF (NUMB .LE. 5)  GO TO 210
          STOP
          END
```

```
data
 1.9
 0.4
 0.9
 3.9
17.5
 2.8
 4.5
 4.1
 3.2
 5.8
 6.9
 4.5
 3.7
 2.9
 5.2
-1.0
```

output
```
DISTANCE   17.5 IS OUT OF RANGE
DISTANCE    6.9 IS OUT OF RANGE

BAR    HEIGHT
 0       2
 1       1
 2       2
 3       3
 4       3
 5       2
```

ANSWERS TO EXERCISES 6 4

1 `INTEGER A(100,3), B(3,100),I` legal; declares two INTEGER arrays A and B

`REAL QRT(3,49)` legal; declares a REAL array QRT

`LOGICAL P(10), Q(4,2)` legal; declares two LOGICAL arrays P and Q

`REAL X(N,100)` illegal; length declarators must be constants

2 `A(4,2) = 0` legal

`B(4,2) = 0` illegal; 4 is too large

`A(3,50) = 0` illegal; 50 is too large

`I = 10`

`Q(I/3,I-8) = .TRUE.` legal (first subscript is non-ANSI, however)

`P(8) = Q(3,2)` legal

3
```
COMMENT:  PROGRAM TO PRINT POLITICAL POLL SUMMARIES
          REAL POLL(7,5), AVERGE, SUM
          INTEGER COLUMN, ROW, I
C         STORE DATA
          I = 1
  100     READ(5,1000) ROW, COLUMN, POLL(ROW,COLUMN)
 1000     FORMAT(2I4, F7.0)
          I = I+1
          IF (I .LE. 35) .GO TO 100
```

```
C
C      COMPUTE AVERAGE SUPPORT IN EAST-WEST SLICES OF AREA
       ROW = 1
200    SUM = 0.0
       COLUMN = 1
250       SUM = SUM + POLL(ROW,COLUMN)
          COLUMN = COLUMN + 1
          IF (COLUMN .LE. 5)  GO TO 250
C         FINISHED SUMMING ROW--COMPUTE AVERAGE
       AVERGE = SUM/5.0
       WRITE(6,2500) ROW,AVERGE
2500   FORMAT('0THE AVERAGE SUPPORT IN SLICE', I3/
      +         ' FROM THE NORTH IS', F7.2, ' PER CENT')
       ROW = ROW +1
       IF (ROW .LE. 7)  GO TO 200
C
```
```
C      COMPUTE AVERAGE SUPPORT IN SOUTHEAST QUARTER
       ROW = 4
300    SUM = 0.0
       COLUMN = 1
350       SUM = SUM + POLL(ROW,COLUMN)
          COLUMN = COLUMN + 1
          IF (COLUMN .LE. 3)  GO TO 350
       ROW = ROW + 1
       IF (ROW .LE. 7)  GO TO 300
       AVERGE = SUM/(4.0*3.0)
       WRITE(6,3500) AVERGE
3500   FORMAT('0AVERAGE SUPPORT IN SOUTHEAST QUARTER:',F8.2)
       STOP
       END
```

data

```
1    1       7.
1    2      40.
1    3      91.
1    4      18.
5    4      25.
5    5      24.
2    3      44.
3    4      75.
3    5      28.
6    1      93.
6    2      94.
2    4      99.
4    1      27.
4    2      12.
6    3      45.
6    4      40.
6    5      57.
4    3      88.
4    4      79.
4    5       1.
1    5      81.
2    5      52.
7    1      33.
2    1      88.
3    1      44.
5    1      24.
3    2      79.
5    2      82.
```

```
3    3    31.
7    2    90.
5    3    52.
2    2    68.
7    3    74.
7    4    86.
7    5    37.
```

output

```
THE AVERAGE SUPPORT IN SLICE   1
FROM THE NORTH IS  47.40 PER CENT

THE AVERAGE SUPPORT IN SLICE   2
FROM THE NORTH IS  70.20 PER CENT

THE AVERAGE SUPPORT IN SLICE   3
FROM THE NORTH IS  51.40 PER CENT

THE AVERAGE SUPPORT IN SLICE   4
FROM THE NORTH IS  41.40 PER CENT

THE AVERAGE SUPPORT IN SLICE   5
FROM THE NORTH IS  41.40 PER CENT

THE AVERAGE SUPPORT IN SLICE   6
FROM THE NORTH IS  65.80 PER CENT

THE AVERAGE SUPPORT IN SLICE   7
FROM THE NORTH IS  64.00 PER CENT

AVERAGE SUPPORT IN SOUTHEAST QUARTER:    16.42
```

5   Add the declarations

```
INTEGER FOR, AGIN, SBLOCK, EBLOCK
REAL RFOR, RAGIN
```

and change statement 100 to the following sequence of statements

```
100    READ(5,1001) SBLOCK, EBLOCK, FOR, AGIN
C          COMPUTE SUBSCRIPTS CORRESPONDING TO BLOCK NUMBERS
           ROW = SBLOCK/100 - 20
           COLUMN = EBLOCK/100 - 47
C          CONVERT VOTES FOR AND AGAINST TO REALS FOR DIVISION
101        RFOR = FOR
102        RAGIN = AGIN
           POLL(ROW,COLUMN) = 100.0*RFOR/(RFOR+RAGIN)
```

Statements 102 and 103 involve conversions from INTEGERs to REALs.
(See Section 4 3.)

```
1  300   S=C(29-17,1,2)+C(29-17,2,2)+C(29-17,3,2)
         WRITE(6,3000) S
   3000 FORMAT('0THERE ARE', I4, ' 29 YEAR OLD, LONG HAIRED',
        +          ' MEMBERS')


2        S = C(21-17,1,1)+C(21-17,1,2)+
        +    C(21-17,2,1)+C(21-17,2,2)+
        +    C(21-17,3,1)+C(21-17,3,2)
         WRITE(6,4000) S
   4000 FORMAT('0THERE ARE', I4, ' 21 YEAR OLD MEMBERS')
   C
         STOP
         END
```

data

18	DEMOCRAT	LONG
20	OTHER	LONG
26	DEMOCRAT	LONG
24	DEMOCRAT	LONG
21	OTHER	SHORT
21	REPUBLICAN	LONG
27	REPUBLICAN	SHORT
27	DEMOCRAT	SHORT
20	OTHER	LONG
23	DEMOCRAT	LONG
22	OTHER	LONG
28	DEMOCRAT	LONG
22	DEMOCRAT	SHORT
27	REPUBLICAN	SHORT
18	DEMOCRAT	SHORT
22	DEMOCRAT	SHORT
29	DEMOCRAT	LONG
25	REPUBLICAN	LONG
26	OTHER	SHORT
24	DEMOCRAT	LONG
18	OTHER	LONG
28	DEMOCRAT	SHORT
18	DEMOCRAT	LONG
29	REPUBLICAN	LONG
24	DEMOCRAT	LONG
0		

output

```
THERE ARE    2 29 YEAR OLD, LONG HAIRED MEMBERS

THERE ARE    2 21 YEAR OLD MEMBERS
```

3 Ignore Alien Orders.

4 Vernor Vinge.

5 Why is a raven like a writing desk?

ANSWERS TO EXERCISES 6 6

1
```
    READ(5,5000) A(1),A(2),A(3),A(4)
     WRITE(6,1000) A(4),A(6),A(8),A(10),A(12)
     WRITE(6,3000) A(2),A(6),A(10)
    READ(5,2000) B(1,1),B(2,1),B(3,1),B(4,1),
   +              B(1,2),B(2,2),B(3,2),B(4,2)
    WRITE(6,4000) Q,R, S,B(3,1),A(1), S,B(3,2),A(2), BC,
   +              A(1),A(2),A(3),A(4)
```

2
```
    WRITE(6,1000) (A(I), I=1,5)
    WRITE(6,1000) (A(I), I=2,10,2)

    READ(5,2000) ( (B(I,J), I=2,3), J=1,3)
```
or

```
    READ(5,2000) (B(2,J),B(3,J), J=1,3)
```

3
`WRITE(6,2000) (A(J), J=1,N-1)`	N−1 is illegal; expressions not allowed as implied do list parameters
`READ(5,7000) (J,A(J), J=1,N)`	implied do list parameters may not be changed while the list is being used. This READ would change J by giving it a value from a data card
`WRITE(6,1000) (A(J), J=1,C(N))`	C(N) is illegal; only constants and *simple* INTEGER variables may be parameters in implied do lists

4 Trouble. We should test for that case too. Here's one way.

```
    300  THISB=BAR(NUMB+1)
         IF (THISB .LE. 0) GO TO 310
    304  IF (THISB .LE. 60 ) GO TO 308
    C       MORE THAN 60 ITEMS IN THIS BAR.
            WRITE(6,3000) NUMB,(XCH,COUNT=1,60)
            THISB=THISB-60
            GO TO 304
    C       BETWEEN 1 AND 60 ITEMS
    308     WRITE(6,3000) NUMB,(XCH,COUNT=1,THISB)
    3000    FORMAT(' BAR',I1,':',100A1)
            GO TO 400
    C       NO ITEMS AT ALL.
    310     WRITE(6,3000) NUMB
    400     NUMB=NUMB+1
            IF (NUMB .LE. 5) GO TO 300
         STOP
         END
```

This makes fat bars if there are more than 60 items in a bar, like this:

```
BAR0:XXXXXXXXXXXXXXXXXXXXXXXXXXXXXXXXXXX
BAR1:XXXXXXXXXXXXXXXXXXXXXXXXXXXXXXXXXXXXXXXXXXXXXXXXXXXXXXXXXXX
BAR2:XXXXXXXXXXXXXXXXXXXXXXXXXXXXXXXXXXXXXXXXXXXXXXXXXXXXXXXXXXXXXXXX
BAR2:XXXXXXXXXXXXXXXXXXXXXXXXXXXXXXXXXXXXXXXXXXXXXXXXXXXXXXXXXXXXXXXX
BAR2:X
BAR3:XXXXXXXXXXXXXXXXXXXXXXXXXXXXXXXXXXXXXXXXXXXXXXXXXXXXXXXXXXXXXXXX
BAR3:XXXXXXXXXXXXXXXXXXXXXXXXXXXXXXXXXXXXXXXXXXXXXXXXXXXXXXXXXXXXXXXX
BAR3:XXXXXXXXXXXXXXXXXXXXXXXXXXXXXXXXXXXXXXX
BAR4:XXXXXXXXXXXXXXXXXXXXXXXXXXXXXXXXXXXXXXXXXXXXXXXXXXXXXXXXXXXXXXXX
BAR4:XXXXXXXXXXXXXXXXXXXXXXXXXXXXXXXXXXXXXXXXXXXXXXXXXXXXXXXXXXXXXXXX
BAR4:XXXXXXXXXXXXXXXXXXXXXXXXXXXXXXXXXXXXXXXXXXXXXXXXXXXXXXXXXXXXXXXX
BAR4:XXXXXXXXXXXXXXXXXXXXXXXXXXXXXXXXXXXXXXXXXXXXXXXXX
BAR5:XXXXXXXXXXXXXXXXXXXXXXXXXXXXXXXXXXXXXXXXXXXXXXXXXXXXXXXXX
```

```
5        WRITE(6,3000) NUMB, (NUMB, COUNT=1,THISB)
      3000 FORMAT(' BAR', I1, ':', 100I1)
```

ANSWERS TO EXERCISES 7 2

1   The first two are legal.

The third is illegal. The name POMEGRANATE is too long.

The fourth is illegal. A parameter must be listed by name only. If it is an array, the parameter declarations will say so. If it is only a memory cell, it doesn't need a subscript.

2   They are all legal.

3   It would PRINT the line

     9   16   25

4   It would PRINT

     A= DOG NONE BAT

ANSWERS TO EXERCISES 7 3

1   Change the second argument in the CALL statement (at statement label 100) to X**2.

ANSWERS TO EXERCISES 7 4

1   Memory cell A will take the values 1.0, 4.0, and then 1.0 again. (We're pretty sure that last 1.0 is correct.)

2   A FUNCTION must have at least one parameter.

3   TAX (3.49) is 0.21; TAX (1.03) is 0.06.

4   2, 1, and 3.0. The expression rounds the result to the nearest whole number. In computing taxes we wanted to round, not truncate.

```
5  REAL FUNCTION OURABS(A)
   REAL A
   OURABS = A
   IF (OURABS .LT. 0.0)  OURABS = -OURABS
   RETURN
   END
```

ANSWERS TO EXERCISES 7 5

1 ONE: legal

   TWO: legal

   THREE: illegal—LENGTH isn't in the parameter list of the SUBROUTINE
   THREE, so it can't be used as an array size declarator in the
   SUBROUTINE's parameter declaration section.

2 It is illegal to change the value of an array size declarator. Thus, the statement N=N+1 is illegal in this context.

3 Change the FUNCTION LOCBIG so that the second IF statement becomes
   `IF (A(I) .LT. A(LOCBIG)) LOCBIG = I`
   It would also be nice, although not strictly necessary, to change the name
   of the FUNCTION (and all references to it) to LOCSM since it now
   LOCates the SMallest element in the array.

4 After execution of the CALL statement, the cells ONE and TWO would
   both have whatever value TWO had before execution of the CALL
   statement.

5 The statement CALL BADSWT (1,2) lists two *constant* values as arguments, yet the SUBROUTINE BADSWT *changes* the values of the
   arguments given to it. It is immoral to change the value of a constant
   (according to the standards of ANSI).

ANSWERS TO EXERCISES 8 1

1 The output will be

NUMBER	SQUARED	CUBED
1	1	1

   since the test to see if the index has exceeded the upper bound is placed
   after the statements in the range (post-test). Actually, the ANSI standards
   do not require this result; DO-loops with starting values larger than upper
   bounds are illegal and the results unpredictable. But most compilers
   implement DO-loops in post-test form, hence giving the result we show
   above.

2 In no way.

3 As near as we can tell, eight.

4 The IF statement includes an illegal transfer of control into the range of
   the DO-loop.

1 Chapter 3:

None of the loops were counting loops, so DO-loops aren't appropriate.

Section 6 1:

The first program has no loops at all. Both the READ loop and the WRITE loop in the last program are counting loops and could be written profitably as DO-loops.

Section 6 2:

The loop which computes the average and the WRITE loop are counting loops and would make good DO-loops. The READ loop, on the other hand, is not a counting loop. It's termination condition doesn't test the loop index (N) against a predetermined count.

Section 6 4:

All the loops in the political poll program are counting loops and are, therefore, good candidates for DO-loops.

Section 6 5:

The loops of statements 100 and 310 could be written as DO-loops, but not the READ loop of statement 200.

Section 6 6:

The READ loop in the bar graph program is not a counting loop because its termination condition does not depend on N reaching a predetermined count. The WRITE loop, however, is a counting loop and would make a good DO-loop.

2 Change all references to memory cell MINIM to MAX. Change the COMMENTs appropriately, and most importantly, change the IF statement in the range of the DO-loop to IF(ROSE(HERE) .LE. MAX) GO TO 300.

3 Add an INTEGER memory cell NUMB, then use these statements (or equivalents):

```
COMMENT:  THERE'S ONLY BEEN ONE ELEMENT SO FAR, SO THE FIRST
C         ELEMENT IS THE SMALLEST, AND THE CURRENT MINIMUM
C         HAS BEEN ENCOUNTERED ONLY ONCE.
      MINIM = ROSE(1)
      NUMB = 1
C
C     LOOK AT ALL OTHER ELEMENTS IN "ROSE" LOOKING FOR
C     SMALLER VALUES.  KEEP TRACK OF THE NUMBER OF TIMES THE
C     CURRENT MINIMUM HAS BEEN ENCOUNTERED.
      DO 300 HERE=2,N
        IF (ROSE(HERE) .GT. MINIM)  GO TO 300
        IF (ROSE(HERE) .LT. MINIM)  GO TO 200
C         CURRENT MINIMUM ENCOUNTERED ANOTHER TIME
          NUMB = NUMB+1
          GO TO 300
C         FOUND A NEW SMALLEST VALUE--UPDATE
  200     MINIM = ROSE(HERE)
          NUMB = 1
  300   CONTINUE
```

```
C       DONE
        WRITE(6,4000) NUMB, MINIM
   4000)FORMAT(1X,I3, ' ROSES HAVE', I3, ' PETALS.',
       +             ' NONE HAVE FEWER.')
        STOP
        END
```

ANSWERS TO EXERCISES 9 2

1 See Section 9 1 1 ; four steps.

2 *Step 1* was the problem statement on the first page of this section.

Step 2 was the input-output description which followed.

Step 3 involved all of the analysis of the conversion process and the gradual refinement of the algorithm from the original form (Conversion Algorithm), through the Digit Conversion Algorithm and the Digit Selection Algorithm.

Step 4 was the last, coding the algorithm in Fortran and debugging it.

3 The problem is in the spacing in front of the input INTEGER. If the input INTEGER is 9, then the output line will be

```
THE ROMAN NUMERAL FOR   9 IS IX
```
—too many spaces before the 9.

One (of many) ways to fix this is to put the digits of the input INTEGER *individually* into an array, leaving off leading zeros and keeping track of the number of digits. If the digits are stored in array IN, and the number of digits is ND, then the WRITE statement would be as shown below.

```
      INTEGER IN(4),R(16),J,ND,IS1,IS2,B
      DATA IS1,IS2/1HI,1HS/, B/1H /
         .
         .
         .
      WRITE(6,1002) (IN(J), J=1,ND), B, IS1,IS2, B,
     +              (R(J), J=1,N)
 1002 FORMAT('0THE ROMAN NUMERAL FOR ', 24A1)
```

4 a `GO TO (10,20,30), K`

   b `GO TO (200,200,100,100,200,300), I`

ANSWERS TO EXERCISES 9 3

1
```
   COMMENT: NOW SORT ON NAMES
           CALL INDSRT(NAME,X,N)
           WRITE(6,5000)
 5000 FORMAT('0CHILDREN IN ALPHABETICAL ORDER'/
     +         ' NAME        AGE      WEIGHT      HEIGHT')
  410  WRITE(6,3000) (NAME(X(I)),AGE(X(I)),WGT(X(I)),
     +                                HGT(X(I)), I=1,N)
```

2 Put a test to assure that N never gets larger than 100 (the length of our arrays) in the loop that READs in the data.

3 No, it won't cause an error. As long as N does not exceed the actual declared length of the array (100 here), the SUBROUTINE can just use the

lower parts of the array (up to position N) with no problem. However, this can cause unexpected problems when the array is multidimensional. But that's covered in Chapter 11.

ANSWERS TO EXERCISES 9 4

1 Change `IF (DICE .EQ. 7)   GO TO 20`

   to   `IF (DICE .EQ. 7 .OR. DICE .EQ. 11)   GO TO 20`

2 Declare an INTEGER array WLR(12)—WLR for win, lose, or roll again—and an INTEGER memory cell D. Immediately after statement 40, insert the following statements.

```
     WLR(1) = 1
     DO 41 D=2,12
41      WLR(D) = 4
     WLR(POINT) = 2
     WLR(7) = 3
```

These statements set up a jump index array with 1 standing for an erroneous dice roll, 2 for win, 3 for lose, and 4 for roll again. Now replace the two IFs and the GO TO after statement 45 with the following statements.

```
D = WLR(DICE)
GO TO (10,20,30,45), D
```

These statements select among the four alternatives.

ANSWERS TO EXERCISES 9 5

```
1  1 2 3 4 5
   2 3 5 4 1
   3 2 5 4 1
   5 4 2 3 1
   5 4 3 1 2
```

```
2  1 2 3   FOR T RAN
   1 3 2   FORRAN T
   2 1 3   T FORRAN
   2 3 1   T RANFOR
   3 1 2   RANFOR T
   3 2 1   RAN T FOR
```

ANSWERS TO EXERCISES 10 2

```
1  LOGICAL EXOR, ONE, TWO
   EXOR(ONE,TWO) = (ONE .AND. .NOT. TWO) .OR.
   +                (TWO .AND. .NOT. ONE)
```

```
2  REAL SDIST, X1,Y1, X2,Y2
   SDIST(X1,Y1, X2,Y2) = SQRT( (X1-X2)**2 + (Y1-Y2)**2 )
```

```
3  REAL ADIST, X1,X2, Y1,Y2
   ADIST(X1,Y1, X2,Y2) = ABS(X1-X2) + ABS(Y1-Y2)
```

```
4   REAL TRNCD, R1,R2
    TRNCD(R1,R2) = AINT(R1/R2)


5   INTEGER ROUND, RNDDIV
    ROUND(X) = INT(X+SIGN(0.5,X))
    RNDDIV(I1,I2) = ROUND(FLOAT(I1)/FLOAT(I2))
```

ANSWERS TO EXERCISES 10 3

1 None of the answers are correct. The EXTERNAL statement appears in the program unit which has a subprogram reference in which an argument is the name of another subprogram.

2 It wouldn't hurt anything.

ANSWERS TO EXERCISES 10 4

1 A:18, B:1
A:1, C(1):7, C(2):7, C(3):7, D:4.0
A:3, E:3.0, F(1):3.0, F(2):3.0, F(3):3.0, F(4):3.0
illegal: E is REAL and can't have the value 2, an INTEGER.
C(2):2−no other cells initialized
illegal: subscripts must be constants.

ANSWERS TO EXERCISES 10 5

1

	ONE	TWO	THREE
BLK1	A(1)	C	Q(1)
	A(2)	B(1)	Q(2)
	A(3)	B(2)	Q(3)
	B	B(3)	Q(4)
BLK2	C(1)	D(1)	R
	C(2)	D(2)	S

2 It will print the values of A, B, C, D, E, and F, which will be 2.0, 1.0, 2.0, 3.0, 1.0, and 3.0, respectively.

ANSWERS TO EXERCISES 10 6

1 A, X, Y(1)
B, Y(2)
C(1), Y(3)
C(2), Y(4)

1 (1X,8 (5X), 3 I5)

The blanks are ignored and were inserted for our convenience.

ANSWERS TO EXERCISES 11 2

1

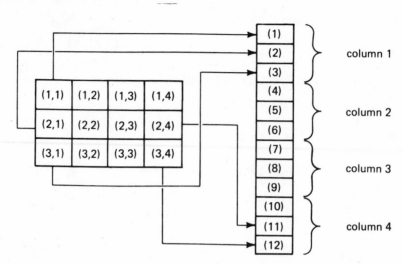

2 In order to refer to elements (in a two-dimensional array) "by columns," you must know *how long* the columns are. (It doesn't matter how long the rows are.) An *m*-by-*n* two-dimensional array has columns of length *m*. Therefore, you could set up the array as long as you knew *m* and an upper bound on the total amount of room you'd need for the array. Thus, knowing *m* exactly and that $n \leqslant 100$ is enough.

3 (I, J) corresponds to element $N*(I-1)+J$
Note that N is the value you need to know precisely.

4

A

1			
1			

i.e., in A(1,1) and A(4,1)

ANSWERS TO EXERCISES 11 3

1 You would not want to store a triangular array by columns because then you would need to know how long the first column is in order to skip around it to reference the other columns.

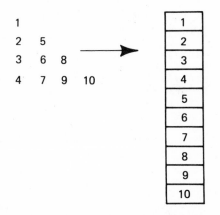

If the first column has four elements, then

$$(\text{row, col}) \longrightarrow \frac{4*(4+1)}{2} - \frac{(5-\text{col})*(6-\text{col})}{2} + \text{row} - \text{col} + 1$$

2 Store it by columns. Then

$$(\text{row, col}) \longrightarrow \frac{\text{col}*(\text{col}-1)}{2} + \text{row}$$

3 It's probably not worth it. Even if the shortest route were recomputed the maximum number of times, it would add less than 25 percent to the running time since less than that proportion of each loop iteration is spent in recomputing the shortest route length. Your time would be far better spent in fixing up the permutation generator, since it is fairly slow, or better yet, in reducing (by more careful analysis) the number of routes you need to look at.

ANSWERS TO EXERCISES 11 4

1 The declaration of the array STACK would have to be changed to REAL. Also the parameter VALUE in SUBROUTINEs ADD and REMOVE must be a REAL.

2
```
      SUBROUTINE REMOVE(QUEUE,FRONT,BACK, VALUE)
      INTEGER QUEUE(500), FRONT,BACK, VALUE
COMMENT:  "FRONT" MOVES ONE PLACE
      FRONT = FRONT + 1
COMMENT:  WRAP AROUND IF NECESSARY
      IF (FRONT .GT. 500)  FRONT = 1
COMMENT:  STORE "VALUE"
      VALUE = QUEUE(FRONT)
      RETURN
      END
```

3   Add a test to see if FRONT equals BACK right after the wraparound
    statement.

ANSWERS TO EXERCISES 11 5

1   Every place EMPTY is altered. Since this happens in three different places,
    it would be best to write a subprogram which does the test and STOPs if
    STRING is filled up. Here's one way to do it:

```
        SUBROUTINE BUMPMT(EMPTY)
        INTEGER EMPTY
          EMPTY = EMPTY + 1
          IF (EMPTY .LE. 1000) RETURN
C            IF WE HAD A GARBAGE COLLECTOR, WE'D CALL IT HERE..
C            BUT WE DON'T, SO...
             WRITE(6,1000)
1000         FORMAT(' SORRY, OUT OF ROOM IN STRING SPACE')
             STOP
        END
```

2

```
37 C O M E   O N   P E O P L E   S M I L E   O N   Y O U R   B R O T H E R
```

3

```
28 A S P I R I N   I S   T H E   B E S T   A S P I R I N
```

4
```
        SUBROUTINE PRINTS(STR)
        INTEGER STR
        INTEGER EMPTY, STRING(1000)
        COMMON EMPTY,STRING
        INTEGER CH,LEN
          LEN = STRING(STR) - 1
          WRITE(6,1000) (STRING(STR+CH), CH=1,LEN)
1000      FORMAT(1X, 120A1)
          RETURN
        END
```

ANSWERS TO EXERCISES 11 6

1   None. It does restrict the system to using no more than 1000 list elements
    at any one time, but as time goes on, elements can be reused time and
    time again.

2 One possibility is:

SLIST	KLIST	FREE
6	11	1

	N1	N2	N3	N4	QUANT	NEXT
1						4
2	SUGA	R			1	5
3	PEAC	HES				0
4						10
5	FLOU	R			5	0
6	EGGS					9
7	PEAS				3	12
8	WHEA	TIES				3
9	BUTT	ER				8
10						13
11	OLIV	ES			1	7
12	JELL	O			6	2
13						14
14						15
15						0

3 There's a crude way to do it—just enter a phony BOUGHT command and then a phony USED command to make the system think we're now out of the item.

The right way to do it involves just two changes. First, add a new command ADD into FUNCTION COMMAND, associating it with the number 6. Second, add statement number 359 in the computed GO TO list between 358 and 360, and insert

```
C       "ADD ITEM TO SHOPPING LIST"
  359   CALL ADD(L1,L2,L3,L4, 0,FREE, SLIST)
        WRITE(6,3590) L1,L2,L3,L4
 3590 FORMAT('0ADDED ', 4A4, ' TO THE SHOPPING LIST.')
        GO TO 300
```

immediately after statement 350.

E COVER PROGRAM

```
COMMENT:  PLOT PRIME SPIRAL PROJECTED STEROGRAPHICALLY
C            ONTO SPHERE
      INTEGER P(4000),PLEN
      REAL BORDER, R, X,Y
C  VARIABLES:
C     BORDER--RADIUS OF PROJECTION SPHERE
C     R--RADIUS OF BOXES TO BE DRAWN
      DATA PLEN/4000/,  BORDER/3.45/, R/0.45/
C     ...SET SCALES FOR IMAGE
      R = R/BORDER
      CALL MAP(-1.0,1.0, -1.0,1.0,  0.,1.,0.,1.)
C     ...GENERATE PRIMES
      CALL PRIMES(P,PLEN)
C     ...PLOT PRIME SPIRAL
      DO 150 K=1,PLEN
        CALL COORD(P(K), I,J)
        X = FLOAT(I)/BORDER
        Y = FLOAT(J)/BORDER
        CALL BOX(X,Y, R)
  150   CONTINUE
      STOP
      END
```

```
       SUBROUTINE PRIMES (P,NP)
       INTEGER NP, P(NP)
C      INPUT-    NP--NUMBER OF PRIMES DESIRED
C      OUTPUT-   P--ARRAY FILLED WITH FIRST NP PRIMES
       INTEGER J,LISTLN,OFFSET,CNP
       LOGICAL LIST(1000)
C      VARIABLES ...
C         LIST,LISTLN -- ARRAY WHERE PRIMES ARE BEING STORED
C         J -- POSITION IN P OF PRIME WHOSE MULTIPLES ARE BEING
C             MARKED OFF LIST
C         CNP -- NUMBER OF PRIMES CURRENTLY STORED IN P
C         OFFSET -- POSITION I IN LIST REPRESENTS THE NUMBER I+OFFSET
C         LIMIT -- POSITION LISTLN IN LIST REPRESENTS THE NUMBER LIMIT
       DATA LISTLN /1000/
       OFFSET = -LISTLN
       J = 1
       CNP = 1
       P(1) = 2
       CALL SETLST (LIST,LISTLN,OFFSET,LIMIT)
 100   IF (J .GT. CNP)  GOTO 999
          CALL MRKOFF (P(J),LIST,LISTLN,OFFSET,LIMIT)
          CALL SELECT (P,NP,CNP,J,LIST,LISTLN,OFFSET,LIMIT)
          IF (P(J)**2 .LE. LIMIT)  GO TO 110
            CALL SETLST (LIST,LISTLN,OFFSET,LIMIT)
            J = 0
 110      J = J+1
          IF (CNP .LE. NP)  GO TO 100
       RETURN
 999   WRITE (6,9990) CNP, (P(J),J=1,CNP)
 9990  FORMAT (*0ABORT-  AFTER GENERATING THE*, I6,
      +          *PRIMES-*/(10X,10I10))
       STOP
       END


       SUBROUTINE MRKOFF (PRIME,LIST,LISTLN,OFFSET,LIMIT)
COMMENT -- MARK OFF ALL MULTIPLES OF PRIME FROM LIST
C         NOTE:  LIST(I) REPRESENTS THE NUMBER I+OFFSET
       INTEGER PRIME, LISTLN,OFFSET
       LOGICAL LIST(LISTLN)
       INTEGER M
C      LET M+OFFSET BE THE FIRST MULTIPLE OF  PRIME  WHICH
C         IS STRICTLY GREATER THAN OFFSET
       M = (MAX0(OFFSET/PRIME,1)+1)*PRIME - OFFSET
 100   IF (M .GT. LISTLN)  RETURN
          LIST(M) = .FALSE.
          M = M+PRIME
          GO TO 100
       END


       SUBROUTINE SETLST (LIST,LISTLN,OFFSET,LIMIT)
       INTEGER LISTLN,OFFSET,LIMIT
       LOGICAL LIST(LISTLN)
COMMENT -- INITIALIZE LIST TO .TRUE.
C         BUMP OFFSET AND LIMIT TO REFLECT NEW MEANINGS FOR
C         POSITIONS IN LIST
       DO 100  I=1,LISTLN
 100      LIST(I) = .TRUE.
       OFFSET = OFFSET+LISTLN
       LIMIT = OFFSET+LISTLN
       RETURN
       END
```

```
      SUBROUTINE SELECT (P,NP,CNP,J,LIST,LISTLN,OFFSET,LIMIT)
      INTEGER P(NP), CNP,J,OFFSET,LIMIT
      LOGICAL LIST(LISTLN)
COMMENT-  SELECT PRIMES FROM LIST
C         NOTE-- PRIMES MUST BE IN THE RANGE P(CNP) < PRIME <= P(J)**2
      INTEGER K,KMAX
      K = P(CNP)-OFFSET+1
      KMAX = MIN0(P(J)**2,LIMIT) - OFFSET
 100  IF (K .GT. KMAX)  RETURN
         IF (.NOT. LIST(K))  GO TO 110
           CNP = CNP+1
           IF (CNP .LE. NP)  P(CNP) = K+OFFSET
 110     K = K+1
         GO TO 100
      END


      SUBROUTINE COORD(N, I,J)
      INTEGER N, I,J
COMMENT:  THIS ROUTINE COMPUTES THE CARTESIAN COORDINATES
C             (I,J)   OF THE NUMBER  "N"  IN THE SPIRAL
C         NUMBERING OF THE LATTICE POINTS IN THE PLANE
      INTEGER SQRTN, R, CNR, RES, RESRES, QUAD, SR
      INTEGER RSGN(4), DSGN(4), ISIGN
      DATA RSGN(1),RSGN(2),RSGN(3),RSGN(4)/-1,+1,+1,-1/
      DATA DSGN(1),DSGN(2),DSGN(3),DSGN(4)/+1,+1,-1,-1/
C
C     N=1 GOES IN CENTER
      IF ( N .GT. 1 )  GO TO 100
         I = 0
         J = 0
         RETURN
C     FIND THE NUMBER "R" SUCH THAT "N" IS IN THE R-TH
C         CONCENTRIC SQUARE ABOUT THE ORIGIN
 100  SQRTN = INT(SQRT(FLOAT(N))) +1
      IF ( (SQRTN-1)**2 .EQ. N )  SQRTN = SQRTN -1
      R = SQRTN/2
C     FIND THE SPIRAL NUMBER OF THE LOWER LEFT HAND CORNER
C        OF THE R-TH CONCENTRIC SQUARE
      CNR = (2*R-1)**2 +1
C     FIND THE NUMBER OF STEPS, COUNTING COUNTERCLOCKWISE
C        ALONG THE CONCENTRIC SQUARE FROM THE LOWER LEFT HAND
C        CORNER
      RES = N-CNR
C     DETERMINE EDGE NUMBER OF SQUARE (QUAD) AND
C        DIRECTION FROM ORIGIN (SIGNED RADIUS)
      QUAD = RES/(2*R)
      SR = ISIGN(R,RSGN(QUAD+1))
C     FIND SIGNED DISTANCE ALONG EDGE (RESRES)
      RESRES = DSGN(QUAD+1)*(MOD(RES,2*R) -R)
C     COMPUTE COORDINATE
      IF ( MOD(QUAD,2) .EQ. 0 )  GO TO 200
         I = SR
         J = RESRES
         RETURN
 200     I = RESRES
         J = SR
      RETURN
      END
```

```
          SUBROUTINE BOX(XC,YC, R)
          REAL XC,YC, R
C   PARAMETERS:
C       XC,YC--CENTER OF BOX (CARTESIAN)
C       R--RADIUS OF BOX
C   OUTPUT:
C       PROJECTION OF BOX OF GIVEN CENTER AND RADIUS ONTO
C       SPHERE BY STEROGRAPHIC PROJECTION.
C       DRAWN ON MICROFILM.
C           VIEWPOINT:  (0,0, -INFINITY)
C
          REAL X(5),Y(5)
          REAL STEREO, SQNORM, SDIST,  DIAGA,DIAGB
          COMMON /RSLUTN/ RESO
          DATA RESO/0.007/
          SQNORM(X,Y) = X**2 + Y**2
          STEREO(X,S) = 2.0*X/(1.0+S)
          SDIST(A1,B1,S1, A2,B2,S2) =
     +        SQRT(SQNORM(STEREO(A1,S1)-STEREO(A2,S2),
     +                    STEREO(B1,S1)-STEREO(B2,S2)))
C       ...COMPUTE CORNERS OF BOX
          X(1) = XC-R
          Y(1) = YC-R
          X(2) = X(1)
          Y(2) = YC+R
          X(3) = XC+R
          Y(3) = Y(2)
          X(4) = X(3)
          Y(4) = Y(1)
          X(5) = X(1)
          Y(5) = Y(1)
C       ...REPRESENT SMALL BOXES BY SINGLE POINTS
          DIAGA = SDIST(X(1),Y(1),SQNORM(X(1),Y(1)),
     +                  X(3),Y(3),SQNORM(X(3),Y(3)))
          DIAGB = SDIST(X(2),Y(2),SQNORM(X(2),Y(2)),
     +                  X(4),Y(4),SQNORM(X(4),Y(4)))
          IF ((DIAGA+DIAGB)/RESO.GE. 2.0)  GO TO 10
            S = SQNORM(XC,YC)
C           CALL POINT(STEREO(XC,S),STEREO(YC,S))
            CALL POINT(STEREO(XC,S),STEREO(YC,S))
            RETURN
C       ...BOX HAS SIGNIFICANT INTERIOR--DRAW EDGES
   10     DO 100 I=1,4
            CALL EDGE(X(I),Y(I), X(I+1),Y(I+1))
  100     CONTINUE
          RETURN
          END
```

```
        SUBROUTINE EDGE(X1,Y1, X2,Y2)
        REAL X1,Y1, X2,Y2
COMMENT:  DRAW LINE FROM (X1,Y1) TO (X2,Y2) PROJECTED
C         STEROGRAPHICALLY ONTO SPHERE
C         VIEWED FROM (0,0, -INFINITY)
        REAL SX(101),SY(101), X,Y, DX,DY, S, EDGELN,GRAIN
        REAL STEREO, SQNORM, SDIST
        INTEGER LEN, MAXLEN
        COMMON /RSLUTN/ RESO
        DATA MAXLEN/101/
        SQNORM(X,Y) = X**2 + Y**2
        STEREO(X,S) = 2.0*X/(1.0+S)
        SDIST(A1,B1,S1, A2,B2,S2) =
     +      SQRT(SQNORM(STEREO(A1,S1)-STEREO(A2,S2),
     +                  STEREO(B1,S1)-STEREO(B2,S2)))
C       ...CALCULATE DEGREE OF APPROXIMATION TO LINE
        EDGELN=SDIST(X1,Y1,SQNORM(X1,Y1), X2,Y2,SQNORM(X2,Y2))
        LEN = INT(EDGELN/RESO) + 1
        LEN = MAX0(2,MIN0(LEN,MAXLEN))
        GRAIN = FLOAT(LEN-1)
C       ...COMPUTE POINTS IN PIECEWISE LINEAR APPROXIMATION
        DX = (X2-X1)/GRAIN
        DY = (Y2-Y1)/GRAIN
        X = X1-DX
        Y = Y1-DY
        DO 100 I=1,LEN
          X=X+DX
          Y=Y+DY
          S = SQNORM(X,Y)
          SX(I) = STEREO(X,S)
          SY(I) = STEREO(Y,S)
  100   CONTINUE
C       ...PLOT LINE
        CALL CURVE(SX,SY, LEN)
        RETURN
        END
```

Boolean algebra 82
Boss Tweed 146
box cars 235
bridge 252
Brown, Basset 275
Brown, Clarence I 275
Brown, Clarence II 275
Brown, Ida 275
buffering 323
bug 5
built-in FUNCTION 72, 416
built-in operator 71, 72
burst 162

C in column 1 34
calculator 43
CALL statement 162, 412
CALLing sequence 412
candidate 134
canyon 113, 194
Captain Hawkbill 150
card
    data 41, 42, 380
    layout 34
    reader 16
    sorter 16
cardgames 251
carpenter 1
carriage control 31, 32, 35,
    403, 409
cascade of errors 118
case statement 361
cell 16, 21
census 31
chad 371
change 109
character 88, 371, 383
    comparison 90
    FORMAT 408
    Fortran 366, 371
    I/O 98
    ordering 90
    relation 90
    storing 92, 296
    string 295
chard 371
Charlie 93
chess 353
Chevy, '54 62
Chicago 148
Chicago Peace 206
chlorine 62
CHOOSE 191
chop 74
chunk 164
circuit 282
class roll 148
classify 285
clumsy appendages 8

COBOL 348
code 159, 323
coding 117
collating sequence 90
column 136
    major form 276
    1 34, 379
    6 34, 379
    7 34, 379
    73–80 34, 42, 379
come on people 299
comma alert 376
comma, one lousy 118
comment line 34, 379
committee 8
COMMON
    blank 388
    extension by
        EQUIVALENCE 389
    labeled 388
    names 264
    safety 264
    statement 263, 388
comparison, character 90
compatible, type 395
compile-time error 116
    initialization 387
compiler 4, 118
COMPLEX 80, 97, 382
    FORMAT 408
    I/O 97
compound interest 14
computed GO TO statement
    223, 396
computer 3, 15
    dating 3, 154
    girl 354
    graphics 172
    language 3
con 78
concatenation 298
conceptual computer 15
conditional statement 48, 55,
    85
confetti 371
connected 318
CONNIVER 350
continuation field 34, 379
CONTINUE statement 205,
    400
controller 16
conversion 33, 69, 72, 77,
    157, 192, 219
    chart 395
    I/O 93
Cooke, Louis 275
COORD 196
COS 72
cosine 72, 154

counting 50
counting loop 200, 399, 444
CPU 16
craps 235
Crotalus viridis viridis 215
cup 157
cycle 194
cypher 159, 323

D FORMAT 96, 408
D-notation 79
dare-devil 113
data card 38, 41, 42, 380
data descriptor **32**, 33, 92,
    407
    A 89, 98, 408
    alphameric 98
    character 98
    COMPLEX 97, 408
    D 96, 408
    DOUBLE PRECISION 96
    E 95, 408
    F 33, 43, 94, 407
    G 96, 407
    I 33, 93, 407
    INTEGER 33, 93
    L 97, 408
    LOGICAL 97
    P 98, 408
    REAL 33, 43, 94, 95, 96
    repeat 101
DATA statement 91, 259,
    387
data structure 274, 276
data type **22**, 69, 78, 81
    chart 386
dating, computer 3, 154
debate 78
debug 116, 121
decimal point shift 63
decision table 85
deck setup 37
declaration statement **23**, 385
declarator, array 127, **138**,
    387
declarator, length 127, 186
decode 159
Democrat 139
Denver Mint Tea 59
descretization 173, 174
descriptor, data (see data
    descriptor)
descriptor, literal **32**, 92, 409
designing programs 117, 218
desk 440
desk calculator 43
detergent 8, 50
DIMENSION statement 387
distance table 280

LOGICAL (*cont.*)
    expression 81, 83, 87, 393
    FORMAT 97, 408
    I/O 97
    IF statement 397
    precedence 85, 394
loop 10, 358, 43
    control 360
    counting 200, 399, 444
    entry 53
    exit 53
    indentation 55
    nested 55, 56
    writing 53
.LT. 48, 83
Lubbock 280
lumber yard 324
L*w* 97, 408

machine language 3
Madam, I'm Adam 148
magnetic tape 16
main program 380
mantissa 62
map of U.S. 212
Marner, Silas 165
mathematical induction 226
matrix operation 194
Maurer, W. D. 345
maximum 72
maximum, finding 185
MAX0 72
McCarthy, John 350
McKeeman, W. M. 216
McQuistian, Marie 275
mean 111, 193
media 353
memory 16, 21
    cell 16
    cell name 21, 78, 384
    location 16
    unit 386
    word 16
Menlo Park 74
message 295, 323
Midland 280
Midville 134
mileage chart 280
minimum 72, 177
minus 26, 68
MIN0 72
mirror printing 121
misconceptions, array 132
mixed mode 67, 392
Mondo Verde 44
Morris, R. 345
Morse Code 323
motorcycle 113, 194
mow 45

multiple errors 118
multiple-branching 396
multiplication 26
multiplication table 150

name **16**, 21, 78, 384
naming memory cells 21, 384
national debt 62
.NE. 48, 83
Nerdly 90, 199
nested loop 55, 56
nesting 143
no good 1
nonstandard subscript 234
.NOT. 83
not equal 48, 83
number, statement 47
numeric field 43
numerical analyst 64

object of IF 55
odd sum 315
Odessa 280
odor 250
one 32
one entry, one exit 53
one lousy comma 118
operating system 373
operator 68
    built-in 72
    extended 72
    infix 72
    prefix 72
opinion 352
.OR. 83
OR, exclusive 88
order of evaluation 66, 85,
    391, 394
Orvedahl, Walter 213
output 31, 36
output-list 31
overflow 28, 62, 64
overprint 403, 409

P scaling FORMAT 98, 99,
    100, 408
pain 300
palindrome 148
parachute 113
parallel process 209
parameter 163
parameter array 186
parameter of DO 201, 399
parenthesis 28
PASCAL 348
path 318
PAUSE statement 400
Pecos 280
peripheral device 269

permutation 239, 281
pharmaceuticals 279
phase 5, 6
pi 113
pillow 84
Pineapple Sliders 420
pint 157
pirate 151
pizza 63, 197
PL/I 349
PLANNER 350
Plauger, P. J. 123
plotting 172, 175, 194, 257
plus 26, 68
pointer 287
polar array 315, 316
polynomial 152
polystyrene 149
pong 355
popping 287
POS 419
position of I/O unit 271, 405,
    406
post-test 53
powerful statement 400
pre-test 53
precedence 28
    arithmetic 66, 391
    logical 85, 394
prefix operator 72, 180
pregnant 84
pretzel 136
prime number 153, 196
prime spiral 196
print 36
PRINT statement 403
printer **16**, 30, 35
printing, mirror 121
pro 78
pro football 85
problem solving 5
problem statement 117
processor 17
program 3, 17, 18
    design 117, 218
    testing 120
    unit **161**, 381
    verification 218
programming 161
    languages 9
    structured 358, 373, 375
proof 226
pseudorandom 190
pumpkin 213
punch 403
purest statement 400
purl 11
pursuit 151
push-down stack 287

supermarket 301
switch 188
symbol manipulation 3
syntax error 376

T, data 97
tablespoon 157
tangent 72
tax 124, 130
tea 59
team 85
teaspoon 157
testing programs 116, 120, 121
thermostat 114
things you've never seen 2
three-dimensional array 138, 279
three-way IF 398
Tide-XK 293
tiebreaker 67
time limit 20
timing diagram 346
top down design 218
trace 120, 122
tracking down errors 122
traffic light system 319
transfer of control 396
trapezoidal rule 110
travel service 155
traveling salesman problem 281
tree 274, 333, 335
triangle 109
triangular array 279
tricky language 106

trigonometric functions 72
.TRUE. 81, 82, 97
truncation 28, 73, 74, 77, 107
tsernotec 213
TSORT 343
two-dimensional array 133, 134, 276
type 22, 78
type compatible 395
type statement 23, 385

unary operator 84
underflow 62, 64
unformatted
    I/O 270, 405
    READ 270, 405
    record 270, 405
    WRITE 270, 405
unit
    of storage 386
    positioning 271
    vector 154
    5 39, 404
    6 30, 403
    7 403
Unruh, Jess 248
upper bound, DO 201
U.S. census 31
U.S. map 212

value 16, 21
Van Horn 280
variable FORMAT 272
variable length array 186
variable, simple 384

variable, subscripted 384
variance 111
vector 154
verbal description 11
verification 218
vigilance 376
Vinge, Vernor 440

warranty 177
watershed 215
WATFIV 36
Waxley, Milton P. 108
wazoo 35
weather report 111
while-loop 360, 364
white lies 8
Whiz Kids 159
Wichita Falls 280
Williams, J. W. J. 346
Williams, Ralph 248
wing-tipped shoes 141
word 16
wrap-around 293
WRITE
    binary 270, 405
    list 31, 142
    statement 31, 402, 403
    unformatted 270, 405
    FORMAT 33
writing desk 440

X FORMAT 100, 409

ZAPDIA 278
Zappa, Frank 17
ZAPPO algorithm 9
zero 32

See Quick Reference Index on page 468

*

```
C                       QUICK REFERENCE INDEX

C   USING THE QUICK REFERENCE INDEX:
C       SCAN THE PAGE FOR THE TYPE OF STATEMENT YOU WANT.
C       SEEING IT IN PRINT MAY ANSWER YOUR QUESTIONS.
C       IF NOT, USE THE PAGE NUMBER TO FIND MORE INFORMATION.
C
C   TYPICAL STATEMENT                                 PAGE NO.
C
C   SPECIFICATION STATEMENTS
        INTEGER A, BASE, C12                             23
        REAL RATE, SPEED                                 23
        LOGICAL PLATO, NOT1ST                            81
        REAL X(25), Y(15,100)                        127,138
        END                                              37
        SUBROUTINE CLEAR(TXT, A, B)                     163
        REAL FUNCTION FIRST(LIST, S, F)                 179
        DIST(RATE,TIME) = RATE*TIME                     254
        DATA A/3HCAT/                                    91
        DATA X/1.4/, A,B/3HCAT,3HDOG/                   259
        DATA X,Y,Z /3*0.0/                              259
C
C   ASSIGNMENT AND I/O STATEMENTS          .
        N = 1                                            26
        QWKREF = THANKS**DDM                             26
        BASE = R*COS(THETA)                              71
        P = .FALSE.                                      87
        Q = A .LT. 0.0  .OR.  B .GT. 10.3                84
        READ(5,1000) A, B, C                             40
        READ 1000, A, B, C                               41
        READ(5,1000, END=999) A, B, C                    53
   1000 FORMAT(2F10.0, I3)                           40,101
        PRINT 2000, A, B, C                              36
        WRITE(6,2000) A, B, C                            31
   2000 FORMAT(' DIMENSIONS:', 2G11.4/              40,102
       +        25X, 'PART NUMBER:', I4)                 34
        READ(5,3000) (X(I), Y(I), I=1,N)                143
   3000 FORMAT(2F10.0)                               40,101
        WRITE(6,4000) (TITLE(I),I=1,10),                143
       +             ((D(I,J),J=1,8), I=1,N)            144
   4000 FORMAT('1', 20X, 10A4/                          102
       +       (1X,8G20.6)     )                        101
        READ(9) ARRAY                               270,143
        WRITE(NT) XARRAY, YARRAY                    270,143
        ENDFILE NT                                      271
        REWIND NT                                       271
        BACKSPACE 9                                     271
C
C   CONTROL STATEMENTS
        STOP                                             37
        GO TO 100                                        47
        IF (N .LT. 1000)  GO TO 10                       48
        IF (X.GT.A .AND. X.LT.B) CALL PLOT(X)            85
        IF (X .GT. 10.32)  Y=X-10.32                     55
        GO TO  (10,20,50,30,400), JTH                   223
        CALL SUBR(R*B, 5HFINIS, A)                  162,168
        Y = F(X)                                    178,254
        Z(J) = COS(ATAN(FLOAT(J)*PI/4.0))               178
        T = ALOG(ALOG(X))                                71
        RETURN                                          164
        DO 100 I=1,N                                    204
    100 CONTINUE                                        205
```